SOCIAL ORDER
AND THE LIMITS
OF LAW

SOCIAL ORDER
AND THE LIMITS
OF LAW

〚A THEORETICAL ESSAY〛

IREDELL JENKINS

PRINCETON UNIVERSITY PRESS
PRINCETON, NEW JERSEY

FOR
LAWSON

CONTENTS

PREFACE

This book has a double intention. It means first to develop a systematic theory of positive law, with close attention to the circumstances that bring law into being, the purposes that law is intended to serve, and the structure of a legal system. Second, it proposes to apply this theory to an examination of the problems that law faces and the conditions that it must satisfy if it is to be an effective force in society. The earlier part of the book is therefore devoted to the formulation of a general theory of law. The first and most important step in this enterprise is to place law within the total environment from which it emerges as an operative element, and from which it derives its nature and functions. All of the contents that law deals with and all of the ends that it serves have both their original and their eventual loci in extralegal sources: they issue from and refer to things, forces, situations, needs, and purposes that are independent of and prior to law itself. As an explicit and organized mode of administering man's affairs, law is a late emergent that serves generally to extend and refine the reach of already existent ideas and institutions.

This insight has been too widely recognized to be announced as a discovery. It has served as the common point of departure for radically divergent lines of thought. The schools of historical, sociological, and psychological jurisprudence, the adherents of natural law doctrine, the legal pragmatists and realists, those who regard law as an instrument of political power and those who view it as an agent of policy formulation—all of these agree that the path to an understanding of the law leads through a study of the larger context from which law inherits its facts, its goals, and its problems.

However, the crucial element in any such study is the context in which law is examined. The various schools of thought mentioned above have contributed greatly to our knowledge both of the multiple facets of law and of the intricate interplay of law with life. But they have also been somewhat specialized in their focus and isolated from one another, so that their collective impact is a series of fragmented insights rather than a coherent vision. What is now desirable, I would suggest, is a speculative approach that seeks a synthesis of the available scholarship and that attempts to reach a systematic theory of the origins and ends of law and of the essential structure of the legal order.

This book is intended as a step in that direction: it attempts to trace the total framework within which law functions and to exhibit the circumstances that give rise to law and determine its tasks. I am assuming that the effective context of positive law is quite simply and inclusively the human enterprise as a whole; and I am further assuming that this enterprise itself is conducted within the setting and under the conditions defined by that even more inclusive whole, reality or the universe. This is the context in which I mean to envisage law and from which I shall derive it. I shall then seek to exhibit law as a specific development within far larger evolutionary and historical processes. If it were possible to cut through the pejorative sense of contemporary usage and to recover the classical meaning of the concept, the book could be described as an exercise in natural law: that is, as a search for those objective principles that define the conditions of man's being and well-being and so determine the origins, the ends, and the functions of law.

With this theory as a framework, the latter part of the book explores the role of law in the social order and the conditions of legal effectiveness. Law is a practical activity, having a decisive impact on the structure of society and the affairs of individuals. Viewed from this perspective, two facts about the present legal scene stand out conspicuously. First, law is being employed in ways and toward ends that are unprecedented: the legal apparatus is being asked to intervene in areas of social and personal life that have hitherto been handled by other agencies in other ways. Second, these employments of law have achieved only a small part of what had been hoped for from them: the massive machinery of the law is put to work, but all too often its quotient of efficiency is disappointingly low.

When we are thwarted in our use of some instrument (whether this be a tool, a machine, a human agent, or a social institution), it is natural to suspect that we have misunderstood its character and capacity. I think that it is this mistake that underlies many of our failures in the employment of law: we abuse the legal apparatus because we have inadequate notions both of what law is and how it acts. We have misconstrued the ontological status of law—its mode of being and the factors upon which its effective existence depends. In turn, this has led us to an erroneous view of law's operational status—of its mode of acting and of the range and limits of its power.

Identifying the nature of these misconceptions is not difficult. We are inclined both to oversimplify the nature of law and to exaggerate its power. We envisage law as constituted exclusively of its visible institutional and professional features: as composed of documents (a constitution, statutes, precedents), an apparatus (legislatures, courts, executive departments), and a personnel (judges, lawyers, administrators, police-men). And we are so overawed by the sovereignty that law exercises in principle that we treat it as omnicompetent in fact: since it voices deci-sions from which there is no appeal, we regard it as able to decide and effect anything at all. In short, we conceive of law after the manner of Aristotle's Unmoved Mover: we think of it as an autonomous and self-sufficient force upon which the rest of the social order depends but which itself depends upon nothing.

But law is very like an iceberg: only one-tenth of its substance appears above the social surface in the explicit form of documents, institutions, and professions, while the nine-tenths of its substance that supports its visible fragment leads a subaquatic existence, living in the habits, at-titudes, emotions, and aspirations of men. In a sense we all know this perfectly well, being quite aware that both the actual contents and the successful operations of law are heavily predicated upon such prior fac-tors as custom, morality, religion, tradition, and many other institu-tions, both private and quasi-public. However, we easily forget this. Be-guiled by the sovereignty and the massive presence of law, we turn to it, as a child to its mother, to solve all of our problems and secure all of our purposes. The result is analogous to our frequent mishaps with electrical appliances: we so overload the legal apparatus that it short-circuits, creating a spectacular display of fireworks but effecting nothing save its own wreckage.

Given the importance and the potential of law, this misuse is tragic. To work law to death for seemingly quick and sure results is the social equivalent of killing the goose that lays the golden eggs. If this outcome is to be avoided, we must come to a better understanding of the nature of law and of its proper place in the social order. The theory developed here hopes to be a contribution to that end.

A perceptive reader of the manuscript of this book remarked that it is rather an extended essay than a work of scholarship. As a concentrated statement of a theory of law, the argument is carried on at a rather high level of generalization and abstraction and in relative isolation (in its ex-position, though certainly not in its origin and development) from prac-tical issues and from the work of other writers in this same field. I am anxious to preserve this essaylike quality: to have the book be the unin-terrupted exposition of an interpretation of law and its place in the social order. But despite this intention, I have thought it advisable to introduce matter of two kinds that is foreign to the essay genre. First, recognizing that a theory is supposed to have repercussions on practice, I have elabo-rated briefly on the disposition of certain critical issues that loom large on the contemporary scene: particular instances will be found in the discussions of rights, of social disorder and conflict, of the nature of authority, of the distinctive characteristics of a legal system, and of the very important problem of the consensus—the bond, or agreement, or acquiescence—that lies at the basis of any society. Second, when the occasion presented itself I have tried to compare my view of the law with the views of certain prominent contemporary thinkers. Works with which this book most obviously invites comparison fall into two groups: the writings of such men as Hans Kelsen, H.L.A. Hart, Lon Fuller, and Ronald Dworkin; and those of such thinkers as F. A. Hayek, Alexander Bickel, Roberto Unger, and Theodore Lowi. However, there are important differences of intention between theorists of these groups and myself, which makes comparison somewhat difficult. The first group is primarily concerned with the internal structural characteristics of a legal system, how it is constituted, and the principles that govern its administration. The second group is very largely concerned with criticizing the present legal-social order, offering a model of a better one, and effecting a realization of the latter. My own basic concern is to analyze the context from which law derives, the environment within which it exists and acts, the enduring problems with which it has to deal, and the conditions it must satisfy if it is to succeed.

These three enterprises (which might be said to be directed respectively toward the formal structure of legal systems, the ideal form of the legal order, and the actual matrix of law) are certainly not sharply distinct. All of the writers mentioned above have at least some concern for all of these broad areas, some of them notably so. But there are significant differences of emphasis at play here, with problems that are central for some being peripheral for others. So works of these three types often touch one another only tangentially, with each pursuing its own way after but slight contact. Because of these differences in focus and thrust, comparisons cannot be forced without the danger of distortion and injustice. In all events, I would emphasize that these references to practical problems and to the work of other thinkers are in a real sense digressions from my theme: they are meant only to throw light on my ideas, and are not advanced as definitive solutions of the issues discussed nor, far less, as adequate treatments of the views of others.

ACKNOWLEDGMENTS

IN THE WRITING of this book I have received much kind help, and it is a pleasure to acknowledge this. The work would hardly have been possible without the support afforded me in the form of a fellowship from the Rockefeller Foundation, a year as a senior fellow in the Law and Behavioral Sciences Program at the University of Chicago Law School (funded by the Ford Foundation), grants from the University of Alabama Research Committee, and finally a grant from the National Science Foundation (grant number SOC75-16102). The Office of Academic Affairs and the Philosophy Department of the University of Alabama have kindly provided me with secretarial help and the duplicating of material. For all of this generous assistance I am duly grateful.

I am obliged to Ms. Caroline Plath and Mrs. Tabitha Tapley for the skill and patience with which they have typed—and retyped and retyped—my manuscript, and to my wife for her help in reading proof. I owe a special debt of gratitude to Professor Beryl Levy for reading proof and for valuable suggestions of substance.

The staff of the Princeton University Press have been uniformly helpful, and their skill has done much to make the book what it is. I owe a particular debt of gratitude to Mr. Sanford Thatcher, the assistant director of the Press, who has been a constant source of sound advice and cheerful encouragement from the time he first saw the manuscript through the months that I was making revisions and additions to the text. Finally, I am also obligated in a way and to an extent for which no acknowledgment can be adequate to Professor Sanford Levinson of the Department of Politics of Princeton University, who was the principal reader of the manuscript for the Press. He has made criticisms and suggestions that were always positive in tone and specific in content, leading me to deal with issues that were glaringly neglected and to repair errors that were glaringly present in the original draft of the book. I deeply appreciate his generous help. Finally, I owe many thanks to Catherine Dammeyer, whose skillful and conscientious copyediting has saved me from numerous errors of grammar and infelicities of expression. Needless to say, I alone am responsible for what mistakes and omissions still remain.

Parts of several chapters have been previously published, although that material as it appears here has been significantly enlarged, revised, and rearranged. A much condensed version of Chapters I-IV appeared as an article, "The Matrix of Positive Law," in the *American Journal of Jurisprudence* (then the *Natural Law Forum*) 6 (1961). Small parts of Chapters V and VI appeared as an essay, "The Modes of Law," in *Experience, Existence, and the Good: Essays Presented to Paul Weiss*, ed. Irwin C. Lieb (Carbondale: Southern Illinois University Press, 1961). A sketch of the argument developed in Chapters VII and IX was presented as a paper at the World Congress of the International Association for Philosophy of Law and Social Philosophy in 1967 under the title, "The Ontology of Law and the Validation of Social Change," and was published in a special issue, "Validation of New Forms of Social Organization," of the *Archives for Philosophy of Law and Social Philosophy* (ARSP), 1968; a part of Chapter VIII appeared in vol. 50 (1964) and a part of Chapter XIII appeared in vol. 53 (1967) of the same journal. A brief statement of the doctrine developed in Chapters X and XI was published as an article, "Authority: Its Nature and Locus," in the *Southern Journal of Philosophy* 8 (Summer-Fall): 1970; it was reprinted in *Authority: A Philosophical Analysis*, ed. R. Baine Harris (University, Alabama: University of Alabama Press, 1976). Small parts of Chapter XIV appeared in two different articles: "From Natural to Legal to Human Rights," in *Human Rights*, ed. Ervin H. Pollack (Buffalo: Jay Stewart Publications, 1971) and "The Concept of Rights and the Competence of Courts," *American Journal of Jurisprudence* 18 (1973). A brief and different version of Chapter XVII was an article of the same title in *Nomos VI: Justice*, ed. Carl J. Friedrich and John W. Chapman (New York: Atherton Press, 1963). A brief statement of one of the ideas developed in Chapter XVIII was presented as a paper, "The Human Person and the Legal Person," at the 1975 World Congress of the International Association for Philosophy of Law and Social Philosophy and was published in the proceedings of the congress, *Equality and Freedom: International and Comparative Jurisprudence*, ed. Gray Dorsey (Dobbs Ferry, New York: Oceana Press, 1977). I am obliged to these several editors and publishers for permission to use this material.

SOCIAL ORDER
AND THE LIMITS
OF LAW

[CHAPTER I]

THE CONTEXT OF
POSITIVE LAW

THE MOST OBVIOUS WAY to launch this inquiry is with the question, What is law? But I think that this would be a mistake. The phrasing of this question—as of many similar ones, such as What is reality? or What is life? or What is good?—is linguistically simple. This is apt to delude us into thinking that the question must have an equally simple answer. So we are led to seek that one essential—and elusive—characteristic that is constitutive of law and to frame a definition that will embrace this in a single phrase. In this search, and even more in the triumphant identification in which it culminates, we overlook far more than we find; excessive emphasis is thrown on some one aspect of law, with a consequent neglect or even denial of other equally significant aspects. For if there is one thing that is clear about the term "law," it is that the phenomena to which it refers are extraordinarily rich and complex: the best proof of this is the variety and disparity of the definitions of the term that have been advanced and of the schools of jurisprudence that have been built on these definitions. The mere recital of the more prominent of these schools makes clear the diversity of these interpretations of law: we have the doctrines of historical, sociological, and interest jurisprudence; theories of natural law and legal idealism; adherents of the pure theory of law, of analytical jurisprudence, and of legal realism. The futility of this search is aptly summarized by H.L.A. Hart when he says of the question, What is law?, that "nothing concise enough to be recognized as a definition could provide a satisfactory answer to it."[1]

I think that a more fruitful point of departure lies in the question, Why is law? For "why" questions are open-ended, pointing in various directions: rather than asking for definitions, they demand explanations. We answer these questions in different ways on different occasions, and even in several ways on the same occasion. We may explain the phenomenon in question—the event, action, situation, or institution—by

[1] H.L.A. Hart, *The Concept of Law* (Oxford: The Clarendon Press, 1961), p. 16.

referring to causes, origins, reasons, purposes, motives, or to several of these. Furthermore, our attitude toward these various ways of answering is tolerant: we regard them not as contradictory but as complementary, exhibiting the same phenomenon from different perspectives and exposing different of its aspects.

The contrast between these two kinds of questions can be clearly illustrated if the reader will simply imagine the answers he would give to the questions What is marriage? and Why is marriage? The first would elicit a definition such as this: marriage is a more or less permanent union of a man and a woman, certainly regularized by civil law and probably sanctified by the church, in which the parties assume certain rights and duties toward one another. The civil and religious regulations governing marriage, the rights and duties associated with it, and the consequences of various delinquencies could be further specified. But our answer would be cast in largely formal terms, and its continued expansion would merely add technical details. Our definition would be a catalogue of the internal characteristics of marriage. On the other hand, the question Why is marriage? would launch us upon a long and complex explanation, in which we would refer to such varied factors as biological demands, social needs, anthropological and historical circumstances, and moral values. As our answer was expanded, it would place marriage in a larger and larger context, explaining it in terms of its causes and origin, its tasks and purposes, its development and varieties, the human needs it serves, and its weaknesses and limitations.

To ask *why* instead of *what* is to throw the emphasis on the genetic, functional, and teleological aspects of law rather than on its formal and structural characteristics; without denigrating these latter, it treats them as derivative of the former. So when we ask, Why is positive law?, we generate a series of questions. What conditions call law into being, and what purposes lead it on? What problems must it solve and what difficulties does it encounter? What are its powers and its limitations? On what other factors does its effectiveness depend? What sort of apparatus does it require—what must any legal system be like—if it is to be equal to its tasks? To deal adequately with these questions we must look well beyond the confines of mature legal systems, back to the general human conditions in which law is grounded and to the historical circumstances from which it has emerged.

The theory of law that I shall develop to deal with these questions rests upon two metaphysical assumptions, one jural or legal postulate, and one fact. I shall first give brief separate statements of these elements of my theory and then bring them together and draw out more fully their collective meaning for law.

The two metaphysical assumptions (or general philosophical principles) on which I rely are *the postulate of the uniformity of nature* and
the theory of evolution. The first of these asserts that there is a single
embracing reality that is complex and variegated but still coherent
throughout its parts; that there are basic forces and conditions that pervade existence; that there is a single pattern of connectedness that runs
through the universe, binding all things into a single systematic scheme
of things; that there are general principles and structures that apply
everywhere in nature, while manifesting themselves in different specific
guises in different regions of nature. This postulate advises us to be prepared for continuities rather than radical disjunctions in nature; to look
for the gradual transformation of structures and processes, of ideas and
institutions, rather than their sudden initiation; to expect that all modes
of existence are contained within one set of broad and flexible categories
rather than a congeries of narrow and rigid concepts. Above all, this postulate teaches us that man and society are parts of the panorama of nature: and this means that human institutions—including law—inherit
their major problems and purposes from the general condition of man.

The second of my metaphysical assumptions, the theory of evolution,
asserts that man, along with all living creatures, is the outcome of organic evolution; that the common problem with which nature confronts
life is that of adaptation; that man has been fashioned by the continuing
necessity to adapt himself to the demands of the environment and the
conditions of life. The whole of the human enterprise, therefore, in its
psychic and social as well as its organic aspects, and including man's
higher and distinctively human activities as well as those that he shares
with other creatures, is most adequately conceived as a massive process
of adaptation.[2] This means that the human psyche and human culture
have become what they now are and have developed their present structures and functions in response to the conditions of life. Both mind and
society play very significant roles in the answer that man gives to the
challenge of life. The operations of mind, and the social and cultural institutions in which these issue, are the principal instruments that man
employs to come to grips with the world and to solve the problem of
adaptation as this occurs at the human level. Prominent among these institutions is positive law. Therefore the most realistic manner in which
to get at the roots and the matrix of law is by an examination of its
source and development as an adaptive agent.

We are well accustomed to the idea that law is a means to an end and

[2] I have argued this thesis at length and developed its implications on a broader scale in a
book entitled *Art and the Human Enterprise* (Cambridge, Mass.: Harvard University
Press, 1958). See esp. Chapters I-III and XII.

that its operations are governed by its purposes. But we need to be reminded that law is a solution to a problem long before it is a means to an end and that its purposes are themselves a reflection of the conditions that it faces and the demands that these impose. Obviously in its first occurrence, and prominently throughout its career, positive law is retrospective rather than prospective: its concern goes more to repairing the inadequacies of the actual than to preparing the realization of the ideal. This is to say that the essential structure of the legal order is determined far more by pressing necessities than by beckoning goals. Law is practical before it is visionary, and its visions must always be tempered by reality if they are to be fruitful. The future is uncertain, so it must be approached experimentally. We can never be sure of what ends are best or what means are most effective until we have put them to the test.

But we can be sure of the tasks that are committed to law. Law arises because certain features of the human situation require it, and these requirements can be discerned by an analysis of the human condition and the human potential as these emerge in the course of evolution. I think that by an inquiry into these matters we can define quite exactly and systematically the essential tasks of law, and this certainly is the indispensable basis for an intelligent consideration of the many—and often competing—values and purposes that are proposed as the goals of law.[3]

The jural postulate that I shall accept and analyze is the following: *Law is a principle of order.* There are two reasons that recommend this idea as a point of departure: it is almost universally accepted as an unquestioned truism, and it has rarely, if ever, been systematically examined. One encounters this notion everywhere in legal literature, and almost always it is stated as a self-evident fact that requires neither substantiation nor explanation. This is a postulate in the true sense that a vast amount of legal thinking depends upon it, and virtually no legal thought seeks to go behind it.[4] Since the argument of my theory rests very heavily on this notion that law is a principle of order, I will cite the

---

[3] I have stated these postulates quite briefly and abstractly for reasons of economy. Their relevance and implications will soon be developed in detail.

[4] To my knowledge, the most notable exception to this practice is to be found in Huntington Cairns's acutely perceptive book, *The Theory of Legal Science* (Chapel Hill: University of North Carolina Press, 1941). But Mr. Cairns's treatment runs in quite a different direction from my own: he is concerned chiefly with the sociology of disorder, while my principal interest is in the metaphysics of order. Reference should also be made to a most stimulating and suggestive article by K. N. Llewellyn, "The Normative, the Legal, and the Law-Jobs: The Problem of Juristic Method," in 49 *Yale Law Journal* 1355 (1940). Professor Llewellyn's approach and treatment are again quite different from the present analysis, but some of the conclusions are very similar. Cf. esp. pp. 1373-1395 of the article cited.

literature rather widely, to the end of establishing its ubiquity in legal discussion. These citations will at the same time serve to exhibit at least the general core of meaning that the postulate carries.

Hans Kelsen introduces his general theory of law in these words: "Law is an order of human behavior. An 'order' is a system of rules."[5] Eugen Ehrlich, looking for the essential element of law on which to base his sociological theory, rejects the traditional ideas that define law by reference to the state, the courts, or the fact of compulsion, and then says: "A fourth element remains, and that will have to be the point of departure, i.e., the law is an ordering."[6] Reflecting on the nature of the discipline that he practiced with such tact, Justice Benjamin Cardozo speaks in a similar vein: "The study of law is thus seen to be the study of principles of order revealing themselves in uniformities of antecedents and consequences. . . . As in the processes of nature, we give the name of law to uniformity of succession."[7] Max Weber bases his studies in the sociology of law on the same insight: " 'Law,' as understood by us, is simply an 'order system' endowed with certain specific guarantees of the probability of its empirical validity."[8] Gustav Radbruch's neo-Kantian analysis rests on this same postulate:

> The validity of positive law, then, is based upon the certainty which it alone possesses; or, circumscribing the sober term "legal certainty" by weightier verbal formulae, upon the peace it creates between conflicting legal views, upon the order that terminates the struggle of all against all. . . . Justice is the second great task of the law, while the most immediate one is legal certainty, peace, and order.[9]

Rudolf von Jhering very similarly defines law as "the form of the security of the conditions of social life."[10] Paul Vinogradoff adopts this same position, but he expands it somewhat:

[5] Hans Kelsen, *General Theory of Law and State*, trans. Anders Wedberg (Cambridge, Mass.: Harvard University Press, 1945), p. 1.

[6] Eugen Ehrlich, *Fundamental Principles of the Sociology of Law*, trans. Walter L. Moll (Cambridge, Mass.: Harvard University Press, 1936), p. 24.

[7] Benjamin N. Cardozo, *The Growth of the Law* (New Haven: Yale University Press, 1924), pp. 37, 40.

[8] Max Weber, *On Law in Economy and Society*, trans. Max Rheinstein (Cambridge, Mass.: Harvard University Press, 1954), p. 13.

[9] Gustav Radbruch, *Legal Philosophy of Lask, Radbruch, and Dabin*, trans. Kurt Wilk (Cambridge, Mass.: Harvard University Press, 1950), p. 118.

[10] Rudolf von Jhering, *Law as a Means to an End*, trans. Isaac Husik (Boston: Boston Book Co., 1913), p. 330.

Man is an essentially social being. . . . We can go a step further: if social intercourse is a requirement of man's nature, *order* of some kind is a necessary condition of social intercourse. . . . It is evident that laws take their place among the *rules of conduct* which ensure social order and intercourse.[11]

In his *Theory of Legal Science*, Huntington Cairns is yet more explicit and detailed on this point:

Order is omnipresent, so far as appears to us, in nature and human thought. . . . Order is a necessary condition of human social life, and it is impossible to imagine a society in which order of some sort does not exist. . . . Law is primarily a system of order, a system of purposefully controlled human conduct. . . . The rules of law which obtain in any society operate to establish a system of order in that society.[12]

Alf Ross, expounding the views of the Scandinavian realists, gives this same postulate a central place:

Such a demand ("That the norms of the law shall be formulated by means of objective criteria") results from the character of the law as a social, institutional order as opposed to the individual moral phenomena. Without a minimum of rationality (predictability, regularity), it would be impossible to speak of "a legal order," which presupposes that it is possible to interpret human actions as a coherent whole of meaning and motivation and (within certain limits) to predict them.[13]

In his analysis of the problem of just law, Max Rheinstein makes this postulate the basis of his treatment:

Recognizing that there exist wide divergencies even within the Great Tradition, we can still say, however, that *the just law is that which reason shows us as being apt to facilitate, or at least not to impede, the achievement and preservation of a peaceful and harmonious order of society*, in whatever shape this peaceful and harmonious order is visualized in detail.[14]

---

[11] Paul Vinogradoff, *Common Sense in Law* (New York: Henry Holt, 1914), pp. 12-13. Emphasis is in the original.

[12] Cairns, *Theory of Legal Science*, pp. 14, 15, 55, 135.

[13] Alf Ross, *On Law and Justice* (Berkeley: University of California Press, 1959), p. 281.

[14] Max Rheinstein, "What Should Be the Relation of Morals to Law," 1 *Journal of Public Law* 298 (1953). Emphasis is in the original.

In a very different context, Sir William Anson begins his classic analysis of contract in these words:

> The object of law is order, and the result of order is that men can look ahead with some sort of security as to the future. Although human action cannot be reduced to the uniformities of nature, men have yet endeavoured to reproduce, by law, something approaching to this uniformity.[15]

Echoing Blackstone across the centuries, Sir John Salmond opens his systematic treatment of law as follows:

> In its widest sense the term law includes any rule of action, that is to say, any standard or pattern to which actions (whether the acts of rational agents or the operations of nature) are or ought to be conformed.[16]

Hooker, speaking against the positivists and voluntarists of his day, begins his argument thus:

> They who are thus accustomed to speak apply the name of *Law* unto that only rule of working which superior authority imposeth; whereas we, somewhat more enlarging the sense thereof, term any kind of rule or canon, whereby actions are framed, a law.[17]

This same view had been stated by St. Thomas Aquinas with a slightly different emphasis:

> Law is a rule and measure of acts, whereby man is induced to act or is restrained from acting; for *lex* is derived from *ligare*, because it binds one to act. . . . Consequently, law must needs concern itself mainly with the order that is in beatitude. . . . Law is nothing else than an ordinance of reason for the common good, promulgated by him who has the care of the community.[18]

And long before any of these inquiries, Justinian had invoked this postulate in announcing the *Corpus Juris Civilis*: "Of all subjects none is more worthy of study than the authority of Laws, which happily dis-

[15] William Anson, *Principles of the English Law of Contract*, ed. Jerome C. Knowlton, 2nd American ed. (Chicago: Callaghan and Co., 1907), p. 1.

[16] John Salmond, *Jurisprudence*, ed. Glanville Williams, 10th ed. (London: Sweet and Maxwell, 1947), p. 20; Sir William Blackstone, *Commentaries* (Oxford: The Clarendon Press, 1765-1769), I:38.

[17] Richard Hooker, *Ecclesiastical Polity*, ed. R. W. Church (Oxford: The Clarendon Press, 1905), I, iii, 1.

[18] St. Thomas Aquinas, *Summa theologica* I-II, 90, 1, 2, 3.

poses things divine and human, and puts an end to iniquity."[19] Finally, the best of all evidences of the close association of these ideas is found in the fact that the expression *law and order* has virtually ceased to be a phrase for us and has become a single word.

I have purposely cited authorities of widely divergent interests and persuasions, with a view to providing a broad basis for my claim that the proposition "law is a principle of order" does occur pervasively as a postulate of legal theory.[20] In addition to this elemental point, these quotations also reveal (though rather loosely and largely by indirection) the common core of meaning that legal thought attaches to the notion of order. As I have said, this concept is nowhere explicitly and systematically explored, and it will be one of my chief concerns to make good this hiatus of inquiry.

For jurisprudence, order has the status of a primitive term. As such, it is deemed to be beyond the reach of definition or analysis, but the ostensive meaning that it is assumed to carry is clear. The notion of order embodies our recognition of pattern and regularity in nature. It refers to the fact that we discern some thread of connectedness and uniformity that runs between discrete objects and occurrences. When we say that order holds or is exemplified, we mean that we are in the presence of some stable body of relationships, some systematic structure, such that we can count upon a temporal recurrence of antecedents and consequents and a settled spatial arrangement. In minimal terms, order means continuity and predictability. And to assert that law is a principle of order on this level is to define law as an organized body of statements that describes the structure of things and so enables us to anticipate the course of events. Jurisprudence transforms this view only slightly when it identifies positive law as a prescriptive body of rules or norms rather than a descriptive body of statements. This is a familiar interpretation, and it is clearly present in many of the previous citations.[21]

[19] Constitution "Deo Auctore." Quoted from A. P. d'Entreves, *Natural Law* (London: Hutchinson's University Library, 1951), p. 19.

[20] It reaches, in fact, much farther than legal theory. In whatever context the concept of law is employed, it is defined by reference to the notion of order. Thus, speaking primarily as a metaphysician and considering the nature of law in the broadest sense, A. N. Whitehead sums up his conclusions in the form of this equivalence: "The notion of Law, that is to say, of some measure of regularity or of persistence or of recurrence. . . ." See *Adventures of Ideas* (New York: Macmillan and Co., 1933), p. 139. And speaking as a philosopher of science and at the outcome of a detailed analysis of the various meanings of law, Karl Pearson comes to the same conclusion: "In the conception of order or sequence, therefore, we see the historical origin of law in all its senses." See *The Grammar of Science*, Everyman's Library (1949), p. 83.

[21] It is of course best known as embodied in the writings of O. W. Holmes and J. C.

But these authorities obviously intend the term order to mean more than continuity and predictability, for they assert not only that order is an actual characteristic of the scheme of things but also an eminently desirable and even indispensable one. And, in addition, they recognize that order is never more than relative: *disorder* is an equally real characteristic of the world, especially in the human context. Disorder means that the pattern and regularity of events blur and dissolve, that uniformity of recurrence is interrupted, that the accidental and unforeseeable intervene in the course of events. And from this it results that man can no longer plan and predict with confidence. Thus according to these authors, when disorder occurs it become necessary for men to take steps to secure and preserve the order that is threatened. Order now becomes an ideal goal as well as an actual fact—something to be accomplished as well as a *fait accompli*. And to assert on this level that law is a principle of order is to define law as an instrument through which men seek to ensure a regularity and uniformity of conduct in human affairs that will enable them to anticipate and rely upon a settled course of events, a stable pattern of relationships. In a word, law is here regarded as a principle that determines (in the double sense of defining and guaranteeing) a rule of order, a uniformity and regularity, that would not otherwise exist.[22] This is the content of the jural postulate that law—here meaning positive law—is a principle of order.

This latter discussion has unavoidably anticipated the identification of the fourth and final element on which my argument is to be based. This consists in the fact—the empirical datum—that *positive law is a strictly human phenomenon*. It does not, at least in an institutional sense, occur outside the human context. There are other regions of nature where the behavioral patterns of individual entities and the relations between them

---

Gray and in the work of Hans Kelsen (although with a radically different specific basis and meaning in the latter).

[22] This theme of the dual status and role of law runs throughout the literature and is found in most of the authors whom I have just quoted. Law carries the double sense and has the double task of being both a measure and a sanction. The very words *order* and *rule* convey both of these meanings, and emphasis continually shifts—often without notice—from one of them to the other. Law is both a norm of order and a force for securing it. Theoretical jurisprudence has usually centered its attention on the first of these aspects. The latter was at the focus of the work of Jhering, and it has been stressed more recently by Cairns and, in a more limited and practical fashion, by the legal realists. The thesis that law has as its principal function to "établir un ordre durable" and to protect this against the disorderly dynamism of life and of other social forces is argued with great brilliance and thorough documentation in the successive works of Georges Ripert, particularly in *Les Forces créatrices du droit* (Paris: Librairie générale de droit et de jurisprudence, 1955). See esp. Chapters I and II.

are established and maintained without the intervention of positive law. Indeed, as we have seen, order is omnipresent in nature: wherever we look, we find regularity of arrangement, uniformity of occurrence, and a pervasive and systematic connectedness that holds things and events together. There are obviously some real forces or factors that operate to produce this condition of order wherever it occurs, but it would be universally agreed that below the human context this happens without any conscious, purposeful, or organized effort on the part of the entities concerned: that is, it is effected by other means than those of positive law or similar explicit agencies. With reference to most regions of nature, when we say that law is a principle of order we mean this in only a descriptive sense: such laws as the "laws of nature" or "scientific laws" we regard as elucidating an order that is primordial and preestablished. We do not think of these laws as creating or maintaining the order that they describe.

All of this changes radically in the human context. Here when we say that positive law is a principle of order, we mean more than that positive law merely describes an order of events that is already simply in existence. Of course a mature legal system, securely embedded in its society, does describe quite accurately the usual course of happenings in all those areas of life with which it deals. The behavior of persons, the relations that hold between them, the transactions in which they engage, the results that follow upon various courses of action—very much of this is "described" by the relevant bodies of positive law and so can be "predicted" by a sufficient acquaintance with this law. In short, law does trace a pattern of antecedents and consequences—of causes and effects—that usually holds; so it can be employed to plan arrangements that can be expected to lead to desired outcomes and to avoid undesired ones. It is in this sense that law is a "fact," in Olivecrona's usage, and this is all that the "bad man" of Holmes's famous example is interested in, just as he would similarly be interested in the laws that describe the tensile strength of iron bars and hemp rope. But we nevertheless conceive of positive law as standing in quite a different relationship to the events it predicts than do scientific laws. For when we say that positive law is a principle of order, we mean that it has the additional tasks of defining, prescribing, and forwarding the pattern of order that should be established. Positive law is an institution that definitely does have a responsible role in creating and maintaining the order that it also describes, and these apparently are tasks that confront only man among all the inhabitants of nature.

This fact that positive law is a strictly human phenomenon is so obvious and familiar that it is difficult to take it seriously and scrutinize it for its significance. But I shall immediately seek to show that it is acutally of the highest importance, especially when taken in conjunction with the other three elements of my argument: the doctrine of the unity of nature, the theory of evolution, and the postulate that law is a principle of order.

Taken together, these four principles suggest very strongly both that changes of a crucial sort take place at the human level, producing novel conditions and problems, and that positive law arises as a means of dealing effectively with these unique circumstances. If we accept this conclusion, then, as I previously indicated, the question that should occupy inquiry is not What is law? but rather Why is law? Our investigations must follow a line that is primarily genetic and teleological, with substantive and formal matters occupying only a secondary role, for law is functional before it is technical, and the necessary structure—the inner logic—of legal systems is to be sought in the conditions that engender and the purposes that animate them. And let me reemphasize that I am not here referring particularly to the relations of law with actual social, economic, psychological, and political circumstances, which are relatively superficial and transitory. Rather, my concern is primarily with fundamental metaphysical issues and with factors of a broad cultural and anthropological character. The first step in this undertaking is to identify the central problems it confronts and to isolate the precise questions that we need to ask. To this end, we must bring together the four elements that have heretofore been discussed separately, and we must also make explicit their collective meaning for legal theory. Accepting these basic tenets, what can we reasonably infer about the origins and the functions—the beginnings and the ends—of positive law?

It follows from the postulate of the unity of nature that man is an element within the embracing context of reality, sharing its essential attributes, subject to its determining conditions, and related to its other parts. But it should also be remembered that man exhibits significant specific differences that mark him off as a distinct type of entity occupying a distinct niche within reality. From this postulate it follows that positive law is a special agent whose function is to procure in the human context the same general effect that is produced elsewhere in nature by other instrumentalities. Positive law is not an isolated or solitary phenomenon; it is not absolutely unique in either its characteristics or its functions; it is not an artificial and arbitrary human construct. On the contrary, it must be regarded as having close affinities with other agencies that occur in the human context and even with forces and factors that operate in other regions of nature. And once again it is to be re-membered that positive law exhibits important specific features that differentiate it from similar phenomena to which it is related.

If we now join to the postulate of the unity of nature the principle of evolution, we can carry the argument an important step further. For it now follows that man is a temporal development, or emergent, within the processes of nature. Due to a complex concatenation of circum-stances (which will soon be analyzed in detail) man develops distinctive faculties and capacities, exercises powers that are not found in any other creature, and stands in a unique relationship both to the environment and to the other members of his species. As a result of these changes, man disposes of potentialities and confronts problems that do not occur in any other context of nature. But he must still meet the demands of the natural order in general, as well as those posed by his special status and attributes: he must satisfy the conditions of life if he is to survive and make his way toward the realization that is open to him. And if nature does not furnish the instruments that are necessary to this end, then man must devise them by his own ingenuity.

It now also follows that positive law is similarly a temporal develop-ment within nature: it emerges gradually out of the same circumstances as man and develops concurrently with him; it is a reflection—a cre-ation—of his faculties and capacities, a means to administer his new-found powers and sustain the novel position in which he stands. In short, positive law is an instrument through which man is aided in realizing his special potentialities and solving his special problems, and it is indispensable if man is to take advantage of his unique status and at-tributes rather than being overwhelmed by them. Positive law is a natu-ral occurrence that is at first largely unconscious and spontaneous and that arises as a means to procure the same generic conditions and out-come in human affairs that are procured elsewhere in nature by other forces and agencies (although with important specific differences). In short, on the basis of these two principles of the unity of nature and evo-lution, one is led to suspect a continuity of essential character and func-tion between positive law and other modes of law—such as laws of na-ture or scientific laws, laws of instinctual behavior, laws of imitation, natural law, moral law, customary law—that drive in the same direction and toward the same ends.[23]

_____

[23] This theme of the continuity of positive law with other modes of law, and of positive law as being somehow derivative from and a further development of other more protean modes of law, is by no means novel. It is frequently encountered in the literature of both philosophy and jurisprudence, but it is rarely if ever examined and developed in detail. I

My interpretation and use of the evolutionary concept can be sharpened by comparison with some interesting recent work by F. A. Hayek.[24] Hayek's purpose is strongly—and explicitly—polemical and reformist: he is concerned to expose what he regards as mistaken and dangerous doctrines that pervade contemporary thought on political and social issues and hence distort practical efforts to solve the problems we face. Hayek develops his analysis through a series of distinctions, with the elements on each side of the pattern being closely related to one another and sharply separated from their corresponding elements on the other side: indeed, these distinctions are sometimes treated almost as though they constituted antinomies.

The most fundamental of these contrasts is between the "two schools of thought" that Hayek identifies as "evolutionary rationalism" and "constructivist rationalism."[25] The first of these views, which is Hayek's own, holds that the human mind is "the product of the same evolutionary process to which the institutions of society are due."[26] Constructivist rationalism, on the other hand, is seen by Hayek as deriving from the thought of Descartes, and it regards mind as an autonomous entity, imposing its structures and purposes upon social life. Hayek then argues that since mind and society are evolutionary developments, many of the most important arrangements, modes of behavior, relationships, and institutions that we find in even the most complex and highly developed societies are "spontaneous formations" or "self-generating orders": they are the outcome of a gradual and largely unplanned process of adaptation; they result not from design but from collective actions that have proved successful; they are what they are because of the functions they perform, not because of any preconceived purposes that they serve. By contrast, constructivist rationalism holds that all important social forms and institutions are and should be "deliberate constructions" or "organizations" that are consciously based on rational principles, intended to further clearly defined purposes, and governed by explicit and systematic bodies of rules.[27]

---

will discuss the matter fully in Chapters V and VI, with special attention to its meaning for the nature and history of positive law.

[24] See particularly F. A. Hayek, *Law, Legislation, and Liberty: Volume I, Rules and Order* (Chicago: University of Chicago Press, 1973).

[25] Ibid., p. 5.   [26] Ibid.

[27] There is an interesting family resemblance as regards both intention and technique between Hayek's argument and that of Roberto Unger as presented in his stimulating books, *Knowledge and Politics* (New York: Free Press, 1975) and *Law in Modern Society* (New York: Free Press, 1976). Unger's views will be referred to in the discussions of later chapters.

The thrust of Hayek's evolutionary argument is directed against this constructivist view. It is his basic contention that "the complex, spontaneously formed structures with which social theory has to deal, can be understood only as the result of a process of evolution."[28] When we try to understand the forms and institutions of social life as deliberately conceived and planned, we inevitably simplify and misinterpret them. Further, and more disastrously, when we try in this way to control the collective activities of men, to alter their arrangements, and to redefine their relationships, we are very apt to make matters worse instead of better, for this represents the imposition of an alien regime of abstract design upon a more basic substratum of concrete adaption. Hayek contends that it is precisely this rationalistic and constructivist hybris that is responsible for many of our troubles, for it leads us to embrace two mistaken conclusions: that only explicit conscious human design can create workable social arrangements, and that there is no limit to our ability to understand and control social life by such purposive designs.

There are obviously close resemblances between Hayek's ideas and my own. But there are also at least two important differences. In the first place, I would not draw so sharp a distinction as he seems to between "self-generating orders" and "organizations," between "spontaneous formations" and "deliberate constructions." I would regard all conscious human activity, and consequently all the arrangements and institutions that result from such activity, as a synthesis of these two modes of action. For it is my thesis that even the most sophisticated of man's instrumentalities and techniques—including positive law—have an evolutionary origin and an adaptive function. The problem we continually face is that of maintaining a balance between the lived patterns and social arrangements that men have gradually and unreflectively adopted in direct response to the conditions of existence and the highly organized and purposive institutions through which we intervene in these activities, seeking to plan them more rationally and so improve their effectiveness. However, I fully agree with Hayek that all too often we tend to exaggerate the power of these institutions and to use them in a way to *supplant* rather than *supplement* the more spontaneous and informal modes of social life.[29] Furthermore, the difference between our views in this regard is one of degree rather than of kind, and Hayek's strong emphasis on his distinctions is, I would think, largely due to his polemical and reformist purpose.[30]

[28] Hayek, *Law, Legislation, and Liberty*, p. 24.

[29] This is in fact one of the principal themes of this book. It will be developed especially in Chapters XIII, XVIII, and XIX.

[30] This interpretation is strengthened by Hayek's explicit rejection of the "false

This leads me to the second difference referred to above: this is more fundamental, as it goes to the particular and distinctive employments to which the evolutionary motif is put. Hayek relies upon the occurrence of evolution to explain the origin and character of the more basic modes of collective behavior and social order and to justify his insistence that planned organizations should not trespass too much upon these. But he does not appeal to evolution in any systematic way to identify just those changes that occurred in human nature and the human situation that called law into being, constituting its setting, posing its problems and tasks, and defining its limits. This is precisely the way in which I intend to use evolutionary theory: to trace the rise of law, to exhibit its relation to other social forms and forces, and to identify its necessary structures and techniques. As I have already suggested, the differences in this respect derive largely from our different purposes, and they might be roughly summarized as follows: Hayek uses evolution as a weapon with which to restrain the encroachments of law upon social life; I use it as a scalpel to dissect the role of law in life.

We have already seen that the notion of law in all of its manifestations is always closely associated with the notion of order. This is as true of its use in the human context as in any other. Indeed, we think of large areas of this context as exhibiting the same sort of order and exemplifying the same types of law as those that we encounter in other regions of nature. We treat many of man's physiological and neurological characteristics and modes of action in strict physical and biological terms, assimilating them with no hesitation into the field of natural science. That is, we assume that the regularities and uniformities that we find here are inherent in the structure of man as a living and sentient creature, and we accept the laws of neurology, pathology, and other such disciplines as being altogether on a par with those of physics and chemistry. The same holds true even well up into the areas of human phenomena that are studied by the psychological and social sciences. Admittedly, the uniformities of structure, continuities of relationship, and regularities of behavior that we find in these areas are less constant than in others, and our assertion and employment of them are subject to important qualification. But it is nevertheless widely felt that man's emotional and intellectual processes—indeed, his psychic activities as a whole—take place in settled if intricate ways and in accord with general principles, that men react to situations and respond to one another along common lines, that human motives and actions are subject to definite forces and unfold in

dichotomy of 'natural' and 'artificial.' " See Hayek, *Law, Legislation, and Liberty*, pp. 20-21.

patterns that are at least roughly if not altogether precisely ascertainable. We accept the fact that order is quite simply an ingrained characteristic of large parts of the human domain, exhibiting itself in regularities of human behavior and uniformities of human relationship without any conscious or organized control on the part of men, and even in defiance of such control. We regard this order as being somehow produced and supported by a variety of forces or factors: instinct, reflex, stimulus and response, conditioning, imitation, habit, and so forth. And we express this order through laws that are empirical descriptions of observable structures and sequences. In short, in many areas of the human context the relation of law and order appears to be the same as in those other contexts of nature that we refer to as "subhuman."

But this is not the whole story. For as we have seen, disorder is also a prominent characteristic of the human context. We find as a simple matter of fact that much of man's behavior is vagrant and variable: many human relations are unstable; men indicate by word or deed that they will act in one way and then act in another; men waste their powers in worthless pursuits, dissipate their talents to false purposes, and fall short of the realizations and values they should achieve; excessive friction and inefficiency often mark men's common undertakings; individuals assert their private interests against the interests of the group. I do not pretend that this is either an exhaustive description or an adequate explanation of disorder. And I would particularly wish to avoid the usual implication that disorder is inherently and utterly undesirable, a condition that is pregnant only of evil and not at all of good. An exact analysis of this concept, of the factors responsible for it, and of the treatment it requires, will be offered shortly. For the moment, I am merely calling attention to the fact that disorder does appear in the human context in all of these and many other guises. Further, it is apparently only in the human context that disorder becomes a conspicuous feature; and it is only man who is at once challenged and equipped to deal purposively with it.

One further step will now bring me to the crux of the argument that is woven of my four original strands. When and to the extent that disorder appears, it immediately threatens to disrupt the pattern and regularity that are as necessary in the human context as they are elsewhere in nature. Less directly and obviously, it also produces a situation that is full of promise for man. So the most basic and persistent problem that man confronts is the dual one of maintaining the order that is the necessary matrix of human careers while at the same time exploiting the advantages that disorder offers. It is the occurrence of this problem that differentiates man from the rest of nature and that stands at the origin of the massive phenomenon that we call culture. Confronted with disorder, man must take steps to correct and utilize it. Notable among these steps is the institution of positive law.

I can now state the major hypothesis that is suggested by the conjunction of the four elements with which my argument commenced: *Positive law is a supplemental principle of order that arises and develops in the human context when other agencies and forces become inadequate to the conditions and the challenge that man confronts.* According to this hypothesis, positive law is called into being by certain pecularities of human nature and the human situation, and its task is to assure a stable and fruitful order in which men can plan securely, carry on effective transactions among themselves and with the world, and reap the benefits that are latent in their nature and position. In short, positive law is an instrument that man creates as a means to promote the realization of potentialities that nature opens before him but does not automatically secure to him.

This is the hypothesis to which we are led when we ask the question, Why is law? It in turn leads to two more specific questions. First, What is order? What are the elements among which order holds and the referents that the concept requires? What is the systematic structure of the order that positive law is called upon to secure? Second, what are the changes that take place at the human level—in human nature and the human situation—that require positive law as a supplemental principle of order? These questions form the subjects of the next two chapters. And I would emphasize that throughout the analyses that they offer of the origin and function of law—of the circumstances that call law into being and of the ends that law is called upon to serve—the discussion is cast in strictly formal and abstract terms. I am concerned to dissect both the actual problems that law has to deal with and the ideal conditions that it is intended to promote. I do not mean to imply that any legal system achieves a perfect solution for these problems, much less that every such system seeks to make the advantages of order available on equal terms to all those persons who are subject to it. Some legal systems are more effective and successful than others, and some legal systems are more faithful than others to the demands of morality, justice, and equity. Finally, a particular legal system may be quite effective but highly iniquitous: it may secure a stable order, but one that is repressive and exploitative as regards some segments—and even large segments—of the society it serves. Ideally, law is consensual and beneficent: obviously it is so for those who control its apparatus and operation, but it may be quite the opposite for some who are controlled by it. These points will be fully discussed in later chapters, but it is important that they be borne in mind as my abstract schema unfolds.

[CHAPTER II]

THE CONCEPT OF ORDER

I HAVE PREVIOUSLY called attention to the failure of jurisprudence to submit the notion of order to systematic analysis. When the question of the meaning of the term arises, the standard procedure is first to identify this meaning by reference to various roughly synonymous terms, such as stability, uniformity, regularity, security; then to give several examples of the areas of human affairs in which order is at once necessary and precarious, such as sexual and family relations, property, protection of the person; and finally to cite the factors in human nature and in surrounding circumstances that cause disorder, such as greed, lust, selfishness, carelessness, scarcity, and so forth. Such a treatment is usually adequate for the solution of immediate practical problems, where the nature, the cause, and the corrective of some actual social disorder are apt to be—or at least to appear—quite obvious. And since law is a preeminently practical science, concerned with the evils of the day and willing to take these as more than sufficient, it is understandable why legal thought has not felt the need to scrutinize more closely the concept of order.

But such a treatment is not adequate as the foundation of legal theory. What is required for this purpose is an investigation that is more profound in its quest for law's basic elements, more precise in its identification of these elements, and more systematic in its analysis of the relations in which they stand. The ultimate setting of positive law is the framework of reality; the entities with which law deals, the conditions that give rise to it, the functions it serves, and the problems it faces, all derive from the structure and processes of reality. Positive law certainly deals with a context of a quite special type: men living in groups. But this context is a specification within the embracing framework of reality as a whole. So we must begin with a strictly metaphysical inquiry.

With this orientation in mind, what do we mean by the term order when we say that law is a principle of order? I would suggest this answer: Order refers to *regular and determinate sequences* that are exhibited in *the behavior* of *distinct entities* that are so related among themselves as to constitute *organized wholes*. The italicized items in this statement are the four constituents that are necessarily entailed by the concept of order. When these constituents occur, we have the type of situation or state of affairs that is orderly and lawful. This is the context that is required if order and law are to be meaningful concepts. These terms presuppose a plurality of distinct entities, a unification of these into a series of higher-order entities, energy expended and activity engaged in by these entities, and all of this taking place in a way that is characterized by uniformity and regularity. Order is the name by which we identify this general condition. Law is the name we give to that type of proposition that formulates the structures and relationships, the sequences and similarities, the constancies and recurrences that are contained within this condition and make up its specific details. Therefore law is a principle of order in the sense that laws are propositions that refer to and explicate the lines of connection that run through orderly contexts. Thus, the laws of motion formulate the ways in which physical objects moving in a common space act upon and react to one another; the laws of genetics plot the courses through which genes and chromosomes are recombined in the act of sexual reproduction that issues in a new individual; the laws of grammar and syntax depict the procedures that men are required to follow in talking and writing if they are to create a world of shared meanings; the laws of morals lay down the norms and patterns of conduct to which men who share a common humanity should conform in their treatment of one another; the laws of contract define the rules that men in any particular society must follow in making and executing private agreements.[1]

In view of what was said in the previous chapter and in the light of the foregoing examples, it is probably unnecessary to make the following point, but to avoid any possible misunderstanding I should say that when I speak of *order* I mean to include its correlative, *disorder*. That is, I am treating order and disorder as comparative terms, not as contradictories. Both concepts refer to contexts containing the elements and exhibiting the characteristics just described: they indicate differences in the degree to which the integrity of individual entities, the stability of patterns, the regularity of sequences, and the coherence of wholes are realized. This is clearly in accord with common usage, for when we

---

[1] The various statements in this paragraph, employing such terms as "refer to," "formulate," "depict," "should," "must," and so forth, are purposely and systematically ambiguous as regards the relation of "law" to "order." That is, they are intended to leave open the question whether law describes order, or prescribes it, or produces it, or evaluates it, or is merely a convenient device for understanding it. This problem will be treated fully in Chapters V-VII.

speak of disorder we imply our recognition of these four constituents and our feeling that they are imperfectly realized. Order is never absolute, and disorder is never total. These terms represent segments along a continuum: one end point sometimes seems to threaten us, and we call it chaos; the other is so unimaginable that we do not even have a name for it.

It will now be useful to give more abstract and generalized names to these four elements that form the context of order and law—to identify them by terms of art that can be precisely defined. I shall refer to the plurality of distinct entities as *the Many*; to the wholes (the complexes, or fields, or groups) of which these entities are parts as *the One*; to the activities in which these entities engage (the flux in which they are caught up) as *Process*; to the uniformities and regularities that run among these entities as *Pattern*. These are the basic categories that define the concept of order and constitute the matrix of law, and they must therefore be subjected to a closer scrutiny.

But first I would like to pause for a moment to confirm this analysis by reference to the work of previous legal theorists. For though these thinkers have usually centered their attention on concrete problems of order, they have still caught glimpses of the abstract nature of order as the general and pervasive object of legal thought and action. Having discerned this, they have not sought to follow up and develop their vision because it has not seemed to them to be necessary or relevant to their more limited and practical concerns. What particularly interests me is the fact that their insights—reported quite casually and as though they were merely a recording of the self-evident—agree point by point with one another and coincide with the analysis I have just suggested. A few quotations will illustrate this.

Benjamin Cardozo epitomizes his conception of law in these terms: "Law is the expression of a principle of *order* to which *men* must conform in their *conduct and relations* as members of *society*.[2] Speaking of law in a broader and more general sense, A. N. Whitehead repeats this thought: "The notion of law is that there are *many things* in *the world*, whose *behavior* towards each other always exemplifies *fixed rules*."[3] Huntington Cairns echoes the same formula: "In this *complex whole* (society or culture) *the behavior of human beings* is ordered in accordance with the requirements of the *relations established in the* struc-

[2] Benjamin N. Cardozo, *The Growth of the Law* (New Haven: Yale University Press, 1924), p. 140. In this and the following quotations I have italicized the crucial terms.

[3] A. N. Whitehead, *Adventures of Ideas* (New York: Macmillan and Co., 1933), p. 51.

ture."[4] Paul Vinogradoff speaks in the same terms: "I think we may say that the aim of law is *to regulate* the attribution and exercise of *power* over *persons and things* in social *intercourse*."[5] K. N. Llewellyn expresses the same idea:

> The law jobs are in their bare bones fundamental, they are eternal. Perhaps they can all be summed up in a single formulation: such *arrangement and adjustment* of *people's behavior* that the *society* (*or the group*) remains a society (or a group) and gets enough *energy* unleashed and coordinated to keep on with its job as society (or a group).[6]

Finally, when it is taken in its entirety and not cut off after the first clause, John Austin's famous imperative definition of law is seen to be cast in terms of these same four elements: "law is *a command* which obliges *a person or persons*, and obliges generally to *acts or forbearances* of *a class*."[7]

None of the authors just quoted have subjected the concept of order to any close or systematic analysis, nor have they given it a particularly prominent place in their doctrines. As I have suggested, order—along with disorder—is so obvious as a fact and so pressing as a problem that one ordinarily feels no need to examine it but rather to set about finding ways to deal with it. However, the concept does have a central position in the recent work of two thinkers who take it very seriously, study it closely, and exploit it purposefully. A brief account of their views is worthwhile, both to further illuminate the analysis given above and to exhibit the differences in their and my own employment of the concept.

In his book *Law, Legislation, and Liberty*, F. A. Hayek defines the term in a way that perfectly reflects the model I have exposed. He says:

> By "order" we shall throughout describe *a state of affairs in which a multiplicity of elements of various kinds are so related to each other that we may learn from our acquaintance with some spatial and temporal part of the whole to form correct expectations con-*

---

[4] Huntington Cairns, *The Theory of Legal Science* (Chapel Hill: University of North Carolina Press, 1941), p. 18.

[5] Paul Vinogradoff, *Common Sense in Law* (New York: Henry Holt, 1914), p. 36.

[6] K. N. Llewellyn, "The Normative, the Legal, and the Law-Jobs: The Problem of Juristic Method," in 49 *Yale Law Journal* 1355 at 1373 (1940). This article is especially valuable for its discussions of what is involved in the doing of these "law-jobs."

[7] John Austin, *Lectures on Jurisprudence*, vol. 1 (London: J. Murray, 1869):98.

*cerning the rest, or at least expectations which have a good chance
of proving correct.*[8]

But Hayek does not further explore and analyze the elements and relationships that this definition exposes: he does not seek to clarify the
meaning of order as such and the demands that it imposes. His interest
lies elsewhere. As with his use of the theory of evolution, he is here
concerned with contrasting two different ways in which order can be
achieved and with emphasizing the limitations of rationalistic planning,
with its exclusive reliance on organizations that are purposely designed
and constructed. He himself makes this perfectly explicit in a passage
following closely upon the definition. "This matching of the intentions
and expectations that determine the actions of different individuals is the
form in which order manifests itself in social life: and it will be the question of how such an order does come about that will be our immediate
concern."[9] The ensuing discussions of the disparate characteristics of
"spontaneous orders" and "organizations" throw a good deal of light on
the general concept of order and especially on the relative effectiveness
of these two ways through which social order is sought and achieved.

In his most recent work, Roberto Unger develops a theory that is quite
similar to Hayek's in both its broad structure and general intention, although there are significant differences in detail and treatment. Unger
does not advance an explicit definition of order: he accepts it as a fact that
poses a problem, that problem being its existence as a fact. He puts the
matter this way: "The problem of social order arises from a deep puzzlement one may experience about the very existence of society. . . . Can
we discern beneath the changing forms of association something basic to
the social bond?"[10] It is this social bond, which underlies and supports
the social order, that is Unger's central concern and the governing theme
of his work: he seeks to understand its character and structure, its
source, the means by which it can be maintained and strengthened, the
forces and circumstances that threaten it. Unger's examination of these
matters centers on his description and critique of two radically different
theories of social order and the social bond, which he refers to as the
doctrines of consensus and instrumentalism. I believe that when his
analyses of these doctrines are considered in conjunction, they exhibit
the same four elements that I have identified as the constituents of order
and, further, that they expose these doctrines as being partial and unbal-

[8] F. A. Hayek, *Law, Legislation, and Liberty: Vol. I, Rules and Order* (Chicago: University of Chicago Press, 1973), p. 36.

[9] Ibid.

[10] Roberto Unger, *Law in Modern Society* (New York: Free Press, 1976), p. 23.

anced because—as Unger himself emphasizes—each recognizes only certain of these elements and neglects the others.

The doctrine of consensus holds that persons are bound together by the values and beliefs that they share and the common activities in which they engage. Here, the community is taken as the basic entity, and a meaningful human existence consists of participation with others in pursuits and toward purposes that are those of the community as a whole and are recognized by all of the members as being also properly theirs. In Unger's words, one of the principal keys to community is "joint participation in a shared universe of discourse about man and his good."[11] The doctrine of instrumentalism stresses the ultimacy of the individual, holding that "men are governed by self-interest and guided by judgments about the most efficient means to achieve their privately chosen aims."[12] Men being so constituted and motivated, their interests and objectives often conflict; therefore it is necessary that definite rules be promulgated and enforced in order that an acceptable degree of peace and cooperation can be assured. The whole of Unger's book is a careful working out of the merits and demerits of these two theories of order, of their origins and development, of the tension between them, and of the possible solutions to the problem of the social bond that neither of them alone can solve.

Admittedly, there is always the danger that anyone discussing another's work will misconstrue this by interpreting it in terms of his own modes of thought and absorbing it into his own conceptual framework. But I do not think it is a forced reading to see Unger's analyses of consensus and instrumentalism, when taken together, as conforming to my analysis of order. Consensus stresses what I have called the elements of One and Process; instrumentalism, those of Many and Pattern. Furthermore, I would hope that reference to my abstract schema will show just how each of these doctrines is incomplete and so must be inadequate and will thus point the way toward a true solution of the problems of the social bond and of social order. But that must wait for later chapters.[13]

I will close this phase of my argument with a brief reference to the work of a man who has exerted a strong influence on American jurispru-

[11] Ibid., p. 168. The other key is "the capacity to perceive and to deal with others as whole persons rather than as jobholders" (ibid.); that is, to regard others not as isolated individuals but as partners in a shared enterprise.

[12] Ibid., p. 24.

[13] I should perhaps point out that the manuscript of this book was completed before I had any knowledge of the previously cited works of Professors Hayek and Unger. Indeed, the argument of the first four chapters of the book is an expansion of a long article, "The

dence, Lon L. Fuller. So far as I am aware, Fuller nowhere couches his discussions in the vocabulary of order, but much of his doctrine is developed within a similar frame of reference. This is true of the major theses and analyses of *The Morality of Law*, where Fuller defines law as "the enterprise of subjecting human conduct to the governance of rules," and a legal system as "the product of a sustained purposive effort."[14] In an important article, Fuller conceives law as being fundamentally "a language of interaction," and he immediately defines the conditions of interaction in these terms: "To interact meaningfully men require a social setting in which the moves of the participating players will fall generally within some predictable pattern."[15]

The equivalences among the key terms in these definitions and their correspondence with the more abstract concepts that form the context of order and law (Many, One, Process, Pattern) are, I think, too clear to require comment. These quotations offer persuasive evidence that the present explicit and generalized analysis of order and of law as an adjunct of order exposes an interpretative schema that is deep-rooted and pervasive (if usually only implicit) in a great deal of legal theorizing. It seems that whenever one thinks about law in a sufficiently persistent and coherent manner, regardless of the approach, this thinking is cast in terms of the categories of Many–One–Process–Pattern. What I intend to do is to analyze this schema closely for the insight and understanding it can yield.

The thesis that I am advancing holds that these categories of Many, One, Process, and Pattern represent the ultimate dimensions of being or reality. The difficulty that arises in developing this thesis is that of presenting the meaning and content of the categories in a manner that is neutral and general. They must be introduced and treated serially, but this serial arrangement does not indicate any order of precedence, since these categories are equally basic and significant. Further, they must at

---

Matrix of Positive Law," that appeared in 1961 in *The Natural Law Forum* 6:1-50 (now the *American Journal of Jurisprudence*). I became acquainted with these recent books when making certain revisions to my manuscript suggested by the publisher. To read them under these conditions was quite startling—a succession of recognitions and surprises. The experience can best be compared to that of seeing your face reflected in water: you recognize yourself, but your features are changed and rearranged. So your face—or your theory—loses the particular structure and symmetry to which you are accustomed, and you see your features—or your ideas—in a new light.

[14] Lon L. Fuller, *The Morality of Law* New Haven: (Yale University Press, 1964), p. 106.

[15] Lon L. Fuller, "Human Interaction and the Law," 14 *American Journal of Jurisprudence* 1 at 2 (1969).

first be described in very general terms, as indicating pervasive aspects or attributes of reality that take on different concrete forms in different contexts of the real. That is, each of the categories embodies mind's recognition of an ultimate and protean dimension of the universe. And these dimensions assume various specific characters and exhibit distinctive features in various local regions of nature.

Since these categories are so broad and fundamental, they permit of various interpretations concerning their individual characteristics and the collective structures that they form. Philosophers identify and describe these dimensions of being in different ways, and they advance different theories of the relationship in which they stand to one another. Thus it is largely conflicting views on these points that constitute the differences in metaphysical doctrines. These differences then reverberate further and exert a strong, if largely subterranean, influence on legal theory. That is, I would suggest that the various schools of jurisprudence are most basically distinguished by the interpretations, and especially the relative emphases, that they place on these several categories. Each school tends to select one of them, to find in it the essential reference of law, to assign to this essential feature a certain definite character, and then to reduce the other categories to this chosen item. In describing these dimensions, I will simultaneously mention the legal doctrines and schools of thought that seem to me to be closely associated with each. Although this has obvious dangers, it should serve to make somewhat clearer the character of these dimensions, and it will certainly bring closer to home the legal relevance of this abstract metaphysical analysis.

The category of the Many embodies mind's recognition of the existence within nature of a plurality of distinct entities. Reality is composed of particular things and occasions, each having a determinate character and asserting itself in definite ways. Wherever we look in the world, we find ourselves confronted by a manifold. In the human context, this means that society is a mass of individual men, each of whom is a unique person intent upon the pursuit of his own career. Men are viewed as egoists and rationalists, and society is regarded as only a convenience. Where this dimension is emphasized, positive law is conceived as a passive and neutral public device, having no intrinsic purposes or structure of its own. It stands exclusively at the service of and is only activated by private interests. The function of law is to facilitate the achievement of personal ends and the execution of mutual agreements. (Classical liberalism. Legal individualism. Emphasis on rights and liberty. The era of private law, free contract, and liability only for fault. Theories that stress the element of will.)

The category of the One embodies mind's recognition that reality exhibits a hierarchial arrangement. All things exist and occur as parts or episodes of some larger whole. Actual particulars are elements within systems, and their character and behavior are strongly conditioned by the positions they occupy within these. Throughout reality things must accommodate themselves to one another and must be subordinated to the interests of the wholes, or Ones, of which they are parts. In the human context, this means that the group is an entity in its own right, having a foundation in reality and a career through history. Men are viewed as both needing and needed by society, which they nevertheless resist through ignorance and willfulness. Where this dimension is emphasized, positive law is conceived as an instrument that the social whole creates to serve its own interests and purposes. Here the function of law is to guarantee the integrity and effectiveness of the One, or State: to this end it coerces men and organizes their efforts. (Imperative theory of law. Public law dominates private law. "Socialization du droit." This position proliferates subspecies, depending upon the manner in which the group and its interests are conceived: *raison d'état*; the welfare state; the garrison state. Doctrine of social solidarity. Stress on duties and equality.)

The category of Process embodies mind's recognition that reality is fluid and dynamic, an arena of becoming. The universe is charged with energy: the being of things is their power, the modes of activity through which they express and assert themselves. Wherever we look in the world, we find things engaged in complicated processes of expenditure and transfer of energy in various forms. In the human context, this means that men in society (or a group and its members) constitute an enterprise rather than an entity: individual life is a striving, and group life is a series of exchanges (whether competitive or cooperative) of efforts and their products. Where this dimension is emphasized, positive law is conceived as a technique through which the diverse interests and forces at work in society are at once fostered and regulated. Here, the function of law is to promote the manifold transactions that are necessary to maintain society as a going concern. (Legal stress is now laid on factual situations and outcomes as much as on abstract relations and obligations. Arbitration procedures become prominent. Law seeks to facilitate those arrangements that are spontaneous and efficient. Legal realism. Social engineering. Historical and sociological jurisprudence—with radically different interpretations of the forces to which law should be sensitive and responsive. Jurisprudence of interests.)

The category of Pattern embodies mind's recognition that reality exhibits structure and stability. The universe is an intricate but coherent web of connectedness, in which every particular thing is of a definite kind, occupies a settled place, and sustains constant relations with other particulars. Though things are unique, similarities run among them; though each pursues its own course, they follow common paths. Wherever we look in the world, we find things interacting with one another in ways that are extremely complicated but that still exhibit marked uniformities and regularities. In the human context, this means that society is a system of relationships through which status and function are assigned and the course of events is assured. Here positive law is conceived as a body of rules that defines courses of conduct, determines rights and duties, and establishes sanctions. The function of law is to prescribe a nexus of antecedents and consequences, such that men can anticipate the outcomes of their actions and plan accordingly. (Stress is now placed on the formal and technical aspects of law, as it is only through these that law can effectively fill its role as a conserving and stabilizing force. Law conceived as a normative rather than a descriptive discipline. Doctrine of the logical plenitude of the law. Analytical jurisprudence. Pure theory of law. Legal conceptualism. Law as reason.)

This analysis, I would claim, exhibits the real meaning of order, the setting of which law is "a principle." Law always occurs within and has reference to a context in which there are many distinct entities, in which these entities assert themselves in action and exchange energy and carry on transactions among themselves, and in which there are definite patterns of regularity and uniformity. That is, law always has to deal with a Many, a One, a Process, and a Pattern. These categories depict the ultimate dimensions of being, define the framework of all becoming, and so constitute the matrix of law in all of its modes as a general principle of order. It is through a closer analysis of these categories that the exact nature and functions of positive law are to be found.

One further point must be emphasized now, though I shall explore it more fully in a later chapter. This is the fact that these dimensions are intimately connected with and interpenetrate one another. The world is at once a manifold, a universe, an arena of change, and a structured system. The same is true of society. Every particular thing is at once a unique entity, an element in various larger wholes, a locus of energy that is engaged in constant transactions with other things, and an item that occupies a definite place in a scheme of relationships. The same is true of men. This fact is vastly important for legal theory, for it means that positive law cannot deal with individual men, with the state, with social processes, or with human relationships in isolation from one another. Any action that positive law takes with respect to any one of these dimensions is inevitably going to reverberate throughout the others, and it is essential that these repercussions be anticipated.

[CHAPTER III]

THE MATRIX OF
POSITIVE LAW

I TURN NOW to the other central problem mentioned earlier: What occurs at the human level that occasions the development of positive law as a supplemental principle of order? It follows from my original postulates that certain significant changes gradually take place in evolution, finally marking off human nature and the human situation as a distinct local region of nature; that these changes place man in a novel condition and confront him with a radical challenge; and that positive law slowly emerges out of this condition and in response to this challenge. Further, relying on the preceding analysis of order as the framework of reality, we can infer that these changes occur within the dimensions of the Many, the One, Process, and Pattern. The problem now is to discern the precise character of these changes and of the situation in which they issue, for it is this course of change and its outcome that defines the full matrix of positive law.

The first step toward a solution of this problem is to call attention to the familiar fact that these pervasive dimensions of being take on different specific characters and exhibit distinctive features in various regions of nature: for example, in the realms of the inorganic, the organic, the vital, the psychic, the social. The universe clearly does contain different sorts of entities, wholes, energies, and structural relationships. Whether we are thinking in the field of physics, chemistry, biology, psychology, anthropology, mathematics, or political and legal science, our thought and the laws it frames are cast in the mold of Many–One–Process–Pattern. But the precise meanings of these categories change radically as we move among these realms. It is equally familiar that in most of these realms the characteristics of the entities, their modes of behavior, their organization into wholes, and the relations among them are established and maintained without the intervention of positive law. There are manifold realms of existence where positive law has no footing. Moreover, even mature legal systems do not take the whole of the human context within their purview. No one has ever equated law with life.

The extrahuman and human contexts in which positive law does not appear are often extremely complex. The billions of atomic particles in a piece of radium move in their orbits, react with one another and with the environment, and live out their collective career of radioactive decay, all in a thoroughly orderly manner; a multitude of individual organisms belonging to hundreds of plant and animal species inhabit a common ecological region, share in its resources, compete with and contribute to one another, and together constitute a delicately balanced whole; the thousands of ants or bees in a single nest or hive maintain the group economy, raise successive generations, pursue their distinct lives and cooperate in many enterprises, engage in mutual help and common work; the cells that compose a newly conceived human fetus grow, reproduce, and multiply millions of times, develop into specific organs and perform highly specialized functions, and are coordinated with the greatest fineness and economy to issue in a mature human being.

Furthermore, many of man's most vital activities and affairs are beyond the reach of positive law. The very idea of passing laws to standardize pulse and metabolism rates, to exclude female issue from the inheritance of blue eyes, to require the full-term human fetus to give proof of certain minimal mental and physical assets before it is born, to establish statutory limits to the age at which infants can or must walk and talk, to prohibit organic degeneration below designated limits, to define standards of parental and filial devotion—any of these proposals would strike us as satire after the manner of Samuel Butler. Yet, as a little reflection will reveal, we successfully employ law as a means to ends very similar to these in other closely related areas of human affairs. Even where it figures so prominently and importantly, positive law is only a supplemental principle of order, and there are definite limits to legal effectiveness. These are facts that we often forget, always to the detriment of both law and life.

Now, all of the contexts just discussed obviously contain the elements of Many–One–Process–Pattern. They satisfy the conditions indicated by the concept of order, and they clearly exemplify the presence and operation of some mode or modes of law. But this certainly is not positive law. There undoubtedly are some real forces and factors that are responsible for securing the state of affairs of order in these contexts. And it is commonly agreed that below the human level, and even quite widely at this level, this is done without any conscious, purposeful, or organized effort on the part of the entities (atoms, molecules, cells, molar bodies, organisms) that exist in these contexts. As to how this is done and through what agencies, there is radical disagreement. The responsibility would be variously assigned to the divine will and intellect, the inherent nature of things, the primordial principles of being, a preestablished causal nexus, and so on. Fortunately, this dispute about ultimate explanations need not concern us here. My immediate interest is sheerly descriptive, and it goes in two directions: toward discerning the significant changes that take place in the dimensions of being as evolution progresses toward the human level, and toward identifying the essential characteristics and structures of the human context as distinguished from other contexts of nature where order is a function of other modes of law.

The essence of the answer that I propose to these problems can be stated quite briefly and then elaborated. It consists in the hypothesis that the entire scheme of the process of becoming, including that segment of it that we know as "organic evolution" and that culminates in man, passes through three main stages of development, which I shall designate as *Necessity*, *Possibility*, and *Purposiveness*. As this process unfolds, gradual but important changes take place in each of the dimensions of being—that is, significant and characteristic alterations occur in the entities that compose different regions of reality, in the fields or systems or environments or milieus in which these exist, in the processes in which they take part, and in the pattern of relationships that runs among them. This is the very meaning of evolution or becoming. These changes accumulate, interrelate, and finally eventuate in man and the human condition. This is an obvious fact, and my hypothesis is simply an attempt to discern the general course and the principal phases of the process through which it has occurred.

Before expanding the hypothesis, two preliminary remarks are in order. First, the categories of Necessity, Possibility, and Purposiveness are here employed in a purely descriptive sense, not an explanatory one. I am using these concepts merely as names to summarize the essential characteristics of different types of situations that are generally familiar to us in different contexts of nature. I am not positing any esoteric forces that produce these situations. This matter can be put most exactly by saying that these terms designate *regimes*, or states of affairs, that actually hold and can be empirically described. Also, these situations are not radically distinct or sharply separated from one another. The sets of characteristics designated by these categories pervade reality and are compresent throughout nature; there is continuity in evolution, and these situations, or regimes, merge into one another. But as these characteristics are present in different proportions, various regions of nature become significantly different. The immediately important meaning of this fact is that all three of these factors pervade the human context, and man is subject to each of them. I shall deal later with the important consequences that this fact has for positive law.

There would be little point in trying to frame definitions of these categories. Instead, I shall describe the changes that are brought about in the dimensions of the Many, the One, Process, and Pattern as the contexts in which they occur exhibit a predominance of Necessity, Possibility, or Purposiveness. That is, I shall trace the movement and the transformations that take place as these conditions are superimposed on one another.

Those regions of nature of which we say that "necessity holds" or "determinism prevails," and of which the fields of physical and chemical phenomena are the most familiar examples, exhibit the following general conditions.

The outstanding feature of the dimension of the Many is the *similarity* of things of the same kind. Throughout great parts of reality the natures of things are relatively simple, and their powers are correspondingly limited. The structure of a molecule, a stone, a star, and even a plant is such that its range of variation is restricted, so that the distinctive individual character of any entity counts for very little as compared with its class characteristics. Things of the same type or kind exhibit the attributes of the type in such a uniform manner that without serious distortion they can be regarded and treated as identical. Individual variations are no doubt real among all things, but here they are so slight and unimportant that they make no real difference.

Under this regime, the significant feature of the dimension of the One is the *subordination* of things to the milieus of their existence. Each entity has its status and function largely defined for it and imposed on it by its position within its context—by the whole of which it is a part. Physical bodies are dominated by the fields in which they occur; biological structures are absorbed in the organisms to which they belong; these organisms in turn are closely dependent upon their environment. In these regions, things have little power over their surroundings and slight influence on the arrangements under which they live. The integrity of separate things is eroded and their effectiveness undermined by the massive pressures that are brought to bear upon them by their surroundings.

Under such conditions, the Processes that take place are largely describable in terms of *action and reaction*. The behavior of things is determined by the external forces that bear upon them and by their own inherent characteristics, so that things release energy but do not direct it. It is antecedent events and prevailing conditions within the field, rather than the active intervention of separate entities, that control the actual occasion. We acknowledge this state of affairs even in the human context in such phrases as "stimulus and response," "instinct," "conditioning," "habit," and "the weight of circumstances." In other contexts, where Necessity prevails, things are caught up in processes that they can neither guide nor arrest: they can only submit. Here, individual initiative and spontaneity have little scope in the face of the chain of events.

Finally, the Pattern that pervades such contexts is characterized by extreme *rigidity*. As things come into existence they take their places in a system of relationships that is already prepared for them, and they are henceforth held fast in this web. Consequently, encounters between similar things under similar conditions follow regular courses and lead to roughly identical results. The structure of the field or environment in which they exist dominates separate things, defining the relations in which they stand to other things and the courses they are to follow. Even in the human context we now have been made vividly conscious of the lasting influence exerted on us by the surroundings in which our early years are passed. Elsewhere in reality this effect is all but absolute: things inherit with existence an environment that forges indissoluble links between them and a horde of other things. This monolithic pattern leaves no opening for the private plans or mutual arrangements of individual entities.

These four conditions—similarity, subordination, action and reaction, rigidity—which are summarized under the category of Necessity, nowhere hold absolutely and without qualification, but they are an accurate description of the state of affairs that is exemplified throughout the region of the inorganic, well up into the domain of life, and even in significant portions of the human context. The outstanding characteristics of a great part of nature are sheer persistence and recurrence: things simply endure through their allotted intervals, they are replaced by closely similar things, change is uniform and sequential, and origination is a rare event. If we generalize the Newtonian concept, we might say that in these contexts inertia holds sway. We can further say that in all regions of nature, including the human, inertia plays a prominent part and Necessity is an important factor.

But however pervasive these conditions may be, they certainly do not by themselves provide an adequate account of the human situation nor of that of many other creatures. As evolution moves toward the human level, a new factor that I have termed Possibility and that is present throughout nature becomes dominant and introduces significant changes into each of the dimensions of being. The concept of Possibility refers to and summarizes certain concrete facts that compel our attention. The basic recognition that is embodied in the term is that of a loosening or easing of the conditions of Necessity, with the result that individual entities are able to participate more meaningfully and effectively in the course of events. In common usage, possibility carries with it the idea of open alternatives and variation, of future outcomes that are not pre-determined, of flexibility and change, spontaneity and novelty, of relations that are defined and can be altered by the things that stand in these relations, of room for arrangements to be made at the discretion and in the interest of those who are immediately concerned. This rather vague but widely felt meaning will at once be rendered more precise by an analysis of the outcome of this new regime in each of the dimensions of the Many, the One, Process, and Pattern.

But lest the transition from the regime of Necessity to that of Possibility be seen in false perspective, two preliminary remarks are in order. In the first place, it must be stressed that Possibility is present throughout reality, tempering the conditions of Necessity as they previously were described. Every individual thing is unique, it asserts itself, it exerts an influence, and it makes a difference to its surroundings. Such modern scientific findings as those of genetic mutations and quantum phenomena have accustomed us to these ideas, and they have made us aware that "pure" or "absolute" Necessity is an abstraction. Possibility does not appear suddenly or *ex nihilo*: it has a foothold throughout reality, and it extends its sway gradually.

The second point to be stressed is that Necessity is equally present throughout reality, and there is no region of nature in which this regime is not largely exemplified. Even in the human context, the conditions I have summarized under the concepts of similarity, action and reaction, subordination, and rigidity always make themselves felt and sometimes dominate the situation. These two points can be summed up in one conclusion: the regime of Possibility does not supersede that of Necessity but only complements and modifies it. By tracing this movement and its outcome, we can move appreciably closer to a systematic view of the essential characteristics of man and his place in nature, and thence to the conditions that give rise to positive law.

In the dimension of the Many, the basic outcome of Possibility is *differentiation*. The higher forms of life—especially man—develop complex structures and specialized functions and become capable of a wider range of activity. Individual differences become vastly more important. Members of the same species share a common nature and exhibit many similar attributes, but the room for variation is greatly increased. Individual men differ in their capacities and temperaments;

they are sensitive to varied interests and seek varied careers; they develop different skills and put these in the service of different purposes. The human endowment is extraordinarily plastic. This plasticity has two important consequences: first, it means that the inherent powers of men are generalized, thus permitting various realizations within a wide common ambit; second, it means that these powers do not develop and come to fruition automatically but that they require training and discipline in order to mature properly. As differentiation and complexity proceed, the potentialities of things become greater but also more precarious. In this course, the individual gradually emerges as the primary locus of existence and value.

The immediate repercussion of this in the dimension of the One is to transform subordination into *participation*. In the life they make and share together, men are not mere parts of wholes: they are members of groups. The essence of this relationship is its unresolved ambivalence. Throughout the human context, the individual is conscious of his personal identity, jealous of his integrity of character and freedom of action, and concerned with his own affairs. Therefore he thinks of the groups to which he belongs as devices for the furtherance of his own purposes, whether through exploitation or protection. But it is equally true that he feels himself closely tied to these groups by complex bonds of sentiment, reciprocity, imitation, and obligation, and so he thinks of himself as an element in the larger designs and destinies that they represent. That is, men regard their groups both as instruments to their personal ends and as continuing common undertakings that deserve their allegiance. The meaning of participation resides precisely in this ambivalent attitude and this reflexive relationship. To participate is to share in the decisions that the group takes and in the goods—in the widest sense of that term—that it has available. It is also to cooperate in group efforts even if we disapprove of them and to contribute to the needs of the group. In a word, participation means that individuals must stand to the group as both ends and parts and that the group must stand to individuals as both means and whole. This is obviously a subtle and fragile relationship. After thousands of years it remains at best a theoretical paradox and a tenuous reality.[1] It also poses a problem that cannot be evaded: in becoming the human group, the One requires to be transformed into a vehicle for the conduct of a mutual enterprise.

---

[1] I have discussed this particular problem quite fully in two previous papers, "The Analysis of Justice," 57 *Ethics* 1 (1946) and "Ethical Values and Legal Decision," 12 *Ohio State Law Journal* 36 (1951).

In the dimension of Process, the basic outcome of Possibility is *self-determination*. As the capabilities of things increase, they are able to enter more effectively as separate and distinct agents in the causal process. The nexus of action and reaction is loosened, alternatives open up, there is room for spontaneity within the actual occasion, and the individual takes a larger part in determining the course of the events in which he is engaged. This movement culminates at the human level. Men can store energy in the present and direct its use in the future; they can select the transactions they mean to carry on; they can control or change their environment; they can plan and persevere. In other words, men attain to a measure of independence from the pressure of circumstances, and they can themselves determine what they are to do and to be. Life becomes a career to be forged instead of a destiny to be fulfilled.

Finally, Possibility introduces a large degree of *flexibility* into the Pattern of relationships that holds among men. Like all other things, men are born into a system of relationships that is antecedent to them. Existence places them immediately in certain surroundings, brings them into intimate contact with other features and inhabitants of these surroundings, and ties them to these in a complex web of connectedness. In the human context, however, this web of connectedness is open, fluid, and only generally defined rather than being closed, rigid, and minutely determined. Its broad structure is of course established and transmitted through time by what we call custom, tradition, the social order, and the group way of life. But this social structure does not absolutely engulf men from the moment of birth: it exerts only a general influence over their training and development, and it requires only that they occupy some status and perform some function. Within broad limits, the system of social relations leaves men options and provides them opportunities to select their goals and to conduct their separate and joint undertakings as they themselves deem best. The supremely important result of this flexibility is that men can enter into private agreements through which they define what their relations are to be, what transactions they are to carry on, what outcomes they are to seek. In short, the social environment is not only a milieu of existence but also—and much more—a medium through which men can pursue their separate careers and arrange their mutual enterprises. Within broad limits, the details of the social order are left quite vague, are always variable, and are continually being reshaped.

As a name for these four outcomes, Possibility is a *fait accompli* with which man is confronted. It is something that simply happens to man, without any intention or effort on his part. Indeed, it is exactly this series of happenings that prepares the human context and inaugurates man as a distinctive kind of creature. But once Possibility has occurred and has made itself felt on an appreciable scale it must be seized and exploited. The most immediate and compelling consequence of these conditions is the shattering of the type of order that has hitherto prevailed and that I have described in terms of Necessity. It must be remembered that this does not mean that Necessity is superseded and expelled from the human context: it is merely supplemented and so modified by the emergence into prominence of characteristics that have all along been present but hitherto inconspicuous. Though this transition takes place very gradually, its cumulative outcome is spectatular. When and as men become differentiated and self-determining participants in flexible social groups, the nexus of sheer persistence and recurrence is disrupted, and inertia gives way to initiative. Spontaneity, uncertainty, conflict, and change enter prominently onto the scene. This means that the situation that issues from Possibility is fraught with both advantages and dangers. It opens the way to further radical developments, but it also threatens confusion and incoherence. Possibility opens the door of disorder upon a new realm of both positive and negative values, thereby at once demanding supplemental principles of order. Positive law arises gradually as one among many such principles. In this sense, Possibility is the ultimate ground, the essential precondition, of positive law.

The most significant feature of Possibility is that it requires that a proper use be made of it. It challenges man to give it a form, a content, and a direction. Man replies to this challenge with Purposiveness. When the action to be taken in the present is not rigidly determined by the past and by surrounding circumstances, then it must either be left to accident or defined by reference to the future. The first of these courses is certainly not unknown to us: we often hesitate, vacillate, and resign the direction of events. But the second is at least as familiar and far more significant: we do as a matter of fact deliberate upon and intervene in the course of events in order that this may lead to certain outcomes and consummations that we have in mind. As the name for this process of deliberation and intervention, Purposiveness is man's response to Possibility, through which actualizations are chosen, prepared, and brought about. Purposiveness thus recognizes and identifies the fact that in much of the human context the present state of affairs is permeated by future considerations. A good deal of human conduct embodies an intention and destination that lie beyond itself. Purposiveness therefore entails the ability to envisage the future, to discriminate within this various alternatives, to choose among these sensitively and intelligently, and to muster one's resources behind the realization of the alternative chosen. Activity is purposive just to the extent that it is controlled and directed in a coherent and persistent manner toward some possibilities and away from others.

Nature has conferred upon man a situation that offers him great opportunities. But these are not realized automatically or haphazardly; if they were, they would not be opportunities but either fates or accidents. If man is to exploit the opportunities that Possibility presents him, instead of succumbing to them, he must choose purposes with care and pursue them with diligence. It is only by such Purposiveness that man can rescue his life from necessity and protect it against chance.

We can now sketch more systematically the nature of Purposiveness by tracing its occurrence and outcome through the four dimensions of the human context. In the dimension of the Many, Purposiveness manifests itself as the quest for *cultivation*. If differentiation is to be fruitfully exploited, the integrity of individuals must be guaranteed and their proper development assured. Human personalities and careers are not the products of spontaneous maturation but of careful nurture. Most men have neither immediately discernible abilities nor compelling goals: these are only implicit and amorphous, requiring to be quickened to life and given direction. The plasticity that is such an outstanding human characteristic means not only that any man has varied potentialities but also that those which are to be realized and the extent to which realization will occur are matters that depend largely upon the intelligence and perseverance that are brought to bear upon them. If differentiation is not cultivated, it must move in one of two directions: it may relapse toward similarity under the awful guise of mediocrity, or it may issue in a theoretical relativism that denies all standards and in an actual heterogeneity that shatters the unity of the group into a mass of cliques. So differentiations must somehow be judged, selected, and trained, and the raw potentialities of men must be disciplined and educated. Cultivation represents the organized human effort to reap the advantages of differentiation by providing both the environment and the nurture that will enable men to realize their best potentialities.

In the dimension of the One, Purposiveness manifests itself as the effort to create and maintain *authority*. In the uses they make of possibility in the pursuit of their own ends, men often run counter to one another, waste their energies in friction or inefficiency, and come into open conflict. If these abuses of participation are to be avoided, the behavior of individuals must be regulated and their separate undertakings coordinated. To achieve this, the human group organizes in order that it can act as an entity. The affairs of the group as a whole must be planned, its interests administered, and its decisions carried out from a central source: it is only in this way that the private lives of men can be made to serve the public welfare. Authority issues from man's recognition that spontaneous mutuality and persuasion must often be supplemented by organized cooperation and force. It serves as a device through which the group seeks to restrain recalcitrant individuals, to assign roles and functions, to distribute the burdens and benefits of group life, and to distill common programs out of separate purposes. This effort, of course, is never completely successful. Authority is corrupted by those who hold it, resisted by those who are subject to it, and frustrated by the complexities with which it has to deal. So it often aggravates the compulsion, exploitation, and incompetence that it is intended to alleviate. But still the challenge must be accepted, for authority is instituted precisely in order that human efforts may be integrated rather than dispersed.

In the dimension of Process, Purposiveness manifests itself as the sense of *responsibility*. Self-determination means that individuals have a voice in deciding what their actions are to be: they give to the course of events a direction and a content that it would not have had without their intervention. In short, men make a difference in what is to be. This being the case, it is incumbent upon them to anticipate the outcomes they prepare, to execute these with care for others, and to acknowledge themselves accountable for the differences they make. Man commits himself to future goals: he must therefore persevere in his efforts and accept their consequences. Furthermore, men rely upon one another's commitments in planning their courses, and because of this all must adhere to their declared intentions. Man is a responsible creature to the extent that he recognizes and submits to the fact that he is a creative agent. This is evidently a burden that men often assume reluctantly and seek to evade. To combat such dereliction, duties are defined and penalties imposed. This is done on the ground that if men cannot be made responsible, at least they can be held liable. The logic of this argument is compelling, and practical considerations require its adoption. But this is a second-best solution, and our use of it should not be allowed to obscure the further goal. For here society assesses men, after the event, for whatever evil follows from their actions, and the shortcomings of this procedure are familiar. The sense of responsibility inclines a man, before the event, to act in such ways as will issue in good. In sum, responsibility is the acceptance of both the logical implications and the practical consequences of the self-determination that man exercises. To be responsibile is to care and to take care.

In the dimension of Pattern, Purposiveness manifests itself as the quest for *social coherence and continuity*. Men are finite creatures, and so are dependent upon the support of their fellows. If the resources that the world makes available are to be effectively utilized, individuals must cooperate with one another and coordinate their efforts. Flexibility has the previously cited advantages of leaving room for individual initatives and private arrangements, but it also threatens the integrity and effectiveness of the social order. To obviate this, a vast number of separate undertakings must be brought together. This requires planning, whether private or public; and this in turn requires anticipation. If men are to commit themselves to joint and future outcomes, they must have confidence that established arrangements will be maintained, that obligations will be enforced, that intrusions of the arbitrary and the accidental will be eliminated, and that they can be secure of the results of their labor. The social order should be sufficiently pliant and indeterminate to accommodate various and novel undertakings, but at the same time it must be sufficiently organized and stable to assure the security of these undertakings through large reaches of space and time. For without such continuity, the expectations that men found upon their foresight, prudence, and patience will be frustrated.

By summarizing the preceding analyses we can comprise at a glance the metaphysical, moral, and human framework of positive law. The regimes of Possibility and Purposiveness, supplementing and modifying the fabric of Necessity (of sheer persistence and recurrence), move through the dimensions of being and gradually inform them with the distinctive characteristics of the human context. Possibility introduces into these dimensions the special features of differentiation, self-determination, participation, and flexibility. Acting concurrently, Purposiveness orients these dimensions toward the forms of cultivation, responsibility, authority, and continuity. It is these two processes and the conditions that are their outcome that set the stage for the emergence of positive law.

On the basis of these conclusions we can give a more systematic answer to the question, Why is positive law? At an early stage of the investigation I proposed the hypothesis that positive law is a supplemental principle of order that arises in and is due to the peculiarities of the human context: its function is to assure man's being and promote his well-being under the conditions that prevail in this context. We now know that these conditions issue from the operation of Possibility and

Purposiveness, so the hypothesis can be restated in more concrete terms: Positive law is an organized instrument through which man seeks to refine and discipline his native purposiveness and thus to meet the challenge with which possibility confronts him (that is, to realize the values and avoid the dangers that his situation opens before him).

We have already exposed the basic structure of this problem. Possibility ushers in the peculiar conditions with which positive law must deal: highly differentiated and self-determining individuals who insist upon participating in the affairs of the groups to which they belong and who demand a flexible social order that will allow for private undertakings and arrangements. Purposiveness embodies man's recognition—sometimes vague and tenuous, sometimes clear and tenacious—of what these conditions require of him: human potentialities must be cultivated, men must be trained to responsibility, authority must be established, and a stable social milieu must be provided. It is from this complex of conditions and values that there issues the special materials and forces with which positive law deals, the special ends it should further, the special functions it serves, and the special problems it must somehow solve in its furtherance of the human enterprise insofar as this is committed to its care. This is the matrix of positive law.

DIMENSIONS OF ORDER	REGIMES OF BECOMING		
	Necessity	*Possibility*	*Purposiveness*
Many	Similarity	Differentiation	Cultivation
One	Domination-Subordination	Participation	Authority
Process	Action-Reaction	Self-determination	Responsibility
Pattern	Rigidity	Flexibility	Continuity

[CHAPTER IV]

THE FIELD OF
LEGAL ACTION

THE PRECEDING ANALYSIS has been carried out on a high level of abstraction and generalization. Like any such investigation, it has had to reduce its subject matter to sharp categories and to organize these in a rigid schema. Therefore it inevitably has strong static and divisive tendencies, threatening to reduce the situation law deals with to a collection of inert and isolated elements. This danger must now be countered by insisting upon the dynamism and cohesiveness of the field in which law operates and legal action takes place. This will also afford me the opportunity to put at least some slight legal flesh upon the bare bones of this philosophical scaffold.

The general point that I want to elaborate in the present chapter is that law functions at the focus of tensions that come simultaneously from all of the dimensions of being and all of the regimes of becoming as these occur and make themselves felt in the human context. This has two important meanings for law. The simpler of these is that the problems of cultivation, responsibility, authority, and continuity always interpenetrate. Although theoretically these tasks are distinct, in fact they merge and overlap in the practical difficulties they raise. The real men and the actual human situations with which law deals spread through these dimensions and involve these problems concurrently. Individual men, the activities in which they engage, the groups that contain them, and the relations that run among them cannot exist and so cannot be understood save as aspects of a single total state of affairs. It is therefore impossible to deal with these elements or the difficulties they pose in isolation. Any failure or unsatisfactoriness that appears in the human condition will at once betray a lack of cultivation, reflect a denial of responsibility, expose the discontinuity of the social order, and exhibit the weakness of authority. Each of these shortcomings is both cause and effect of all of the others, and since the difficulties they pose are reciprocal and cumulative, the efforts to repair them must be coordinated. As law goes about its tasks it inevitably touches all of these aspects of the human situation, though its attention is apt to be concentrated on only one of them. Any steps that law takes, any concepts, rules, and procedures that it develops in dealing with one of these problems, will bring about repercussions on its treatment of the others. And its neglect of any of them creates a vacuum that spreads through the human context and undermines the whole legal structure. We are naturally tempted to hope that if we can overcome just one of these difficulties, the others will automatically be corrected. But this hope is as futile as it is inviting. For to act in this way is to treat what are really aspects of a single problem as though they were separate issues.

The second point to be made is that each of the problems with which law deals is itself internally complicated to an extreme degree. The source of this complexity lies in the fact—the importance of which I have several times emphasized—that Necessity, Possibility, and Purposiveness are compresent throughout reality. Purposiveness is not an autonomous and self-subsistent regime or state of affairs. It does not supersede and abolish the regimes of Necessity and Possibility: it only supervenes upon these and modifies them with its own characteristics. Just as the dimensions of being interpenetrate, so do the phases of becoming. The human context forms no exception to this principle. Man is subject to each of these regimes, and he exists under each of these sets of conditions. If law is to be adequate to its role in the human enterprise, it must be sensitive to the pressures and requirements of each of these regimes alike.

The injunction that law must respect Necessity runs in two directions. In the first place, it must honor (in the bare sense of acknowledging and accepting) the demands and the limitations that necessity sets. There are some things that men cannot do, others that they are impelled to do; there are conditions that men will not long abide, others they insist upon; there are changes that men welcome, others that they resist, and still others that they will acquiesce in if skillfully managed. The human potential is marvelously pliant, but it has inherent orientations and resistances as well as critical breaking points. It is incumbent upon law to know these and to take them into account.[1]

[1] This argument becomes a good deal more familiar and obvious when we transpose it into terms of the concrete "Necessities" that a particular legal system confronts in the actual social, economic, and physical conditions in which it operates. I will touch on this point later. For the moment, I am concerned only with Necessity in its most general and pervasive form, as an essential ingredient of the human situation and so as bearing upon all law always.

But Necessity does more than merely set limits beyond which purposive intervention is ineffective or ill-advised. It also constitutes the substratum of human existence, and so defines the framework within which such intervention acts. As they were defined earlier, the conditions of similarity, action and reaction, subordination, and rigidity are indispensable to man's existence. Man must be able to rely upon them to satisfy his most vital needs, and they serve as the stable and sustaining base for his further adventurings. Law must respect these conditions by assuring their maintenance and preserving them against the threats of both erratic possibilities and wayward purposes.

Far from being always harsh and niggardly, Necessity is a regime that supports human development. Without the conditions it secures, the human enterprise would soon lose all coherence and impetus, and it would disintegrate into a series of disjointed episodes. One major task of the law as a principle of order, therefore, is to serve as a surrogate of Necessity, maintaining its inherent values when men too often seek to deny or evade them.

Law stands under an equal obligation to respect Possibility. Until quite recently there would have been no need to emphasize this: we have traditionally regarded Possibility as an unqualified blessing that should always be promoted, just as we have tended to regard Necessity as an unmitigated evil that should be eliminated when possible. Possibility was translated into the hallowed concepts of freedom, opportunity, and progress, and so was thought of as an intrinsic and absolute good. This attitude has lately undergone a radical change. As the uses men made of Possibility issued in exploitation, corruption, arrogance, and uncertainty—in sum, as they began to undermine the regime of Necessity without sufficiently supplementing this with a Purposiveness that was rationally and morally acceptable—there was a revulsion of feeling and a reversal of practice. It was widely felt that under the rules of open competition and the free play of individual initiative there were far too many losers and the few winners won far too much. The conviction grew that men needed to be protected against misfortune and their own mistakes as well as against one another. Social Darwinism, with its naive interpretation of "the struggle for existence" and "the survival of the fittest," effectively dug its own grave. Possibility came to be regarded as a threat to security and justice (it was virtually treated as a principle of disorder), and it was held to be an intrinsic evil that must be eliminated.

Both of these views are incorrect. The value of Possibility is real and very great. But this value is extrinsic and contingent: it lies in the initiatives and potentialities that Possibility unleashes, the alternatives and opportunities it provides, the enterprise and imagination that it elicits from men. Possibility can certainly be abused: it can lead to failure as well as success, regression as well as progress; misfortune or miscalculation can foil our efforts to seize the chances it gives us. Therefore the values that Possibility confers are contingent and often frustrated, but the conditions that it inaugurates are indispensable to the exercise and realization of the full human potential. By sacrificing these conditions, man might make himself secure of much that he now wants, but he would condemn himself to a lower level of existence and would forfeit all further freedom and creativity. So the challenge we face is that of maintaining Possibility and schooling ourselves to use it properly.

It is these regimes of Necessity and Possibility that provide the materials and set the conditions of our purposive pursuits. What we do at the level of Purposiveness (largely through law and other institutions) is to give form, content, and direction to our lives, both individually and collectively. But these activities are dependent upon the stable framework that Necessity provides and the fresh potentialities that Possibility makes available. Cultivation presupposes both the common substance of humanity and the plasticity of human beings. Responsibility presupposes both individual initiative and a causal nexus through which this can anticipate its outcomes and make itself effective. Authority presupposes men who acknowledge their status and duties as members of society at the same time that they claim their rights as participants. Continuity presupposes a framework that will maintain its general structure while undergoing changes of detail. These are the presuppositions of Purposiveness—the matter upon which it must impose form. The function of Purposiveness is to build upon this foundation in a way to promote the realization of the human potential that is bequeathed to it still incomplete.

Consequently, each of the four great tasks of law is in effect a triple task, and all of them are aspects of a single enterprise rather than isolated undertakings. Since law relies upon the regimes of Necessity and Possibility, it must take care to preserve their essential conditions. Since law acts within a tightly integrated four-dimensional field, its separate actions must be closely coordinated. In all of its employments, law faces a double challenge: it must solve the paradox of administering a regime of Purposiveness that will give form and direction to man's uses of Possibility without thereby reconstituting the rigid conditions of Necessity; and in dealing with particular problems in local regions of the human context (which is the usual business of the law), it must take into account the further effects that its actions will have as they spread through all of the dimensions of this context (as they surely will). In more traditional terms, this is to say that law is continually called on to solve the riddle of freedom and order (of change and certainty, progress and stability) and in doing so to resist the temptation of the single cause and simple cure. The crux of this matter lies in the paradox just mentioned—that of instituting a regime of Purposiveness that gives direction to the future while respecting the general conditions set by Necessity and preserving the potential for initiative and innovation that resides in the regime of Possibility. Because this is a highly abstract analysis that may seem remote from legal and social reality, it may help to compare and contrast this summation of the setting and the tasks of law with some similar analyses that are cast in more concrete terms and rooted in contemporary situations. The ideas of F. A. Hayek and Roberto Unger can serve this purpose admirably.

I believe that this same paradox constitutes the central problem to which Hayek and Unger address themselves in the works referred to previously;[2] and as I interpret these doctrines, they collapse my complex analysis into a simpler form: what I interpret as the interpenetration of four elements and the task of synthesis that law confronts, they see as a conflict between two competing forces and the conciliatory or balancing task of law. Hayek and Unger approach this issue from different points of view, they derive their ideas regarding it from different contexts, and they envisage it in different terms. But there is a close similarity in their analyses of our present failure to solve the problems posed by this paradox and in the proposals that they offer for a more satisfactory solution. And there is virtually a point by point correspondence of Hayek's basic concepts of "spontaneous orders" and "organizations" with Unger's central contrast of "consensus" and "instrumentalism" as competing principles of social order.

When we scrutinize these two pairs of concepts—these two dichotomies—I think it is clear that the first term in each pair is constituted of my categories of One and Process and that the second term in each pair is comprised of my categories of Pattern and Many. Hayek then conceives the problem we face as that of holding the two principles of order in a proper balance and especially of controlling the encroachments of ra-

---

[2] See F. A. Hayek, *Law, Legislation, and Liberty: Vol. I, Rules and Order* (Chicago: University of Chicago Press, 1973); and Roberto Unger, *Knowledge and Politics* (New York: Free Press, 1975) and *Law in Modern Society* (New York: Free Press, 1976).

tionally planned organizations upon the social arrangements that men have developed gradually as ways of adapting to the conditions of life and satisfying their own needs. Unger conceives the problem as that of reconciling the two sides of human nature that express themselves as sociability and individuality and thus of creating a social order in which instrumental rules can cushion the conflicts that arise when consensus weakens, without at the same time destroying these intimate personal bonds. I state the problem more abstractly: Purposiveness must intervene upon and guide Possibilities, but it must not suppress these by reconstituting a second-order regime of Necessity nor must it ignore its obligation to preserve the essential conditions of Necessity.

As a final illustration of the point I am making, I will refer briefly to the ideas of Theodore Lowi as they are set out in his interesting book, *The End of Liberalism*.[3] This work is avowedly a polemic, a powerful critique of what Lowi refers to as the "out-moded ideology" of the modern liberal state, which has made the fatal error of regarding its hypotheses as though they were "inviolable principles."[4] Lowi's indictment of contemporary liberalism contains two counts. He charges it with having wholeheartedly embraced two false and dangerous doctrines, the first of which holds that there neither can nor should be any effective limit to the scope of governmental power: the state is to be unlimited. The second holds that the ends that this unrestrained power is to serve and the means it is to adopt can best be determined simply by the play of organized pressure groups: as Lowi puts it, liberalism accepted "the pluralist notion that the pulling and hauling among competing interests is sufficient due process."[5]

Here again, I do not think it is a forced interpretation (or translation) to see Lowi as charging liberalism with basing itself on a legal and political ideology that recognizes only those constituents of order that I have identified as the Many and the One. Further, the One—the state or government—is virtually abolished as an independent element, since it acts in accord with no regular procedures and toward no settled purposes. That is, government is little more than a reservoir of power; every organized group seizes as much of this power as it can to serve its own interests; and no effort is made to coordinate these competing claims, to direct them toward a common end—the general welfare—or even to consider the feasibility of satisfying all of them. In short, what Lowi is describing is a mode of legal and political behavior (it cannot be

---

[3] Theodore Lowi, *The End of Liberalism* (New York: Norton and Co., 1969).
[4] Ibid., p. lx.   [5] Ibid., p. x.

dignified by ascribing to it a plan or policy) that abolishes the regimes of Necessity and Purposiveness and simply exploits the regime of Possibility, ignoring the restraints of actuality and indifferent to the claims of the ideal. Under these conditions, the social order becomes an amorphous field of conflicting forces, and law ceases to be a principle of order and becomes an instrument through which power is exercised. That is, the matrix of law dissolves into its separate elements, none of which has any stable character and among which no settled relationship holds.

As with any polemic, this indictment is probably a bit strong, but if the shoe is not a perfect fit, it is close enough for us to wear it and feel the pinch. Furthermore, Parts II and III of the book constitute a detailed and shattering documentation of the failure of ad hoc planning by concentrated power to solve any of the problems it deals with. This goes far to support Lowi's central theses, and it confirms the insistence of Hayek and Unger on the limitations of "constructivist rationalism" and "instrumentalism," with their reliance on "planned organizations" in the pursuit of "subjective values." And in Part IV of his book, Lowi sketches a theory of "juridical democracy" that would restore the rule of law, return a larger role to local regions and functional groups, and establish a senior civil service to administer general policies and common purposes instead of being at the beck and call of various pressure groups. As I would put it, Lowi intends to reconstitute the matrix of law by reasserting the integrity of its elements.

I think that the overriding lesson of all of these doctrines is the same: the later and more formal and explicit modes of ordering society (which are valuable developments) should not be allowed to erode and supplant the earlier and more personal and direct modes. In short, I would suggest that the analyses of Hayek, Unger, and Lowi are both special and limited interpretations of the paradoxical situation that law faces and specific proposals for dealing with this situation. If I am correct, it is easy to understand why these men seek to reduce and simplify the complex nest of tensions and problems that the matrix of law exposes: since their concerns are strongly practical and reformist, they simply have to coalesce some of the elements of this paradox in order to convert it to a more manageable form.

The difficulties that law encounters and the strategies that it employs in dealing with these complexities can clearly be seen in the checkered careers of legal concepts and doctrines. In instance after instance a legal doctrine will be enunciated in order to deal with what seems to be a specific and local problem; the legal treatment of this problem will then uncover or create other problems, more or less closely connected with the original one; and as the doctrine develops it will extend or retract its reach, retrace its steps, and engender a whole family of concepts and applications, members of which may contradict one another as they are applied in different contexts. This is to say that legal doctrines are inherently dynamic: almost any doctrine, however local and limited its origin, is soon apt to find itself engaged throughout the dimensions and regimes of the social structure. A few brief illustrations will exhibit this dispersion effect in the field of legal action.

The concept of liability—civil and criminal—is perhaps the most important tool with which law works in its efforts to institute a regime of responsibility in the dimension of Process. There is very little if anything that law can do directly to make men responsible agents in the moral sense of the term—to imbue them with a spirit of good will that will lead them to care about the differences they make. But law can quite effectively hold men accountable for the consequences of their actions: it can fine, imprison, impose damages, force reparation, and punish in other ways. This is precisely what the law of torts and the criminal code are designed to accomplish. Through these devices law is able to create an apparatus and a set of conditions that will, within limits, induce men to act with forethought and caution, if not with benevolence and concern. In general, law does this by decreeing an artificial order of antecedents and consequences with which to supplement and repair the natural order of cause and effect.

The problem that law now faces is how far to carry this new order. If we are to accept the weight of opinion of legal historians, liability was at times all but absolute, and it was certainly strict: a man was held accountable for virtually all of the differences that he produced, however unintended, inadvertent, or indirect they might be. Here, law apparently set out to fill up what it regarded as unfortunate lacunae in the causal nexus: if men did not naturally expiate and repair the ills they produced, then law would see to it that they did. There was a strongly felt need to hold men to established courses and thus to minimize the intrusion of the arbitrary and erratic into human affairs, and as a result law attempted to preserve the condition of action and reaction that characterizes the regime of Necessity. In the course of time it developed that this had—or was thought to have—the effect of stifling human energies and efforts: if anything that men did might adversely affect others, and so themselves, then it was best to do nothing. So law then developed the doctrine of no liability without fault. Given the complex interrelations of human lives and actions, men were bound to suffer from the mere fact of

the collisions of their efforts and interests, without intention or carelessness on anyone's part. Since enterprise must be encouraged, men were
absolved of the consequences of their actions unless these clearly fell
within the categories of *dolus* or *culpa*. In short, men were told to
exploit Possibility. In the course of more time, and with further changes
in the conditions of life, this doctrine was found—or thought—to create
various and familiar hardships. Thereafter law sought a way to mend
these without discouraging enterprise on the one hand or dissolving ac-
countability on the other. Law is still seeking for this *via media*, through
such concepts as negligence, liability for risk created, society as the ultimate bearer of risks, insurance, and others.

Two further remarks are in order here. First, it is obvious that these
various devices that law adopts in dealing with the dimension of Process
have an immediate impact on the other dimensions of the human context. As liability is more or less strict, the range of individual differentiation is narrowed or widened, the power of the state is strengthened or
weakened, and the web of social relationships becomes closed and rigid
or open and flexible. Second, I previously indicated that there is little
that law can do directly to promote responsibility, but this requires some
qualification. The mere fact that law enjoins some forms of behavior and
forbids others confers on these something of the aura of moral approval
and disapproval. Due to the respect men have for law, these conducts
cease to be simply lawful and unlawful and come to be felt as just and
unjust. They can then exert a positive influence on our sense of right and
wrong and so on our behavior: in effect, we value and follow legally approved behavior for itself, instead of only fearing and avoiding the consequences of illegal behavior.

The history of contract offers another example of law creating new
problems as it solves old ones and causing repercussions in areas far removed from its original source and intention. Contract has its primary
locus in the dimension of Pattern: it is a device by which men can specify
private relations and arrangements among themselves within the general framework of public relationships that is defined by the state. The
legal power to contract was granted only reluctantly and gradually. The
great necessity that pressed on the law was that of preserving the fabric
of society. This required a settled and stable pattern of social relations,
with the status and function of the individual within the group made
explicit and permanent, and this precluded private agreements and
transactions. But as men pressed for greater freedom of action and as the
advantages of individual initiative became apparent, certain forms of
contract were recognized and the concept was steadily extended. Once it

was accepted, contract gained a momentum that eventually carried it to the position of preeminence expressed in the famous provision of Article 1134 of the French Civil Code: "Les conventions légalement formées tiennent lieu de loi à ceux qui les ont faites." This same general intention is embodied in much of the legal apparatus of testamentary disposition, property, and trusts, to name but a few devices.

Of course, this apparently absolute freedom was from the first made subject to broad considerations of policy and morality, as in Article 6 of the French Code, which provided that nothing should be done that might contravene "l'ordre public et les bonnes moeurs." And this prohibition was made progressively more precise through rules having to do with good faith, fraud, illicit cause, mistake, unjust enrichment, the protection of weaker parties, and so forth. The cumulative impact of these rules, as interpreted by courts and extended by further legislation, has been to more narrowly restrict the freedom to contract. The general technique that is employed in this operation is the substitution of the will of the state (guided by some public policy or program that it has in view) for the wills of the contracting parties (guided by their views of their private interests). This process has now carried so far that commerce and industry have taken organized steps to escape the reach of the law by obviating the need to appeal to it: they in their turn establish substitutes for the legal order in the form of trade associations and private systems for arbitrating and settling disputes. And this continued encroachment of the law has produced the final irony of what the French call *le contrat marché noir*, that strange orphan of the law that is privately honored, and even enforced, though officially unrecognized and unenforceable.[6]

To take a final example, the concept of legal personality exhibits the play of these same tensions. From the start, this concept seems to have served two purposes, with first one and then the other becoming more prominent. On the one hand, the legal person could be defined quite precisely as regards status, function, and duties: since he was a creature of the law, law could assign and withdraw characteristics as it saw fit. On the other hand, the person regarded as the bearer of inherent or natural rights that demanded legal recognition was protected against discrimination and harassment by the state and was guaranteed a large measure of privacy and freedom.

In the course of its long history, the doctrine of legal personality has

[6] The course of this development in French law is brilliantly traced by R. Savatier, *Les Métamorphoses économiques et sociales du droit civil d'aujourd'hui* (Paris: Dalloz, 1948). See esp. Chapter III.

been—and still is—used variously to promote similarity, differentiation, and even, though less directly, cultivation. The existence of a sound society is dependent upon the maintenance of certain basic similarities among its members. The more significant of these include a common language, tradition, and culture, a widely accepted body of moral practices, well-established customs and habits, shared aspirations and expectations, and a general belief in the essential fairness of the social system, seen as a structure of rules and rewards that offers the same opportunities to all the group members. This common social background is so obvious and is taken so much for granted (until it begins to break down) that we are largely unaware of its presence and influence. When positive law first arises, all of this is certainly already there, and therefore law's early concern in assuring these similarities is chiefly formal and procedural. This concern finds expression in the concept of equality and in the maxim that all men are equal before the law, and it is made effective in practice through the doctrines of due process and equal protection. Within a firm and pervasive social structure, where the dissimilarities are generally accepted as fair and reasonable, this is all that law needs to do: here law is only a subsidiary principle of an order that is chiefly maintained by other means.

But this concern for essential similarities—for equality—becomes more positive and specific as the social order loosens, dissimilarities become more glaring, and men complain more fiercely. When inequalities, in the forms of exploitation, inequity, and exclusion, grow too prominent, law moves to correct them. Measures embodying this intention have long been familiar to us: indeed, we have all but forgotten that law had to decree such steps as those providing for minimum wages and working conditions, compulsory education, a progressive income tax, and mandatory basic health procedures, such as vaccination and sanitary standards. Within more recent experience we have had the extensive Civil Rights legislation and court decisions of the 1960s, directed to procuring such fundamental equalities as open housing, fair employment opportunities, and effective access to the electoral process. And on the contemporary scene we have proposals for a guaranteed minimum income to put a floor under poverty and for an Equal Rights Amendment to overcome discrimination against women. In all of these measures law is seeking to eliminate dissimilarities that are seen as prejudicial to various groups and as threats to the social order.

Law is equally solicitous in its concern for differentiation. This struggle is waged under the banner of liberty, and its weapons are the many rights that guarantee the integrity, privacy, and freedom of action of the individual. Men are protected against undue intrusion into their lives and affairs; they are made secure against various forms of harassment and discrimination; they are assured of freedom of speech, assembly, movement, choice of career, and much else. Law forges an additional and powerful weapon with the creation of nonnatural legal persons. Through these artificial entities, men are enabled to assert themselves as individuals while overcoming many of the limitations of individuality. By means of such legal persons as the labor union, the corporation, and the trust, men can combine their efforts, maintain their group identity indefinitely, avoid onerous personal responsibilities, and even enforce their wills after death.

It is inevitable that these legal efforts on behalf of similarity and differentiation should often clash and contradict one another. It is all but impossible to make men more equal without severely limiting the play of individuality. When we create new rights or extend the range of old ones, we impose corresponding duties. If this network of rights and duties becomes too detailed and complete, it tends toward the social analogue of physical entropy: all personal spontaneity and quest for excellence would then be smothered by this blanket of imposed relationships, and while all would be equal, they would be equal to very little. The end result would be a human desert of mediocrity and passivity. Conversely, as differentiations multiply and become more extreme they threaten the essential similarities of outlook, interest, and behavior on which the social order depends. It is now argued that no beliefs, practices, life styles, or moral codes are better or worse than any other— they are all merely different—so everyone must be allowed to go his own way unmolested. With the power to judge (to praise and condemn) thus called into question, the outcome would be a chaos of individual eccentrics and social factions. Here as elsewhere law, along with society, is torn between a harsh conformism that rejects individuality and a lax relativism that denies all discriminations. (In this context it is indicative of the contemporary state of mind that both of the terms *conform* and *discriminate* are now used in an exclusively pejorative sense. One does not conform to a model or standard of excellence but is made to conform to senseless and oppressive rules. And we now discriminate not "between" but only "against".)

The ideal resolution of this dilemma consists in establishing a regime of cultivation that can impose standards and institute disciplines that will assure the nurture that human plasticity requires, while at the same time leaving room for this plasticity to express itself in various ways and to seek novel outlets. To this end, differentiations must be judged, selected or rejected, and trained. For the most part, law intervenes in this process only indirectly, through the medium of other institutions over which it exercises a general power of supervision. Among the more important of these institutions that law both protects and oversees are the family, schools, churches, labor unions, private foundations, charitable organizations, and the communications media. In their different ways, all of these serve to maintain both a solid foundation of similarities and a loose superstructure of differentiations: they have borne the brunt of the work in society's efforts to assure itself of a properly cultivated citizen body. But all of these institutions are subject to legal control, which can be exerted to extend or retract their field of action, to increase or limit their powers, and to redefine their functions. And when it is felt to be necessary, there is available to law an array of devices by which it can intervene more positively in this process: the licensing power and regulatory agencies through which it can set standards and monitor performance; the interpretation it chooses to put upon such concepts as public policy, due process, equal protection, individual rights, reasonable care, and many others; and, more recently and actively, programs to support both the disadvantaged and the exceptionally talented.

In all of the dimensions of the human scene, law faces the same general task of manipulating the regimes of Necessity and Possibility in such a way as at least to permit and hopefully to promote the development of the regime of Purposiveness. Perhaps the most familiar instance of the tension that accompanies this effort is found in the dimension of the One. The group must be able to assure social order and its own integrity: individuals have to be subordinated to group power. But central arbitrariness and despotism must be prevented: individuals have to be able to participate effectively in group decisions and actions. This is of course the traditional problem of at once instituting and controlling power. And the devices that law employs to solve it are equally traditional: on the one hand there are such concepts and doctrines as sovereignty, the prerogative, public policy, the general welfare, and police power; on the other hand there are written constitutions, the doctrine of the separation of powers, representative government, and guaranteed rights. It is hoped that from these there will issue an authority that is both effective and responsive.

The complexity of the field of legal action is threefold: law deals with a plurality of elements and issues; these are intimately interconnected; and law transforms them in dealing with them. Every legal concept—every doctrine and dictum, every procedure and rationale—has its primary locus at some specific point within the grid that is formed by the dimensions and regimes of being: it has been developed as a solution to some concrete problem or as a means to some particular end. But since the problems and purposes that challenge man—and law—are never sharply defined and demarcated, the content and reach of legal concepts tend also to remain open and flexible. Whatever their original source and objective, these concepts are almost sure to encounter situations, to have repercussions, and even to create problems that were not foreseen when they were first enunciated. The ambiguities, vacillations, and subtle distinctions that are so characteristic of any mature legal system are therefore not the loose ends and incommensurables that they may appear to be. Rather, they are law's answer to the complications and tensions that it encounters as it goes about its tasks. Legal concepts do not embody eternal truths, absolute values, or categorical solutions—they are never static and complete. These concepts are both the summations of the past achievements of Purposiveness and the indications of its present intentions. They should always be thought of as subject to future correction.

It is, however, understandable that law should be continually tempted to reduce this task to simpler and more static terms. The most obvious temptation that Law faces is that of disposing of its problems once and for all by a return to the regime of Necessity. Since possibilities are always uncertain in their outcome and unsettling to the established order, their future occurrence would be eliminated by a program projected far into the future and rigorously adhered to. The human scene would be minutely regulated, and law would henceforth be only a passive agent of the status quo. When the fallacies of this procedure are realized, there is always the temptation for law to shirk its problems by installing a regime of pure Possibility: law would renounce the task of defining and directing the uses that men are to make of Possibility and would act only as an impartial arbiter of the conflicts that inevitably arise out of the private uses that men determine for themselves. Law here conceives itself in purely procedural and formal terms and absolves itself of responsibility for the content that gains expression and actualization through its forms.

These conceptions of law have had both theoretical and practical ascendancy at various times in the past, and they still exert an influence in the present. But the inadequacy of these ways of dealing with the issues that law faces is now widely recognized, and they are rejected in principle, although I believe it can be shown that legal action still falls into these errors in concrete cases where the theoretical path that it is following is disguised, even from itself, by the maze of facts through which it is moving. Instances of this have been suggested in the preceding discussions of various legal concepts. I shall discuss the matter very fully in Chapters XIV and XV, with particular reference to the doctrine of rights and its recent extension into vast and novel regions.

To adopt the first of the views above would be to maintain that the purposes of law are already so clear and certain that they require no further refinement and permit of no deletions or additions. To adopt the second would be to maintain that these purposes are so personal and arbitrary that they can be neither anticipated nor disciplined. Both of these views depend upon the supposition that it is the function of law to serve purposes that somehow come to it from elsewhere already complete. And this supposition is altogether a mistake. For law does not inherit its purposes ready-made: it has to fashion them. The human purposiveness of which law is an agent is very far from being a completely coherent and lucid force: it is often inchoate and inarticulate. Law is one of the major institutions (though by no means the only one, and I shall turn to this point in a moment) that gives shape and direction to this force. Law cannot therefore sit idly by and await the outcome of the interplay of Necessity, Possibility, and Purposiveness as these weave their way through the dimensions of the Many, the One, Process, and Pattern. Since law helps to preside over these regimes, it must take an active role in determining both the contents and the conditions of the major goals toward which they are striving—cultivation, responsibility, authority, and continuity.

This analysis completes the statement of my theory of the basic elements and structure of law: it is my thesis that this system of interrelated elements constitutes the matrix from which law emerges and the field within which legal action takes place. Before fleshing out the body of my theory, it will be well to consider two related objections that might be urged against it.

In the first place, it might be objected that the preceding analysis and argument issue in an interpretation of law that is extraordinarily intricate and fluid, and it might be complained that it is difficult for law to embrace all of the tasks and goals that I have assigned to it. Both charges must obviously be admitted. The only answer to them is to insist that this is, as a sheer matter of fact, the matrix within which positive law must and does operate. And to substantiate this claim, it can easily and convincingly be shown that law does, as a further matter of fact, undertake each and all of these tasks as it goes about its daily work (though all too often, alas, it deals with them separately and intermittently, and as though unaware of their interconnectedness). This complex involvement

of the law has been concretely illustrated in some of the preceding discussions, and it will be more fully documented in later chapters.

Since this matrix is the context and the challenge of law, it is well that
law be aware of it, so that it can act with a clear and coherent consciousness of its total role. My defense on this charge can most tellingly be
made by pointing out that it has long been a commonplace that law is a
tissue of paradoxes. No one has been more alert to this characteristic of
law, or has given it a more central place in his legal thought, than Mr.
Justice Cardozo. In the last of his major works, he has this to say on the
subject.

> The reconciliation of the irreconcilable, the merger of antitheses,
> the synthesis of opposites, these are the great problems of the law.
> "Nomos," one might fairly say, is the child of antimonies, and is
> born of them in travail. We fancy ourselves to be dealing with some
> ultra-modern controversy, the product of the clash of interests in
> an industrial society. The problem is laid bare, and at its core are
> the ancient mysteries crying out for understanding—rest and mo-
> tion, the one and the many, the self and the not-self, freedom and
> necessity, reality and appearance, the absolute and the relative. We
> have the claims of stability to be harmonized with those of prog-
> ress. We are to reconcile liberty with equality, and both of them
> with order. The property rights of the individual we are to respect,
> yet we are not to press them to the point at which they threaten the
> welfare or the security of the many. We must preserve to justice its
> universal quality, and yet leave to it the capacity to be individual
> and particular. . . . Deep beneath the surface of the legal system,
> hidden in the structure of the constituent atoms, are these attrac-
> tions and repulsions, uniting and dissevering in one unending
> paradox.[7]

We may deplore this situation, but it is futile to deny it and irrespon-
sible to evade it. It is surely better to seek for a comprehensive grasp of
the tensions that law must reconcile—the paradoxes it must resolve—
than to deal with them in isolation. The latter procedure usually raises at
least two problems for every one it settles; the former should enable us
to anticipate and measure the outcomes we are preparing and so equip
us to act with a larger and a longer view.

The whole intention of the preceding analyses has been to give a systematic exposition of these "ancient mysteries" of the law to which Jus-

---

[7] Benjamin N. Cardozo, The Paradoxes of Legal Science (New York: Columbia University Press, 1928), pp. 4, 5, 7.

tice Cardozo paid such eloquent testimony. I would maintain that the results of this inquiry do no more than exhibit what is actually involved in the deceptively simple dictum, "law is a principle of order." When we analyze this apparent truism, this is what we find. I do not think that I have invented complications. I hope that I have merely exposed those that are usually covered by a too facile acceptance of a familiar formula.

A second possible objection follows immediately from the first. This can best be put in the form of several obvious questions that might be asked of the analysis presented here: Can so complex and abstract a theory be of any possible guidance in dealing with concrete issues? How would a judge or legislator apply such a theory in reaching a decision? How would the theory effect the practice of those who make and administer the law? In a word, could the theory make a difference, and if it did, what would the difference be?

A satisfactory answer to these questions can only emerge from the book as a whole, but I can offer a general response that might serve to allay these doubts for the present and at the same time to indicate the form in which a fuller answer will be cast. I would suggest that this theory can and should—indeed does in fact—function in the making of legal decisions in much the way that Jeremy Bentham held that his famous hedonic calculus should and did function in moral judgments. Bentham first describes what would be involved in a complete or theoretical application of the calculus in a specific case: this is spelled out in detail through six steps. Roughly summarized, it would require the determination of the total amounts of pleasure and pain, as measured against each of the seven points of the calculus, that would be produced for all of the persons affected by each of the actions among which a choice is being made. The right action is that which would lead to the greatest balance of pleasure over pain. But Bentham was enough of a realist to recognize that this could never be done with precision and that it would rarely even be attempted: his theory is therefore advanced as an ideal model to be kept in mind and not as an actual procedure to be followed. His views on this question, brief and to the point, are worth quoting in full:

> It is not to be expected that this process should be strictly pursued previously to every moral judgment, or to every legislative or judicial operation. It may, however, be always kept in view: and as near as the process actually pursued on these occasions approaches to it, so near will such process approach to the character of an exact one.[8]

---

[8] Jeremy Bentham, *An Introduction to the Principles of Morals and Legislation* (Oxford: The Clarendon Press, 1876), Chapter IV, paragraph vi.

My answer to the questions posed above is the same as Bentham's. I would argue, in the first place, that all of those who work in the law, especially in making and applying it, actually carry on their deliberations within the framework that I have analyzed. Such a conception of the field and the tasks of the law is quite simply an integral and basic part of the heritage—the intellectual furniture—of anyone who is trained in the law. Three points should have been firmly established by the previous discussions and citations: "law is a principle of order" is a postulate that pervades all legal thought; the concept of order carries implicitly and in concrete terms the meaning that I have formulated explicitly and in abstract terms; and law must assure stability, provide for change, and envisage future goals. This being the case, it is natural and inevitable that anyone trained in the law thinks of it in this way.

I do not, of course, mean to suggest that lawyers, judges, and legislators always have such a formula clearly in mind. They do not need to: they simply apply the formula without being conscious of it. In doing this, they do not necessarily, or even usually, survey the entire field of legal action as I have plotted it: they do not run through the dimensions of Many–One–Process–Pattern and the regimes of Necessity, Possibility, and Purposiveness. But they are at least peripherally aware of all of these constituents that comprise the matrix of law. Put more concretely, they are aware of the impact that their contemplated decision is apt to have on the parties who will be affected by it, on the state and its relations with its citizens, on the activities and enterprises that men undertake, and on the established body of human relationships and the social fabric in general. Furthermore, they will be aware that they must preserve the present legal and social orders, accommodate new forces and circumstances, and channel these toward certain outcomes. In the vast majority of instances, events and conditions in some small number of these areas of the total field will stand out sharply as being of decisive significance; the decision will then be reached by explicit consideration of the demands they impose and the solution they require, with the other elements never being weighed, at least consciously.

In short, this is the framework in which legal thought moves, and those trained in the law think in these terms and apply this seemingly complicated and artificial formula as naturally as all of us employ the multiplication tables and the rules of grammar. It is only on rare occasions that a legal problem is so involved and obdurate that a lawyer or judge has to withdraw from its concrete facts and dissect it by reference to this schema. Here, as so often elsewhere, familiarity surprises us when we are made to realize the complexity of operations that we carry out quite spontaneously. As a final word in this regard, it is interesting to note that Bentham made exactly the same point about his hedonic calculus when he said: "Nor is this a novel or unwarranted, any more than it is a useless theory. In all this there is nothing but what the practice of mankind, wheresoever they have a clear view of their own interest, is perfectly conformable to."[9]

This leads to the second part of my answer. I think that legal decisions involving complex problems and having serious and far-reaching consequences should be made with all of the elements of my analysis clearly in mind. All too often such decisions are reached with consideration of only those areas of the legal field in which the issue arose, with a neglect of the repercussions that may follow in any other areas or even in other regions of the area in question. Decisions made in this way cannot be anything but partial and short-sighted in their view of the issues at stake and the outcomes they prepare. As Bentham argued, if we are serious in the search for pleasure (the pursuit of happiness is a more imposing way to put it), then we should weigh all of the dimensions of the pleasures we are comparing, not only such immediately obvious ones as their intensity, duration, and easy availability. Similarly, I would urge that if those who serve the law are seriously concerned to achieve justice and further the general welfare, they should hold clearly before their minds the entire matrix of law and not allow their attention to be monopolized by some apparent and self-proclaimed "compelling interest" of the here and now. For it is only such consideration that can assure decisions that are balanced in their weighing of competing claims, farsighted in terms of future consequences, and consistent with the web woven by the past. This counsel is the more important because it is precisely when judges have to decide "hard cases" and when legislators have to bite the bullet on a highly controversial issue that they are the most likely to hear only the party with an immediate claim to urge or the interest that can exert the greatest pressure.

Finally, with regard to this question, I must enter an urgent disclaimer. I certainly do not mean to assert that this theory can automatically generate correct solutions to the concrete problems with which law deals. The theory is not advanced as a logical schema from which sound conclusions can be deduced. It cannot indicate the one right decision in a case, or guarantee beforehand the efficacy of a legislative enactment, or point the precise path toward justice. As in questions of morality, so in those of public policy, no theory can dictate a "right"

[9] Ibid., paragraph viii.

answer. The most it can do is to expose the complexity of the problem and the framework within which it must be resolved, to clarify the issues at stake, to direct attention to repercussions and consequences that are not immediately apparent, and to protect deliberation against the appeals of sentiment and expediency while guiding it toward an outcome that is reasoned and principled. But, like any other, this theory is helpless to identify exactly and certainly either the proper goal to be pursued or the best course toward this goal—all of which is simply to recognize that universals can never exhaust particulars.

These relative powers and limitations will be exposed more clearly in later chapters, when I apply this analysis and framework to certain vexed and important contemporary problems. But now I want to elaborate the theory I have sketched by looking at law from another point of view: that of its actual genesis and development in time. I shall seek to place law more exactly in both its natural and human contexts: as related to other modes of law in nature and to other principles of order in human society.

[CHAPTER V]

THE MODES OF LAW

IN THIS and the following chapters I want to consider three closely related topics: the modes of law, the continuity of law, and the genesis of
positive law. The broad issue of which these topics are aspects is that of
the relationship—if any—between positive or civil law and various other
kinds of laws, such as laws of nature, moral laws, and customary law.
This issue is still an open one, even despite all of the centuries it has been
debated. There are those who claim that positive law is sui generis, having no real relationship with other kinds of laws but merely sharing a
verbal umbrella with them. And even those who agree that such a relationship does exist often disagree radically regarding both its precise nature and the other terms to which it runs.

On this issue I shall argue that there is an essential and intimate connection between positive law and other types of law. I have of course
already suggested this (in Chapters I and II) in elaborating the notion of
law as a principle of order. Now I want to develop more fully this principle of the continuity of law, which holds that all laws are coherent members of one vast "realm and rule of law," as ancient writers called it. My
discussion will focus on three points: the systematic identification of the
basic modes of law, the continuity that runs among these different
modes, and the genesis of positive law within this field, with particular
attention to the complex nature of such law.

To obviate at once a possible serious misunderstanding, I should make
it clear that I do not mean to "reduce" positive law to some more primitive phenomena or to derive it from some higher and more authoritative
body of law. These things have been done in the past, to the justifiable
anger of legal scholars and men of the law. I regard positive law as having distinctive characteristics that distinguish it from other types of law,
and I will pay full due to these later. I also think that positive law shares
equally important traits and has intimate relations with these other
types of law, and these are my immediate concern. A proper understanding of these common characteristics and relationships will do much to
clarify the nature and tasks of positive law and to explain its role in
society.

The first step in this inquiry is to confront the thesis of the continuity of law with the array of facts that it encounters and must account for. The term law has a rich employment in our thought. It occurs in a multiplicity of phrases, batteries of qualifying words are attached to it, it refers to dissimilar contexts, and its exact attribution varies with its range. I have earlier presented argument and evidence that in its most general and inclusive sense and in all of its usages, law is a principle of order. As I then put it: "Law is the name we give to that type of proposition that formulates the structures and relationships, the sequences and similarities, the constancies and recurrences that are contained within this condition [order] and make up its specific details. Therefore law is a principle of order in the sense that laws are propositions that refer to and explicate the lines of connection that run through orderly contexts." But the fact still remains that this generic meaning of the concept occurs in a variety of specific forms: for laws and the orders to which they refer exhibit quite different characteristics in different contexts.

This rich and diverse employment of the term law can best be brought out by merely listing some of the kinds of laws to which we frequently and familiarly refer. A random catalogue displays such items as these: descriptive laws, prescriptive laws, normative laws, imperative laws, scientific laws, laws of nature, natural law, divine law, moral law, positive law, civil law, international law, primitive law, customary law, common law, laws of motion, laws of thought, laws of learning, laws of war, laws of heredity and of inheritance, laws of status and of contract, the law of the jungle, the law of the marketplace, the law of supply and demand, and even bylaws and in-laws.

This is certainly a heterogeneous array of items, and it might seem foolhardy to assert that there are any real continuities among these terms and any classification that can relate them systematically. It is therefore comforting to realize that if the claim appears foolhardy, it is at least not novel. For this notion of the continuity of law is one of the favorite themes of jurisprudence and philosophy, and it has a long history. It was adumbrated by the earliest Greek philosophers. It was developed in various directions, though never systematically, by Plato and Aristotle. It became one of the central tenets of the Stoics, and from them passed to the Roman jurists, where it first served as a fruitful legal doctrine; here it found expression in the famous triad of *jus naturale*, *jus gentium*, and *jus civile*. The principle of the continuity of law probably received its most complete and refined statement in the thought of Thomas Aquinas, where it was systematically expounded in terms of the four types of eternal law, natural law, divine law, and human law. It played an influential part in the development of international law at the hands of Grotius and Pufendorf. It had a central place in the thought of John Locke, both in its classical form and in the modern guise of natural rights; and through the American disciples of Locke, this principle was given a prominent role in our own legal thought and practice. Finally, this notion of the continuity of law can readily be seen to have a necessary and important place in all of the varied doctrines of historical and sociological jurisprudence, with their emphasis on the derivation of positive law from some prior factors.

The wide occurrence of the principle of the continuity of law and the general meaning that it carries can be illustrated by quotations from jurists of varying schools of thought and different periods of time. Aquinas spoke in behalf of centuries of philosophers when he said that "Law is a measure and rule of acts."[1] And he elaborated in these terms, adopted from Tully: "Justice has its source in nature; thence certain things came into custom by reason of their utility; afterwards these things which emanated from nature, and were approved by custom, were sanctioned by fear and reverence for the law."[2] Blackstone speaks in similarly broad terms: "Law, in its most general and comprehensive sense, signifies a rule of action; and is applied indiscriminately to all kinds of actions, whether animate or inanimate, rational or irrational. Thus, we say, the laws of motion, of gravitation, of optics, of mechanics, as well as the laws of nature and of nations."[3] Montesquieu states the same idea with a somewhat different emphasis: "Laws, in the widest signification of the term, are the necessary relations that derive from the natures of things; and in this sense, all things have their laws."[4] Hooker embodies this principle in a theological form when he says that "the being of God is a kind of law to His working,"[5] and so he terms "any kind of rule or canon, whereby actions are framed, a law."[6]

Karl Pearson develops the same idea in a more scientific manner and greater detail:

Tracing historically the growth of civil law, we find its origin in unwritten custom. The customs which the struggle for existence

[1] St. Thomas Aquinas, *Summa theologica*, I-II, 90, 1.

[2] Ibid., 91, 3.

[3] Sir William Blackstone, *Commentaries* (Oxford: The Clarendon Press, 1765-1769), I:38.

[4] Montesquieu, *De l'esprit des lois* (Paris: Garnier Frères, 1927), p. 1.

[5] Richard Hooker, *Ecclesiastical Polity*, ed. R. W. Church (Oxford: The Clarendon Press, 1905), I, ii, 2.

[6] Ibid., I, iii, 1.

have gradually developed in a tribe become in course of time its earliest laws. Now, the farther we go back in the development of man,
through more and more complete barbarism to a simply animal
condition, the more nearly we find customs merging in instinctive
habits. But the instinctive habit of a gregarious animal is very much
akin to what Austin would have termed a natural law. The laws re-
lating to property and marriage in the civilized states of today can
be traced back with more or less continuity to the instinctive habits
of gregarious animals.[7]

We find another advocate of this idea in John Austin. He writes:

Every act or forbearance that ought to be an object of positive law,
ought to be an object of the positive morality which consists of opinions or sentiments. Every act or forbearance that ought to be an object of the latter, is an object of the law of God as construed by the
principle of utility. But the circle embraced by the law of God, and
which may be embraced to advantage by positive morality, is larger
than the circle which can be embraced to advantage by positive law.
Inasmuch as the two circles have one and the same center, the
whole of the region comprised by the latter is also comprised by the
former. But the whole of the region comprised by the former is not
comprised by the latter.[8]

Finally, one finds contemporary echoes of this principle in two of our
greatest jurists, Justices Cardozo and Holmes. Cardozo is particularly
explicit on this point for a modern, so I will quote him at some length. In
The Growth of the Law he puts it thus:

When there is such a degree of probability as to lead to a reasonable
assurance that a given conclusion ought to be and will be embodied
in a judgment, we speak of the conclusion as law, though the judgment has not yet been rendered. . . . I think it is interesting to reflect that such a use of the term law strengthens the analogy between the law which is the concern of jurisprudence, and those
principles of order, the natural or moral laws, which are the concern
of natural or moral science. . . . If once I figured the two families as
distant kinsmen, tracing their lines perhaps to a common ancestor,
but so remotely and obscurely that the call of blood might be ignored, I have now arrived at the belief that they are cousins ger-

---

[7] Karl Pearson, *The Grammar of Science*, Everyman's Library (1949), p. 77.

[8] John Austin, *The Province of Jurisprudence Determined*, ed. H.L.A. Hart (London: Weidenfeld and Nicholson, 1954), p. 163.

man, if not brothers. . . . The study of law is thus seen to be the study of principles of order revealing themselves in uniformities of antecedents and consequences. . . . As in the processes of nature, we give the name of law to uniformity of succession.[9]

In the closing sentences of his famous essay, "The Path of the Law," Holmes puts the matter more succinctly and enigmatically: "The remoter and more general aspects of the law are those which give it universal interest. It is through them that you not only become a great master in your calling, but connect your subject with the universe and catch an echo of the infinite, a glimpse of its unfathomable process, a hint of the universal law."[10]

But despite its long history and the strong influence it exerted in the past, the principle of the continuity of law has been undergoing a steady attenuation in recent decades. The schools of legal realism and positivism, analytical jurisprudence, and the pure theory of law have largely dominated the scene for some time, and all of these, in their different ways, have put the legal system itself at the center of attention. Their precise reasons for doing this have varied, but they have shared a general motive: they have wanted to exclude questions of the origins and ends of law in order that they might focus their studies on such internal questions as the logical structure of legal systems, the manner in which these systems actually operate in practice, and the ways in which they produce effects in society. Thus, whereas the outlook of legal scholars used to be philosophical, it is now scientific: like the scientist in his laboratory, they isolate their phenomena and study them under artificial conditions as a means of gaining more detailed knowledge. There is nothing to be said against such a procedure and much to be said for it if the investigator remembers to put his phenomena back in their context. But the proviso is vital, and contemporary jurisprudence largely fails to meet it.[11]

Of course, these scholars recognize the connections of law with morality, justice, social conditions, human aspirations, and what H.L.A. Hart

[9] Benjamin N. Cardozo, The Growth of the Law (New Haven: Yale University Press, 1924), pp. 33-40.

[10] O. W. Holmes, Harvard Law Review 457 (1897). It must be acknowledged that this is more the rhetoric of a peroration than a serious statement of doctrine. The view that Holmes systematically expounds in his legal writings and relies on in his judicial opinions is quite different. Cf. footnote 12.

[11] A notable exception is the work of Lon L. Fuller. See especially his books, The Law in Quest of Itself (Chicago: The Foundation Press, Inc., 1940) and The Morality of Law (New Haven: Yale University Press, 1964), which are sustained and eloquent arguments for placing law in a larger context.

calls "natural necessities;" but they are not really interested in these, and their attitude appears to be that although such factors played a role in the past development of law, they are no longer relevant or influential. Now that law is mature, they seem to feel, it can stand on its own feet.[12] This point of view finds a typically matter of fact expression in one of the most influential of modern texts, Sir John Salmond's *Jurisprudence*, which went through ten editions between 1902 and 1947. Salmond introduces his treatment of this question by distinguishing eight kinds of law: imperative, physical or scientific, natural or moral, conventional, customary, practical or technical, international, and civil (positive). He explicitly insists that this list is a "simple enumeration" of the kinds of law, not a "logical scheme of division or classification"; and he strongly implies that to search for this latter is to tilt at windmills. Salmond's general position is well summarized in his conclusion that "the relation between the physical laws of inanimate nature and the moral or civil laws by which men are ruled has been reduced . . . to one of remote analogy."[13]

From its position as a living principle that guided inquiry, the principle of the continuity of law has fallen to the point where it usually receives at best only casual lip service and often open denial. That this should have happened is understandable, for the search for a thread connecting the diverse types of law listed above is at least as frustrating as it is fascinating. As long as thought was cast in religious terms, this diversity did not cause serious problems, for then all things and all of the orders of nature were regarded as creatures of God, and they all, in their various ways, obeyed His laws. Modern thought, with its naturalistic turn, finds it far more difficult to accommodate these different kinds of laws within a single schema, for such thought is unwilling either to give up its materialistic and mechanistic bias or to extend this comprehensively into its explanations of man and the human scene. Therefore a bifurcation results.

But though the contemporary neglect of this principle may be natural, it is also regrettable, for its outcome is to isolate man from the rest of

---

[12] For instance, the only "natural necessities" that Hart mentions as constituting "the minimum content of natural Law" are the provision of "sanctions" for the "protection of persons, property, and promises." See H.L.A. Hart, *The Concept of Law* (Oxford: The Clarendon Press, 1961), p. 195. A similarly impoverished interpretation of the tasks and goals of law is often expressed by Holmes. Cf. especially the two essays, "Ideals and Doubts" and "Natural Law," both reprinted in *Collected Legal Papers* (New York: Harcourt, Brace and Howe, 1921), pp. 303-307 and 310-316.

[13] John Salmond, *Jurisprudence*, ed. Glanville Williams, 10th ed. (London: Sweet and Maxwell, 1947), pp. 20, 26.

nature and law from the rest of the social order. Simply as a matter of logic, this is a violation of two postulates that stand at the heart of modern thought, the unity of nature and evolution. And, more importantly, it has the practical effect of depriving us of a powerful tool for understanding the full nature of positive law and its connections with other social elements and institutions. We come to think of law simply as "sovereign," "logically complete," and guided only by its own "*grundnorms*"; and thus we close our minds—if we cannot quite shut our eyes—to the extralegal forces that do so much to create and direct law. So I intend to take the principle of the continuity of law very seriously, to carry it to its logical conclusion, and to see if a satisfactory contemporary meaning can be given to it and some constructive results derived from it. But the first step in this inquiry must be to get a clearer and more systematic view of the kinds of laws among which this continuity runs.

Law is always "a principle of order." This defining phrase has two constituent parts, and we have so far analyzed only one of these, the concept of "order." We must now examine the first part, and ask what is meant by saying that law is "a principle of" order. What is the relation of "law" to "order"? How are laws connected with the orders of which they are principles?

In raising this issue, we recognize at once that the sense in which law is a principle of order is not the same in all contexts and usages. There clearly are different kinds of law: witness the list given earlier in this chapter. Just as clearly, we do not think of all of these laws as standing on the same footing, either in themselves or in relationship to the orders to which they refer. We recognize laws of personal health and public sanitation, of moral responsibility and contractual obligation, of learning and school attendance, of genetic heredity and legal inheritance, of prenatal development and postnatal duties. But we certainly feel that these laws are differently related to their phenomenal fields: that they have different statuses, serve different functions, operate in different ways, and are differently compelling. As my main thesis indicates, I think that we exaggerate these distinctions and make them too sharp. But this point must wait, for differences of some sort are present here, and these must be clarified separately before we can trace the continuity between them.

This task can be approached most simply through a classification of laws. I would argue that there are three fundamental modes of law: expository, prescriptive, and normative. These categories embrace all laws whatsoever. The following descriptions of these modes of law and the distinctions to be drawn between them are too rigid to be faithful to the facts: they are tainted with the artificial. This is a temporary sacrifice to clarity, and will shortly be repaired with the qualifications that truth in its turn requires. For the moment, then, I am describing abstract types of law rather than actually operative laws.

Expository laws describe an *actual* order of things and events. We think of them as reflecting a state of affairs that is pre-established and self-sustaining. The characteristics of objects and the course of happenings that they report appear to be invariant and predetermined. Typical cases of laws of this mode are what we call scientific laws or laws of nature: for example, the laws of gravitation and acceleration, of molecular structure, of genetic and chromosomal recombination, of good and bad money, of instinct and learning, of supply and demand, and perhaps more doubtfully (and already anticipating complexities soon to be considered), conventional and customary laws. We usually regard such laws as expounding an order that is prior to and independent of the laws themselves: they embody and depict what is, but they do not determine, or create, or maintain this. Expository laws describe how things are ordered: they consecrate what we accept as fact.

Normative laws describe an *ideal* order of things and events. We think of them as defining states of affairs that should be but as of yet are not and that command our efforts in their behalf. The most familiar examples of this mode of law are the moral law, divine law, and natural law. All of these serve to depict to us the realm of what ought to be—the goals for which we should strive and the standards to which we should conform. Other examples, in the very different context of the arts, are the laws of proportion, of harmony, of metrics, and of the dramatic unities. Codes of legal and business ethics, of scholastic honor systems, of sportsmanship, are also of this type. Many of the statements found in political proclamations, such as the American Declaration of Independence, the Communist Manifesto, and the Preamble and Bill of Rights of the United States Constitution, are primarily normative in character: they describe the salient features and structures of the ideal community that we are called on to build. At a level still closer to common sense, the stereotypes, ambitions, and heroes that we hold before the young are covert normative laws: they are implicit descriptions of the happiness, virtue, blessedness, or success that we seek to inculcate as the ideal end of man and the proper content of his purposes. All laws of this mode expound an order that represents the perfect completion and realization of tendencies which, if left to themselves in this world, often go astray or meet frustration. Normative laws describe how things should be ordered: they consecrate what we accept as value.

Prescriptive laws describe the *passage* from the actual to the ideal order. They embody what we take to be the most effective methods for transforming what is into what ought to be. Familiar examples of this mode are traffic regulations, rules governing academic behavior, codes of manners, international law, the laws of plant propagation and cultivation, of eugenics, of bodily and mental health, of animal breeding, of financial investment, of business management, and the rules set out by federal regulatory agencies. Also of this kind are the regimes and disciplines established to promote the success of such disparate types as professional athletes, would-be scholars, and operatic tenors. Laws of this mode trace the courses that we should follow if we are to attain our goals. They are always hypothetical in character: they assume certain ends (the ideal order as described at least implicitly by normative laws) and point the way to their achievement. They are also contingent, assuming the structure of the actual order (as described by expository laws) as the setting in which they must operate.

Prescriptive laws occur in two subtypes: advisory and imperative. Laws of the first kind assume that those to whom they are addressed have certain ends in view, and they merely depict the means to achieve these ends; their sanction is simply the success or failure that will follow upon their acceptance or rejection. The laws of animal breeding, voice control, business management, and weight control through diet are of this type. Prescriptive-imperative laws command some patterns of behavior and prohibit others on the ground that these observances are necessary to achieve some valuable goal but are apt to be challenged by individuals, either because these individuals reject the goal in question or because they resent the efforts and restrictions it demands. This leads to the introduction of explicit and artificial sanctions and to the creation of an apparatus to enforce these sanctions and thus to secure a conformity that might otherwise be withheld. It is in this category that most people would spontaneously place positive or civil law, and an influential legal theory has been based on this characteristic of imperativeness: as John Austin said, "law is a command." I do not question the importance of this element, but I would insist that the true hallmark of prescriptive laws—including positive laws—lies in the fact they are practical counsels or recommendations regarding the courses to be followed if certain results are to be attained. The element of command, however significant, is secondary and supportive: it is introduced to make the recommendation effective. In considering the character and conditions of effectiveness of positive law, I will have a good deal more to say on this matter later.

These prescriptive subtypes of advisory and imperative are not sharply separate; they merge into one another, and the form of a law often changes—in either direction—while its substance remains constant. The government may at first merely appeal to labor and management to consider the good of the country, the interests of the consumer, and the horrors of inflation in their contract negotiations and pricing policies, but if this appeal fails to win accord, wage and price controls may be instituted. When we train children in the habits necessary to their health and when we instruct youths in such skills as writing, mathematics, music, and laboratory techniques, the rules and practices that we lay down for them to follow are supported by various external sanctions of reward and punishment: the laws that we issue and they obey are imperatives. When people become mature, they are assumed to be concerned for their health and dedicated to success in their careers, so they are expected to adhere voluntarily to the prescribed regimens: the laws they follow are advisory, whether framed by themselves or their physicians and coaches. Whether a law is to have an advisory or imperative status depends upon the importance we attach to the ends its promotes, the urgency we feel to realize these ends, and the resistance we anticipate in achieving the ends. Prescriptive laws describe how things can be ordered as they should be: they consecrate what we accept as the prudential.

This view, which ascribes primacy to the prescriptive character of positive law, can be seen to underlie all legal theories when these are examined closely with an eye to what they largely assume as well as to what they expound. This is obviously the case with those doctrines that explicitly regard law as derivative from and supportive of some prior principles of order: classic natural law theories and the modern schools of sociological jurisprudence and the jurisprudence of interests are clear cases in point. But it is equally true of those doctrines, such as the imperative theory, legal positivism, and the pure theory of law, from which such a view might seem utterly remote and even alien. This claim needs some substantiation, which can be briefly supplied.

H.L.A. Hart's work is usually—though I believe mistakenly—taken as the prototype of positivism. But his account of the origin and function of positive law, as contained in his well-known and important distinction of primary and secondary rules, clearly gives pride of place to law's prescriptive role. Hart identifies three defects of customary law, with its reliance on only primary rules: such law is uncertain, static, and inefficient. Positive law arises precisely to repair these deficiencies: its three basic secondary rules of recognition, change, and adjudication are prescriptions for achieving the desired results of constituting authority, providing for modifications of and additions to the body of primary rules, and settling disputes and enforcing the will of society through organized sanctions.[14] I think that my analysis is simply a more systematic and complete statement of the same position, with the outcomes in both cases being rather similar. And Hart was not concerned to be systematic or complete on this matter. For his purposes, he needed only enough to establish a legal order, not to explain fully the tasks imposed on it.

Hans Kelsen, who sedulously avoids all questions of the social and moral bases of law—of its connection with the actual and ideal orders—nevertheless recognizes that law, in its origin and function, is a means to an end, a prescription for bringing about certain desired results. Not being interested in the specific defects that law is called on to repair, he does not consider the question as Hart does. But he is still perfectly aware that it is this need to transform what is toward what ought to be—to achieve a goal or purpose—that brings law into being. This comes out clearly in such a passage as the following: "The word 'law' . . . refers to that specific social technique . . . which consists in bringing about the desired social conduct of men through the threat of a measure of coercion which is to be applied in case of contrary conduct. What the social conditions are that necessitate this technique is an important sociological question. I do not know whether we can answer it satisfactorily."[15]

Indeed, this view that positive law is primarily and fundamentally prescriptive in character is again found where we might least expect it—in the theory of John Austin. Austin is usually treated, and his doctrine expounded, as the advocate par excellence of the imperative theory. It is understandable, if not excusable, that this should have happened. For Austin's avowed subject is positive law, with its essential internal or constitutive features of command, sovereignty, sanction, and might. So it is this part of his teaching that is emphasized—and criticized—in most accounts of his theory. But this is to forget that Austin was an almost devout admirer of Jeremy Bentham and a committed adherent of the doctrines of utilitarianism. As he himself makes perfectly clear, he draws the sharp and insistent distinctions that he does—between the is and the ought to be, between positive law and morality—because he is concerned to demarcate positive law as a separate field of inquiry, so that he can better study it and thus reach an understanding of what it is and

[14] H. L. A. Hart, *The Concept of Law*, (Oxford: The Clarendon Press, 1961), Chapter V, section 3.

[15] Hans Kelsen, *General Theory of Law and State*, trans. Anders Wedberg (Cambridge, Mass.: Harvard University Press, 1945), p. 19.

how it operates. And all this solely in order that positive law can be made to serve more effectively its proper functions and ends, for it does have these purposes beyond itself, upon which it is dependent for its content. And these ends of positive law are defined and identified by the principle of utility.

Austin's thought on these matters can be summarized in four points. First, he does insist upon distinguishing sharply between legislation and jurisprudence, the former of which is concerned with what the law ought to be, the latter with what it is. Second, he is equally insistent that these two sciences "are connected by numerous and indissoluble ties."[16] Third, he declares that jurisprudence is dependent on legislation, and he explains the dependence in this way: "It is impossible to consider Jurisprudence quite apart from Legislation; since the inducements or considerations of expediency which lead to the establishment of laws, must be adverted to in explaining their origin and mechanism. If the causes of laws and of the rights and obligations which they create be not assigned, the laws themselves are unintelligible."[17] Fourth, he identifies the standard that is to be used in making laws and in judging of their worth; it is the "principle of utility which is the test of positive rules"[18] and which "not only ought to guide, but has commonly in fact guided the legislator."[19] The strength of Austin's commitment to utilitarianism, and his reliance upon it, stand out clearly in such a statement as the following: "To the adherent of the theory of utility, a human law is good if it be generally useful, and a human law is bad if it be generally pernicious. For, in *his* opinion, it is consonant or not with the law of God, inasmuch as it is consonant or not with the principle of general utility."[20] For Austin, as for any disciple of Bentham, it is simply a self-evident truth that the role of the legislator in making laws is analogous to that of the physician in treating his patients: he is to prescribe those regimens that will promote the health—the good or pleasure—of the body politic.

As a final word on this subject, to illustrate how this same principle is used by those who do make the laws, reference might be made to the famous "mischief rule" of statutory interpretation. The guidelines that this rule lays down are concisely expounded in Heydon's Case:

> It was resolved by the Barons of the Exchequer that for the sure and true interpretation of all statutes in general (be they penal or

---

[16] Austin, *Province of Jurisprudence*, p. 6.

[17] Ibid., p. 373.

[18] Ibid., p. 260.

[19] Ibid., p. 59.

[20] Ibid., p. 128. Emphasis is in the original.

beneficial, restrictive or enlarging of the Common Law) four things are to be discussed and considered: 1st, What was the Common Law before the making of the Act; 2nd, What was the mischief and defect for which the Common Law did not provide; 3rd, What remedy the Parliament hath resolved and appointed to cure the disease of the commonwealth; and 4th, The true reason of the remedy.[21]

This discussion can be summarized briefly. Positive law assumes an ordered social context that exhibits certain deficiencies; it envisages a more desirable—an ideal—ordering of this context; it prescribes the steps to be taken in order to move the actual toward this ideal; and it orders that these measures be instituted. That is, positive law is at once expository, normative, prescriptive, advisory, and imperative. But it is positive law in its role as a means to an end—as prescribing and thus ordering human conduct in certain ways toward certain outcomes—that dominates the situation.

My prime concern is to use this doctrine to clarify the nature of positive law and especially to reinforce the view that positive law is fully three-dimensional, having expository, normative, and prescriptive elements, all of which are equally important. That is, I want to appeal to these ideas in arguing the thesis that positive law is a gradual development within the whole field of law, is continuous with other kinds of law, and is a supplementary principle of order. But if this argument is to have full value, there must first be a consideration of broader areas and more basic issues, for the principle of the continuity of law asserts that *all* laws whatsoever have these same three aspects. And this entails that all regions of reality have a mixed character that requires normative and prescriptive as well as expository laws to yield an adequate description of them; that is, it entails the view that the order that holds in every context of nature is at once an established actuality, a transitional stage of becoming, and a movement toward a fuller realization. This raises vexing metaphysical questions that cannot be avoided if the nature and function of positive law are to be solidly grounded. I shall deal with these necessary matters as briefly as possible in the next chapter.

[21] *Heydon's Case* (1584), 3 Rep. 7a.

CHAPTER VI

THE CONTINUITY OF LAW

IT WILL BE WELL to begin this discussion by summarizing for ready comparison the preceding accounts of the modes of law. Laws of the kind that I have designated expository refer to an order that is actual and observable in some phenomenal field. The regularities of character, structure, behavior, and relationship that they describe give every evidence of being prior to and independent of our formulation of them as laws. We regard such laws as describing an order that is somehow preestablished (we casually gloss over this "somehow") and that we need only discover. Laws of the kind that I have designated normative refer to an order that is ideal but unactualized in phenomena. They depict what ought to be, and they propose this as a model and guide to what is to be. We regard such laws as describing an order that is advantageous and/or obligatory for us to work toward. Laws of the kind that I have designated prescriptive refer to an order of becoming that is intended to transform the actual in the direction of the ideal. They mean to regulate the character, structures, behavior, and relationships of the phenomena with which they deal. We regard such laws as defining patterns of conduct and rules of procedure that will secure the order we seek.

To state the matter in this way—which is, I think, the way in which it is now usually conceived—is almost to make out a prima facie case for the position that these modes of law are radically different. What I have described under the rubrics expository, prescriptive, and normative laws, modern thought would identify respectively with scientific law (or the laws of nature), positive or civil law, and moral law; and it would regard these as having no relationship save the tenuous one of sharing a linguistic label. To think in these terms is to pose a virtually impassable gulf between expository laws on the one hand and normative and prescriptive laws on the other. The first are "discovered," are immutable, and are beyond the control of the entities that fall under them. The second are "made," and can be changed, revoked, and disobeyed by those who made them and to whom they apply. There are certainly real and important differences here. But the current view grossly exaggerates these differences and issues in a distorted picture. In particular, it introduces a sharp disjunction between nature's laws and the laws of man. If the claim that there are essential similarities and a broad continuity between these modes of law is to be rendered plausible, then the first necessity is to uncover and correct the misconceptions on which this current view is based. And the most important—and difficult—step in this undertaking is to reach a sounder appreciation of the true character and status of expository laws, or laws of nature.

The position that I shall develop in dealing with these issues can be summarized in four propositions.

1. What I have called expository law, with certain crucial refinements of meaning, is the primordial and pervasive mode of law.

2. The character of such laws is actually a synthesis of expository, prescriptive, and normative elements; their status with respect to the phenomena (the orders) to which they refer is one of immanence; and their reach is universal, covering all regions of reality.

3. Prescriptive and normative laws are supplemental to this basic mode, and they issue into explicitness in response to distinctive characteristics that develop gradually in certain regions of reality, especially the human context.

4. These other modes of law are already implicitly exemplified and effectively functional in expository laws.

The argument in support of this position is based on themes that have been developed in earlier chapters. The most fundamental of these is the postulate that defines law as "a principle of order." As we have seen, this applies to all laws whatsoever. It follows from this that the kinds of laws that are exemplified in any part of nature are a function of the type of order that holds there: that is, laws embody and reflect the characteristics of the phenomenal fields of which they are laws. This notion was expounded and made more precise by identifying the three regimes of Necessity, Possibility, and Purposiveness as referring to states of affairs, or sets of conditions, that we can readily recognize as present in nature.

In the course of my discussion it must already have become evident that there is an intimate correlation of these modes of law with these previously identified regimes of becoming. Insofar as the state of affairs in any region of reality approximates closely to the conditions of Necessity (similarity, subordination, action-reaction, and rigidity), then the order that holds within this region effectively expresses itself, and so can be adequately rendered, through the medium of laws in which the expository element is preponderant. As the conditions of Possibility (differentiation, participation, self-determination, and flexibility) manifest themselves and threaten to disrupt the established order, laws will acquire a prescriptive character in order to limit and direct the uses that are to be made of Possibility: that is, to define which possible modes of behavior will in fact be adopted. When the challenge of Possibility becomes sufficiently intense and the conditions of Purposiveness (cultivation, authority, responsibility, and continuity) develop to meet this challenge, then laws with a strong normative cast will emerge to define explicitly the goals and the courses of behavior: that is, the open order that Possibility ushers in is given standards and models to which to adhere and is directed toward future outcomes.

The final step in this argument is the thesis, elaborated and defended in Chapter III, that these regimes are present throughout nature. Every region of nature embodies all three of these sets of conditions, representing a particular synthesis of them, which will differ from one region to another. Since this is the case, and since the modes of law reflect and are correlated with these regimes, it follows that these modes of law are also compresent throughout reality. That is, every law is at once expository, prescriptive, and normative, combining in itself elements of each of these abstract types. In some laws the expository element will predominate, even to the apparent (but only apparent) exclusion of the other elements. In other laws, prescriptive or normative aspects will become predominant, with the same apparent result of exclusiveness. But such appearances are delusory: since the order that holds in every context of nature is at once an established milieu, an arena of change, and a movement toward a fuller development, every law refers at once to actual conditions, a process of becoming, and an ideal outcome.

If the premises of this argument were accepted as materially sound and the argument itself as formally valid, my point would be established without more ado. The principle of the continuity of law and the claim that all laws embody expository, prescriptive, and normative elements would be acknowledged. But that is too much to expect. For the seeming gap between the laws of nature and those of man is too wide to be bridged merely by theory and logic, and common sense needs more than this to persuade it that the laws of nature are in any way prescriptive or normative. These doubts can be overcome only by clear empirical evidence—by a close scrutiny of both scientific and positive laws that will reveal to direct inspection what the preceding argument claims as a logical entailment. And as I have already remarked, it is scientific laws, or the laws of nature, that present the greatest difficulty and require the most careful examination.

Much of the difficulty here springs from the fact that our notions regarding the character, status, and function of laws of nature are characterized by a high degree of vagueness and complacency. We can give a satisfactory account of the mode of being of positive and moral laws—at least, an account that satisfies us. Such laws are made, decreed, or enunciated by persons who are in one way or another endowed with authority; and they are intended to control and direct the behavior of men. But if we are asked to give a similar account of the laws of nature, we have nothing better to offer than loose analogies. To make matters worse, this inability does not bother us. Our interest in such laws is overwhelmingly pragmatic: we value them for the powers of prediction and control that they afford us. We therefore largely ignore the question of their status in reality: as long as they serve our practical needs we do not worry about their metaphysical credentials.

But this is precisely what we need to do. How is it that there are laws of nature: laws of motion, of thermodynamics, of chemical valence, of genetic heredity, and so forth? What is the ground of such laws? What brings them into and conserves them in existence? To what do these laws refer, and how are they connected with the phenomenal fields of which they are principles of order? In a word, what is the mode of being of laws of nature, or scientific laws?

We normally think of such laws in strictly subjective terms, and we assign to them an exclusively epistemological status and function. Looked at from this human point of view, these laws merely summarize our findings about the states of affairs and the course of events in various phenomenal fields. They formulate temporal sequences, spatial relationships, uniformities, regularities, and patterns of behavior that our inquiries have disclosed as existing in nature. We do not think of them as referring to any real forces or factors in nature or as in any way causing the phenomena to which they refer. The laws of motion, for instance, are not held to be responsible for things tending to continue in their state of motion or rest unless disturbed therefrom, nor do they determine that action and reaction shall be equal and opposite. And the laws of genetics do not dictate the elaborate rituals of mitosis and meiosis. We naively refer to these formulas as "laws of nature," though our attitude toward them would be more faithfully rendered by calling them "rules of interpretation."

But let us shift perspective and ask what these laws are from the point of view of nature itself—from the point of view of the actually existent things whose laws they are. I think that only one answer is reasonable: they are expressions and reflections of the characters of things and of the ways in which things behave and carry on their existences. These laws are not imposed on things from some prior source, nor are they merely ascribed to things by posterior human scrutiny. Rather, they are integral and coeval with the existence of things—atoms, molecules, cells, stars, plants, animals, men—that cannot exist without simultaneously forming a particular mode of order. In the act of existing, things assume a certain structure, combine to form wholes, stand in certain relations, and act upon one another. And it is these structures, combinations, relations, and processes that are expressed by laws. Things other than men do not proclaim and administer laws. But all things "make" laws in the sense of serving as their ground, and they do this in the very act of existing in their own specific way.[1]

Consequently, the modes of law that are relevant to any particular region of nature will be a function of the characteristics of things—the type of order—that holds within this region. Insofar as the situation in any part of reality approximates closely to the conditions of Necessity, the order that holds within this region can be adequately rendered by laws that seem to be purely expository. Within such contexts, we find that strict uniformity and regularity are the prevailing characteristics. Inertia, in the full sense of the term, appears to hold sway: things repeat themselves, fields maintain their integrity, the course of event continues without interruption, and relations are constant: what now *is* confines closely what is to be. We describe this state of affairs objectively by saying that the presently established contents and courses, structures and connections, of the actual perpetuate themselves indefinitely as a function of what is already inherent in them and with only minor and casual

---

[1] In the work previously referred to, F. A. Hayek emphasizes this same point. In discussing the nature of "spontaneous orders"—"self-organizing" or "self-generating" systems—he calls special attention to the type of rule that determines such an order. Citing examples from the fields of physics and biology, he says that these

> are instructive because they clearly show that the rules which govern the activities of the elements of such spontaneous orders need not be rules which are 'known' to these elements; it is sufficient that the elements actually behave in a manner which can be described by such rules. The concept of rules as we use it in this context therefore does not imply that such rules exist in articulated ('verbalized') forms, but only that it is possible to discover rules which the actions of the individuals in fact follow.

In the next paragraph, he points out that the same is true of "many of the rules which govern the actions of men and thereby determine a spontaneous social order." See *Law, Legislation, and Liberty: Vol. I, Rules and Order* (Chicago: University of Chicago Press, 1973), p. 43.

variations from type or deviations from routine. We describe it subjectively in terms of highly general class concepts, systematic models, equations that formulate invariant temporal sequences, and abstract relationships.

The laws in which we summarize these findings have the air of being absolutely general and final, in the sense that the phenomena to which they refer conform perfectly to the formulas that they embody: that is, these laws appear to be purely expository. We now know that this is a false picture of nature, even at the simplest physical level. But we still have great difficulty in finding the terms in which to cast a more accurate account. What causes most of the trouble here is our habit of thinking of the world in a quaint mixture of mechanistic and theological terms. The conceptual apparatus that dominates thought at any time is inevitably outdated and inadequate to contemporary knowledge: the formation of intellectual habits is a slow process, always lagging behind empirical inquiry. Thus we still tend to picture the world as it was depicted by classical physics.

This world is already perfectly categorized. Things follow public courses, but they have no private existences; similarity equals identity; and possibility is only statistical probability, not real opportunity. Parts are therefore engulfed in their wholes, spontaneity is smothered by determination, and the present is absorbed into a seamless temporal continuum. This is a world where, since everything is caused, nothing can happen.

Two tenets lie at the heart of this creed. One of these is the persistent notion that physical reality is altogether passive and inert, with no inherent capacity save sheer persistence and incapable of exercising any initiative of its own. The other, which is the reverse of the same medal, is the reification of the causal nexus. Together, these ideas tell us that existent things are static and impotent, acting only in accord with laws that are somehow imposed on them from without. Since we no longer accept God as the source and conserver of the world, we reify causation, call it the causal nexus, and make it our *deus ex machina*. To state this in another way, what we do quite innocently and unconsciously is to capitalize Nature and regard it as prior to natural objects and processes.

Once these ideas are made explicit, their absurdity is manifest. It is ridiculous to speak about "cause and effect" and the "laws of nature" as though these were real forces that were independent of existent things and determined their character and behavior. It is actually existent things—Aristotle's primary substances—that are ultimate. Nature is the whole of these, and the laws of nature are expressions of what they are and do. Furthermore, as I have said, we now know that this earlier view of the world is false. We have been brought up on the ideas of the convertibility of mass and energy, the principle of indeterminacy, quanta jumps, genetic mutations, radioactive decay, and short-lived elements—all of which point to the conclusion that all things are ingredient with energy, they act out of the needs and resources of their own natures, they fashion their own courses, and through their existences they become what they were not in their beginnings. In short, we are vividly aware that the order that holds throughout nature is dynamic and directed as well as settled. And from this it follows that all laws, including the laws of nature, reflect a perpetuation of the past, an exploration of the present, and an anticipation of the future. In the language I have used earlier, this means that every region of nature is a synthesis of the regimes of Necessity, Possibility, and Purposiveness and so expresses itself through laws that are themselves a synthesis of expository, prescriptive, and normative elements.

But despite this more sophisticated knowledge and its implications, the classical world view still dominates our thought. As I just indicated, the responsibility for this lies partly in our inability to shake off old intellectual habits and partly in the seeming lack of a conceptual apparatus that can accommodate these new findings. Yet the nucleus of such an apparatus lies ready to hand in the category of *potentiality*. Potentiality means that things have certain inherent characteristics and capacities, which are present from the beginning but are at first only latent. For their realization they require certain series of acts and chains of events: they dispose the things in which they inhere to the actions that will realize them. This concept has a wide and familiar usage. We say that the fertilized ovum is potentially the child, and the child the man; that an acorn is potentially an oak tree; that a stone poised on high and a gas under pressure are potential with energy; that situations are potentially promising or threatening, and relationships potentially creative or destructive. In brief, potentiality means that things act in accord with their natures and in so doing fulfill these natures. Things are as truly their existences as their essences.

It is potentiality that links together the various regions of reality and renders intelligible the principles of the continuity of nature and of laws. Seen from the point of view of its origins, potentiality is simply the explication of the true meaning that is disguised by the simpler concept of energy: by asserting that it is actually existent things, not a fictitious "nature," that are the moving forces in the world, it recognizes and guarantees the pervasiveness of those conditions that I have described as the regime of Possibility. For if all things are loci of mass-energy, then each is a unique entity that asserts itself, exerts an influence, and reacts with other things. Seen from the point of view of its outcome, potentiality is the primitive form and the progenitor of the state of affairs that I have described as the regime of Purposiveness. Potentiality means that existence is a process of actualitization, not a mere state of persistence, and this process expresses itself in the conditions of that regime. These latter statements require a slight elaboration.

Everything undergoes cultivation in the elemental sense that it has a history through which it expresses and develops its native capacities, whatever these may be. To hold otherwise is to suppose that the basic elements of things are small, compact, inert, unchanging pellets of stuff, and this view has long been discarded. Everything acknowledges authority in the elemental sense that it is influenced by its surroundings—the field, system, organism, or environment in which it exists—and acts in a manner to stabilize and sustain this milieu. Everything exhibits responsibility in the elemental sense that its nature and history are adjusted to those of its neighbors. In its simplest form, to be responsible is to be sensitive and responsive. Since things are never isolated but impinge upon one another in many ways, they must exercise these traits or mutually destroy one another. Everything promotes continuity in the elemental sense that it tends toward a situation where energy can be accumulated and exchanged on the most favorable terms. Unless things maintain such relationships, energy would soon be dissipated in friction or would be hoarded in isolated packets and so would become unavailable.

These are the primitive conditions from which Purposiveness, as we know it in experience and exercise it in conduct, emerges. And these conditions must be universal. This world would not be what it is, no matter what region of it we examine, if things were utterly subject to a rigid and extraneous necessity: under those conditions novelty, change, development, and evolution could not occur, and they obviously do. Nor is this account made adequate by the mere addition of Possibility, in the sense of occasions on which things were relieved of all restraints, both internal and external, so that the outcome of such occasions would be altogether unconditioned: this would reduce the world to a chaos of random and erratic events, which it obviously is not. What is required beyond this is potentiality, in the sense just analyzed. It is only by stipulating the compresence of these regimes that we can give an intelligible account of reality.

The order that we always find in nature is at once a stable actuality, a transitional stage of becoming, and a movement toward a fuller development. So all the regimes of nature manifest themselves through laws that have prescriptive and normative as well as expository characteristics and functions. This is not to say that we find throughout nature, in even its simplist regions, three distinct sets of laws: as I indicated in the four introductory postulates, these modes of law become separately explicit and distinct only in certain regions of nature, and especially in the human context. Rather, it is simply to say that even those laws that we regard as strictly expository—the laws of nature—are in fact a synthesis of all three modes. That is, such laws are expressions of an order that is at once settled, dynamic and directed.

Because of the complexity and plasticity that characterize man, prescriptive and normative laws are gradually analyzed out of this primitive synthesis and given separate formulation; thus they appear to take on a distinct and independent mode of existence. We can readily identify the presence of laws of these different modes in the human context, and we appeal to each of them in our quest for order. Indeed, we do this so casually that we overlook the fact that these laws were manifested in human behavior before men discovered them or even suspected their existence. This point is so important to my argument that it needs illustration.

Take first the elemental human activity of seeking food for nourishment. Originally—say half a million years ago in East Africa—this was a composite activity in which it would be impossible to distinguish the separate presence of expository, normative, and prescriptive elements. These were thoroughly synthesized, but were nonetheless present. Foods that can and cannot be digested, poisonous substances, the relative nutritive value of different foods and their ease of digestion—all of this is determined by chemical and physiological factors. That is, it could be formulated in laws of nature—expository laws. But these early men lacked the ability to discover these laws, or even to envisage their presence. In the course of time, through trial and error and the accumulation of experience, men learned a good deal about what foods to eat and what to avoid. They got an inkling of these laws of nature, and could then frame prescriptive laws that would lead to behavior in conformity with these natural facts and demands. All of this was so far very vague: men had only a rough acquaintance with the processes of feeding, digestion, and nourishment; their end in view was only the general and negative one of avoiding sickness or death; and the rules that they taught their young concerning what foods to seek and what to avoid were entirely the result of experience. In the long course of time, men enlarged and refined their knowledge of this whole field. They learned a good deal about the physiological processes involved, and they obtained a clearer idea of what constitutes health, so that they were able to make more specific dietary recommendations. In short, men became able to formulate at least rough expository, normative, and prescriptive laws.

Once these laws are formulated, they play back upon one another, and the mastery of this field accelerates rapidly. Now we can define quite exactly what constitutes the peak of physical efficiency and well-being for different types of persons engaged in different sorts of activities. We acquire an exact knowledge of the chemistry and physiology of nourishment, so that we can prescribe detailed diets and regimens tailored to typical and even individual needs: for weight lifters, fashion models, prospective mothers, and operatic tenors. Expository, normative, and prescriptive laws are now in full bloom, explicitly formulated and systematically applied. The important fact to notice is that all of these modes of law are implicitly present and operative from the very beginning. Once man emerged, his nature and circumstances grounded the processes of feeding and digestion, directed him toward the goals of survival and enhanced energy, and guided his choice of foods. And all of this without any formulation or even an awareness of these laws, although they could readily have been discerned and formulated by a being of superior intelligence—say a visitor from a more advanced planet who was studying human behavior as we study the behavior of animals and formulate our findings in lawlike statements.

As another example, take the very different field of economics—the production, exchange, and sale of goods and services. Very early on men certainly became aware of the relation between supply and demand, even though they could not yet formulate this as a law. There was also some general agreement on the sort of economic-social situation that was desirable—every man should have useful work, the tools he needed, and the assurance of the necessities of life. At the same time there were certainly disagreements about the detailed structure of the best type of social order—primitive capitalists, socialists, and communists were already expounding their views. Finally, various measures were gradually developed to try to correct the more blatant economic ills that occurred: policies were adopted regulating prices, wages, means of production, land use, and currency. Gradually these elements became differentiated and more refined. The simple laws of supply and demand and the open market became the elaborate formulae of contemporary economic theory, symbolized, quantified, and finally computerized. Clear, but certainly not common, norms regarding the distribution of wealth arose, and the machinery of economic control became highly sophisticated if not highly efficient. And again the important fact to notice is that the processes, the goals, and the methods that ground our present expository, normative, and prescriptive laws were present and fully operative long before these laws were formulated.

These examples could be multiplied indefinitely, and they are all so familiar to us as history and in the conduct of our own affairs that we take them for granted and overlook their lesson. Man's character and circumstances, his purposes and his strivings, were all actively on the scene long before he was in a position to formulate laws regarding them. His capacities, his goals, and the avenue to their achievement were roughed out by the interplay of his nature and the natural environment. As the human adventure begins, it is a close synthesis of the regimes of Necessity, Possibility, and Purposiveness; these are not clearly distinguished either in fact or in thought. Man's instincts and appetites dictate definite courses of action, these are pointed toward certain outcomes, and in their pursuit they try out various paths that conditions make available. He gradually learns more about himself and his surroundings: he gets a clearer view of what makes life satisfactory, and by a slow progression through trial and error, experimentation, insight, forethought, and planning he creates more effective means for the pursuit of his ends. As the anthropologist puts it, culture now supplements biology as a vehicle through which man inherits the past and evolves toward the future. What man discovers about the necessities that press upon him, the purposes he should pursue, and the best use to make of his possibilities, becomes embodied in such forms as habit, tradition, mores, and custom. In all of these there is a close synthesis, if not identification, of what will later become the ideas of the actual, the ideal, and the possible. Even when the social order has become quite complex, the customs that define its structure are regarded as determining at once what is, what ought to be, and what must be. It is only very much later that these aspects of existence will be recognized as such and man will set out to explore them systematically, giving rise to the enterprises that can be roughly identified as science, morality, and technology, which in turn formulate their findings in laws that are predominantly—but not exclusively—expository, normative, and prescriptive.

What all of this means is that man attains a high level of biological and social development without having discovered any of the laws that were embodied in—that grounded and guided—this development. He spontaneously adopted forms of behavior, pursued ends, and devised practices that constituted a structured order that was thoroughly "lawful" and would later be expressed and regulated through explicit laws. But the order preceded the laws; or, more exactly, the human order exhibited laws before human beings discovered them. This order is a function of the human potential, and it is being realized in action before the human intelligence has developed sufficiently to recognize it and embody it in laws. Man lives his expository, normative, and prescriptive laws long before he frames them.[2]

All that I am arguing is that this same situation holds true throughout nature. The point that I am anxious to make—and perhaps I have already labored it too much—is simply this: laws have their basic ground in the characteristics and behavior of things. They are primarily principles of an objecitve order and only secondarily subjective formulations of the mind. They are embodied in nature as expressions of its structure before they are formulated in propositions as expressions of our knowledge. The most obvious witness to our recognition of this fact is found in the way in which we refer to eminent scientists as discoverers of this, that, or the other law. If men are to discover laws, the laws must themselves already exist. It would take an extreme realist to hold that they exist in some "heaven of concepts." The only alternative is that their existence is a function of and is integral to the order that holds in nature.

If we bear this clearly in mind we can give a perfectly straightforward interpretation to the thesis that even those laws of nature that seem to be purely expository actually have a prescriptive and normative character. For this merely means that all regions of nature, even the simplist, exhibit the characteristics of the regimes of Possibility and Purposiveness as well as Necessity. That is, the panorama of nature is an ongoing function of the potentialities of things, not a settled product of the causal nexus.

There are regions of nature in which the established order appears to be perfectly determinate and permanent: things seem only to persist and the course of events seems only to repeat itself. Deviations from type are slight, variations of patttern are infrequent, and change is extremely slow; therefore we write these off as "exceptions," "accidents," or "experimental errors." But we now know that such a dismissal of these phenomena is unwarranted, for in fact they are manifestations of the inherent dynamism of things and of the processes through which poten-

---

[2] Cf. again ibid., pp. 74-75, where, speaking of man, Hayek points out that the comparative study of behavior has "made it clear that individuals [men] had learned to observe (and enforce) rules of conduct long before such rules could be expressed in words." And again, speaking of the early stages of human and social development, he says: "At this stage, it is sufficient to see that rules did exist, served a function essential to the preservation of the group, and were effectively transmitted and enforced, although they had never been 'invented', expressed in words, or possessed a 'purpose' known to anyone."

tialities seek actualization. The world is throughout an arena of becoming, moving toward a future that is foreshadowed in general outline but indeterminate as to its details. The laws that reflect nature always have a prescriptive element; they are principles of an order that is in a state of flux and transition in which varied originations are occurring, the direction of events is indefinite, and the future pattern that is to be established is still uncertain. These laws mark the paths that potentialities explore tentatively, exploiting the possibilities that occur and awaiting the outcome. Stated metaphorically, the prescriptive element in these laws represents experiments through which reality moves toward realization.

In a similar way, the normative aspect of laws of nature reflects the outcome to which potentialities point. The potentiality of a thing is a function of its nature: indeed, it is this nature regarded as having a future reference and as at once specifying and supporting a certain course that will lead to its completion. The laws that are expressed in the behavior of things are normative in the simple sense that they depict the outcomes to which things tend.

It is partly prejudice that blinds us to the dynamism and direction that characterize all of nature, but appearances also contribute to this illusion. Our encounters with the physical world are preponderantly at the molar level as given in ordinary perception. To further distort the impression we receive, this encountered world is largely an artificial one of our own creation: it is composed of buildings, furniture, tools, instruments, gadgets, and other artifacts that we have made for our own convenience by interrupting the careers of natural substances, removing them from their natural environment, and imposing on them a foreign form. The epitome of this interference with natural things and processes is man's creation of substances that are nonbiodegradable. In short, the world of our daily familiarity is a world of nature arrested.

In this molar and artificial world, the outcomes that existence seeks are so familiar and uniform and the passages of becoming so regular and secure that we can predict them with assurance; they appear to us as necessary and predetermined. Under these conditions, a close scrutiny of present actualities leaves aside very little in the way of future contingencies and undisclosed potentialities: the sun sets in the west, the temperature drops when the sun sets, the furnace goes on when the temperature drops, and lovely warm air pours from the registers. Effect follows cause, and once we know the formulae we ignore the entities whose activities are really responsible for these sequences. In the abstract, we know that iron rusts, wood rots, leather wears out, stone erodes, cloth disintegrates, and elements decay. But all of this happens so gradually in the concrete that we notice only the end conditions and ignore what goes on between them. Our language reflects this: we say "this pipe is rusty," "that plank is rotten," "my shoes are worn out," "your shirt collar is frayed." We tend to see nature as a series of static states connected by abstract formulae.

To correct this impression empirically we need to examine nature at the microscopic and macroscopic levels and through the medium of time-lapse cinematography. When we do this we realize that nature in all of its parts is alive with energy and that all natural entities are continually in the process of exerting themselves, acting upon and interacting with one another, becoming different and making a difference. This is dramatically exemplified in genetic mutations, the rise of new strains of viruses, quanta phenomena, short-lived particles, the process of sub-speciation as a plant species spreads into new environments, and the panorama of evolution and adaptation as a whole. Indeed, scientists now speak of the evolution of chemical elements, of the solar system (and by extension of the universe), and even of the laws of nature, although these scientists usually cover themselves by putting the term "evolution" in quotation marks.

The existence of all things is a synthesis of persistence, passage, and project. In many regions of nature this synthesis is so close and firm that the latter aspects of existence appear to be absorbed into the former. The potentialities inherent in such regions are very largely expressed and exhausted in what is already actual: the limited resources of things and the scarcity of alternatives in the surroundings conspire to keep both the range and the tempo of change at a minimum. Even here existence strikes out spontaneously along new paths and toward new outcomes; but these are very quickly either rejected as destructive (for example, lethal mutations) or established as routine (so that we notice them only in retrospect and regard them as predetermined).

In the course of time, the natures of things grow more complex and plastic, and the conditions they face become more open and flexible. These enhanced potentialities continually generate finer instruments to serve them. We call this process evolution, and we can trace its general course and identify some of its principal stages: giant chemical molecules, replication, regeneration, sexual reproduction, sensitivity, more effective ways to utilize energy, improved perceptual apparatuses, mind and consciousness. When we recognize these outcomes, they appear to us as so many *faits accomplies*. We regard them simply as states of affairs that we can locate at different points in space and time—in different parts of the panorama of nature. We forget that in their actual occurrence they were happenings, developments, accomplishments; that they came into being gradually, over long spans of time; that they are the successful outcomes that existence achieved by laboriously exploiting the openings it found. We picture evolution after the manner of those strip-cartoon paintings of an earlier day that depicted several incidents of an historical event or several occasions in the life of a man as though they were static episodes that were all present at the same time.[3] Thus evolution becomes for us a tableau. But in itself it is a process.

It is the essence of this process that as it continues, the outcomes that things project and the passages that actualize them become at once more intricate and more vulnerable. These aspects of existence now begin to separate. The present manner of existence—the actual order—now becomes distinguishable both from other and fuller manners of existence and from the steps through which these are to be achieved. Different futures lie equally open, and different courses can lead toward them. In sum, the earlier synthesis of persistence, passage, and project—of the regimes of Necessity, Possibility, and Purposiveness—is disrupted.

As a result, things now confront a problem that remains essentially the same in structure but grows increasingly more difficult of solution: this ruptured synthesis must be repaired. That is, existent things must find ways to preserve a coherent relationship between the elements of persistence, passage, and project, for these now threaten to become dissociated from one another to such a point that things adopt courses and goals that are inappropriate to their actual natures. An effective synthesis of these elements must be maintained, but it must also be sufficiently flexible to accommodate novelty and change. One is reminded of the old adage that counseled that in holding hands with a young lady the clasp should be gentle but firm, and anyone who lived and courted in that more innocent age will recall how difficult a feat this was.

This balance can be struck at different points and maintained in different ways. Below the level of life, phenomena appear to have solved the problem by settling into routines that are permanent and unalterable, although to assume this is to overlook not only the past process by which these phenomena reached their present states but also the changes that may lie in the future. As the potentialities (the natures) of things grow in complexity, with a consequent increase in plasticity, such a solution is no longer available. Existence now becomes both more volatile and more

---

[3] A typical and charming example is *The Life and Death of Sir Henry Unton* in the National Portrait Gallery, London.

vulnerable. Things have the power of attaining richer and more diver-sified modes of being, but in doing so they sacrifice much of the stability and security they formerly had. In a seemingly paradoxical manner, as things extend their mastery of themselves and their environment, the established order becomes more fragile and a sound existence more dif-ficult to maintain. (This outcome presents a striking analogy with the social and individual ills that contemporary man has created for himself just when his technological powers appeared to be absolute.) In short, as evolution proceeds, things move through different adaptive courses to-ward new forms and modes of being. Success and failure now emerge as significant features of existence.[4]

We describe this situation and its outcome in language that is frankly normative and prescriptive: we say that various orders of existent things engage in a process of adaptation through which they evolve toward higher forms of development and more advanced manners of existence. We also recognize that this process can lead to decline and extinction. When biologists, paleontologists, and ethnologists depict the course of evolution and the behavior of evolving things, they find it impossible to avoid such evaluative language: in referring to the new forms that ap-pear and the adaptive devices that they employ, these professionally cau-tious scientists continually have recourse to such terms and phrases as "higher," "superior," "more advanced," "more developed," "more ap-propriate," "better adapted," "more effective," "refined," "complete," "improvement," "progress," and the like.

Even at the level of plant life we speak of geological and climatic changes making new ecological niches available and of established species as giving rise to new subspecies that are able to exploit these openings. Further, we identify the conditions and developments that are most favorable to such exploitation and expansion: the maintainance of genes in a recessive state until such time as they prove advantageous; polyploidy; the ideal size of breeding populations; flower structures that prevent self-fertilization; more effective methods of seed dispersal.

---

[4] In *Law in Modern Society* (New York: Free Press, 1976), Roberto Unger emphasizes this same point. He returns again and again to the theme of the precariousness of this transition from early to advanced societies and to the challenge that it poses to law and politics. In a typical passage, after speaking of the similarities between the "instincts" and "drives" of animals and the customary patterns of behavior of men, he says: "Unlike the regularities of conduct based on the genetic code, these [customary] patterns are taught. Though neither deliberately made nor articulated as rules, they become shrouded in sym-bol and attached to belief. Because it can never be wholly dissociated from reflection, cus-tom is always on the verge of falling prey to distinctions between regularity and norm, or between social practice and individual conscience" (p. 133).

When we reach the level of animal behavior, the use of such evaluative modes of thought becomes the more compelling and explicit. For here the elements of persistence, passage, and project have clearly separated from one another and are distinguishable as distinct aspects of existence that the animal must now reintegrate. The behavior of things is no longer controlled by action-reaction, genetic coding, stimulus-response, and other built-in mechanisms that largely determine the course of existence. Instead, animals have to exercise initiative in specifying ends and selecting means within a rather wide ambit that is constituted by their potentialities and the circumstances they confront. The facts compel us to recognize that animals seek certain goals and outcomes, such as self-preservation, reproduction, adequate food supply, peace within the group and protection against other groups. We also recognize that animals take definite steps and devise various methods for securing these goals: the establishment of orders of dominance (pecking orders), careful rearing and training of the young, marking of a territory, submission gestures, division of functions. We even discover that when a usual way of reaching a goal is thwarted, animals will seek other ways toward it. In these cases, animals are clearly behaving normatively and prescriptively—they are living laws of these kinds, although they lack the faculties to frame them.[5]

We thus ascribe to other things the achievements that we propose to ourselves in normative laws and the practices that we impose on ourselves through prescriptive laws. But no sooner do we describe the ways of things in these terms than we recant, insisting that of course things have not really done them. Even when the misunderstandings based on inadequate ideas and superficial observation have been removed, we find it impossible to conceive of normative and prescriptive laws as having any meaning and footing beyond the human context. The root of this difficulty lies in the fact—or rather mystery—of consciousness and the activities that it makes possible. Explicit and refined consciousness (especially self-consciousness) colors our own lives so intensely that we become obsessed with its significance. We therefore come to believe that goals and the courses that lead to them—ends and means, purposes and plans—can exist only if entertained in consciousness. And from this it follows that a law is not a law until it is recognized and proclaimed as such.

This is to ignore the points I have argued above: that laws are em-

[5] The ideas advanced here find wide expression in the current literature of ethology, anthropology, and comparative behavior. They are familiar through the writings of such men as Konrad Lorenz, Niko Tinbergen, Claude Levi-Strauss, and others.

bodied in the behavior of things before they are formulated in proposi-tions, and that even man lived his laws long before he framed them. We are so used to saying that we "make" and "obey" normative and pre-scriptive laws and so conscious of the contrived processes through which this is done that we come to regard such laws as strictly the creatures of mind and consciousness. But normative and prescriptive laws are neither "made" nor "obeyed" in a vacuum, and they are not arbitrary pro-nouncements. Like expository laws, they are functions of our own na-ture and the circumstances that we confront, and our role with regard to their formulation is far more passive than is usually recognized: they are largely the making explicit of goals and patterns of behavior that have been adopted without serious forethought or intention. In their original occurrence, these laws reflect far more than they create. And their origi-nal content largely embodies the ways in which human potentialities have spontaneously expressed themselves and exploited the opportuni-ties they have found.

The significant point here is that these earliest normative and prescrip-tive laws simply reflect potentiality that has become conscious of itself and the conditions of its fulfillment. That is, the primary basis and source of such laws—as of expository laws—lies in objective potential-ity, not subjective formulation. As the potentialities and plasticity of things increase, the original synthesis of persistence, passage, and proj-ect becomes steadily looser, and these aspects of existence become less sharply defined individually and less closely linked collectively. Goals become ambiguous and the means toward them uncertain, and even facts (the actual order) become less obvious and compelling. As this movement continues, more intricate and effective instrumentalities must be developed to protect against these incoherences and to re-establish the ruptured synthesis. The principal stages of this transition are thoroughly familiar to us: action-reaction is supplemented—but not replaced—by reflex, and this in turn by instinct, imprinting, imitation, habit, learning, tradition, custom, morality, and finally by the horde of institutions, including religion, education, and positive law, that consti-tute a human culture. These are names that we give to different forces and factors that serve to regulate the behavior of things. They represent faculties, powers, practices, modes of organization, and, finally, institu-tions through which things at different evolutionary levels assure that existence will be orderly. In the course of this transition, things gradu-ally acquire the capacity to recognize the laws that they have been living, to conform to them more successfully, to inculcate familiarity with them in the young, to devise means to insure their observance, and at last to supplement them when necessary by framing new laws: that is, by defining and enforcing novel patterns of behavior intended to improve the quality of existence. Man "makes" positive law consciously and purposively, and he uses it as an instrument both to support the established order when it is threatened and to create a better order.

This passage of laws (expository as well as normative and prescriptive) from implicit to explicit principles of order is slow and gradual. Its various stages from instinct to positive law are moments in the unfolding of a single primal impetus, the quest for order. All that prevents our seeing this is the fact that when we consider positive law it is all but impossible for us, however we may try, to avoid the conceptual fallacy. Positive law *is* for us the legislative enactment or judicial decision duly inscribed in the statute book or reported cases. That is, we reify the declared law just as in other contexts we reify the causal nexus. In thinking of law in these inert and abstract terms, we leave aside two sets of very real forces and processes: those that have led to these official pronouncements and those that must be applied to make them effective. The legal realists have certainly done their best to drive home this lesson, and if we can only remember it we can learn to see positive law not as an autonomous and self-sustaining proclamation but as a complex apparatus. This apparatus is composed of the various legal institutions (legislatures, courts, regulatory and enforcement agencies) and the professional personnel (legislators, judges, attorneys, sheriffs) who operate these institutions. The function of this apparatus is to regulate individual and social affairs in a way that is responsive to actual conditions and in furtherance of ideal goals. Positive law is therefore a principle of order in the very real sense of being an instrument through which order is achieved.

The similarities between law and such other human institutions as religion, morality, and custom have often been remarked. I think this analogy can be pressed much deeper, and we can properly regard law as an extension and refinement of the central nervous system and of even more primitive mechanisms: it is a device through which the body politic organizes its efforts and adapts to its environment. To "make" positive law is to define statuses, functions, relationships, and patterns of behavior that are intended to promote the attainment of desired goals under actual conditions. To "enforce" positive law is to create officials and sanctions that will induce people to behave in prescribed ways. Promulgated positive law is simply the point at which the output of the first of these systems is transferred as input to the second: it is similar to the synapse between afferent and efferent nerves.

It is this apparatus as a whole, not marks on paper, that we should bear in mind when we think of positive law. Promulgated positive law plays a part analogous to that played by formulated laws of nature: it describes to us the usual patterns of behavior and courses of events in the context to which it refers and so allows us to predict the consequences (outcomes) of different actions and situations. It is in this sense that positive law is, in Cardozo's phrase, "cousin german" to laws of nature. Law is here a principle of order in only a passive and detached sense, reporting how men should and usually do behave. When we think of the legal apparatus in its entirety and in its setting, quite different similarities come to mind. Law is now seen as analogous to and a direct descendant from those devices and procedures mentioned above, from instinct through the "big brain" to learning and custom. Law (the legal apparatus) is here an active and effective *instrument* of order, serving to organize and administer human affairs. Man's potential is so plastic, the projects he proposes so various, and the passages toward these so uncertain that they require for their governance a highly explicit principle of order. Thus it is that in the realistic sense of the legal apparatus positive law arises as a natural evolutionary development, taking form gradually to supplement these earlier instruments of order when they prove inadequate to the human condition.

This metaphysical excursus has certainly been too long an interruption, and even so it is probably too fragmentary an argument. But I would hope that it is sufficient to lend credence to the major themes with which I have been concerned. First, the thesis of the continuity of law, which holds that there are real and significant similarities of character and function among positive law and other types of law. Second, the claim that positive law (the legal apparatus) has expository, normative, and prescriptive elements: its function is to promote an orderly passage from the order that is actual to the order that is being sought. These matters should become clearer as we now leave these alien fields and return to more familiar legal ground to examine the manner in which positive law comes into being and operates as a principle and instrument of order.

CHAPTER VII

THE BEING OF
POSITIVE LAW

OUR VERY FAMILIARITY with positive law tends to divert our attention from two significant facts: positive law is both a human and an historical phenomenon. It does not occur beyond the human context, and even within this context it is a relatively late arrival. As I have already argued, positive law is a supplemental principle of order that is called into being and takes shape gradually in response to special conditions that develop in man's manner of existence: it arises to support and complement earlier principles of order when these prove inadequate to the task. This means that the characteristics and functions of positive law reflect both the structure of the human situation in general and a particular series of changes that this situation undergoes in time. I want to examine these matters in turn as a means to throw light on the nature of positive law.

It is a principal characteristic of man's nature and situation that he exists under the three regimes, or sets of conditions, that I have identified as Necessity, Possibility, and Purposiveness. The life order (both individual and social) that man constructs is a composite of these distinct orders that he inherits with existence. I shall describe these only briefly to refresh recollection, since I have analyzed them in detail in Chapter III.

We exist, in the first place, in a closed actual order. Our existence is strongly influenced and limited by our inherent nature and the external environment. This actual order has both natural and social components: we are conditioned by inescapable physical, biological, and psychological forces, and we are also conditioned by a complex social structure that assigns status and duties, imposes patterns of behavior, defines common relationships, and inculcates a body of habits and beliefs. As the existentialist philosophers like to put it, we are "thrown" into "the world." This is the regime of Necessity, and it represents the stable and persistent milieu of our existence.

We exist, in the second place, in a projected ideal order. Our lives are perpetually directed toward the future, seeking to escape the grip of the past and to change the present. We direct our conduct toward certain goals and in accord with certain norms in the effort not merely to exist but to improve the quality of existence. Melioration, rather than mere preservation, is the driving force of human life. Again, as the existentialists put it, man is the creature who is not what he is, who is what he is not, and who is always reaching beyond himself. Our existence is pervaded by anticipation and intention. This is the regime of Purposiveness, and it represents the order that we seek to make real.

We exist, in the third place, in an open provisional order. We find that our surroundings, both natural and social, have a certain flexibility, allowing us some freedom of movement. Human existence is characterized by real indeterminacy, so that we must decide what to do with our lives and how to manage them. This is the regime of Possibility, and it represents a tentative unfinished order that invites us to make of it what we will.

This same triadic character is of course mirrored in social existence. Every society has an established structure that covers the whole range of human interests, activities, and relationships and that is embodied in and supported by a complex of institutions. A society is a closed actual order that imposes a certain way of life upon its members. Further, every society is animated by a shared dream of a better and more just life, although the content of this envisaged future may vary radically from one case to another. Societies do more than just change: they move purposefully toward defined goals and conditions. Even with hesitation, uncertainty, and dissent, any society is continually in the process of realizing its vision of an ideal projected order. Finally, this structured society is always to some degree indefinite and incomplete, leaving some room for its members to arrange their individual pursuits and their mutual affairs as they see fit. And any society is in a continual state of transition, as men adventure down new paths at the behest of new interests and in search of larger satisfactions. A society is thus an open provisional order, forever in the process of changing its structure.

As a principle (instrument) of order, positive law reflects this triadic structure that pervades the human context in both its individual and its social aspects. It is the compresence of these three regimes of Necessity, Possibility, and Purposiveness—of these actual, provisional, and ideal orders, of these factors of persistence, passage, and project—that lies at the source of positive law and that poses its problem, which is to assure a satisfactory measure of coherence and harmony among these facets of human existence. And so it is that positive law embodies the three elements that I have designated as expository, prescriptive, and normative.

Positive law is expository in the sense that it reflects, and reflects back upon, the order that already holds in its society. Positive law is always to a marked degree a principle and an instrument of an established state of affairs: much of its content is a description of practices, relationships, and arrangements that exist prior to and quite independently of it, and one of its major tasks is that of maintaining stability, regularity, and continuity in human affairs and thus assuring that the structure of society is not disrupted. Positive law derives from and expounds an actual order.

Positive law is normative in the sense that it embodies the ideals men cherish, the standards they respect, and the values they seek to realize. It is thus an agent of Purposiveness, looking toward a future that is better than the present: men employ positive law both to guarantee themselves against undue intrusions or discriminations and to secure for themselves the material goods and conditions that they now lack and deem desirable. It is here that such concepts as equity, justice, rights, liberty, equal protection, and the general welfare enter the body of law. Positive law envisages and proclaims an ideal order.

Positive law is prescriptive in the sense that it defines and enforces the arrangements, relationships, procedures, and patterns of behavior that are to be followed in its society. It is an answer to the twofold challenge posed by Possibility: it must prevent the conflict and chaos that any misuse of Possibility threatens, and it must chart the course of change that will take the best advantage of the opportunities that Possibility offers. Positive law is prescriptive in the quite literal sense that it prescribes what is to be done under present conditions in order that certain future results may be accomplished. That is, it posits a mediating order—a passage—between the actual and the ideal.

This thesis that the character of positive law is fully three-dimensional has two facets: it means to advance a statement of legal fact and to provide a standard of legal effectiveness. It claims that the existence of positive law has its source in actual conditions and ideal considerations as well as in the authority that enunciates it. It also claims that the effectiveness of positive law—its ability to win assent and command obedience—depends upon its adequacy in relation to these actual and ideal factors. Its prescriptive content—the imperatives it issues—even though grounded in legitimacy and supported by force, cannot be realized in the behavior of men and the fabric of society unless a proper account is taken of the conditions men face and the goals they seek. I am here concerned only with the first of these claims, leaving the second for a later chapter.

This first claim confronts us directly with the ontological question, What is the mode of being of positive law? What is its status in reality, and on what does its existence depend? Or, most directly and realistically, whence does positive law derive its being? There is an obvious and prevalent answer to this question: from the person who proclaims it. That is, positive law is brought into being by the act of promulgation. It is an order issued by someone, and in turn it orders human affairs. This theory has had a persistent history, in the course of which the human source of law has been variously identified. According to the doctrine of divine rights, law derived from the anointed king, who held secular authority under God. All later forms of this imperative theory can be seen as so many attempts to place limits upon such absolute power. According to medieval natural law doctrine, the law "promulgated by him who has the care of the community" must be in accord with divine law. With the advent of the modern era, attention shifted to more human and mundane methods of control. In the form made famous by John Austin, it is the sovereign whose commands make laws; and the sovereign that Austin obviously had in mind was the king in parliament. Populists, romanticists, and metaphysicians of various schools have held that law is the expression of the general will, whether spontaneously shouted in public unison or secretly divined by an inspired leader. Taking a colder and harder look, the American and Scandinavian legal realists have found the source of law in judges: the law is what courts say it is. Recognizing that courts, legislatures, the sovereign, and even the assembly of the people have some manner of official status and derive their lawmaking power from a prior source, Hans Kelsen and H.L.A. Hart have sought the true basis of law in a "basic norm" or a union of "primary and secondary rules" that transform mere pronouncements into legitimate laws.[1] And Lon Fuller has extended and refined this notion in his careful analysis of the "inner morality" of law.[2]

There is an important measure of truth in this position. In a sense,

[1] See Hans Kelsen, *General Theory of Law and State*, trans. Anders Wedberg (Cambridge, Mass.: Harvard University Press, 1945); and H.L.A. Hart, *The Concept of Law* (Oxford: The Clarendon Press, 1961).

[2] Lon L. Fuller, *The Morality of Law* (New Haven: Yale University Press, 1964).

positive laws are certainly man-made: they are enacted by legislators, proclaimed by executives, or announced by judges. And they are the outcome of highly formalized and institutionalized procedures. But these men are not so much the creators of law as the agents through whom it finds expression. And when we scrutinize it closely, the process of lawmaking turns out to be rather a translation than an original production.

The laws that issue from these human persons and procedures are not made arbitrarily, whimsically, or *ex nihilo*. Indeed, the entire legal apparatus—substantive, procedural, and personal—is designed for the express purpose of preventing such erratic human intrusion and of insuring that the process of lawmaking follows its appointed course to its proper outcome. The very use of such phrases and concepts as "due process," "correct procedure," "sound interpretation," "*ultra vires*," "valid order," "reasonable provision" (and there are many such) indicates that we think of the acts through which men make laws as being animated by forces, directed toward goals, and judged by standards that do not originate in these acts themselves but exist independently of them. Furthermore, those who are officially engaged in the process of lawmaking insist vehemently upon this point. Administrators and police officers merely "apply" and "enforce" the law; judges "find" the law; legislators "take cognizance of" physical circumstances, economic conditions, social needs, and human demands, and give them legal form and status; and even constitutional conventions declare that they are simply ratifying and codifying what is somehow already law. In fact, the closer we look and the harder we press the more difficult it becomes to find any human acts or agencies through which positive law is made. None of them will acknowledge that it *makes* law; each insists that in one way or another it *declares* law.

This brings us back to the crucial point that was discussed at length in the previous chapter. For insofar as they are declared, *all* laws are man-made. This is equally true of scientific laws, civil laws, and moral laws—of the laws of heredity, inheritance, and charity. It is extremely interesting to consider, for instance, whether the law of gravity existed before Newton noticed apples falling to the ground in the orchard at Woolsthorpe Manor or whether the laws of genetics existed before Mendel carried out his experiments in the monastery garden at Brunn. From one point of view, they obviously did. Material bodies were attracting one another in a definite manner and genes and chromosomes were engaging in their elaborate maneuvers long before Newton and Mendel were even aware of them. So these laws "existed," in the sense that certain organized structures, stable relationships, patterns of behavior, and courses of events were already established in nature; that is, existent things had definite characteristics, behaved in set ways, and pursued constant paths. Therefore all of the content that these laws were to express—the situations, processes, and states of affairs to which they refer—were already there: these laws were "embodied," and to that extent they "existed."

But from another point of view they just as clearly did not exist. Considered as statements and formulations, as explicit recognitions of what is the case, they had no existence at all. There was no awareness on the part of anyone—apples, genes, or men—of these precise structures, processes, and relationships. No one knew with any exactitude how things had happened, were happening, or were going to happen, and therefore no one was able to intervene with real effectiveness in these happenings. These laws had not been discovered and formulated, so they could not be "applied": they were not available to be used as instruments to understand and change the state of affairs and the course of events. As I have already argued, laws are lived long before they are framed. Laws are embodied in the nature and behavior of things and are even taken account of by man before mind recognizes them for what they are and uses them to intervene in the order of things. To plait the simplist rope of vines as a means of crossing a ravine—or even to take a running start for a leap—is to acknowledge and counter the *force* of gravity, but to plot the course of the planets or to launch a spaceship to the moon requires a precise formulation of the *laws* of gravity. And there is a wide difference, as well as a basic similarity, between the selective reproduction that takes place in nature and the scientific breeding that is practiced in a racing stable. So long as these laws of nature are only implicit, they afford no power of prediction and control. To put it so, they are "principles" but not yet "instruments" of order.

We find a similar situation, I think, when we consider moral laws. Long before these are expressly proclaimed, the facts and forces to which they refer are real and active: men exist in situations, they encounter one another, they enter into relationships and engage in transactions, they are subject to a multitude of needs, appetites, desires, sentiments, and intentions that drive them along certain courses toward certain outcomes. With regard to these matters, men already make primitive distinctions of "good" and "bad," based on such compelling but imprecise feelings as pleasure and pain, desire and aversion, duty and remorse, pride and guilt. Therefore moral laws already "exist" prior to their proclamation in the sense that the behavior of men is animated by emotions, attitudes, and purposes that cluster around the poles of approval and dis-approval: this point is stressed by those schools that locate the basis of morality in "conscience" or a "moral sense." But it is only after these laws have been systematically formulated and preached that they can be "applied" as models and standards to motivate and direct the conduct of men. Moral laws, like scientific laws, now take on a richer mode of exist-ence, becoming instruments as well as principles of order.

I would urge that the situation is essentially similar in the case of posi-tive law. When we are asked whether positive law exists before it is pro-claimed, we tend to give an immediate and emphatic negative answer. We think of such law as necessarily issuing from a human agent: as enacted by a legislature, ordered by an administrative body, or an-nounced by a court. We also think of it as necessarily enforced by other human agents: by sheriffs, police officers, bailiffs, probation and parole boards, and so forth. In a sense, as I have already acknowledged, this view is entirely sound: positive law—like scientific and moral law—attains to a full measure of existence and becomes effectively real only when it has been explicitly formulated and institutionalized. Fur-thermore, one is perfectly entitled to insist as a sheer matter of defini-tion that nothing is to be termed and classified as positive law until it has been officially declared to be such. And this insistence stresses an impor-tant point, which we will soon explore.

But to tie the whole existence of positive law to the act of promul-gation—to the fact of its being officially proclaimed—is quite another matter. This view, like any half-truth, is dangerously deceptive: in fas-tening our attention upon certain features of the matter at issue, it blinds us to other features that are equally important and even equally obvious. For we all know perfectly well that there is a real sense in which positive law exists prior to and independently of its enunciation as such. This prior manner of existence is twofold, having both expository and normative roots.

The expository existence of positive law is rich and varied: it is em-bodied in the habits, practices, usages, traditions, and settled relation-ships of people—in short, in what we call their customs or ways. These constitute the existential roots of positive law, supplying very much of both its content and its strength. A great deal of positive law consists simply in the acceptance and prescription of arrangements that already hold in society. Men are in fact ordering their lives and their affairs in certain ways, conforming to certain standards, enforcing certain rules, before these have any legal status and sanction. As Eugen Ehrlich put it, positive law arises when this "inner order of associations" is transformed first into "legal norms" and then into "legal propositions."[3] Positive laws have an expository existence in just the same sense as do scientific laws, which we think of as the prototype of this mode: they formulate structures, relationships, and patterns of behavior that are already established in the phenomena to which they refer. In familiar legal language, this aspect of law is acknowledged in all of those acts by which courts and other bodies "recognize" and "receive" custom and give it legal status.

Positive law has a similar normative existence that is embodied in the ideals and principles that men cherish, the purposes and aspirations they pursue, and the notions they hold to of fairness, reasonableness, and common decency. These constitute the existential goals and guidelines of positive law: they furnish many of the rules and standards that positive law obeys itself and applies to others, they define the social conditions that it seeks to realize, and they determine the human values it is to respect and promote. This Normative existence of positive law was traditionally given explicit recognition in the doctrines of natural law and natural rights. These have recently fallen almost completely out of fashion, but it is difficult even now, save in the most routine cases, to find a legislative enactment, a judicial decision, or an executive order that does not appeal to, or at least assume, the principles and maxims that these doctrines set forth. And the doctrines themselves are still openly invoked in moments of legal crisis, such as the Nuremberg trials, the post-Nazi war crime cases in German courts, and the civil rights decisions in the United States in the 1950s and 1960s. All that we have done is to substitute "human rights" for "natural rights," writing them in lower-case in accord with our nominalistic bent.[4] As the expository content of positive law comes to it by way of custom, its normative content is largely derived from common morality.

But this is still far from the whole story, and the central character is yet to be introduced. For positive law is more than an echo of custom and morality, and it does more than simply acknowledge and enunciate what is and what ought to be the case. Though these actual and ideal orders contribute greatly to the being (the substance) of positive law, they do not constitute it as such. For positive law also has a prescriptive dimension: it exists as a set of prescriptions having the force of imperatives

[3] Eugen Ehrlich, *Fundamental Principles of the Sociology of Law*, trans. Walter L. Moll (Cambridge, Mass.: Harvard University Press, 1936).

[4] As I shall argue in Chapter XIV, this seeming advance toward a sophisticated realism is in fact a retreat toward a naive utopianism, since it affords absolutely no criteria to determine what is a "human right."

that are intended to secure the passage from the actual to the ideal order. And its effective existence as an instrument of order depends not only on these expository and normative materials but also upon a highly formalized apparatus through which these prescriptions are formulated and enforced.

In its prescriptive role, positive law is a principle of an open and transitional order. It declares the order that we intend to establish in the world, the manner in which we propose to effect a passage from the order that is to the order that we think ought to be. Man's character is distinguished by its plasticity and his manner of existence by its openness and indeterminacy. Both individually and collectively, men are continually confronted by options: different goals and different paths are open to them; and there are alternative ways in which they can organize themselves, arrange their affairs, and define their mutual relationships.

As I stated before, this means that human existence is permeated with Possibility. Man is not closed in by the actual, nor is he preordained to any single ideal outcome. He certainly has specific potentialities: Necessity limits him, and his purposes lie in certain directions. The field of human action is loosely structured, pliant, and fluid, leaving much room for men to decide for themselves on their goals and courses. But this freedom has its price: stated generally, it opens the way to mistakes and conflicts. Men misconstrue their natures, worship false gods, and plan inadequately, with the result that they betray themselves and clash with their fellows. Man's condition thus confronts him with a double task: he must prevent the disorder that continually threatens, and he must create an order that will promote the realization of his potential and enhance the quality of life. In short, Possibility challenges man to make proper use of it.

Positive law prescribes this use. It administers the human effort in both its individual and social aspects. It defines the general goals and conditions to be promoted, as well as the courses to be followed in furtherance of these goals and conditions, it lays down rules and standards of behavior in various contexts, it regulates the transactions that men carry on and the relationships that they form, and it imposes sanctions to support its policies and decisions. Of course, positive law does not shoulder this burden alone; it is but one participant in the larger undertaking that we call culture, and it shares its task with many other institutions and organizations, such as religion, education, the family, science, morality, and economic and industrial enterprises. But positive law has increasingly become the dominant partner in this effort, exercising a general supervision over the other members and even assuming more and more of their functions. One cause of this shift of power has been the decline in influence and effectiveness of several of these other institutions, notably the family, the church, common morality, and the local community as a spontaneous source of order. But of at least equal importance has been the high development and effectiveness of positive law as an instrument of order. With the erosion of these other institutions, the obvious thing to do was to call on the legal apparatus to fill the power vacuum that resulted.[5]

This apparatus of law is complex and diversified. Institutionally, it comprises the various officially constituted bodies for making, interpreting, administering, and enforcing its prescriptions, the formalized procedures that these must follow, and the accumulated mass of its previous prescriptions (the body of substantive law, whether legislative enactment, judicial decision, executive proclamation, or administrative order). Professionally, it comprises all of those officials who assist in the operation of this apparatus: legislators, administrators, judges, attorneys, bailiffs, sheriffs, and other "officers of the law."

As I have repeatedly insisted, there is a real and important sense in which positive law exists prior to its formulation and implementation by means of the legal apparatus. But these expository and normative modes of existence are incomplete: both custom and morality are conservative, uncertain, without sufficient provision for change, and lacking strong sanctions, so that their enunciation of what is and what ought to be tends to be static, while the actual forces and ideal aspirations that seek expression through them are dynamic and volatile. There comes a time, therefore, when these earlier principles of order prove inadequate to the conditions they confront. It is then that positive law in its prescriptive aspect and in the form of the legal apparatus comes into being. Its task is to discover the direction sought by these social forces and aspirations, to criticize and correct them, and then to implement their realization.[6] Positive law now exists in a fully three-dimensional sense, serving as an explicit principle and an effective instrument of order.

This whole matter can perhaps be illuminated if we refer back to the discussions of the preceding chapter and draw from them an analogy. Positive law can then be seen as supplementing custom and morality in

---

[5] I shall have more to say about this development in Chapters XIII and XVIII.

[6] This theme of the eventual inadequacy of custom and morality and the emergence of law to make good these failures is a familiar one in the literature. I shall deal with the matter in more detail in the next chapter. Cf. also Hart, *Concept of Law*, pp. 89-96; and Fuller, *Morality of Law*, pp. 33-94. The Latter is particularly detailed and helpful.

much the same way as the formulated laws of science supplement the embodied laws of nature. Once these laws have been discovered and made explicit, they can be used as tools to predict and control the course of events. That is, they make possible the development of the various technologies that play so large a part in our lives and allow us to intervene so effectively in the world. Similarly, once the contents of custom and morality—the patterns and standards of conduct they impose—have been recognized as factors that control human behavior, they can be examined critically and then corrected or reinforced, as the case may require. When we not only follow the edicts of custom and morality but are aware of them as expressions of human nature and experience, accumulated slowly over a long past, we are in a position to measure their appropriateness to our present needs and purposes and to the circumstances we now confront. And then we can take steps to define and secure more adequate patterns and standards of conduct. Positive law is a supplemental principle of order through which this is accomplished.

This is to say that positive law—always in the realistic sense of the legal apparatus—is a case of technology. It is a highly organized device for predicting and controlling the course of events in the human world. Its purpose and function are purely practical: it is an instrument of order, intended to assure that certain conditions, arrangements, relationships, and patterns of behavior are realized and adhered to. In short, it is a practical or applied science.

But no sooner have we said this than we begin to reflect, and then to have reservations. For all of the more familiar applied sciences—from engineering and agriculture to medicine and education—are clearly dependent upon other disciplines and institutions. In fact, they have a double dependence, they depend upon various theoretical sciences—physics, chemistry, biology, psychology—for the knowledge that they apply, and they depend upon outside sources—in general, the clients they serve—for the purposes to which this knowledge is to be applied and the outcomes it is to secure. In the usual case, both the facts that a practical science uses and the ends that it serves are given to it ready-made: pure science furnishes the theoretical principles and the empirical data that it needs, and the uses to which these are put are dictated by the client (whether private or public) who employs the technology. People demand that their doctors keep them healthy; such basic medical sciences as biochemistry, physiology, bacteriology, neurology, anatomy, pathology, and others study the multiple factors that condition health and sickness; the medical profession acknowledges this responsibility, accepts this information, and devotes its efforts to helping people stay well and live long.

We can now see how positive law at once resembles and differs from most technologies. Like any such, it is heavily dependent upon sources beyond itself both for the ends it serves and for the information upon which it relies in devising means to secure these ends. Positive law—any particular legal system—is subject to pressures coming from everywhere within the society it serves: some of these, such as the demands for due process and equal protection, embody moral claims; some represent the common aspirations of the people; some—probably most—express the private interests of various groups and factions. And the legal apparatus, alike in its legislative, executive, and judicial branches, relies upon information and advice from any and all of the theoretical sciences that are relevant to the point at issue, from economics and sociology to meteorology and nuclear physics.

But there are three facts about positive law that taken together make its position and its responsibilities unique. In the first place, the purposes that are proposed to law are always diverse and often contradictory. The interests that the legal apparatus is called upon to serve—the ends it is expected to secure—are perpetually in competition, with every concerned party being able to make out a strong case for the particular cause that it espouses: conservationists seek to protect the environment, the oil companies insist that they need to increase their supplies, and the general public demands both more power and less pollution. In the second place, the sciences upon which the legal apparatus depends for information and advice—especially the social or "soft" sciences—often give testimony that is incomplete and conflicting. The exact causes and cures of such social ills as poverty, inflation, discrimination, functional illiteracy, gross inequalities, corruption, and so forth are so complex and obscure that no one can say with any certainty what policy will be most effective or what its outcome will be. Unexpected factors intervene, side effects appear, benefits have their price, and people respond in ways that no one could anticipate. Thus the powers of prediction and control that the law commands are very imperfect. It is one thing to throw a bridge across a river and quite another to get a society to exchange its present habits and values for new ones.

Any practical discipline of course suffers under these same liabilities: its clients often ask the impossible, and the available knowledge is incomplete. But in the case of positive law, the difference in degree is enormous. And there is a third consideration that is a real difference of kind, confronting the legal apparatus with a unique situation. This is the simple fact of the sovereignty of law. As the agent of the state, the legal apparatus has no source beyond itself to which to appeal for a decision among conflicting goals, nor can it excuse itself from action on the ground of incapacity. It must decide and it must act, since even not to do so is itself a decision and an action. Other technologies can say to their clients: "Make up your minds. You can have A, or B, or C, or some compromise among them. But you cannot have all three in the form that you want them. So think it over and let us know." Or they can say: "The knowledge and techniques presently available make it impossible to achieve the results you seek. You will just have to wait."

Neither of these recourses is open to the legal apparatus. Its clients are those tenuous entities, the people and the general welfare. But, as the embodiment of the state, this apparatus is itself the voice of the people and the measure of their welfare. Therefore positive law is, in an effective sense, its own client. Since it represents and acts for the society it serves, it is in the anomalous position of being both principal and agent; or, more exactly, it is an agent that must make all of the decisions for its principal. The legal apparatus, therefore, must make its own judgments regarding the facts it has to deal with and the values it is to promote. It seeks advice where it can get it and it is sensitive to the claims urged upon it, but the final decisions are its own. While positive law is the servant of society, it is also its own master; and so it is the master of society. The only appeal beyond it is to force in the form of revolution.

It is because of this status and responsibility that it carries that the being of positive law is composed of expository and normative as well as prescriptive elements. The existence and effectiveness of any legal system depend on actual circumstances and ideal considerations at least as much as upon the authority that enunciates it. The actual order and the ideal order pose to the legal apparatus the conditions that its mediating order must satisfy. These prior orders contribute greatly to the substance of positive law: to the extent that positive law loses touch with them, or ignores their demands, its being is impoverished.

This largely theoretical account of the being of positive law can be elaborated by an empirical account of its becoming. We can now look briefly at law as an historical phenomenon.

CHAPTER VIII

THE GENESIS OF
POSITIVE LAW

THERE IS BROAD AGREEMENT, at least in general terms, regarding the course of change that elicits positive law: this resides in the transition from primitivism to civilization. The conditions that we refer to by these terms cannot be sharply defined or clearly distinguished. Rather, they are segments along a continuum, and the transformation is gradual. We are in the same predicament here as when we try to say just what life is and when it begins or to mark the line that separates Homo sapiens from other hominids. However, these conditions can be satisfactorily, if roughly, identified.[1]

Under primitivism the human group is tightly knit, unilaterally organized, and cohesive. Individual differences of status, function, training, opportunity, and achievement are relatively slight. The margin of safety with respect to the environment—the human control of the physical surroundings—is small, so that the way of life is largely dictated by the pressure of external circumstances. Conformity and cooperation are required for survival. Under these conditions, *what actually is* tends to become identified with both *what must be* and *what ought to be*. Order is maintained within the group by a complex of forces and agencies: instinct, habit, custom, training, imitation, tradition, the feeling of reciprocity, natural necessity, emotional ties, the sense of personal obligation, moral sentiments, the urge for acceptance and respect, religious influences, and others. These have been variously interpreted and em-

---

[1] There is a vast literature on this subject. I will mention only a few of the more familiar and accessible items. The classic is of course Sir Henry Maine's *Ancient Law* (London: J. Murray, 1861). More recent and more fully supported by field work are: E. A. Hoebel, *The Law of Primitive Man* (Cambridge, Mass.: Harvard University Press, 1954); Robert Redfield, *The Primitive World and its Transformation* (Ithaca: Cornell University Press, 1953); George Peter Murdock, *Social Structure* (New York: Macmillan and Co., 1949); William Seagle, *The Quest for Law* (New York: Alfred A. Knopf, 1941); Bronislaw Malinowski, *Crime and Custom in Savage Society* (New York: Harcourt, Brace and Co., 1926); A. S. Diamond, *Primitive Law* (London: Longmans, Green and Co., 1935). Most of these works contain full bibliographies.

phasized by different investigators, but all agree that primitive groups tend to be homogeneous, to be dominated by personal relationships, and to be characterized by a strongly felt solidarity.

The disruption of primitive conditions, and the trend toward civilization, is a complex and gradual process involving changes on three levels. Physically, groups grow in size, they advance technologically, they attain a larger control of the environment and a greater measure of safety, they come into contact with other groups. Socially, group structure becomes complex, subgroups arise, functional specialization and differences of status become greater, competition for material goods increases, heterogeneity spreads, special interests arise and conflict. Psychologically, self-consciousness and self-assertiveness increase, men envisage their private interests as distinct from those of the group, they form associations, they challenge the relevance of the past and the sanctity of the status quo.

These changes take place gradually, concurrently, reciprocally, and cumulatively. Just where within this process positive law emerges can be determined only in the loosest way, and even then largely by arbitrary definition. But it seems clear that the process that we later recognize as leading to law exhibits two tendencies from its inception: there are definite arrangements for the use of the organized force of the group, and there are explicit rules concerning when this force is to be invoked and how and by whom it is to be employed.

This brief account calls to mind H.L.A. Hart's theory of secondary rules, previously discussed in Chapter V. However, Hart's interest is different from my own, leading to differences of emphasis and treatment in the two cases. His purpose is to identify the basic elements that are necessary to constitute a legal system, and his argument is entirely analytical. He is unconcerned with any actual process through which law emerges and develops, and thus his interest is focused on the abstract characteristics—and especially on the defects—of the situation that calls law forth. One might say that Hart's tactic (quite legitimate for his purpose) is to employ the device of an avowedly hypothetical social contract as a means of getting at the essential structure of a legal system. He can then regard the origin of law as a one-time event, neglecting the question of stages of development. Thus he writes as though the uncertainty, the static character, and the inefficiency of a regime of custom simultaneously elicited the rules of recognition, change, and adjudication.

The thrust of my argument, on the other hand, is genetic and developmental. I am interested not in the abstract situation but in the concrete changes that lead to law and that dictate its development. I do not believe that Hart's secondary rules come into being simultaneously and through a single act. Rather, they emerge gradually and serially. I would suggest that as the customary social order loosens (as the grip of Necessity is relaxed), what is first required is an authority that can maintain the order that is threatened; thus the rule of recognition is established and invested in some person or persons. Then, as men welcome and grasp the opportunities that open before them, asserting themselves and pursuing their private interests (as the regime of Possibility extends its sway), what is required is an apparatus to settle their differences and to restrain aberrant behavior: the rule and apparatus of adjudication are thus introduced. Finally, as these individual pursuits issue in disorder compounded by injustice, exposing the need for explicit social planning (as the regime of Purposiveness makes its demands felt), what is required is a way to provide for orderly movement toward definite ends: thus the rule of change is introduced and implemented.

This schematic account will be expanded and qualified in the discussion that immediately follows. I believe that the progression that it posits is generally faithful to the course of events, but as it stands it is admittedly tainted with the artificiality that attends any such dissection of a synthetic process. I would also point out that given the differences in the interests at work, there is no conflict between Hart's account and my own. I accept his analysis and simply install it in time.

When we first discern the germ that is to grow into positive law, this seems to consist primarily in a technique for effecting a reconciliation between men who have been estranged by some act or occurrence. Both the rules that define who and what is "right" or "wrong" and the agents of decision and enforcement hover very much in the background. In this sense, the first recognizable legal figure is not the legislator, not the executive or sovereign, and not even the judge, but rather the lawyer. He appears in the guise of the mediator and negotiator: he is the "runner," "crosser," or "go-between" of the California tribes, the Ifugao of the Phillipines, the Ashanti on the Gold Coast. Both the function and the power of this figure are largely persuasive. He lacks organized force, and there is no code to which he can appeal: behind him stand only established usage and the tacit support of the group.

When positive law in an institutional sense emerges, with its twin facets of force and form, it largely inherits the status and character of the go-between. As the transition from primitivism to civilization proceeds, there is an increase both in disagreements among individuals and in defiance of group decisions and interests by individuals—disorder threatens. In its first appearance, the function of positive law is to prevent or restrain this disorder: it seeks to repair and maintain the fabric of group life, and it does this chiefly by reiterating and preserving the order that has been. The content of such law comes from established ways and usage: it asserts itself as merely an additional agent—or sanction—by which these are to be kept effective. At this stage, what predominates is law's expository character, with its normative and prescriptive elements in the background, though already certainly present. In this stage, law's ambition is to reflect and maintain an actual order. There is little thought of either an end in view or a process of transformation to be guided by prudence. Such law is retrospective rather than prospective. Its norms, such as they are, are the normal, and what it prescribes is merely the maintainance of the status quo. This situation might be described (in language borrowed from mature legal systems and hence too sophisticated to be altogether applicable) by saying that here the executive function of law is preponderant. There is little felt need or willingness for legislation to create new rules, and adjudication is largely the announcement of the penalty that follows automatically once the facts have been established. The important task that is demanded of law is the enforcement of the rules of the group, so that recalcitrant individuals can be restrained and disruptive acts prevented. This is law in its conservative function, seeking to perpetuate what the past has secured. To revert to the abstract analysis of earlier chapters, law is here dedicated to the task of preserving the regime of Necessity and protecting this against the uncertainty and disorder that the intrusion of Possibility threatens.

But the movement toward civilization cannot be contained. Differentiation and variation proceed; initiative intensifies; social life becomes more open and fluid, both in fact and in man's desire. The loosening of the established order is seen not as a threat but as an opportunity. Under these circumstances, what is asked of law is that it prevent the old order from stifling the new forces that are moving toward a different future: it is expected to encourage change and to protect enterprise by laying open the fabric of society. Law now becomes predominantly prescriptive, with its expository and normative features kept at the periphery of its attention. What such law prescribes is not so much patterns of behavior and schedules of duties and penalties but rather the procedures that men must follow in developing new modes of action and working out new arrangements among themselves: the legal apparatus now serves as an instrument that men employ in creating new relationships and in organizing new undertakings. Maine's famous dictum regarding the movement from status to contract is undoubtedly an oversimplification, but it still contains an important element of truth, for we can detect a period in the life of all legal systems in which their primary concern is to make it easier for men to arrange their affairs as they deem best in pursuit of whatever goals they prefer. Law becomes primarily a principle of an open and provisional order, with only a minor regard for the actual order that surrounds it and with little effort to proclaim an ideal order in any detail. Of course this neglect is not absolute: it would be absurd and even impossible to promote change without some regard for both existent circumstances and ends in view.

But under these circumstances positive law can and sometimes does becomes systematically casual and uncritical as regards these matters. Its goals then become such amorphous futurities as progress, liberty, equality, the pursuit of happiness, growth, the general welfare and individual well-being, and it is content to accept the actual order as a framework that defines in broad and flexible terms the possible avenues of change. What positive law is asked to supply is an apparatus through which men can determine for themselves just what these changes are to be and what outcomes they are to lead to. One might say that the legal apparatus now becomes primarily procedural, accepting uncritically the substantive expository and normative content—the customs and morals—that other forces supply. Or we might better say that what such law prescribes is quite simply the form of freedom within which men are to create their private careers with a minimum of public interference ("that government is best that governs least"). The judicial function now becomes prominent, as the courts are the forum before which men plead their private interests and seek official sanction for their novel undertakings and arrangements. This is law in its liberalizing function, intent upon promoting the conditions of Possibility and thus encouraging men to exploit what the present offers.

As we saw earlier, the regime of Possibility is provisional and incomplete: it challenges men to make use of it. If these uses are left too much to individual discretion, with inadequate central control, abuses soon appear—might makes right, there is ruthless exploitation, and vast inequalities occur. Where positive law becomes too exclusively prescriptive—in the sense just canvassed—energies are left undirected and goals are ill-defined, with the result that men's efforts become erratic and dispersed. The legal apparatus can confine itself to the role of umpire (in the figure of speech that was once so popular) only when the rules of the game are fair and the forces at play are evenly balanced. Otherwise injustice and oppression become widespread. As this occurs, the legal apparatus is called upon to intervene purposively and systematically in the course of events. The main function of law now becomes that of defining and executing policy: its task is to give form and direction to society. If law does not actually propose and fashion the ends it is to serve—and it is usually most reluctant to admit that it does—it decides among those submitted to it, redefining and reconciling them in the process. In the light of these norms, law then devises means intended to transform the actual order. Legislation now becomes a continuing and significant function of the legal apparatus, as this seeks to anticipate and prepare the future. Positive law here undertakes to compose and create—to expound and prescribe—an ideal order.

Though the preceding account is perhaps closer to an abstract schema than to actual history, I believe that it is generally faithful to the course of legal development. But two points merit explicit mention. First, what I have been depicting as a single linear progression has been in fact a cyclical process. Second, as positive law develops and assumes new functions, it still retains its old ones. In becoming a constructive and directive agent, law does not escape the responsibilities of its earlier conservative and liberalizing stages. What varies with time and circumstance is the relative pressure exerted on these functions of law: under different conditions, the primary responsibility of law will be to protect an order that is threatened, to open up and loosen an order that has become restrictive, or to guide society toward a new and better order. But the legal apparatus always faces all three tasks, which are facets of a single undertaking. And simply in the act of responding to one set of conditions and emphasizing one objective, law promotes other conditions that require a different emphasis. Hence the fluctuations that are so familiar in legal history, as law strives to achieve a balance that forever eludes it.[2]

We know full well that this quest of the law for a resting place has proved fruitless in the past, but we still delude ourselves into thinking that there is promise for this in the future. We do this because we oversimplify the dimensions of this quest and the nature of the solution in which it issues. We usually think of legal problems in terms of antinomies: freedom and security, stability and change, individual rights and the general welfare, liberty and equality, private interests and public order—the roll call goes on interminably. Thinking in such dichotomies, we are led to believe that we can find a middle term that will strike a

---

[2] I have discussed several examples of this in Chapter IV, and I shall examine the problem in more detail, and from a different point of view, in Chapters XV and XVI.

balance between the extreme points and reconcile their claims, thus bringing the swing of the pendulum to a halt. What we forget is that this new order—this supposed middle term—at once becomes the established order. And since its very intention is to be static, it soon begins to become restrictive, and so generates the demand that it be opened up. The solutions to old problems generate new problems demanding newer solutions, with law continually having to correct its own successes. The pendulum of legal change swings through three points, not two. Thus the figure needed to describe it is not the Aristotelian Golden Mean but the Hegelian dialectic, with thesis leading to antithesis and this to synthesis, which then serves as a new thesis and a fresh starting point.

This problem can best be clarified by reference to my earlier analysis of the regimes of Necessity, Possibility, and Purposiveness, and of the relation between these. We tend to reduce this schema and to think of it only in terms of a tension between Necessity and Possibility—between forces that are working in contrary directions for stability or change, for economic laissez faire or a controlled economy, for the protection of the rights of the accused or the preservation of public safety, for the demand of officials for the privacy of their deliberations or the right of the people to know, for greater security against personal failure or a larger opportunity for personal success, and so on, and so on, and so on. This leads us to regard law as merely the vehicle through which constituted authority acts to strike a balance between these competing forces. An almost exclusive emphasis is thus placed upon the prescriptive function of law: we conceive the legal apparatus as an instrument that mediates these conflicts, looking always for a lasting compromise.

But this is to overlook the fact that in trying only to mediate, law inevitably creates. In the very act of compromising the rival pressures of Necessity and Possibility, the legal apparatus invokes the regime of Purposiveness: it projects a new order different from the old, and it prescribes the passage that is to lead to this. Criminal procedure is modified, the antitrust laws are changed, pornography is redefined, the welfare system is revised, legislation is enacted regarding fair employment practices and open housing, and new standards of political representation are established. As these prescriptions take effect and the projected state of affairs is realized, it becomes the established regime: it acquires the status of a second-order regime of Necessity. As such, it soon generates new protests and demands requiring new satisfactions. And so the process is continually refueled.

The recent works of Hayek and Unger referred to earlier contain accounts of the development of law that have close similarities to the one just expounded.[3] But the differences in our intentions and manners of treatment stand out very clearly here. Their accounts are more empirically and historically oriented, offering a wealth of important and interesting detail regarding the actual changes that have occurred in the social and legal orders, and as such their books supply much concrete evidence to flesh out my abstract account. Further, these writers are deeply concerned with the problems that the present social and legal situation poses and with the possible solutions to these problems that lie in the future (if they are ever solved, or even solvable). Their discussions of these matters are extremely illuminating and suggestive. Hayek enriches his account with numerous detailed analyses of actual institutional developments and with criticisms of the failures to which these have too often led. Unger enriches his work with illustrations brought to bear on his argument from a wide variety of contexts and with farreaching speculations. Both men open vistas on the future, but they are not concerned to develop a general philosophical theory that could explain exactly why the social and legal orders have changed as they have; nor do they seek a systematic analysis of the character of these changes and the forces that have driven them. These are precisely my central concerns.

This difference in outlook and intention is brought out sharply in a brief passage from Unger's *Law In Modern Society*. At the conclusion of a penetrating discussion of the course and outcome of social change, he mentions two critical problems that his account poses. "First, how could tribal society, which is surely the type most applicable to the earliest forms of human association, ever change? Second, are there any general reasons why one form of society turns into another?" He then continues:

> To answer the first question, one must postulate that in any society that can be characterized as human there is always a potential rift between *ideal* and *actuality*. This inherent possibility is simply a particular manifestation of that more general power to transcend the forms of one's existence which is a defining attribute of humanity.
>
> If there is a solution to the second problem, it might be a speculative hypothesis about the relationship between the way societies change and the way human nature develops in history. . . . It is not

[3] See F. A. Hayek, *Law, Legislation, and Liberty: Vol. I, Rules and Order* (Chicago: University of Chicago Press, 1973); and Roberto Unger, *Knowledge and Power* (New York: Free Press, 1975) and *Law in Modern Society*.

my purpose here to elaborate or to justify this frankly evolutionary idea. I mention it only to suggest the form of a possible answer and thereby to indicate once again how the problems of social theory may force one back to a more basic puzzlement about human nature and its relation to history.[4]

The conceptual and even the terminological similarities of Unger's account and my own are striking. The theory that I have developed in the preceding chapters constitutes a careful and systematic analysis of the "postulate" and "idea" that Unger here suggests—and that he himself richly expands in a more historical and speculative manner.

Throughout its history, law has been perpetually engaged in this restructuring of the social order. At different moments of this on-going task the emphasis will shift, but the structure remains constant. The legal apparatus operates within and upon an actual order that it must respect and preserve. It anticipates and is directed toward an ideal order that must be reasonable and realizable. And it posits a mediating order that must achieve an accommodation of the actual and the ideal, the established and the projected.

[4] Roberto Unger, *Law in Modern Society* (New York: Free Press, 1976), pp. 154-155. I would merely suggest that these problems also "force one back" to an even more "basic puzzlement" about the relations of man and the social order to other forms of life and other modes of being. These are the issues with which I have been concerned throughout the preceding chapters.

[CHAPTER IX]

THE CONDITIONS OF
LEGAL EFFECTIVENESS

As I INDICATED in my Introduction, one of my chief aims in this book is to elucidate the conditions of legal effectiveness, especially as these manifest themselves during those times when law is being used as a leading instrument of social change. I think it is clear that the present is such a time to a spectacularly high degree. As has often been remarked, we have become a legalistic society: we are relying more and more upon the legal apparatus, in its legislative, judicial, and executive functions, to effect reforms of all kinds—social, economic, technological, and even political and moral—and at every level, from the local to the international.

It is painfully apparent that these efforts to achieve social reform through law have met with a large measure of frustration. Considering this disappointing record, I argued that the chief responsibility for these failures lies in the fact that we have been working with inadequate notions regarding both what law is and how it acts. We have first misconstrued the ontological status of law, oversimplifying its nature and exaggerating its power. And this has led us to a similarly mistaken view of the social status of law—of the position that it occupies in society, the role it plays, and the force it is able to exert. Put very briefly, we have been too much beguiled by the doctrine of the sovereignty of law, and we have acted as though this ideal were an accomplished fact. We have thus been led to focus attention too exclusively upon the prescriptions that law issues—the legislative enactment, judicial decision, or executive order—and so we have come to think that a valid legal act must be automatically translated into corresponding social action, just as effect follows cause in nature. In sum, since we regard the legal apparatus as autonomous and omnipotent, we believe that we need only manipulate it to achieve the social changes that we seek.

Our failures in these efforts have been more than sufficient to indicate that something is seriously amiss in this body of doctrine. So, finally, I suggested that if these mistakes are to be corrected we need to reconsider, at a basic level, both the ontological status and the social role of law. That is, we need a theory of law that can better illuminate the conditions of legal effectiveness. I have now presented this theoretical account, and it is time to apply it to examine these conditions that must be met if the legal apparatus is to be adequate to the tasks that are being demanded of it. This should give us a clearer grasp and so a better command of the problems that we face when we seek to use law to change society.

The practical lesson that theory teaches is easily drawn. If positive law is to exist and function effectively as an agent of reform—if it is to be a living force and not merely a dead letter—then its mode of being must be fully three dimensional. This demand springs from the fact that the social order, of which law is a principle and instrument, is dynamic and continually in passage from one state of affairs to another. Society is as restless as the sea, but without the latter's constancy.

Law is therefore perpetually engaged in restructuring the social order. And this undertaking, as we have seen, has three aspects and poses a threefold challenge: the legal apparatus operates within and upon an established social milieu, it projects certain goals and purposes, and it proposes the steps through which the present is to be transformed into the future. The problem that law constantly faces is that of maintaining a harmonious relationship among these elements. The possibilities that law is able to exploit (the measures that it can effectively implement) are limited by the factual situations with which it has to deal and by the aspirations and tolerances of the people whose lives it seeks to change. In sum, the mediating order that law posits—the courses and outcomes that it prescribes—must be commensurate with the actual and ideal orders that circumscribe its field of action.

One would think that the force of this lesson would be as compelling as its meaning is clear. But such has not been the case. To the contrary, our inflated view of the power of law leads us to think of the legal apparatus as an instrument on which we can play whatever tune we wish, with full confidence that all who hear it will dance to its measure. With regard to any contemplated legal action, the question that almost exclusively occupies our minds is that of its validity. Satisfied on this point, we move blithely ahead, secure in the faith that validity assures compliance and efficacy. We thus regard the power of law as defined and limited only by formal requirements, untouched by material considerations.

Two circumstances have played particularly significant roles in fostering this attitude. The more overt and obvious of these has been the temper of those schools of thought that have dominated contemporary legal theory. The doctrines that have exerted the greatest influence—the imperative theory, legal positivism and realism, analytical jurisprudence, the pure theory of law—have all emphasized the formal structure of legal systems and their role as the source of prescriptive norms. It is my belief that all of these schools have been guilty of the same general error: they have confused the differentia of positive law with its full nature. They have been so intent on identifying and describing the specific features that distinguish the legal apparatus as a mode of social control—on exposing the "essence" of law—that they have lost sight of the generic characteristics and functions of law. Thus, Kelsen can say that justice and social fact are alike irrelevant to jurisprudence; and Hart, in speaking of the "minimum content of natural law," can dismiss the question of the purposes of law by identifying these simply with the provision of sanctions to protect person, property, and promises. This technique of isolating law and thinking of it only internally is quite justifiable as a methodological device. And as I have indicated in earlier discussions, both Kelsen and Hart are perfectly aware that law exists in and is limited by its social milieu. But they largely ignore this fact because it is irrelevant to their purposes. Trouble arises when, at the hands of others, this neglect leads to forgetfulness and even denial of this connection and dependence. That is, it breeds the dangerous habit of regarding and treating law as though it were in fact an autonomous and self-sustaining force.

The other circumstance fostering this attitude is the fact that our direct experience of law is limited to mature legal systems functioning in established and cohesive societies. The influence of this circumstance, while less overt and explicit, has been of paramount importance. For it is virtually the definition of an established society that there is a close coordination of law acting in its prescriptive role with the actual and ideal orders within which it functions. When a legal system is indigenous and has grown with and out of its society, it is naturally attuned to the conditions and aspirations that it serves. The legal apparatus, reflecting the circumstances and intentions that gave rise to it, is carefully designed to preserve the existent social structure and to further the values that it seeks. So long as the tempo of change within the society is gradual and its direction is familiar and unchallenged, the prescriptive role of law is derivative from and subordinate to its expository and normative roles. That is, the mediating order that law posits is a reflection of a secure actual order (of established practices and arrangements) and an anticipation of a widely sought ideal order (of goals and intentions that are generally shared). Under these conditions, law is largely the creation and the servant of antecedent social facts and values. The legal apparatus is here a tool that employs already available materials for already agreed upon purposes, so that what it prescribes is assured of acceptance; the only problem the lawmaker faces is that of defining and effecting a passage that is well prepared and widely desired. This symbiosis of an indigenous legal apparatus and an established social order is so familiar to us that we tend to reverse the relationship and to regard law as the creator and master of these facts and values—these social conditions and ideal aspirations—capable of manipulating and even transforming them at will.

We learn better as soon as we undertake to use law to effect radical social change, for here the usual relationship between law in its prescriptive role, on the one hand, and the expository and normative parameters with which it interacts, is reversed. The legal apparatus is separated from the actual and ideal elements—the habits and aspirations of people—that constitute its established setting, and it is employed to redefine and restructure these elements. This means that law is now required to posit not merely a mediating order but new orders of the actual and the ideal. That is, we attempt through law to establish new patterns of fact and value—new practices and purposes—in the society that is being reformed.

This is a formidable task. And we make it virtually impossible when we too much exaggerate law's prescriptive power. As Plato long ago suggested, being is power. The relevant passage reads thus: "I suggest that anything has real being that is so constituted as to possess any sort of power either to affect anything else or to be affected, in however small a degree, by the most insignificant agent, though it be only once. I am proposing as a mark to distinguish real things that they are nothing but power."[1] The converse of this proposition is equally significant: power is being. That is, the kind and degree of power that any real thing can exert are measured by its being.

This means that the power of law is dependent upon its expository and normative modes of being, not merely its prescriptive. The power of law is exercised through the legal apparatus, by means of which its prescriptions are enacted and enforced. But the real source and measure of its power derive not only—or even chiefly—from the efficiency of this apparatus but largely from its being properly adjusted to the manner of life

[1] Plato *Sophistes* 247E.

of its people and able to secure in decent degree the values that they expect from life. That is, if the mediating order that law posits is to be accepted and woven into the social fabric, it must be made congenial to the settled habits and aspirations of people. This requirement is easily and almost automatically met in the normal, day-to-day operations of law, where the modifications that are affected in the social order are relatively minor, being simple adjustments to accommodate slight changes in actual conditions or to satisfy a reordering of the preferences that people express. Here, law merely echoes (recognizes and responds to) shifts that have occurred independently in social conditions and popular expectations. But when law is used as an instrument of social reform, it seeks through its own power to initiate changes in these conditions and expectations, not to sustain them.

The problem that law faces here might be compared with that which medicine confronts in organ transplants. In the latter cases, something is so radically wrong with certain structures of the human body that they cannot be repaired and restored to normal functioning: therefore they must be replaced. The difficulty that arises here is the familiar one of rejection. The defense mechanisms that conserve the body against foreign intruders will not accept these alien elements, which appear to them as germs or viruses that must be destroyed. Two methods are employed to alleviate this difficulty: the transplanted organ is matched as closely as possible with the host body as regards tissue, blood type, and other biological factors, and the host body is prepared in various ways to accept and accommodate itself to the stranger in its midst.

As an initiator of social reform, law encounters a similar difficulty and must employ similar techniques. Since a critical social ill has been diagnosed and radical measures are being undertaken, it is to be supposed that certain organs of the body politic are functioning inadequately: basic needs are not being satisfied, reasonable hopes are being frustrated, and the level of life is lower than it should be. So reform—a transplant of new political organizations, social arrangements, and human purposes—is decreed. But just like the human body, the instinctive response of the body politic is to reject these novel goals and conditions as alien elements that threaten its existence. So these reforms cannot be chosen arbitrarily or imposed dogmatically. The reformer must have recourse to the same methods as the surgeon if he is to disarm this opposition.

First, it is necessary that the proposed reforms be matched as closely as possible to the established social order: they should be an extension or embellishment of the existent pattern of life, not a disruption of it; and they should largely be capable of realization through the present administrative machinery, without conflicting with or requiring elaborate revisions of it. That is, the real changes that are to be introduced must be sufficiently congenial to the broad structure and goals of the body politic to find accommodation within it. Otherwise, the society will adopt the defensive measure of rejection: it will assume a reactionary and conservative posture, which is the social equivalent of rigor mortis.

Secondly, the people of the society must be carefully prepared to accept and support the proposed reform. They are the cells and tissues of the body politic, and it is their way of life that is to be changed. Thus their instinctive hostility and resistance to these foreign elements must be neutralized. Just as with the host body in an organ transplant, the defense mechanism of the citizen body—their suspicion of the new and untried—will need to be lulled into acquiescence. This requires a varied program of persuasion, education, and demonstration, directed toward exhibiting the proposed changes in the most favorable light and making them appear at once necessary and salutary. This program can have many facets: the reforms can be presented as a natural extension of the traditional ideals and commitments of the society, as necessary adaptations to changed circumstances, as more effective means to the ends which the society has always sought, as concessions that must be made if tensions are to be eased and conflicts avoided. But all of these arguments have a common intention: they mean to domicile change within the settled framework of men's practices and purposes and so to make the new seem both familiar and desirable.

The sense of this analogy translates readily into literal discourse, for it means that the effectiveness of law as an agent of social reform depends upon maintaining a balance between its expository, normative, and prescriptive elements. By simple decree, law can prescribe new goals for society and new patterns of behavior for its members. By legislative enactment, executive order, or judicial decision, it can establish rules and procedures, proclaim policies and programs, create administrative bodies and regulatory agencies, impose standards and conditions, and otherwise ordain the organization and the aims of its society. But law cannot win the allegiance and adherence of people to its new actual and ideal orders merely by positing them. A way of life and a body of aspirations are too personal to be invoked by public fiat: if law is really to effectuate social reforms, it must persuade before it prescribes.

The problem posed by this demand is brutal in its directness. It consists in the fact that the benefits promised by social reform cannot be made manifest before the event: the people must desire them and cooperate in working for them if they are to be achieved. You can show people the advantages offered by tools, machines, and even techniques without their understanding and wanting these: an electric pump is obviously more efficient than a rope and bucket, a truck is more effective than a team of oxen, and controlled irrigation is more productive than the annual flooding of fields. You can demonstrate the superiority of these to people who are initially indifferent, skeptical, or even opposed: the advantages speak for themselves, and adoption quickly follows. But the case is quite otherwise with those more private aspects of life, such as the practices people follow, the purposes they seek, and the values they cherish. The supposed benefits to be gained from changing these cannot be realized and made apparent until the changes have themselves been affected. So reform hangs on a promisory note, with no supporting collateral, being honored at its face value.

It is for this reason that the maintenance of a balance between the expository, normative, and prescriptive orders is so important. Every change in one of these orders must be quickly reflected in changes in the others. When we undertake social reform through law, then, by definition, law in its prescriptive role takes the leading part: it animates the process, sets the pace, and points the direction. But it cannot get too much out of step with its partners. The changes that it proposes in the actual way of life must be realized in the practices and behavior of a people, not merely projected. And the aspirations that it has stimulated must be satisfied, not merely aroused. If the discrepancies between what law prescribes and what it accomplishes become too great, the outcome is confusion and frustration. Law then loses its persuasive power (its hold on the allegiance of its people), this drains away its effectiveness, and one of two results occurs: either the program of social reform is rejected and abandoned, or the people dismiss the legal apparatus as an effective method of securing the now desired reforms and turn to other means of achieving them, whether these be civil disobedience, protests and demonstrations, violence, dictatorship, or the solicitation of foreign intervention. Events in the three areas that I referred to earlier—civil rights, the strengthening of the United Nations organization, and the newly-independent states—give abundant confirmation of this prognosis.

When we are engaged in social reform through law we are simultaneously transforming the way of life of a people, the values and satisfactions they seek, and the content and operation of the legal apparatus itself. We are positing a new mediating order through which we hope to create new actual and ideal orders. The problem is to keep these transformations in step and thus maintain a balance among the orders. And the most important fact about this balance is that it does not remain static. Instead, it is volatile and unstable, so that there is no way in which a "proper" balance between actual conditions, ideal strivings, and legal prescriptions can be determined and permanently settled. This balance is in continual flux. The practices and aspirations of people may resist the urgings of law, or, having been initiated, they may gain a momentum that carries far beyond the original intentions of reform. These practices and aspirations themselves may work in unison, or they may clash violently, with custom, habit, and proven utility commanding one line of behavior while accepted ideals and values proclaim another. The legal apparatus may command such resources of power and persuasion that it can win a very large degree of adherence to its programs and proposals, or its claim to authority and its hold on the allegiance of its people may be so precarious that it can only proceed tentatively and on sufferance of immediate results.

I think that the key to understanding and mastering this intricate process of reform through law lies in two concepts: *value* and *authority*. It is a truism that the program of reform is premised on the assumption that it will enhance the realization of human values. The motive and the justification of the effort involved in reform can only be a hoped for improvement of the quality of life. Further, it is all too obvious that the attainment of the values sought by reform is often difficult and delayed. Thus the effort that is required must be guided by an authority that has the trust of the people and is adequate to its task. People will undertake the strenuous work of reform and will accept the sacrifices it may require only if they have faith in the integrity and respect for the ability of their leaders.

Consequently, if the reforms that we attempt through law are to succeed, we must have a clear grasp of these two central concepts. First, we need to understand the nature of value and the conditions of value realization, for only then can we assess the values that are at stake (in both the old order and the new) and the adequacy of the means available to secure them. Second, we need to understand the nature of authority and the factors upon which its effective exercise depends, for only then can we assure ourselves of a leadership that will be acceptable and efficient. I will deal with these matters in turn.

[CHAPTER X]

VALUES AND THE LAW

CLARIFICATION of the problem posed by values depends on first drawing a distinction and then avoiding two opposite errors that this distinction often invites. The distinction itself is familiar and deceptively simple: it differentiates between intrinsic or final value on the one hand and extrinsic or instrumental value on the other. The intrinsically valuable is that which stands on its own feet and needs no further justification: it is the end sought by action, the consummation achieved; it is good or worthwhile or desirable in itself, needing no completion; in a word, it is its own excuse for being. The extrinsically valuable is that which supports and sustains the occurrence of intrinsic value: it is the means to an end, the things and devices we employ to achieve our purposes; it is good and desirable to the extent that it serves as an instrument to procure final values.

The now generally accepted view holds that intrinsic values are exclusively occurrences in experience, having their primary locus in human consciousness. Final values—values in the strict sense—reside in activities and in the enjoyments that inhere in and accompany these activities: they are functions of the exercise of man's abilities and talents, and they reflect the realization of various of man's potentialities. Such values exist only in consummations, never as finished products or secured conditions: as Aristotle put it long ago, happiness is an activity, not a state. As modern terminology puts it, values are pleasures, enjoyments, delights, satisfactions, or gratified interests. In brief, value is always an accomplishment, never a *fait accompli*.

Extrinsic values are all of those "things" (in the broadest possible sense of that term) that we use to support our activities and to secure our enjoyments; whatever contributes in any manner to the attainment of final value falls within this category. The catalogue of such instrumental values is long and varied: it comprises the whole range of physical objects that we employ in our pursuits—tools, machines, appliances, utensils, artifacts, works of art, animals, and even other human beings; the skills and techniques that we develop; the practical and moral rules that we follow and the norms that we hold; the habits and practices that we acquire and transmit, the situations and states of affairs that we create; the organizations and institutions that we establish. All such items (including of course civil and political rights, integrated schools, economic policies, programs for the treatment of criminals, the United Nations) are instrumental values. They are only potentially and provisionally valuable, and their actual value depends upon their success in promoting the achievement of final values. Intrinsic values are hedonic in character, while extrinsic values are utilitarian.

I think that this distinction is on the whole sound, and I subscribe to it, although with certain refinements and reservations that need not here concern us. But its very simplicity and its air of being transparently obvious are apt to induce in us a serious error: we may become so intent upon one of these modes of value that we altogether lose sight of the other. On the one hand, we may become so obsessed with final values—with the enjoyments, satisfactions, and consummations that people seek—that we forget that the attainment of these is utterly dependent upon the whole complex of instrumental values. We are then apt to conclude that whatever intrinsic values people desire and claim both can and should be made immediately available to them, without consideration of the availability of the necessary extrinsic values. When stated thus in naked abstractness, this conclusion is manifestly fallacious and would hardly fool a greedy child. Yet we are often lured into its trap under the pressure of insistent claims that present themselves as justified and so appeal strongly to our emotions.

We may, on the other hand, become so engrossed in the manipulation of instrumental values—in improving the presumably inadequate physical conditions and social arrangements—that we forget that these are only means to human satisfactions and by themselves are sterile unless they can be successfully exploited. The most obvious targets of any program of reform are material, technological, and institutional deficiencies. These deficiencies are often conspicuous, and they are apt to present themselves as both solely responsible for our value troubles and as readily amenable to correction. So it is easy to conclude that if we can only repair these defects and provide more favorable conditions, then the quality of life—the measure of intrinsic value—must necessarily be enhanced. This conclusion is as obviously fallacious as the former one, but impatience and unfamiliarity with the ways of others often lead us into it.

The point that must always be borne in mind is that final and instrumental values are interdependent. It is feckless to project and promise intrinsic values unless we can control the extrinsic values that are indispensable as means to them. And it is pointless to provide instrumental values without also taking steps to ensure that these will issue in the final values that are their true ends. To risk a homily, the essence of the matter is this: means without ends are meaningless, while ends without means are endlessly postponed. Evidently, then, if the reforms that law proposes are to be effective, both of these errors must be avoided. Stated more positively, if these reforms are to lead to the desired enhancement of value, two conditions must be satisfied: the necessary instrumental values must be available, and men must be equipped to use them for the realization of final values. These two conditions of value need a brief consideration, and it will be best to take them up in reverse order.

Intrinsic values are both initiated and consummated in human experience: their pursuit is the issue of men's needs and desires, and their realization is the outcome of men's activities and achievements. When law sets out to effect social reform, its first concern must be to make sure that men are prepared for the intended reforms and that they have the potentialities to profit from them. The final values that are in question—the activities and attainments in which it is hoped men will now share—must be wanted and sought for by these men, not merely dreamed of or demanded; and men must bring to this quest the skills, training, and discipline that are its necessary support. Such values cannot be conferred by some as donors and passively accepted by others as recipients; men must make them their own by direct participation in the process through which they are realized. For example, we can and do confer academic degrees upon graduation: but these are merely testimonials, witnessing to past value achievements and opening paths to further value pursuits. All too often, both the people who have been deprived of certain human values and the reformers who sympathize with them have eyes only for the material benefits and privileges that crown success: the good job that comes with education, the big salary that comes with the good job, and all the good things that money can buy. This compulsion is understandable, and the sympathy it arouses is admirable. But both are often misdirected because they focus attention only on the attainment of value to the neglect of its pursuit. They think to pick the fruit without first cultivating it. And this is a vain hope, for this pursuit of value is usually arduous in itself, uncertain in its outcomes, and long delayed in its achievement. Those to whom law seeks to make new values available must be brought to realize that they will themselves have to make a large contribution to this conquest, for determination, patience, and self-restraint will be needed in large measure if men are to persist in the effort that is required.

Furthermore, intrinsic values can be attained only to the extent that men have the appropriate abilities and cultivation. Since such values reside only in men's activities and the enjoyments that accompany them, the kinds and degrees of value that men can realize are conditioned by the skills, the discipline, and the discernment that they can bring to bear. Education, in all of its aspects, is best conceived as preparation for value achievement: it is only on this foundation that law can build a program of reform, for people cannot be ushered into a new way of life, like guests into a house.

There is a final consideration that hedges in this pursuit of final values, this being the cruel recognition that the realization of value often entails the sacrifice of value. Most obviously, if a larger measure of intrinsic value is to be made available to some men, then others may have to surrender values they have hitherto enjoyed. As certain pursuits and gratifications cease to be the private preserves of the few; as the hitherto underprivileged clamor for a richer life; as the egalitarian ethos intensifies and dictates a more equitable distribution of the world's goods; as more people sense and seize opportunities that were formerly restricted; as increased leisure makes possible wider participation in more varied activities—as all of this happens, values that had been easily and abundantly available to the favored few now become scarcer and less accessible. Men do not always acquiesce in such a loss, and therefore law must take steps to win over or disarm their potential opposition.

Less obvious, but perhaps more critical, is the fact that even those who now achieve new values may have to make commensurate sacrifices. As we have seen, this achievement will certainly demand effort, delay, and discipline, all of which can be inherently unpleasant. And there are other negative considerations. This move toward new realms of value will engage people in situations and surroundings that are unfamiliar and in which they are apt to suffer from insecurity. They will face increased competition, with its certainty of pressure and its threat of defeat. And finally, it may be that the values to which they have looked forward so eagerly and struggled for so hard issue in only disappointment and frustration. That is, people find themselves engaging in activities that are not enjoyable or rewarding but that they feel compelled to pursue simply because it is expected of them in their new role and status. This outcome is so familiar that it is epitomized in the popular phrase, "keeping up with the Joneses."

All of these problems are encountered but not always overcome in the reform movement that overthrew the "separate but equal" doctrine and led to racially integrated schools. We can grant that this process has already led to an increase in final values (a statement that would nevertheless be challenged by some). More blacks are being exposed to a better education, are receiving more intensive training, and are acquiring higher skills. At the same time, familiarity washes away the prejudices of whites, who learn to respond to human beings as such, without regard to color or race. It is even safer to assume that these reforms will yield a steadily larger measure of value in the future, as strangeness wears off, conflicts are resolved, inequalities are eliminated, and the two groups lose their sense of difference. But there can be no doubt that this process has caused some real hardships, entailed some loss of value, and created problems that are yet to be resolved. The bussing that is required to achieve racially balanced schools is itself inconvenient and expensive, and it has the more serious effect of destroying the neighborhood school and thus weakening the neighborhood itself as a significant influence on children. It is often claimed that integration has resulted in a lowering of academic standards, and the violence and tensions that have attended it have inevitably hurt educational programs. And many black children whom the reform is intended to benefit have certainly undergone more or less severely traumatic experiences as they moved into an unfamiliar environment where they encountered hostility and rejection and were handicapped in competition with more privileged children.

As these difficulties and failures mount, they may elicit either of two responses. The public may conclude that school integration is not necessarily an end in itself and is certainly not a panacea (as the Supreme Court seemed to indicate in its decision in *Brown*) but is only a means to an end: if the means proves ineffective, then drop it or reinforce it with other techniques. This response has prompted two recent movements. Many blacks have shifted their emphasis from "integrated schools" to "quality education." Concurrently, parents and teachers all over the country and from all groups have demanded that something be done to reduce the number of high-school graduates who turn out to be functionally illiterate and only marginally employable. The thrust of these movements has led to the practice of "proficiency testing": this seeks to identify and correct deficiencies before it is too late and to assure that graduates do have the basic skills and competences that they need if they are to make their way in the world. This is a positive and healthy response, provided that the measures it dictates are implemented impartially and effectively: it accepts the rebuff of reality, recognizes the limits that constrain the law, and looks for other ways to achieve its goal.

There is, however, another response that the underprivileged can make when their hopes and efforts are disappointed. This has a more complex history, but its origin and course are roughly as follows. The law in its majesty assures these groups that they have certain rights—to an education, jobs, advancement—and that it intends to see that these rights are enforced and these benefits made available. But the law fails to deliver on its promise: minorities find themselves falling behind in school, failing employment tests, and being denied the goods to which they have been told they are entitled. Under these conditions it is altogether to be expected that the disillusioned groups should turn to the law to take further action to implement the rights it has recognized. But the law cannot supply the teachers and facilities that are needed—it does not have them at its disposal. Nor can the law make good by mandate the cultural and educational deprivations of the past. That is, the law is helpless to take positive steps to afford these groups the instrumental and final values—the skills and jobs, the activities and enjoyments—that it has promised they should have.

With their disappointment now turned to frustration and bitterness, minorities turn to an option that is available and tempting: they argue that the tests used by schools to determine admission and proficiency, and by business and government to determine employment and advancement, are "culturally biased" and unfair because they do not take into account the different cultural backgrounds of minority group members. These groups can now appeal to the courts to invalidate these testing procedures on the ground that they are a denial of equal protection and a violation of the Fourteenth Amendment. And this is an appeal that the law *can* answer. It cannot give students an education, but it can see that they are given diplomas; it cannot give people skills, but it can see that they are given jobs.

This response is negative and self-defeating: its outcome is as tragic as its occurrence is natural. Both the law and the minorities who appeal to it are frustrated: the former by its inability to effect changes and secure values that are eminently just and desirable; the latter by their failure to receive the benefits they had been promised as their right. Since minorities find the door to opportunity still closed against them and since they have been assured that they have a right to have it opened, they insist that the guardian be dismissed; since the law finds that it cannot give minorities the password that will open the door, it simply rules that passwords are unconstitutional. The behavior of minorities in this situation is easily excusable: one can understand that they should come to the cynical conclusion that these tests are just another trick of the white man to pawn them off with paper promises that yield no real results. The behavior of the courts is less easy to understand: assuming that the tests are reasonably fair and unbiased—and they are of course subject to rigid scrutiny in this regard—then the courts should recognize that they are legitimate devices that serve the long-run best interests of all parties. The procedure of invalidating such tests on no other ground than that members of minority races do less well on them than members of the majority race is doomed to defeat its own purposes: supposedly committed to reform—to progressive change—the law can only perpetuate the inequalities and deprivations it pretends to cure.[1] I will deal with this issue more fully when I consider the general question of rights in Chapters XIV and XV. I have discussed it at this length here because it illustrates so dramatically the mistakes into which the legal apparatus can fall when, in its determined pursuit of final values, it overlooks the complex conditions that must be satisfied if these values are to be realized.

I should also add that this discussion is in no sense advanced as an argument against integration, still less as a plea to reverse this policy. To the contrary, its intention is to further the process by pointing out the difficulties that legally initiated reforms are apt to encounter and so must be prepared to overcome. The points in which this argument issues can be briefly summarized: the only reason for undertaking social reform is to enhance the realization of final values, and such values have their only being in the activities and experiences of men. So if they are to be realized, the persons whose benefit is intended must have the requisite background, abilities, and training; they must believe that the final values promised them will in fact be available if they themselves make the necessary effort and succeed in what is asked of them; and it is extremely important that the programs that prepare them to realize these values be planned in such a way that those pursuing them can see themselves making progress toward their goals. Good faith and careful planning on the one part, trust and honest effort on the other, are the indispensable keys to success in this endeavor. The legal apparatus can do something to keep the first party up to the mark and to assure the second of its backing, but it clearly is not able to supply any of the essential ingredients.[2]

---

[1] There is an interesting discussion and defense of the "cultural bias" thesis in Justice Douglas's dissent in DeFunis v. Odegaard, 416 U.S. 312 (1974) at 320. The question of the use of tests in determining employment is discussed at length in the three decisions in the case of Washington v. Davis, 348 F. Supp. 15 (1972), 512 F. 2d 956 (1975), 426 U.S. 229 (1976). This is a volatile, even explosive, issue, with those on both sides holding very strong views.

[2] This general problem will be discussed in detail in Chapters XVIII and XIX.

We can turn now to the second condition of value, which is that the instrumental values that are necessary to the attainment of final values must be available. The activities that yield men enjoyment, satisfaction, and a sense of well-being are dependent on the resources of the world. Even the apparently most self-sufficient of these, such as contemplation, appreciation, worship, and love, require leisure, training, and objects upon which to be directed, while most activities stand in more complete and pressing need of outside support. The intrinsic values that men seek require access to the goods of the physical environment, such as land, raw materials, tools, and machines; they require diverse educational, medical, recreational, and cultural facilities that will enable them to develop and express their talents; and they require social, political, and economic institutions through which to make their efforts and their voices effective.

These requirements for effective reform are so obvious and urgent that it is almost impossible to overlook them. But it is nevertheless the case that law, in its reforming efforts, does often misread their character and mistake the demands they impose. These misapprehensions that bedevil the law in its undertakings all proceed from one basic oversight: the legal apparatus fails to consider with sufficient care its ability to control the various instrumental values that it needs to employ in its intended reforms. For if social reform through law is to succeed, it is not enough that the necessary resources—material, human, and institutional—should be available in society and the environment. It is of equal importance that the legal apparatus should have an adequate command of them. It does not suffice for law merely to decree, by legislative, judicial, or executive action, certain changes in the social order: in the goals and practices of people, the relations that are to hold among them, and the ways in which they are to arrange and manage their affairs. In addition, the legal apparatus must have the means to assure that what it directs will in fact be done. Under normal circumstances, and where law is rather the echo than the voice of social change, conformity is largely automatic. But when law seeks to initiate change, it is very easy for it to have an exaggerated view of its power and to underestimate the resistance it will encounter.

There are three levels at which such difficulties can arise. The most persistent obstacle that legal reform encounters is popular recalcitrance. If the changes that law decrees too much disturb the settled principles and practices of people, or too closely invade their privacy, or propose goals of which people do not approve, the resistance that is aroused can thwart the proposed reform. The classic example of this is the failure of prohibition in the United States. Other and more recent cases are found in the difficulties encountered by rationing programs, the revival of the military draft in the 1960s, the enforced bussing of students, fair employment policies, and efforts to control the use of hallucinogenic or "consciousness expanding" drugs.

Secondly, the legal apparatus may find that it cannot mobilize and rely on the institutional and organizational support that is needed to effect the reforms it intends. When the proposed reforms are radically innovative, the necessary institutions are apt to be nonexistent or only rudimentary, it is difficult to create or strengthen them, and if this can be done, it is even more difficult to impose these new institutions and procedures upon the established social order without severe opposition and disruption. These problems are especially acute when the "advanced industrial" nations seek—with the best intentions in the world—to reform and modernize the "underdeveloped" countries or when these advanced nations try to establish international institutions to stand beside or above themselves, as with the United Nations or the European Common Market. But similar problems confront internal reform. For here well-established institutions and organizations may resist the changed practices that law seeks to introduce, either because these conflict with what they regard as their own interests or because their implementation would require effort and expense that are deemed to be inordinate. Thus industry, labor unions, and school boards have actively or passively obstructed and tried to evade the implementation of fair employment policies; no-fault insurance has been fought by lawyers, and "socialized medicine" by doctors; the legal determination of safety standards has been resisted alike by the companies that manufacture automobiles and the people who drive them; police officers have opposed and ignored judicial decisions regarding the rights of those suspected of crime, and prison officials have been equally vehement in their denunciation of legislation regarding the treatment of those convicted of crime; and industry, labor, municipalities, and the public have joined as one—each for its own reasons—in rejecting as misguided meddling the efforts by law to halt pollution and protect the environment.

Finally, even when law is able to command popular and institutional cooperation (or at least acquiescence) and to mobilize the material support it needs, it still faces a further problem that is apt to be yet more formidable. This consists in the fact that if physical resources and human services are allocated as required by the proposed reforms, then other social goals and undertakings, which are equally valuable and urgent, may have to be reduced in scope or altogether abandoned. Physical resources, human energies, and wealth are all finite. If law decrees that these shall be put to certain uses in order to achieve certain ends, then they will not be available for other uses and ends. Such conflict and sacrifices, resulting from legislative enactments or court decisions, have already become familiar occurrences, frequently causing real hardship to communities and groups and arousing intense popular resentment. Thus, money spent on bussing students to achieve racial balance must be taken from other educational services or found through new taxes; legal requirements regarding the control of pollution and the protection of the environment have forced the closing of certain industrial facilities, creating unemployment and undermining the tax base of municipalities; and court decisions recognizing the rights of prisoners and establishing minimum conditions that prisons must meet have imposed serious burdens on the states affected by them.

To call attention to these problems is not to imply that such court decrees are always, or even usually, mistaken in their intention or unreasonable in their demands. To the contrary, they are often the only way to correct situations that have become intolerable through the neglect of those authorities and agencies that are charged with their management; that is, the courts step in only when and because others have shirked their responsibilities. But it is still the case that such legal intervention often fails of its purpose and creates as many difficulties as it removes because it does not take into proper account the conditions that it must satisfy if it is to be effective.

If we look for a particular instance to illustrate these general problems, an excellent one presents itself in the leading case of *Wyatt* v. *Stickney*,[3] in which Federal District Judge Frank Johnson took two momentous steps: he first gave explicit legal recognition to the "right to treatment" of persons who have been involuntarily committed to mental institutions in civil proceedings, and he then issued detailed and stringent orders defining the standards of care and treatment to which such patients are legally entitled. Several considerations make this case especially appropriate as a concrete instance against which to test the abstract suggestions and reservations just advanced. In the first place, the changes (the reforms) that the law seeks to bring about in order to secure the right that it has recognized are spelled out very precisely; to the extent possible, the court framed its decree in quantitative terms, so that there could be no uncertainty about what it required, and compliance with its orders would be easy to monitor. Secondly, the court order was

---

[3] Wyatt v. Stickney, 325 F. Supp. 781 (1971), 344 F. Supp. 373 (1972), sub nom. Wyatt v. Aderholt, 503 F. 2d 1305 (1974).

very local and limited in its application, being addressed directly only to the two leading mental health facilities in Alabama, Bryce and Partlow Hospitals, though of course it had an indirect impact on the state mental health system as a whole. Consequently, the context in which the reforms were to be effected was sharply identified and circumscribed. Finally, more than six years have now elapsed since the original court orders were issued, during which time Bryce Hospital has been under constant pressure to implement these orders and comply fully with the standards they established. In short, the state was told very specifically what to do and where to do it, and a definite procedure and apparatus were appointed to see that it was done.

Due to this combination of circumstances, the history of *Wyatt* v. *Stickney* affords an excellent opportunity to watch the law at work in an actual case as it seeks to realize the reforms it has ordered: we can here get an idea of the kinds of success that are attained, of the difficulties that are encountered, and of the failures that are experienced; and most importantly, we can identify with at least some precision the mistakes—the errors of commission and omission—to which the legal intervention is most prone and the problems that result therefrom. Finally, I shall use the consideration of this case as an occasion to illustrate the practical applicability of my theoretical analysis of the matrix of positive law and the difference that this could make if it were employed as a guide to legal deliberation and action.

It is not my intention here to trace the history of *Wyatt* even in outline,[4] but only to draw its lessons. One of the most interesting points to emerge from this six-year process of implementation—this effort by the court to realize in fact the reforms that it has decreed in its orders—is the marked difference between those areas in which it has been possible to effect notable changes and achieve a high degree of compliance and those other areas in which change has been slow and difficult and compliance is still largely lacking. This difference can be roughly summarized by saying that where the required reforms can be stated in numerical terms and

[4] This is a task that has occupied much of my time since the completion of the first draft of the present work. Under a grant from the National Science Foundation (NSF Grant Number SOC 75-16102), I have been engaged in an intensive study of the character of "human" rights, with particular attention to the problems and conflicts that occur in the implementation of these rights. *Wyatt* v. *Stickney* and the right to treatment have been the centerpiece of the empirical aspect of this study. A huge mass of material is available dealing with the implementation of the court orders in *Wyatt*: the primary sources of this material are the Bryce Human Rights Committee, appointed by the court to monitor compliance with its orders and protect the rights of the patients, the Office of the Superintendent of Bryce, and the Bryce Office of Planning, Research, and Evaluation (OPRE). The account and analysis that follow are based on reports from these bodies.

where the necessary changes are chiefly quantitative, then implementation tends to proceed and compliance to be reached quite rapidly and easily; where the goals set by the court are primarily qualitative and can only be described in general and impressionistic terms—where they have to do with such matters as the "competence" of the professional staff, or the "adequacy" of the treatment programs, or the "comfort" of the physical facilities—then implementation is hesitant and compliance lags.

This difference can be sharpened and clarified by a few examples. Since the original court order, by far the most obvious and dramatic changes at Bryce Hospital have occurred in the patient population and the budget: the former has been reduced from over 5,000 to less than 2,000; at the same time, the budget has more than doubled. Along with these changes, there have been significant increases in the size of the professional staff in certain categories, notably nurses and social workers. Again, there have been marked improvements in several measurable aspects of the physical plant, such as the installation of fire escapes and sprinkler systems, air conditioning, and furnishings. Finally, in this regard, there has been a considerable expansion of the state mental health system as a whole, with the addition of community centers, transitional homes, and other intermediate care facilities. Where reform is largely a matter of effecting sheerly physical and quantitative changes and where the degree of improvement and compliance can be easily measured and established, court orders can be monitored and implemented quite readily and effectively.

As critics of the conditions and programs of Bryce are quick to point out, these quantitative changes may be perfectly real but still altogether irrelevant: what is important, these critics insist, is not the *size* of the patient population, the budget, or the professional staff but rather the *quality* of the treatment that the patients are receiving and the effectiveness of this in returning them to a normal life. The rights and wrongs of matters such as these are evidently much more difficult to establish: criticisms and claims, charges and countercharges, complaints and justifications fly back and forth between the parties in a manner that is as inconclusive as it is contradictory. But without pretending to judge these disputes with exactitude or certainty, it is still safe to say that many of the most significant aspects of the Bryce treatment programs remain to this day in a highly unsatisfactory condition.[5]

[5] The numerous detailed investigations and reports of the Bryce Human Rights Committee and its professional consultant, Dr. John McKee, dealing with every aspect of the operation of the hospital, give solid confirmation to this conclusion. Even allowing for

Probably the most basic shortcoming that is cited, and one that under-lies many of the others, is the failure to make a careful professional classification of the patient population. This population is far from homogeneous: it includes those who are suffering from an acute and identifiable mental illness for which treatment is available, those who have been at Bryce so long that they have become "institutionalized" and need social and vocational rehabilitation, geriatric and adolescent pa-tients, those who have no chance of being returned to a normal life, or even to less restrictive conditions, and for whom the hospital can do no more than provide adequate custodial care, and those who are waiting to be transferred to a transitional home of some sort, where they can be prepared to cope for themselves. Partly because of this failure to classify the patients properly, many of them do not have proper individual treatment plans designed to lead to their cure and release. In the same connection, patient records are woefully incomplete, yielding little in-formation about the therapy the patients are receiving or the progress they are making. In a different but still related context, one of the most serious and persistent criticisms has to do with the excessive use of psychotropic drugs: it is charged that drugs are being used as a substitute for treatment, with no object other than that of keeping the patients docile and with the result that many of them are suffering irreparable harm. Another area of complaint is interesting as illustrative of the ex-treme difficulty of implementing court orders that are couched in vague and general terms. One of the most basic items of the original decree required that Bryce provide its patients with a "humane" physical and psychological environment that would assure them of the "privacy and dignity" to which they are entitled. In cases such as this, where the lan-guage is highly ambiguous, those who actually implement the court order—the members of the hospital administrative and professional staffs—simply interpret the terms as suits their convenience, and they have little difficulty in defending the outcome as "reasonable" under the conditions they confront. Critics may carp at the result, but it is virtu-ally impossible for them to frame their complaints in a way that can per-suade a court to take action, much less advise the court what action to take.

---

some measure of exaggeration in these reports (since they are partly polemical in inten-tion, being meant to move the court to more positive action), the failures they complain of are fully documented. Further, many of these criticisms and complaints are supported by Bryce's own Office of Planning, Research, and Evaluation, although, as would be expected, this body expresses them in a somewhat milder form and cushions them with references to the progress that has been made.

Anyone who studies the history of *Wyatt* finds himself thoroughly perplexed by a basic contradiction—an atmosphere of paradox—that pervades the case. This perplexity expresses itself in a simple question that never receives a satisfactory answer: given the very significant increase in the operating budget at Bryce and the equally significant reduction in the patient population, why has it been so difficult to implement the court order and comply with its standards? With this radical alleviation of the situation at Bryce, it would seem that the general conditions and the treatment programs at the hospital should have undergone a vast improvement. That is, one would think that the reforms ordered by the court should have been realized with relative ease and rapidity. Yet it is the consensus of all save the most partisan defenders of Bryce that this has not occurred: there have certainly been some important improvements, but conditions and treatment programs are still very far short of what the court ordered. One keeps asking why success has been so limited and failure so widespread, but an adequate explanation is never forthcoming.

This question is obviously of great intrinsic interest since it goes to the heart of the problem of the conditions of legal effectiveness. For me it also has an equally great extrinsic interest: its consideration gives me the opportunity to illustrate in a concrete case a matter that I have earlier (in Chapter IV) discussed in abstract terms. This is the issue of the possible usefulness, or applicability, of the theory I have expounded, with its intricate analyses of the matrix of positive law and the field of legal action. In that earlier discussion, I acknowledged that it might well be objected that this theory was too complex and abstract to be of any practical help in dealing with actual cases. The answer that I then offered was in essence very simple. I pointed out that legal decisions involving complicated problems and having far-reaching consequences should be made with explicit attention to all of the elements of my matrix (that is, all of the parties and purposes, all of the factors and considerations, that would be affected by these decisions and would in turn affect their implementation); that all too often such decisions are reached with consideration of only those areas of the legal field in which the issue arose, with a neglect of the repercussions that might follow in other areas; and that, finally, decisions made in this way could not but be partial and shortsighted in their view of the issues at stake and the outcomes they prepared. I then argued that if these mistakes—these shortcomings—were to be avoided, those who serve the law should hold clearly in view the entire matrix of law, not allowing their attention to be monopolized by some "compelling interest" of the here and now. Finally, I pointed out that while this theory (like any other) was incapable of dictating and guaranteeing a "right" answer, it could expose the complexity of the problem at hand and the framework within which it must be resolved, it could clarify all of the various issues at stake, and it could direct attention toward difficulties and consequences that were not immediately apparent and that might otherwise escape notice. In short, what such a theory can do is to protect deliberation against the appeals of sentiment and expediency while guiding it toward an outcome that is reasoned and principled. If it cannot guarantee success, it can at least point out the pitfalls that will lead to failure if they are not avoided.

I now want to illustrate this argument by reference to the decision and orders in *Wyatt* v. *Stickney*. I would suggest that many of the problems and difficulties that have arisen in the implementation of these orders have resulted just because the procedure described above was not followed: the court orders were framed without reference to and hence without the guidance of the sort of theoretical matrix that I have analyzed. For quite understandable reasons, Judge Johnson's attention was sharply focused on the actual wrongs of the mental patients and on the reforms that were necessary to right these. As a consequence, he did not take adequate account of various facts and considerations that must inevitably have an important bearing on the implementation of his orders and the realization of the reforms he envisaged. In the language of my doctrine, his interest was almost exclusively concentrated on a very limited segment of the total matrix of law—on only certain of the dimensions of order and regimes of existence. His orders were framed with only these elements in mind, so that the impact of these orders upon other elements of the matrix, and the reaction of these elements to such orders, were largely lost sight of. Of course, this neglect was not total: as I argued in the earlier discussion of this matter, what I have explicitly and systematically analyzed as the matrix of law constitutes the framework within which anyone trained in the law thinks of it and its problems. So Judge Johnson was perfectly aware that his orders were not automatically self-executing: they would have to be put into effect by an administrative and professional personnel with their own attitudes and habits, in a hospital with long established practices, dependent upon material support from the state, and under conditions that might change in unforeseen ways in the future. But his consideration of these factors, and the allowance he made for them, was peripheral and casual; and this neglect was more than serious enough to lead to the problems and difficulties that have in fact eventuated. Indeed, this is a classic instance of the kind of case referred to earlier, in which the pressure to do something to correct an intolerable situation is most likely to distract attention from both the larger context in which the necessary corrective measures will have to be realized and from the factors upon which success depends.

In amplifying this argument, I do not intend to run through all of the elements of my matrix, one by one and in serial order. I shall content myself with pointing out the more important of the elements that were neglected and the unanticipated—though altogether to be expected—troubles and failures that have resulted from this neglect. In doing this, I shall give the argument a concrete content (which should both illustrate and substantiate it) by showing that the most frequent criticisms made of Judge Johnson's orders, and the deficiencies in these orders that have manifested themselves most forcefully in the effort to implement them, can be clarified and fully understood only when they are put into the framework of the abstract matrix that I have analyzed.

This account can best begin by indicating those elements that occupied Judge Johnson's attention when he framed his orders in *Wyatt*: these clearly were the mental patients themselves and the reforms that were needed to assure them of adequate care and treatment. Conditions in the Alabama mental health institutions at that time were an open scandal: these "hospitals" amounted to little more than human warehouses, providing storage for all those persons who were in any way troublesome or inconvenient to their families and communities.[6] The facts that were brought out at the hearings in the case were so shocking that they froze attention on themselves and the remedy they demanded. It is clear from the court record that these were the matters that held and virtually monopolized Judge Johnson's mind. Thus, after hearing the evidence brought out by numerous witnesses, he referred to Bryce as "a prison" or "crazy house" rather than a hospital. He then identified "three fundamental conditions" that reform must achieve: 1) a humane psychological and physical environment; 2) qualified staff in adequate numbers; 3) individualized treatment plans for each patient.

With these conditions as a framework, Judge Johnson then spelled out, in an appendix to his decree, the "Minimum Constitutional Standards for Adequate Treatment of the Mentally Ill." These standards are the heart of the court order, and they control the process of implementation, for they define with great detail and precision exactly what reforms must be instituted. They run to thirty-five separate headings, most of

[6] It should be pointed out that these conditions were by no means unique to Alabama: they were prevalent in public mental health institutions all over the country, even in those states that were regarded as the most progressive and socially conscious.

which comprise a good many subheadings, and they cover such diverse matters as the fundamental rights of patients (to receive mail and visitors, to consult a lawyer, to be immune from isolation and confinement, and many more), qualifications and ratios of various categories of professional personnel, allowable medication practices, patient labor, physical facilities, treatment plans and patient records (these itemized in minute detail), nutritional requirements, and constant examination of each patient, with review of his present status and progress toward release. This done, Judge Johnson appointed the Bryce Human Rights Committee to monitor compliance with his orders and to ensure that the rights of the patients were secured. Then he left it to Bryce to take the necessary steps to meet the standards he had set and to achieve the reforms he had decreed.

Now, Judge Johnson was perfectly aware that none of this was going to be easy to accomplish. He knew that the hospital was badly run down, that mental health professionals were in short supply and not anxious to accept positions in public institutions, that conditions at Bryce had been so bad for so long that they had come to be taken for granted, so that the staff had inevitably acquired poor habits and attitudes, that patients could not be released to "less restrictive conditions" until such facilities were created, and that his reforms would require large sums of money that were not available just for the asking. And finally, as an extremely intelligent man with long judicial experience, he certainly knew that highly trained administrative and professional personnel are not noted for their servility and amenability to interference from the outside and so could not be controlled like so many automata. But to all of these potential and easily foreseeable difficulties, he adopted a singularly cavalier attitude. This is perfectly exemplified in a casual remark that he dropped in the decree that established the standards and procedures to be adhered to. He said: "From the above, it follows consistently, of course, that the unavailability of neither funds, nor staff and facilities, will justify a default by defendants in the provision of suitable treatment for the mentally ill."[7] In short, since it must be done it shall be done, and a plea of impossibility will not be accepted.

I now want to examine this procedure and expose its shortcomings by placing it in the framework of my matrix of positive law. When we do this, we see at once that Judge Johnson's attention was indeed very narrowly focused: it embraced only the dimension of the Many (indeed, only a small segment of this dimension, the patients) under the regime

[7] Wyatt v. Stickney, 344 F. Supp. 373 (1972) at 377.

of Purposiveness. That is, his efforts—the investigations he initiated, the recommendations he solicited from various professional bodies, and the standards he devised—were concerned exclusively with defining the care and treatment (the "cultivation") to which the patients were entitled and with which Bryce must provide them. As I have acknowledged, this concentration of attention in this one area is understandable, but that does not prevent it from being regrettable and trouble-producing. For, again recalling Bentham's advice, if we take my matrix seriously as the guide to reasoned and balanced decision making, then the areas that the court orders neglected are appalling in their magnitude and significance.[8]

Stating the matter broadly, it might be said that Judge Johnson simply ignored the regimes of Necessity and Possibility in their entirety: he did not allow for the limitations imposed by actual conditions or for the contingencies that might arise in the future. Furthermore, his decree ignored the dimensions of One, Process, and Pattern under the regime of Purposiveness. As we have seen, the detailed orders that he issued were framed with attention focused exclusively on the standards of care and treatment to be accorded the patients. But these standards in turn entailed a precise pattern of relationships and duties to which the hospital staff would have to adhere. So in establishing them, the court usurped much of the authority and many of the responsibilities that were the usual and proper province of Bryce administrative and professional personnel. And Judge Johnson appears simply to have assumed that these persons would acquiesce in this usurpation, abide by his orders, and work willingly to procure the results he had decreed.

In sum, the court orders (the implementation of which would obviously reverberate throughout this matrix, with its twelve elements and its intricate internal relationships) were highly provincial in character, being framed with only one element (cultivation) clearly in mind: it was supposed that the other elements would spontaneously conform to the conditions set by this one dominant element. If they had done so, all would undoubtedly have been well. But they have emphatically not done so, and this has resulted in the problems that are still unresolved after six years. To supply the specifics that this argument requires I shall cite the principal criticisms that have been urged against the Court orders and the more persistent failures in their implementation, and I shall at the same time point out the association of these criticisms and failures

[8] These general remarks and the detailed analyses and criticisms that follow will be more easily understood if reference is made to the diagram of the matrix in Chapter XVII.

with the neglected elements and areas of my matrix. In other words, I shall argue that these criticisms could have been obviated and these failures avoided—or at least minimized—if the court had framed its orders with this matrix in mind.

There is one very broad and basic criticism that is repeatedly urged against the court orders in *Wyatt* and of which all other criticisms can, in a sense, be regarded as specifications in different contexts. This charges that the orders were far too detailed, rigid, and inclusive: they covered virtually every significant phase of the operation of Bryce and the treatment of the patients, they went into great detail about all of these matters, and they did not allow for flexibility or modification in their interpretation and application. Substantively, they were extremely complete and precise in the reforms they posited. Procedurally, they were highly formal and restrictive, limiting the staff's exercise of discretion with elaborate due process requirements. Earlier I discussed the dangers and difficulties that are apt to occur if law identifies too closely the reforms that it proposes and the manner in which these are to be accomplished.[9] When this is done, the regime of Purposiveness that law seeks to institute—the state of affairs it intends to realize—constitutes in effect a second-order regime of Necessity: it dictates its conditions with a disregard of the limitations imposed by present circumstances and the novel adaptations that may be required by changed circumstances in the future. This, I believe, is precisely the fundamental mistake that has vitiated the court orders in *Wyatt*, making their implementation so difficult and eliciting the broad and persistent criticism mentioned above.

We can turn now to some of the more specific criticisms of these orders and to the problems and failures to which they point. I will consider these orders in relation to the several dimensions of my matrix (Many, One, Process, and Pattern) with which different sections of the orders are primarily concerned, and I will interpret their shortcomings as resulting, in each case, from neglect of the regimes of Necessity and Possibility in this dimension. But it must be acknowledged that this tactic is somewhat artificial: given the close and systematic structure of this matrix—and of the field of legal action—an order that is framed with a primary regard for only certain of these elements will have an impact on other elements as well. However, it is still the case that each standard (or group of standards) does have a local origin and reference that can be seen to have a determining influence on its character.

Thus, in the dimension of the Many, the two important parties to

[9] In Chapter IV, especially on pp. 44-47 and pp. 55-57.

which the court orders directly applied are the patients themselves and the members of the professional staff (the Qualified Mental Health Professionals [or "Qs"] and the aides) who are to treat them. And in both cases, critics point out that these standards have created serious problems because they did not take adequate account of either the present constitution of these groups or of changes that might occur, or might be needed, in their constitution. As regards the patients, the standards did not allow for the heterogeneity of this population and did not provide for adjustments to be made as its character changed in time: they assumed a homogeneous and stable group, with every patient requiring some specific course of treatment for a diagnosed mental illness. As was previously noted, this assumption was quite unfounded and unwarranted, but acting on it the court issued detailed standards regarding the professional and support staffs that would be needed to treat this supposititious patient population. These standards identified some twenty categories of staff personnel, they required definite ratios of staff to patients in each category, and they defined in detail the professional functions that *should* and that *could not* be performed by each category. The standards have thus been severely criticized and protested by the administration: they are inappropriate to the present patient population and make no allowance for future changes in the character of this population; the required numbers of professionals in several categories are quite simply unavailable; and, most importantly, the restriction of decisions regarding treatment methods, medication, restraint, review of records, and so forth, to only certain categories is unrealistic and has caused great inconvenience, waste of time, and duplication of effort. In sum, it is charged that the court, with its eyes fixed solely on an artificial model of care and treatment, failed to pay enough heed to the present and potential characteristics of the patients to be treated or of the personnel who would treat them: it was so absorbed in constructing a regime of Purposiveness that it largely ignored the regimes of Necessity and Possibility.[10]

The court orders in *Wyatt* applied directly to only the principal mental health institutions, Bryce, Searcey, and Partlow. But they had important implications for two larger contexts (groups, or Ones) of which these hospitals were but parts: the state of Alabama, with its limited re-

[10] These criticisms are spelled out in detail in two articles in *Hospital and Community Psychiatry* 25, no. 5 (May 1977) in an issue devoted largely to the *Wyatt* case. See Harold W. Heller, "The Wyatt Standards: An Administrative Viewpoint," p. 362 (Dr. Heller was at that time the superintendent of Bryce); and Philip Leaf, "*Wyatt* v. *Stickney*: Assessing the Impact in Alabama," p. 351 (Dr. Leaf was at that time a postdoctoral fellow doing research on the implementation and impact of *Wyatt*).

sources, the varied needs of its citizens, and its governing apparatus, which was accustomed to exercising authority in these matters; and the state mental health system as a whole, with its wide array of facilities. And again in this dimension it is charged that the court did not take sufficient account of the impact of its orders upon these two bodies or of their reactions to such orders.

As regards the former of these parties, the effect of *Wyatt* was to create an adversarial relationship between the court and the state, and so between their respective agents, the human rights committees and the mental health board and its commissioner. As a result, the attitude of the Board and Commissioner toward, and their relations with, the court and committee have from the start been marked by animosity and opposition. That this should have happened is to some extent unavoidable: it is virtually built into the adversary relationship that a lawsuit generates. But it does appear that this spirit and this stance could have been mitigated if the court had given more consideration to the reactions to be expected from these authorities to its orders. The language of the court could have been toned down, criticism muted, the deplorable conditions at Bryce blamed on circumstances and past mistakes, and the cooperation of the present state administration and commissioner at once assumed and solicited. Instead, the court excoriated the state, charged it with dereliction of its duty, made it clear that it expected more of the same behavior, and threatened various more extreme measures if the state did not mend its ways and comply with its orders. In a word, the court demanded obedience where it should have invited cooperation. There was undoubtedly much justification for the court's attitude and remarks, but while it may be that the truth will set you free, it is not always the best instrument to win friends and influence people. And this is what Judge Johnson needed.

In the case of the statewide mental health system, the difficulties have been of another kind: they have arisen from the impact of the court orders upon this system. Here, it is charged that Judge Johnson was so intent on improving conditions and providing for the patients in the major mental health hospitals that he lost sight of the system of which these are parts. The effort to comply with his standards for these hospitals required a very large expenditure, and this inevitably diverted funds from the system's other facilities—community mental health centers, transitional homes, and intermediate and remedial care programs of various kinds. These facilities were largely responsible for two very important services: early preventive treatment and rehabilitation. To the extent that these facilities functioned effectively, they were invaluable adjuncts of the hospitals: they treated the mentally ill in their home communities and before their illnesses incapacitated them, thus obviating the need for hospitalization, and they provided social and vocational rehabilitation for the patients on their release from the hospitals, thus preparing them to lead independent lives. But the loss of funds to these facilities consequent upon the court orders has prevented them from developing to the extent needed.

With regard to the above important matters, the defects in the court decree can be readily translated into the terms of my matrix and briefly summarized. In its anxiety to establish its authority and further the laudable purpose of correcting the gross deficiencies at Bryce and the other hospitals, the court put the state and its agents in a totally subordinate—even subservient—position, thus forfeiting their goodwill and cooperation. At the same time, it did not allow for the participation of the mental health board and commissioner in preparing its orders, and so it did not have a properly full and balanced view of the needs of the state mental health system as a whole.[11]

Similar criticisms have been voiced against the effect of the court orders in the dimension of Process—as regards their impact on the attitude and performance of the professional staff and aides who, in the last analysis, will determine how successfully these orders are in fact implemented. The reaction of these groups has been less inimical and their cooperation more forthcoming, but there can be no doubt that the detailed standards enunciated by the court did intrude upon the independence of these personnel, restricting their self-determination and abridging the responsibilities that they were accustomed to exercise. The fundamental mistake here was the same as occurred with the state of Alabama: it was the court's deep reservations—even suspicion—regarding both the competence and the integrity of the professional staff that created hostility between the state mental health system and the court. Interestingly enough, Judge Johnson was clearly aware that it would be indiscreet to express these doubts, and he even seems to have tried to persuade himself that he did not harbor them, for repeatedly in the series of decrees that he issued, he explicitly affirmed his faith in the ability of the staff and in their commitment to the best interests of the patients. But the very precise orders and standards that he devised conveyed exactly the opposite message: they forcefully implied a lack of

---

[11] This criticism is developed and documented in another article in *Hospital and Community Psychiatry* 25, no. 5. See Layton B. Dorman, "Community Mental Health Services in Alabama After Wyatt," p. 364. (Dr. Dorman is executive director of the Jefferson-Blount-St. Clair Mental Health Authority, located in Birmingham, Alabama.)

confidence in the staff, a fear—if not the conviction—that they would shirk their duties, would violate the rights of the patients, and would not provide the necessary care and treatment unless the court defined just what they were to do and established strict procedures to ensure that they did it.

The professional staff and aides naturally resented this intrusion upon their freedom of action and this aspersion of their integrity. In addition, they complained that the court's detailed standards had two general consequences that seriously interfered with the performance of their duties. In the first place, the standards set very narrow limits on the discretion allowed the staff in making certain decisions and taking certain actions: some were absolutely prohibited; others were hedged round with elaborate procedural requirements. This meant that the staff could not make quick decisions and act on them in emergencies; and, more importantly, it meant that they could not easily introduce new treatment methods or change their practices to adapt to changed circumstances. In the second place, these standards required an excessive amount of paper work, supervision, and duplication of effort. All of this diverted the staff's time and energies from the patients to records, reports, reviews, and recommendations concerning the patients. In short, in seeking to ensure that the professional personnel would be responsible (would "care and take care"), the court overlooked their natural reaction to its orders, and it deprived them of a large measure of the initiative and discretion that were indispensable to the proper performance of their duties. That is, it created a second-order regime of Necessity, and in so doing it transformed responsibility into liability.

The effects of this can be seen more clearly and specifically in the dimension of Pattern, for it is in this context that the court's efforts to define and secure the patients' rights and privileges, to protect them against abuse, and to assure them of humane treatment and effective therapy are spelled out with the greatest care and detail. What the court sought here was to establish a definite set of relationships between the professional staff and the patients, to ensure that the staff would adhere to certain patterns of behavior and procedures, and to guarantee that the patients would be free of interference in certain areas.

This effort found expression in very many ways, of which I will mention only a few that have posed special problems in implementation. Perhaps the most vexatious of these has had to do with patient labor. It is unquestionable that the patients were grossly abused in this respect in the years before *Wyatt*: they were virtual serfs, being used for housekeeping chores, maintainance and repair of the physical plant, farm labor, and anything else that promised to save expenses or turn a profit. To correct these abuses, Judge Johnson laid down very strict rules and standards regarding patient labor. Although these have achieved their purpose, they have also had the unfortunate effect of creating a vast amount of idleness among the patients. Because the rules are so strict and because compensation at the minimum wage rate is required in most cases, the employment of patients in tasks that have value as either therapy or vocational training has been greatly inhibited. This problem, incidentally, provides an illuminating example of the interaction between the different dimensions of my matrix. For what comes into play here are not only these rules themselves but also the attitudes and reactions that the court orders have aroused in the staff. It has been argued with much justification that if these rules are interpreted in a reasonable and intelligent manner, then there is no cause for them to create difficulties. But unfortunately this has not always been the case: some staff members are so intimidated by the rules and by the fear of punitive action by the court that they do not assign the patients any tasks or occupations at all; other staff members, wishing to avoid their own involvement in devising and supervising suitable tasks for the patients, simply use the rules as an excuse for not doing so.

Similar problems have arisen with regard to the use of restraint and isolation as a means to control or discipline the patients. There is again no doubt that these practices had formerly been abused. But they are sometimes necessary to prevent harm, and they can be useful as tools of behavior modification. And here also the strict procedures laid down by the court to prevent the abuse of these techniques have greatly restricted their employment in situations where they would serve a beneficial purpose, whether protective or educational.

Numerous other instances in which the court orders have issued in this same dilemma can be cited. Rules regarding the use of "unusual or hazardous" treatment methods, such as electro-convulsive shock or lobotomy, limiting the use of patients in research experiments, controlling medication, defining the ways in which individual treatment plans must be drawn up and patient records compiled, requiring reexamination of the patients and their release from the hospital unless a definite treatment plan is being implemented—in all of these areas, and in many others, the court-ordered standards have corrected evils only at the cost of sacrificing values.

So again in this dimension we find the same fundamental mistake that we have encountered in the others: the anxiety of the court to assure a projected regime of Purposiveness (a desired outcome) has resulted in

the creation of a second-order regime of Necessity that ignores the obstacles and limitations of the present regime of Necessity (of actual conditions) and fetters the regime of Possibility, stifling initiative and im-
provisation. Speaking more concretely, Judge Johnson overlooked two
factors that must have—and have had—an important bearing on the implementation of his orders and the realization of the quality of care and
treatment that he envisaged: first, the difficulty of overcoming by simple
fiat practices that had for long been common at Bryce and the habits that
had consequently become engrained in many of the hospital personnel;
second, the impossibility of anticipating all future contingencies, and
hence the importance of permitting the professional staff and aides to
exercise a reasonable degree of discretion in many areas of patient care
and treatment.

Two points must be stressed in closing this long analysis of the court
orders in *Wyatt*. In the first place, the tenor of this analysis has been
almost exclusively critical, but that is by no means to be interpreted as
entailing a total condemnation of Judge Johnson's actions. It is, rather, a
simple consequence of my purpose in undertaking such an analysis,
which was to illustrate in a concrete case the usefulness of my analysis of
the matrix of law as an abstract model to alert deliberation to the complexity of the problems with which it deals. My primary concern, therefore, was to indicate the difficulties that have arisen in implementing the
Wyatt decree and that could have been avoided if the court had framed
its orders with this matrix in mind. But the history of *Wyatt* has by no
means been one of unqualified failure. Very considerable benefits have
accrued as the result of the court's intervention, and intolerable conditions have been eliminated. Furthermore, it must be remembered that
Judge Johnson was breaking new ground in his decision and orders, so it
is inevitable that there should be mistakes and oversights. His standards
have since served as guidelines in several other states, and there have
already been significant modifications and improvements in them, precisely as a result of the experience gained at Bryce and the other hospitals. In a problem as complex and unexplored as this, any first attempt to
solve it must be tentative and subject to correction. I have merely sought
to indicate how reference to such a framework or paradigm as my matrix
of law could have obviated some of the deficiencies in these orders and
facilitated their implementation.

This leads directly to a second remark. I certainly do not mean to
argue that reference to this matrix could have dictated in positive terms
and in detail just how the orders should have been framed. With legal

problems, as with moral ones, no rules or models can do more than illuminate the path toward one's goal and the pitfalls that lie in wait: picking a way through the maze and reaching a decision are tasks that can only be carried out by the individual, relying on sensitivity and judgment. In even the most elaborate system of casuistry there are counterarguments to every argument, and commitment cannot wait on certainty. I claim no more for my matrix of law and legal action than did Bentham for his hedonic calculus. It is my belief that my matrix has the power to expose both the complexities of the issues at stake and the factors that bear upon their resolution: while it cannot guarantee a right decision, it can help to prevent a wrong one.

Speaking more specifically, I think that references to such a matrix can afford two great advantages. It can do much to assure that a decision will be reasoned and principled and not unduly influenced by some local and momentary emotional appeal or compelling interest. And, of equal importance, it can serve notice that no set of orders should attempt to give a final and exhaustive answer to the issue with which it deals, since these orders are going to reach into a future where they will encounter contingencies that could not possibly be anticipated. This latter point is of particular significance in the context of the case I have been discussing, because I think that Judge Johnson's crucial mistake lay in ignoring its warning. Due to the detail and stringency with which his orders were framed, the letter of the law was spelled out so fully that no room was left for the free play of the spirit of the law.

In the preceding analysis, it has not been my intention to paint too complicated or too bleak a picture of the problem that law confronts when it seeks to initiate social reform. I have merely wanted to point out that these problems are real and that such reform can succeed only if it recognizes them and takes steps to overcome them. The only rational purpose of reform is to increase the realization of value—to enhance the quality of life. This purpose can be achieved only if the final values that are sought are congenial and accessible to people and if the instrumental values that are needed are available and can be utilized effectively. The legal apparatus needs to be alert and sensitive to these conditions that impose themselves on the realization of value and hence on the success of social reform.

Of all the men who have sought to effect social reforms through law, there can be little doubt that among the most successful were Jeremy Bentham and the utilitarians who applied his principles. In the course of a few decades in the nineteenth century they transformed English society, giving it a new structure and direction. Bentham was an extraordinarily acute person with a sharp eye for the ends that were desirable, the results that were possible, and the means that were necessary and available. It was exactly this rare combination of qualities that enabled Bentham and his followers to accomplish such radical changes with so little perturbation of the social order. More specifically, I think that Bentham's success was based on his firm grasp of three cardinal points to which he constantly recurs in his writings and which govern his legislative proposals. There was, first, his recognition that law and social reform cannot provide happiness but can only promote the conditions that will enable men to procure happiness for themselves. Second, there was his perception that reforms can succeed only if they are appropriate to the circumstances of society, consonant with the feelings, habits, and desires of men, and commensurate with the material resources available. There was, finally, his insistence that no reform measures should be undertaken, or even proposed, without assurance that the legal apparatus had sufficient command of the necessary resources—physical, human, and institutional—to give a high probability that the ends in view could actually be achieved.[12]

For those of us living in the present, who seek to accomplish so very much through law, nothing could be more salutary than to keep these three principles constantly before our minds. The last of these points raises the question of authority, which must now be considered.

[12] There is an illuminating discussion of Bentham and the utilitarian reform movement in A. V. Dicey, *Law and Public Opinion in England in the Nineteenth Century* (London: Macmillan and Co., 1905), Chapters VI and IX.

[CHAPTER XI]

AUTHORITY, LEADERSHIP, AND LAW

THE ATTAINMENT of the final values sought by social reform is often difficult and delayed, and the enhancement of human enjoyment and well-being that is promised for the future is apt to entail effort and even hardship in the meantime. People are generally reluctant to make this effort and accept these sacrifices, and they will be at least suspicious and probably resentful of the changes in their habits, ideas, roles, and manner of life that the reforms are calculated to bring about. The inertia that is generated by these factors can be overcome only if there is present some locus of power and influence that can win the allegiance and secure the compliance of people. If reforms are to be accomplished, and not merely planned, they must be backed by that magic ingredient, *authority*. There must be some single source—some person or body—that can make decisions and issue directives that will be respected and acknowledged by all.

This need for an effective authority is much too obvious to be overlooked, yet many reforms fail just because this need is not met. We proclaim sweeping programs of reform, we create departments, bureaus, institutes, and commissions to oversee these programs, and we staff these with innumerable officials and functionaries. But having done all this, we then fail to endow this apparatus with the authoritative power that alone could render it effective. This is exactly as though we were to fabricate an intricate machine designed to perform many tasks and then to make no provision for any fuel to drive it. There are two contexts in which this shortcoming is most familiar. One of these is international relations: we draft fulsome charters defining the goals, functions, and structures of such bodies as the United Nations and the European Common Market, we build vast organizations to administer these charters and effect their purposes, and then we find that these bodies are incapable of making, much less enforcing, any decisions that impinge significantly on the interests of the parties concerned. A similar situation occurs when the "advanced" nations try to introduce institutions similar to their own into the social fabric of "underdeveloped" countries in order to upgrade the latter: we write constitutions, we send in experts, we recruit bureaucracies—and nothing much happens. Time after time we are forced to recognize that the changes we seek to effect in these areas are merely proposed and never accomplished. They are truly paper tigers, lacking the bite of authority.

But such failures are by no means restricted to these areas: they occur very frequently, if not so recognizably, with internal reform. It does not require a long memory or any deep involvement in politics to recall numerous such cases in the recent history of this country. Inequities and inadequacies in society make themselves felt, those who feel put upon protest, the need for reform is recognized, and a response is initiated at some point in the legal apparatus; a law is enacted or a judicial decision delivered, a commission is appointed and a bureau or department created, a program of reform is announced—and again nothing much happens, or at most only a fraction of what was intended. This has been the story with regard to school integration, equality of economic opportunity for minority groups and women, the welfare system, the postal service, the administration of justice, tax policies, and health care delivery, to name only a few.

Since the need for authority as the support for reform is so obvious and well-known, the failure to provide it cannot be laid to oversight or lack of trying. It must therefore be due to misapprehensions of the nature of authority and of the foundations on which it rests—of the factors that constitute authority. I think that two such misconceptions in particular have bedeviled our efforts: we have regarded authority as a property, and we have thought that law was the source or the creator of authority. These are the errors that must be corrected if legally instituted social reforms are to secure the authoritative backing that they require.

Our first and basic mistake is to treat authority as a *property*, whereas it is in fact a *relationship*. A person does not "have" or "possess" authority in the same way that he has black hair, or great wealth, or a fine mind. Of course, we do commonly speak in this manner, as when we say that a person "has authority" or "is an authority." But a moment's reflection reveals that these expressions are elliptical: they require a reference to other terms to fill out their meaning. The identity of these other terms—or elements—is likewise clear, and when we supply them, we find that the authority relationship is triadic. Authority is vested in some men; it is acknowledged by and exercised over other men; and it is directed to definite purposes or relevant to definite fields. Thus, men with adequate knowledge of physics accept Einstein as an authority with respect to relativity theory. And the citizens of a country (or the members of a primitive tribe) acknowledge the authority of their governors (or chiefs) to issue commands and order affairs for the common good.

It is only if all three of these elements are effectively present and properly balanced that we can establish and maintain authority: there must be officials who are fit to wield it competently and responsibly, subjects who are prepared to recognize it, and common purposes that direct and delimit its uses. Since there can be wide variations both in the character of each of these elements and in the relative influence that each exerts, the exact nature and balance of the authority relationship itself varies in subtle ways. To touch only the surface of this matter, it is apparent that any one of these elements may stand at the focus of the relationship and dominate its partners. Those who exercise authority may enjoy such respect and trust and achieve such success that they have a firm command of power and wide discretion in its use. Those who are subject to authority may be so suspicious of its motives and so doubtful of its abilities that its effectiveness is limited and tenuous. Finally, the purposes for which authority is to be used may be so widely accepted, so urgent, and so severely threatened that they virtually determine both the decisions of governors and the obedience of subjects; or, conversely, opinions about these purposes may be so divergent and so vehement that very little can be decided or accomplished.[1]

The point that must be stressed here is that these elements that ground the authority relationship are all necessary and are equally significant. Authority cannot be established merely on the base of some one, or even two, of them. All must be effectively present, and each must be both fit for its own role and appropriate to the others. Weak, incompetent, or despotic governors, rebellious or divided subjects, and purposes that are unacceptable or unattainable can alike undermine the relationship.

Given this complex situation, the natural tendency is to simplify it by treating some one of these elements as though it were the cornerstone of

---

[1] In arguing against the view of the sovereign as having absolute legislative power (which he attributes to legal positivism), F. A. Hayek suggests a relationship similar to the one here advanced. Hayek insists that sovereignty rests on allegiance, which in turn depends on the sovereign satisfying "certain expectations" held by his subjects regarding the ways in which his power is to be used. He puts the matter in these terms: "The power of the legislator thus rests on a common opinion about certain attributes which the law he produces ought to possess, and his will can obtain the support of opinion only if its expression possesses those attributes." So here too authority is conceived as consisting essentially in a relationship among those who hold it, those who accept it, and what it prescribes—"What is right," as Hayek puts it. See *Law, Legislation, and Liberty: Vol. I, Rules and Order* Chicago: University of Chicago Press, 1973), p. 92.

the relationship, able by its own strength to assure the concordance of the others. That is, men hope that if they can just secure a satisfactory embodiment of one of these elements, the others will necessarily follow from it and fall into line. Because we in this country take a secure social order and an effective legal system so much for granted, we tend to think of authority solely in terms of those who exercise it in virtue of the offices they hold. We equate "authority" with "the authorities," regarding these as the dominant element in the relationship, able to hold the other elements in thrall. History should by now have taught us better than this. A person may succeed to a position of authority ("inherit the mantle of power" is the accepted figure of speech) as a crown prince or a vice-president, but it does not at all follow that he will be able to exercise effective authority, as Mary Tudor and Andrew Johnson learned through bitter experience. Those with other political perspectives will simplify the authority relationship by assigning superiority and supremacy to some other of these constituent elements. Marxist-Leninists dream of the day when the whole society will be animated by the single purpose of making real the maxim "from each according to his abilities, to each according to his needs," so that class differences will disappear and the state will wither away, while anarchists project a time when all men will be so reasonable and so responsible that they will spontaneously integrate their separate purposes and efforts without the need for central control or direction.

These simplifications are equally delusory. The stubborn fact remains that authority can be effectively exercised only when its three elements stand in a proper relationship to one another. This relationship is extremely volatile and is always precariously balanced. The challenge it poses is that of continually readjusting the accommodation among rulers, subjects, and purposes, for if this balance is too much disturbed, and this accommodation disrupted, then authority as such vanishes, to be replaced by despotism, anarchy, or apathy.

Under normal conditions in an established society, this balance is maintained almost automatically: the various institutions that embody and administer the authority relationship and its several elements respond to changing circumstances and to one another in a perpetual process of accommodation. The legal apparatus (the instrument through which the rulers exercise authority) is sensitive to the arrangements and aspirations of the different groups (classes or factions) that are subject to its authority and at the same time maintain it by their support. Each of these groups is itself aware of its dependence upon the others, of the advantages of a stable social order, and of the fact that excessive demands on its part are apt both to arouse general opposition and to upset the balance that is vital to the authority relationship. Finally, so long as the expectations of all—or most—groups are being reasonably satisfied, there is a substratum of generally shared public values and purposes that is broad enough to accommodate the special private ends of the constellation of groups. Under these conditions, and in the language I used earlier, the mediating order that law posits is largely the reflection of a secure and accepted actual order and the anticipation of a widely acknowledged, even if differently interpreted, ideal order. As a result, the prescriptive role of law is subordinate to the expository and normative parameters within which it acts. Thus the authority relationship remains stable, though certainly not static.

However, this depiction of concord and mutuality as the "normal condition" must not be exaggerated. Even under optimum circumstances, when the masses of the people can look back on progress made in the past and are confident of further improvement in the future, tensions are present. Because each of the numerous groups that make up a society has its own special interests to promote and because the influence of each group and the intensity with which it urges its concerns fluctuate, full harmony and stability are forever luring and eluding authority. Change is constant and conflict endemic in all societies at all times. Some measure of disorder is therefore always present, threatening to get out of hand. This threat is normally contained by continual minor adjustments being made by each of the elements of the authority relationship. Groups redefine their goals, moderate or increase their demands, and form various alliances. Those who exercise authority relax or intensify their grip on the social order, listen attentively to some groups and turn a deaf ear to others, look for, or seek to create, a large and lasting consensus that can give a steady direction to the process of change, holding in check erratic or aberrant movements. And all the while, the ideal order—the vision of the future—that is commonly proclaimed even though carrying different meanings for those who proclaim it, is gradually changing itself, so that continuity culminates in transformation.

This process does not follow a steady course. Demands for radical change—for disruption and reformulation of the authority relationship—arise fairly frequently and from various quarters, occasionally resulting in sudden and drastic changes. When any such demand is voiced persistently and passionately and is backed by the threat of action, those in authority—and to a lesser extent those groups whose positions are challenged—must decide how to respond. Actually, the authorities now face a double decision. Normatively, they must analyze the demand, assess the justice (the justification) of the claim it advances, weigh it against competing demands and claims, and evaluate its impact on the social order. Pragmatically, or empirically, they must measure the power of the group making the demand, anticipate the reactions of other groups (especially those adversely affected), take stock of their position and resources, and consider alternative responses.[2]

What those who exercise authority want to do is to keep the demand within acceptable bounds, to maintain control of it, and to effect the changes that they deem desirable or necessary within the context of the present authority relationship: that is, they seek to have the change conducted under their direction, with the cooperation, or at least the acquiescence, of other groups, and in accord with the values and purposes that are supposed to animate and guide the society as a whole. Normally, but certainly not always, this is in the best interest of all parties. The tactic that the authorities thus pursue is that of making the demand their own, of adopting it and so assuming responsibility for it. They seek to absorb and accommodate the demand without disrupting the social order. That is, they transform the threat of revolt into a program of reform to be carried out under the guidance and within the framework of the established authority relationship.

Now, it is obvious that when we initiate any large-scale social reforms through law, we deliberately throw this relationship out of balance. One element, the rulers (those "in authority"), mean to use the legal apparatus to change the life styles, the statuses, and the roles of the subjects and to direct the society toward novel purposes. Law in its prescriptive role is now cast as the leading character, charged with the responsibility of positing a mediating order that will radically transform the actual and ideal orders. This is the very meaning of legally instituted and directed reform. As the earlier discussions in the previous chapters should have made clear, this effort places a severe strain on the legal apparatus and hence on those who hold authority and are the moving agents in this process. These authorities will encounter both the passive resistance of inertia and the active opposition of those who feel threatened by the proposed reforms. If they are to be able to exert the effective authority that will be required to realize these reforms, they will need to command the allegiance and confidence of their subjects, and

[2] Speaking for the moment only in general terms, I would suggest that the most effective way to make these decisions is by analyzing the demand by reference to my matrix of law and thus estimating the possibility, the benefits, and the costs of satisfying it. The model for this procedure would be that which I employed in my discussion of the *Wyatt* case in the preceding chapter.

they will need a sharp sense of what is possible as well as what is desirable.

This being the case, it is a matter of primary importance that we have a correct understanding of the way in which authority is acquired, maintained, and exercised. The question that we need answered can be posed in various ways to bring out its several aspects. What is the origin of the authority relationship as a whole? What are the sources from which he who exercises authority derives his position? How does a person establish himself and come to be accepted as holding authority? What are the essential attributes and status that a person must have if he is to exercise authority effectively, and how are they acquired?

To this cluster of questions there is a simple and commonly accepted answer: authority must be legitimate. That is, a person is endowed with authority and equipped to use it when he occupies an official position that has its functions and powers defined by law. I think there can be no doubt that we do familiarly regard authority as a legal datum and as the creature of law. If faced with the question, common sense would define authority in some such terms as "legalized power," "legitimate government," or "the right to command and be obeyed": in the language of horsemen, authority is by law out of force. And this usage is authorized in the definitions given by standard dictionaries. Thus *Webster's International* defines authority as "legal or rightful power; a right to command or to act; power exercised by a person in virtue of his office or trust; jurisdiction." And Larousse defines it as *"puissance légitime, droit de commander."*

This is our second and even more critical mistake: we have thought that authority was bestowed by law. We have therefore assumed that all that was needed to assure the effective exercise of authority was to define by law the responsibilities, powers, and limits of various offices and the procedures through which these offices were to be filled. The clothing of legality is the king's new suit that only the innocent fail to perceive and respect. This mistake is not obtuse or gratuitous. Rather, it is the very obviousness of this conclusion that makes it so prevalent and dangerous. For in an established and stable society, such as we are chiefly familiar with, legality does very largely determine authority. In such a society and under normal conditions, law is sovereign. These are governments of laws, not of men. Under these regimes, law confers authority on duly designated officials, and law defines both their powers and the purposes for which these powers are to be used.

But this view that identifies authority with legality is nonetheless mistaken and seriously misleading, for, as I hope to have shown, the primary being of authority lies in a complex relationship between rulers, subjects, and purposes. The original sources from which authority draws its strength are personal, psychological, social, and moral; and these sources still retain their vital importance after they have acquired the formal dress and sanction of legitimacy. Legal authority is a latecomer on the scene. As it first emerges and takes shape, it does little more than regularize a state of affairs—a relationship—that is already in full being. And even at the height of its dominance, legal authority is still dependent for its effectiveness upon the presence of these original constitutive sources.[3]

That authority precedes law, rather than being dependent upon it, is a well-attested fact. This evidence is so familiar that it need only be cited and not discussed. We find authority in full bloom and effective exercise in primitive societies, where there is nothing resembling a formal legal apparatus with its body of substantive and procedural law and its designated officials. That is, the authority relationship is solidly established without legal support. On the other hand, we are equally familiar with situations in which there is the richest panoply of law—solemn charters and constitutions, executive, legislative, and judicial organs, and numberless officials—and yet where there exists no semblance of effective authority. The United Nations Organization is but the latest of numerous such cases. And international law is always stigmatized as being "law" only in an extended sense—by "remote analogy"—because, though it exhibits all of the formal characteristics of a legal system, it lacks real authority. Finally, we speak familiarly of authority in contexts where positive law simply has no bearing: scientists, historians, critics, and scholars are regarded and treated as authorities in their respective fields. Reflection will show that the meaning we attach to the term "authority" and the situations in which we apply it are essentially similar in all of these attributions. Authority is manifested in relationships where there are some who accept responsibility for their opinions, decisions, and directives, others who respect and acknowledge the competence of these former, and a more or less definite field within which this mutuality runs and beyond which it does not reach. Officials can thus be charged with acting *ultra vires*, and a physicist has no authoritative standing on political issues. We therefore apply the term authority in contexts where law is unknown and irrelevant, and we withhold it in other contexts

---

[3] This truncated statement of the relation of law to authority will be elaborated in the next few pages.

where the full paraphernalia of a legal apparatus is present. In sum, authority can exist where law does not.

How then is authority acquired, if not through law? By virtue of what qualities, and by what means, is a person enabled to establish himself in a position of authority and to gain acceptance in this role? These questions require a careful answer. In the ensuing discussion, and unless the context indicates otherwise, I will be employing the term "authority" in a restricted sense, to refer not to the whole relationship but only to those who are "the authorities" and who "hold" and "exercise" authority. But even in this restricted sense, I believe that authority is a complex and variable datum, containing several facets or elements and capable of being constituted in various ways. It is also my contention that the essential attribute of authority is *leadership*, which is always present though in different guises.

To exercise authority is to direct and to lead men and to be willingly and confidently followed in the pursuit of definite goals. The leader—the authority—is the person who is accepted as having the attributes and status that equip him above all others to plan and administer the affairs of the group. This common usage is again embodied in standard English dictionaries, which give the following definition: "Power derived from opinion, respect, or esteem; influence of character, office, or station, or mental or moral superiority; acknowledged claim to be believed or obeyed." And Larousse echoes this meaning: "Ascendant, influence résultant de l'èstime." Such authority is confirmed and strengthened to the extent that the results that are jointly intended are in fact achieved. Conversely, it is questioned and challenged when those who are subject to authority and have relied on it come to feel that their expectations have been betrayed or disappointed. Authority is rooted in esteem and trust, but it is finally known by its fruits. In sum, the authority—the leader—is the One who is able and allowed to speak for the Many because of his ability to plan and administer the Processes and Patterns—the activities and the organization—on which the well-being of the social order depend.

This idea that leadership is the seed from which authority grows—the root from which it springs and on which it always rests—is a familiar one, especially in the literature of anthropology and sociology. Many anthropologists regard the holding of authority as synonymous with the exercise of leadership, and they define the leader as the person who can influence group decisions and direct group activities. The legal antropologist Leopold Pospisil, for instance, considers authority and leadership as "functional concepts" defined as adhering in "an individual or a group of individuals who initiate actions in a social group or whose decisions are followed by a majority of the group's members."[4] A very similar idea is expressed by Max Weber, who summarizes the matter in these terms: "The manifested will (*command*) of the *ruler* or rulers is meant to influence the conduct of one or more others (*the ruled*) and actually does influence it in such a way that their conduct to a socially relevant degree occurs as if the ruled had made the content of the command the maxim of their conduct for its very own sake."[5]

And now, what makes a leader? As I indicated above, I think that leadership is variously constituted and acquired, and thus it occurs in different types, or guises. The leader is always he who inspires respect and confidence and commands obedience. But in different situations and contexts, it will be now one and now another set of qualities through which a leader achieves and maintains his position, and he must adopt different procedures and methods in different circumstances. There are various grounds on which leadership is claimed and acknowledged, and the exact status of the leader varies with these grounds. We therefore need to explore these different kinds of leadership-authority and the relations among them.

It is best to approach these matters in an empirical manner, by examining the evidence afforded us by animal ethology and human history. A reading of this record will illustrate that leadership occurs in at least four principal types. They are: 1) the dominant male—the alpha—in an animal group,[6] 2) the paramount chief of a tribal society, 3) the anointed king of a medieval nation, 4) the elected president or premier of a modern constitutional state.

---

[4] Leopold Pospisil, *Anthropology of Law* (New Haven: Yale University Press, 1971), p. 57. Pospisil cites numerous authorities to this same effect: see also ibid., pp. 52-58. With numerous references to the anthropological evidence, the same view is advanced by E. Adamson Hoebel in his work, *The Law of Primitive Man* (Cambridge, Mass.: Harvard University Press, 1954); references can be found in the index under the terms authority, chief, kingship, law, and government.

[5] Max Weber, *On Law in Economy and Society*, trans. Max Rheinstein (Cambridge, Mass.: Harvard University Press, 1954), p. 328.

[6] Throughout the following discussion of leadership, I employ the term "dominant male" and the masculine pronoun. This is purely a linguistic convenience, and is in no way to be interpreted as the assertion of male supremacy or the contention that only males can be leaders. "Dominant male" is now virtually a term of art, taken to include females as well as males, and it is well established that there are numerous animal groups in which it is the females who are dominant and exercise leadership. The same phenomenon occurs in primitive human societies, and it is by no means unknown in modern states. Even a casual

Before examining the characteristics and status of these different types of leadership and the process that leads from one to another, several preliminary remarks are in order. In the first place, I would not insist that this list is exhaustive: it may well be that other distinct types can be identified. Second, these types, like any others, are abstractions. No actual leader conforms perfectly to any of these types—except perhaps the dominant male—but combines the traits of several of them. I have chosen familiar examples to represent each of these types, but other examples could have served, as every type occurs in various specific forms. Third, it is obvious that the leadership—the authority—that each type of leader exercises derives from different personal qualities and stands on a different footing of public acceptance. Fourth, these types mark stages or moments in a cohesive process of development. If we look only at the extreme terms of this series, we might well conclude that there is no resemblance or connection between them. But I would argue that in truth this series represents a continuous progression in time, with no sharp breaks in it. (Interesting confirmation of this claim is found in the fact that we use synonymous words, "alpha" and "premier," to indicate the two extreme types of leader.) Finally, and most importantly, these different modes of leadership *supplement but do not supplant* one another. Thus, if one is to succeed as a leader and to exercise authority effectively, each of the later and more advanced types of leader must embody in himself the specific characteristics of all of his predecessor types. That is (to anticipate and summarize a point that I will immediately argue in detail), the procedures and formalities that we associate with legitimation cannot of themselves create an authority that is capable of leading; all they can do is confirm, support, and define more precisely a leadership that must still rely on the more basic attitudes of dominance, hegemony, and majesty.

Max Weber's well-known classification of the types of domination—the equivalent of leadership—is somewhat similar to that which I have suggested, as is his analysis of the bases on which each type grounds its claim to "legitimation" or "validity." Weber first defines domination in general as "the possibility of imposing one's will upon the behavior of other persons." He then proceeds to distinguish three "pure" types of domination. The "validity" of the first type is expressed "in a system of

---

acquaintance with Elizabeth I of England, Isabella of Spain, or Catherine de Medici in France (not to mention Indira Ghandi of India) will quickly dispel any notions of masculine supremacy. Thus, "dominant male," "alpha," "leader," and the masculine pronoun are to be taken as sexually inclusive.

consciously made *rational* rules (which may be either agreed upon or imposed from above), which meet with obedience as generally binding norms whenever such obedience is claimed by him whom the rule designates. . . . Obedience is thus given to the norms rather than to the person."

But this claim to validity, or a power of command, can also rest upon "personal authority"; of this type there are two subtypes. One of these is "founded upon the sacredness of *tradition*, i.e., of that which is customary and has always been so and prescribes obedience to some particular person." The other subtype has "its source in the very opposite, viz., the surrender to the extraordinary, the belief in *charisma*, i.e., actual revelation or grace resting in such a person as a savior, a prophet, or a hero."

At an earlier stage of this same discussion, Weber had also identified a second general form of domination (distinguished from the previous forms, which rest on "validity" or "authority") that he describes as based on the control of "a constellation of interests": that is, on the influence that can be exerted by the holder of economic, financial, or industrial power, quite apart from any official position or acknowledged preeminence. Finally, he concludes his analysis with a qualification that is similar to one of those that I made above. He says: "The 'pure' types of domination correspond to these three possible types of legitimation. The forms of domination occurring in historical reality constitute combinations, mixtures, adaptations, or modifications of these 'pure' types."[7]

Allowing for differences in terminology, these four types correspond respectively, and rather closely, with my elected official, anointed king, dominant male, and paramount chief. However, this remark requires two qualifications. In the first place, Weber's attention is centered entirely on domination as it occurs in advanced societies. Consequently, his account of the modes of domination is cast in more exclusively formal and sophisticated terms than is mine: for instance, I would suggest that such concepts as "validity" and "legitimation" are effectively present only when the stage of the anointed king has been reached, although they may be incipient before that. This leads to a second remark. Weber is apparently not thinking in terms of a process of refinement and development leading on from one type of domination-leadership to another, with each type exhibiting deficiencies and so becoming in-

---

[7] See Weber, *On Law in Economy and Society*, pp. 323, 336, 324, 336-337, respectively.

adequate as human and social conditions change. Nor does he seem to regard the more formal and official type of domination—that based on "a system of consciously made rational rules"—as necessarily combining within itself the other and earlier modes if it is to be effective. I strongly emphasize both of these points.

This suggested analysis of leadership obviously cries out to be completed by a careful examination of each of these modes of leadership and of the process through which these stages advance, always retaining and synthesizing what has previously been achieved. To do this in detail, taking full account of the empirical and historical evidence, would carry my account too far afield. But it is relevant to my argument to trace the general course of this development and to mark its principal stages.

The earliest and simplest form of leadership is clearly based on personal dominance. The leader is he who is able to impose himself on his fellows and to win their acceptance of the position he has assumed. We associate this kind of leadership primarily with animal groups and with very small and primitive human groups. But it is by no means confined to these contexts. To the contrary, we find such leaders in virtually every human group, persisting even at the most sophisticated levels and in connection with the most recondite activities: in university faculties, scientific societies, political parties, athletic teams, social clubs, charitable and humanitarian organizations, cultural and artistic circles—in all of these and many other cases we find the personal leader playing a dominant role and exerting a preponderant influence, even when he occupies no official position and there is no formal organization to define his status.

The personal qualities on which such dominance is based vary across a wide spectrum, as does the relationship between leaders and followers. In its crudest form, as among animal groups and youthful gangs, we think of it as established by sheer physical force and the fear that this calls forth, though even here there are probably subtle psychological factors that escape our notice or understanding. The next development is probably the ritualized combat, which is common with many animals, reaches its apogee in the jousts of the knights of chivalry, and survives in the bloodless encounters of small boys and the rivalries of adults. Beyond this, it is easier to detect variation than to trace development. Dominance may be based on assertiveness and aggressiveness, force of personality, self-confidence and the confidence that this inspires in others, cunning, the power of persuasion, intelligence and character, age and the wisdom of experience it supposedly confers, wealth, or the indefinable quality that we call charisma. This list is representative rather than complete, but with three additional comments it will suffice. The dominant male—the alpha—will probably combine several of these characteristics. His dominance is exerted in many variants between two extremes: it may be imposed on reluctant and potentially rebellious inferiors, or it may be spontaneously bestowed by enthusiastic followers on a leader who makes no conscious effort to exercise it. Finally, this merely personal dominance anticipates and even contains implicitly the more advanced types of leadership and authority. This will become more clear in the immediate sequel.

Leadership begins with dominance. Such an intimate and direct authority relationship has certain real advantages. Since the leader owes his position almost entirely to his personal qualities—his ability to influence and hold followers, to lead them effectively, and to withstand the challenge of rivals—he will maintain his position only so long as his leadership is sound and successful. Furthermore, leadership based on dominance is apt to be responsive to the needs of the group and quickly adaptable to the circumstances it confronts. Where failure or abuse of leadership is so immediately obvious and responsibility falls so directly on the leader, he can be quickly corrected or removed. However, this type of leadership has serious corresponding disadvantages. Since it is exclusively personal, it is to a high degree volatile and arbitrary; both its manner of acquisition and its uses are ill-defined, so it is apt to exhibit sudden and radical changes. Such an informal and spontaneous—one might almost say, amorphous—relationship of leader, followers, and common purposes is bound to be unstable and discontinuous. It is well adapted to small coherent groups with strong and specific purposes, but it is ill equipped to conciliate diversity or to organize large affairs. Dominance never ceases to be an essential aspect of effective leadership, but it must acquire new dimensions as time brings new demands. It is the necessary but not sufficient condition of authority.

The further history of such leadership—its development into what we more readily recognize as authority—is a continuing attempt to impose form upon the material element of dominance. This attempt faces two basic problems between which there is extreme tension, so it is torn between two poles: it seeks both to institute and assure effective leadership and to define and control the uses of this leadership. Consequently, this passage from spontaneous personal dominance toward formalized public authority exhibits a marked cyclical pattern. Every step taken toward one of these goals threatens the other: as we limit the resources and the reach of leadership, we undermine its effectiveness; and as we enhance its hold on power, it escapes our control. We are still searching for a formula that can reconcile these contradictory demands and resolve these tensions.

I have taken the paramount chief of a tribal society merely as the type of the first step in this passage. He has many counterparts: an early medieval king circumscribed by his tenants-in-chief and other magnates, the Holy Roman Emperor, the dean of a faculty, the leader of a political party, the commissioner of professional baseball or football. The essential thrust of this step is to reduce and regularize the role of the leader. This is a movement toward what might be called corporate or collegiate leadership, with decisions to be made and action taken only after consultation of the leader with his principal followers, who are deemed to share authority with him. The leader is now shorn of his unique position and is regarded as simply "the first among equals": instead of exercising absolute dominance, he exerts no more than a paramount influence. The status and functions of the leader are more or less formalized, with his duties and powers spelled out in some detail and acknowledged in a public and at least semiofficial form, as when they are embodied in custom and the ceremonies of installation. At this stage it is also usual either to make definite provisions for succession to leadership or to define a procedure by which the leader will be designated. Finally, steps are now taken to keep the leader responsible to his followers and accountable for the uses to which he puts his position. What underlies this whole movement and makes it possible is the fact that, as human groupings become larger in size and more complex in structure, the sources of power diversify and power itself becomes more widely distributed. So even an established and acknowledged leader has to deal with colleagues who themselves enjoy both a solid basis and a large measure of independent strength.

Under these changed conditions, the successful leader must moderate his ways and acquire new qualities. Effective leadership is now a matter of compromise and persuasion rather than dogmatic and arbitrary assertion. Since there are divergent interests, each possessing some kind and degree of power, these must be reconciled to one another and their separate efforts must be coordinated. What is required of the leader is the willingness to consult and accept advice and the ability to secure the cooperation of the various parties and to organize them into a coherent whole. Leadership now depends to a great extent on the consent and loyalty of those who are being led. Correspondingly, the leader becomes the coordinator and organizer of forces that are not his own.

This movement toward shared power inevitably dilutes and weakens leadership. It has the merit of making the leader more responsive, but as the voices to which he must respond become stronger and more divergent, his ability to lead is eroded. Factions, so much feared by the Founding Fathers, arise, each seeking only its own interest; alliances are made and unmade, with friend becoming foe overnight; leadership disappears in a welter of conspiracy; and the mob waits in the wings. In short, disorder threatens.

In answer to this threat, the role and attributes of the leader undergo a further transformation. What must now be found is some way to endow the leader with a character that will place him altogether above these conflicting parties, so that he can settle disputes among them before they bring violence and disruption. It is too late to repair the fragmentation of society into contending classes and ranks; and even if it were possible to do this it would be undesirable, since these factions represent legitimate interests and it is precisely the distribution of power among them that serves to assure freedom and mobility. But there still must be a leader whose unique status and absolute authority are acknowledged by all parties, so that he can always count on the allegiance of the greatest number of them and can command the preponderance of power if some subject becomes too arrogant and threatens to seize control and upset the balance.

I have chosen the anointed king as the model of this kind of leadership. He has numerous counterparts, his closest kin being the spiritual leader who has been consecrated by the laying-on of hands. Others who are related to him by more or less "remote analogy," as John Austin would put it, are the prophet who communes with God, the witch doctor who has magic powers, the revolutionary hero, such as Lenin or Tito, who succeeds against seemingly hopeless odds, the founder of a union who first organizes workers and wins for them an independent status and substantial benefits, and indeed any leader who by his personality, his achievements, or a ceremonial rite is viewed with awe by his followers and is seen by them as being absolutely different in kind from themselves.

The king—or his counterpart—knows that in a loose sense he rules only with the tacit approval of his subjects. He must assure the people he leads what they most want: peace, security, justice, and reasonable prosperity. And he must placate his more powerful followers with lands, honors, and offices. If he fails too conspicuously in these respects, he will be deposed. Conversely, every subject of the king, even the most powerful lord, knows equally well that if he challenges the rule of the king, all the rest will unite to crush him.

What we have here is the beginning of legal authority as we understand it. The power of the king—if he is a William the Conqueror, an Edward I, or a Henry VIII—is in a sense absolute and unlimited. At his coronation he is anointed, consecrated, and all but sanctified. He rules by divine right, and he is quite literally transformed into a being of a distinct kind, above and remote from his subjects, having a status and an understanding, powers and gifts, privileges and responsibilities that others cannot even comprehend, much less challenge. But this same king is a man among other men, and he must rule as well as reign. He may reign by divine right, but he must rule by his own sense and strength, his ability to impose his will and command fealty, and his skill in governing his kingdom. The position of the anointed king can be put most graphically by saying that he represents a reincarnation of the dominant male. His ability to rule thus depends upon his possessing analogous traits. Since his subjects regard him as the source of order and justice and look to him in all things, he must be able to inspire in them an attitude that is a compound of fear, awe, and reliance. He needs to be visible and approachable, but only on terms that emphasize the sanctity of his person and the splendor of his position.

Physical presence and bearing are important assets, and they are enhanced by the magnificence with which he surrounds himself. To support his role, the king must have a self-confidence and a sense of his position that border on arrogance and a determination on having his own way that approaches fanaticism. With this, he requires a resiliency that enables him to change his policies radically without admitting past mistakes or arousing doubts of his mastery. In sum, he must be able to create a personal aura such that his decisions, however much they may puzzle or displease, will never be questioned. For although the power of the king is absolute and unlimited in principle, it is in fact hedged in by many conditions: the oath that he takes at his coronation, the power that lies in other hands, and the real if implicit understanding of the limits he must observe. Indeed, it is just because the myth of his supremacy is so seriously challenged by the facts of his situation that such pains are taken to preserve the myth, which is so necessary to social peace and security. This explains the enormous emphasis placed on legitimacy, on the blood royal, and on the lines of succession, for it is only if the king is legitimate that he reigns by divine right, and it is largely this right that enables him to rule in fact. The trappings of regality with which the Tudors, the Valois, and the Hapsburgs surrounded themselves may seem childish, but they served an indispensable purpose: the artificial distance that they put between king and subjects, the ceremony and obeisance that they demanded, and the sense of majesty they created all helped to preserve the fiction that royalty is more than human.

The king—and each of his counterparts—has very little real power at his disposal to enforce his commands. Therefore everything possible is done to endow these commands with the odor of sanctity, to put them beyond the reach of challenge, and to assure automatic compliance. Since it is recognized that in reality the position of the king is so fragile, the dice are loaded in his favor. We are well aware that the preservation of order in a contemporary society depends to a great extent on the habit of legal obedience; the people of late medieval and early modern times were equally aware that it depended almost entirely on the attitude of reverence for the king. In short, legitimacy meant to an earlier time what constitutionality means to us: it certified that the leader (the sovereign) held his position of right, it guaranteed that his commands (laws) were valid, and it placed men under an obligation to obey. For the men of that time, the royal prerogative did what due process does for us.

With this recognition we can see how natural—if not always easy—is the transition from the anointed king to the elected president. For what is happening throughout this process is the slow but steady formalization of power. As societies grow more stable; as more men, and more classes of men, have a personal stake in the preservation of order; as governments become at once more centralized and more representative and hence both better able and more willing to dispense justice; as power and wealth are diluted through wider distribution; as the habit of legal obedience inhibits the impulse to violence; and, perhaps most important if least obvious, as people become more accustomed to abstract ideas and so less dependent on concrete symbols—as these changes proceed, the nature, the conditions, and the exercise of leadership are progressively formalized. As this passage is effected, we reach familiar ground that need not be surveyed in detail.

What essentially occurs here is that the elements of the authority relationship and the terms on which they are related are closely and explicitly defined. The leader, at least in principle, neither reigns nor rules: instead, he governs. He does not hold his position by private and inalienable right, conferred by a higher power, and he is not the source of law, declaring this largely at his discretion. Instead, he acquires his position through a definite procedure, he occupies it for a limited time, and the uses he makes of it are strictly circumscribed. The leader now holds an office, not a crown. His power is formal rather than material. He is an elected official, not an hereditary monarch. It is as an official, not as a person, that he exercises authority and wields power. The conditions under which he holds this authoritative power, the manner in which he exercises it, the purposes to which he is to put it, and the limits of its use are all spelled out in detail. In short, the public power that goes with leadership is limited by the private rights of the people and by the legal definition of the office of leader. The dominant male has been transformed into the chief executive.

With this transformation of his role, the leader must again acquire new qualities and skills. As the anointed king represents a reincarnation of the dominant male, so does the elected president reincarnate the paramount chief. The constitutional leader enjoys certain very great advantages over his predecessor type. In being defined and limited, his authority is at the same time protected by law. As long as he does not act outrageously *ultra vires*, overstep very broad bounds, or fail to meet extremely lenient standards, he is secure in his office. He is not at the constant mercy of the whim of his colleagues or a coalition of his enemies. Furthermore, such a leader has access to enormous resources of military, political, and economic power, so that he is in a strong position to protect himself if he is attacked.

But the elected leader of a modern constitutional state suffers under new disadvantages that are just as real and serious. For one thing, the central authority that he theoretically holds in his hands is in fact fractured into several functions and shared among numerous officials and official bodies. If the leader is really to lead and to accomplish what he proposes, he must be able to control this cumbersome administrative machine and the entrenched bureaucracy that feeds on it while caring for it. Furthermore, the elected leader must answer to a constituency that is extremely heterogeneous and notoriously fickle. Where the paramount chief need placate only a few tribal headmen whose views and purposes run largely with his own, the elected president must win the cooperation, or at least the acquiescence, of powerful groups whose interests always diverge and often clash head-on. Labor and management, agriculture and industry, supplier and distributor, wholesaler and retailer, producer and consumer, urban and rural dwellers, conservationists and manufacturers, exponents of public and private transit—these are but a sample of the pressure groups that tug and haul at the legal system, atop which sits the elected leader, trying to keep his balance as the structure he purports to administer sways to and fro. And to compound his difficulties, there is the opposition party, always snapping at his heels, frequently going for his jugular, and waiting to destroy him if he loses his grip and topples off.

We proclaim that we are a government of laws, not of men. In the terms in which I have been speaking, this is tantamount to saying that personal dominance, the most primitive form of leadership, has been altogether transmuted into the pure gold of legal authority. But this is an illusion. And I shall here take up a theme that I only mentioned earlier: namely, that these several modes of leadership that I have been analyzing are abstract types, with every mode in fact exhibiting characteristics of each type, though certainly in very different proportions; that as this progression unfolds with changing circumstances, these modes of leadership supplement but do not supplant one another; and that even the most "advanced" type of leader must, if he is to be successful, embody the specific attributes of all of his predecessor types.

The fundamental challenge that confronts every leader, whatever his situation, is that of maintaining the authority relationship. The leader must have a sound and sensitive rapport with his followers—the ruler with his subjects, the government with its citizens—and he must move the group or society that he leads toward the satisfaction of its expectations and the achievement of its goals. It is self-evident that mere legal authorization—the simple fact of election to office—is not by itself sufficient to assure success in meeting this challenge. The leader is a person as well as, indeed before, being an official. And it is his personal traits and his ability to fill the several roles of his predecessor types as well as his actual role that will largely determine his capacity to lead.

The leader of a modern constitutional state must combine in himself the essential qualities and have the status of dominant male, paramount chief, and anointed king, as well as legal official. Like the dominant male, he must be capable of commanding respect, imposing his will, and taking decisive action: he must assert and establish his personal supremacy. Like the paramount chief, he needs the subtlety of the serpent if he is to persuade and reconcile followers who hold divergent views. Like the anointed king, he must have the arcane ability to wrap himself in the mantle of near divinity and so to receive allegiance and subservience even when everyone knows that he has neither the capacity for leadership nor the power to enforce his will. As legal official, he needs the political skill to get elected and the administrative ability to manage the cumbersome apparatus of government. What this means, in effect, is that he who hopes to exercise effective legal authority must combine two essentially contradictory sets of characteristics and play two mutually antagonistic roles. As dominant male and anointed king, he seeks to establish an absolute ascendancy and to receive unquestioning obedience. As paramount chief and elected official, he seeks to portray himself as merely a man among men, fallible like all others, anxious only to carry out the wishes of his people and waiting eagerly for the time when he can return to private life. In sum, he who holds legal authority must appear to follow while he is actually leading and must seem to lead when he is really following. His difficult role requires him to be accepted as both sovereign and servant.

It is time to draw together the threads of this discussion and weave them toward their conclusion. Contrary to much current opinion, I have argued that authority is not a simple property that inheres in a person, and that it cannot be conferred by law. Rather, the true being of authority consists in a relationship between those who exercise it, those who acknowledge it, and the purposes that both parties share. It is this authority relationship that is the primary datum. Law does not—indeed it cannot—create this relationship: to the contrary, the relationship is the root from which law grows and which alone can sustain law in effective existence.

We speak of the United States as having been founded either in 1776 with the Declaration of Independence or, more usually, in 1789 when the Constitution was formally declared in effect. But these dates are merely milestones, however important, in a gradual progress from one state of affairs to another. The adoption of a constitution does not create a society: it only "constitutes" a legal order through which a preexistent social order based on an authority relationship is to be organized and administered. It took from 1777 to 1781 for the Articles of Confederation and Perpetual Union to be ratified by the thirteen original states. And the Constitution of the United States, which was signed by the delegates on 17 September 1787, was not officially proclaimed by the Congress until 4 March 1789. Throughout this period, and indeed commencing well before 1776, a new authority relationship was slowly taking shape: new leaders were arising to replace George III and the British Parliament; large numbers of subjects were shifting their faith and allegiance to these new leaders; and the populace of leaders and subjects, in a continuing dialogue, was giving clearer voice both to its grievances and expectations and to defining the values and purposes to which it meant to dedicate itself. Through a gradual coalescence of these three elements, the new authority relationship was cemented. When it had become sufficiently firm and definite, then—and only then—was it ready and able to "constitute" itself in legal form.[8]

Interestingly enough, ideas very similar to those argued in this chapter are advanced by John Austin. It is the imperative element in Austin's

[8] Contrast this natural process with the artificial proceedings that drafted the Charter of the United Nations. The near futility of this body illustrates the vanity of trying to establish a legal order without the support of a vital authority relationship.

theory that is always emphasized, to the almost total exclusion of its other elements. The textbook accounts of Austin tell us that he regarded positive law as the command of the sovereign, backed by force and threatening sanctions if not obeyed; and they tell us little more. But Austin himself was perfectly well aware that much more than this was required if the commands of the sovereign—of the government or the legal system—were to be respected and made effective. In particular, he explicitly recognized three significant facts that are also essential parts of the theory I have been advancing: the sovereign's commands must be willingly accepted and obeyed by the populace; this acceptance depends on the sovereign adhering to certain principles and purposes that might be said to compose the constitution of the state or independent political society; and this constitution is a gradual growth, the formulation of beliefs, practices, and relationships that have developed spontaneously in the society over generations. These aspects of Austin's doctrine are so important and so widely neglected, and they bear so directly on my present argument and its further course, that it is worthwhile to elaborate them at some length.

Austin makes the first point in these terms.

> Now the permanence of every government depends on the habitual obedience which it receives from the bulk of the community. For if the bulk of the community were fully determined to destroy it, and to brave and endure the evils through which they must pass to their object, the might of the government itself, with the might of the minority attached to it, would scarcely suffice to preserve it, or even to retard its subversion. . . . Since, then, a government continues through the obedience of the people, and since the obedience of the people is voluntary or free, every government continues through the *consent* of the people, or the bulk of the political society. . . . As correctly or truly apprehended, the position that 'every government continues through the people's *consent*' merely amounts to this: That, in every society political and independent, the people are determined by motives of some description or another, to obey the government habitually; and that if the bulk of the community ceased to obey it habitually, the government would cease to exist.[9]

And now what are these "motives of some description or another" that induce the people to obey? Austin recognizes that, generally speak-

[9] John Austin, *The Province of Jurisprudence Determined*, ed. H.L.A. Hart (London: Weidenfeld and Nicholson, 1954), pp. 302-303.

ing, these are of two kinds: people may obey positively, "by their special inclination or attachment," or negatively, "by their dread of a violent revolution."[10] The first motive is obviously the more desirable, and Austin speaks directly to the conditions that elicit it. This raises the second significant point in Austin's doctrine—that of the conditions on which allegiance and obedience depend. Austin states:

> In every, or almost every, independent political society, there are principles or maxims which the sovereign habitually observes, and which the bulk of the society, or the bulk of its influential members, regard with feelings of approbation. Not infrequently, such maxims are expressly adopted, as well as habitually observed, by the sovereign or state. More commonly, they are not expressly adopted by the sovereign or state, but are simply imposed upon it by opinions prevalent in the community. . . . In case it ventured to deviate from a maxim of the kind in question, it would not and could not incur a legal pain or penalty, but it probably would incur censure, and might chance to meet with resistance, from the generality or bulk of the governed.[11]

And now to the third point, which is especially relevant to my present discussion. Austin's statement of his position on this issue follows upon a long argument (of some thirty pages) against the hypothesis of a social contract, or "original convenant" as he usually refers to it. He stigmatizes this hypothesis as both logically absurd and empirically, or historically, without foundation. He then continues:

> In a few societies political and independent (as, for example, in the Anglo-American States), the sovereign political government has been determined at once, and agreeably to a scheme or plan. But even in these societies, the parties who determine the constitution (either as scheming or planning, or as simply voting and adopting it) were merely a slender portion of the whole of the independent community, and were virtually sovereign therein before the constitution was determined: insomuch that the constitution was not constructed by the whole of an inchoate community, but rather was constructed by a fraction of a community, already consummate or complete. . . . In most societies political and independent, the constitution of the supreme government has *grown*. By which fustian but current phrase, I intend not to intimate that it hath come of itself, or is a marvelous something fashioned without hands. . . . I

[10] Ibid., p. 303.   [11] Ibid., pp. 257-258.

intend to intimate, by the phrase in question, that the constitution of supreme government has not been determined at once, or agreeably to a scheme or plan: that positive moral rules of successive generations of the community (and, perhaps, positive laws made by its successive sovereigns) have determined the constitution, with more or less of exactness, slowly and unsystematically. Consequently, the supreme government was not constituted by the original members of the society: Its constitution has been the work of a long series of authors, comprising the original members and many generations of their followers.[12]

These three Austinian doctrines constitute a condensed account of the character, mode of being, and manner of development of the authority relationship as I have analyzed it in more detail. Austin is saying that the continuance of a government—of those who exercise authority—is dependent on the habitual obedience, or acceptance, of the people who are subject to this authority; that this acceptance and obedience will be given only so long as the sovereign (the authority) adheres to certain principles and maxims, or what I have called common values and purposes; and that these principles and maxims, which compose the constitution, are the outcome of a gradual growth. Admittedly, Austin himself did not give these ideas any central or prominent place in his theory. He is quite explicit in holding that a sovereign government and the system of law through which its authority is administered cannot come into being or continue in effective control of its society unless these conditions are satisfied. But he does not elaborate on these matters because his interest lies elsewhere. He is concerned to "determine the province" of positive law, to mark it off from other institutions and undertakings, to identify its proper tasks, and to clarify its systematic structure. He therefore carefully notes, and even emphasizes, the fact that these are necessary conditions for the creation and continuance of a legal system. But having done this, he then ignores them in order to set about his chosen tasks.

The legal positivists, the heirs of Austin, have followed his example. They recognize that any legal system emerges from prior and prelegal conditions and that its continued existence depends on other factors than only the norms that it defines. But they give even less attention to these facts and the questions they raise than did Austin. Their interest is focused exclusively on that element that was central for Austin himself: the sovereign, conceived generally as the hinge on whom—or which—the legal system hangs. They agree that there must be some source, or

[12] Ibid., pp. 336-337.

factor, that grounds the whole body of law and by reference to which the status of any particular legal norm or enactment can be established. But, while they acknowledge with Austin the significance of the coercive element in law, they reject the appeal to might, or force, as the distinguishing feature of law: force can only compel people by the harm it threatens, with no pretense of justification; law asserts its legitimacy and imposes duties that are acknowledged as binding. Therefore the positivists emphasize the notions of "validity," "obligation," and "authority" as central to the concept of a legal order. It is these latter concepts that they wish to analyze and clarify, without reference to any extralegal social, political, or moral considerations. This is certainly a legitimate and important undertaking, and the motives of the positivists are understandable: it is their desire to mark off law as a distinctive field, having a structure and operating on principles of its own. In this way they hope to avoid certain confusions and irrelevancies which, in their view, have plagued much legal theorizing. This procedure of narrowing the focus of inquiry has obvious advantages, and it has been skillfully exploited by the positivists to clarify many aspects of the nature of law. But it also has disadvantages and dangers, and it is these that concern me here, as they bear directly on the issues with which I am dealing. That is, I want to expose both the outcome to which a rigorous employment of positivist doctrine leads and the problems that this outcome poses.

This concern of the positivists has led them to seek for an ultimate source of law that could itself be defined by strictly internal criteria. This source has been variously identified. Austin himself found it in the sovereign: as we have seen, he emphasized the features of might and habitual obedience, and his refinements and qualifications of this thesis were not further developed by him, nor have they been followed up by his successors. Seeking to bring analysis closer to intuition and to put the notion of legal obligation on a sounder basis, H.L.A. Hart finds the origin of law in his influential theory of "secondary rules" and especially the "rule of recognition." Hans Kelsen postulates his "basic norm," which generates and justifies all of the other legal norms. Alf Ross identifies this foundation stone with the "inner coherence of meaning" of a legal system. Given this source, whatever it may be, one could then—at least in principle—construct a system of norms or laws by reference to which the validity of any specific act in law, whether legislative, judicial, or executive, could be determined.

But what is the standing of this source itself, and hence of the system as a whole that hangs on it? Since it is the creator and criterion of validity, it cannot itself be either valid or invalid. To ask whether a legal *system* is valid is to ask a meaningless question; or, more exactly, it is to commit what the linguistic analysts would call a "category mistake." To deal with this problem, the positivists introduce a quite different criterion, embodied in the concept of *efficacy*. The ultimate source of law—the sovereign, the rule of recognition, the basic norm—and the system of norms derived from it are established if they are efficacious—if they are generally acknowledged to be binding and are on the whole obeyed. Both Kelsen and Hart are explicit on this point. The former puts the matter in these terms: "The efficacy of the entire legal order is a necessary condition for the validity of every single norm of the order. . . . The principle of validity is restricted by the principle of effectiveness."[13] Hart is equally clear and forthright:

> There are therefore two minimum conditions necessary and sufficient for the existence of a legal system. On the one hand those rules of behavior which are valid according to the system's ultimate criterion of validity must be generally obeyed, and, on the other hand, its rule of recognition specifying the criteria of legal validity and its rules of change and adjudication must be effectively accepted as common public standards of official behavior by its officials.[14]

So validity is a function of efficacy.

And now what of efficacy? Of what is it a function? This question is obviously of critical significance. And the positivists' answer to it needs to be carefully examined, as it invites misinterpretation. At first glance, one gets the impression that they regard it as having neither interest nor importance. They seem figuratively to shrug their shoulders at it, dismissing it as irrelevant to their concerns; and in a qualified sense, which I shall soon discuss, I think that this is indeed the case. Some of the positivists deal with this problem by positing or presupposing the existence of an ultimate source and criterion of law and so of the efficacy of the system as a whole. Kelsen perfectly exemplifies this position, saying:

> The basic norm is not created in a legal procedure by a law-creating organ. It is not—as a positive legal norm is—valid because it is created in a certain way by a legal act, but it is valid because it is presupposed to be valid; and it is presupposed to be valid because without this presupposition no human act could be interpreted as a legal, especially as a norm-creating, act.[15]

---

[13] Hans Kelsen, *General Theory of Law and State*, trans. Anders Wedberg (Cambridge, Mass.: Harvard University Press, 1945), p. 119.

[14] H.L.A. Hart, *The Concept of Law* (Oxford: The Clarendon Press, 1961), p. 113.

[15] Kelsen, *General Theory of Law and State*, p. 116.

Others of the positivists treat the problem in a more realistic manner. Hart, for instance, criticizes these solutions by "postulation" or "hypothesis" on the ground that they are unnecessary, obfuscating, and misleading. He insists that the existence of the rule of recognition is of an "essentially factual character" and can "neither be valid nor invalid but is simply accepted as appropriate for use in this way (i.e., to determine the validity of rules *within* a system)."[16] Hart proceeds at once to elucidate this somewhat enigmatic statement by distinguishing two ways in which a particular rule may be said to exist: first, as a statement of external fact, meaning that people generally accept it as a standard and act in accord with it; second, as an internal statement, meaning that the rule in question is derived from an accepted rule of recognition and so is valid given the system of rules. He summarizes his view in these terms:

> In this respect, however, as in others a rule of recognition is unlike other rules of the system. The assertion that it exists can only be an external statement of fact. For whereas a subordinate rule of a system may be valid and in that sense 'exist' even if it is generally disregarded, the rule of recognition exists only as a complex, but normally concordant, practice of the courts, officials, and private persons in identifying the law by reference to certain criteria. Its existence is a matter of fact.[17]

The positivistic doctrine as embodied in these terms—and these are the terms in which it is usually interpreted by its critics—is obviously incomplete and untenable. Indeed, it is manifest nonsense and is a singularly ingenuous account to be advanced by the highly sophisticated legal positivists. These men make short shrift of the social contract, dismissing it as a fiction that is too naive and unsubstantial to found a political order. But their own concepts of the "basic norm" and the "rule of recognition" as they stand in the passages just quoted are, I would argue, equally naive and even more fragile. Appeal is made to these concepts to found the legal order and to give meaning to such essential notions as validity and authority. But these concepts themselves have no credentials other than their efficacy. And this efficacy is simply a brute fact that must be accepted without explanation or justification. Conceived in these terms, authority is created by law, but law is created arbitrarily and for no reason at all.

I believe that it is self-evident that such an arbitrary and capricious first principle could not possibly found a legal order in any meaningful sense of the term. The most that could be created in this manner and on

[16] Hart, *Concept of Law*, pp. 106 and 105, respectively.   [17] Ibid., p. 107.

this basis is a game that men could play, not a set of laws that men would respect. A legal system with no better foundation than this would never be acknowledged as binding, as creating duties and obligations, as meriting to be observed. Men are reasonable creatures, and they expect to be given reasons for obeying and conforming. Fiat backed by force can only issue commands; it cannot establish a legal order, as men understand that term and respect what it stands for. That "might makes right" is a discredited doctrine, but it hardly seems an advance to replace it with the dogma that whim makes right.

The preceding are the terms in which legal positivism is frequently interpreted and expounded. Such an interpretation is perhaps justified by certain of the writings of the positivists and realists, especially when these are polemical in tone: these thinkers are concerned to distinguish legal issues and considerations from others of a moral, social, and political nature and to clarify the structure of legal systems and processes as such and without reference to other purposes and standards. They therefore sometimes get carried away and deny—or seem to deny—the legal relevance of such extralegal facts and values. But it is extremely doubtful that any reputable legal theorist ever seriously espoused such a truncated doctrine as that just depicted.

Be that as it may, it is clear that thinkers of the caliber of Kelsen and Hart do not hold such an indefensible position. Just a few pages after declaring that the basic norm is "presupposed" simply in order to found a legal order, Kelsen explicitly renounces and retracts this thesis, saying:

> The basic norm of national legal order is not the arbitrary product of a juristic imagination. Its content is determined by facts. . . . Therefore, the content of a basic norm is determined by the facts through which an order is created and applied, to which the behavior of the individuals regulated by this order, by and large, conforms.[18]

Admittedly, Kelsen does not say what these "facts" are, nor does he seem to care. But his general meaning is clear: the character and content of the basic norm of a legal system—the constitution of a national state[19]—is defined by the actual historical situation and human intentions that "determine" it.

Since Kelsen's interest lies exclusively elsewhere, his treatment of this issue is extremely cursory. The case is quite different with Hart, who

---

[18] Kelsen, *General Theory of Law and State*, p. 120.

[19] For this identification of basic norm and constitution, cf. ibid., pp. 115-116.

also is primarily concerned to elucidate the internal structure of a legal system and to make a clear distinction between the legally valid and the morally right. Thus, Hart insists that a specific legal enactment—a primary rule of obligation—can be morally iniquitous and yet legally valid. A statute or an executive order may be enacted by legally constituted officials in accord with legally sanctioned procedures, but it may so outrage our sense of morality and justice that it forfeits our respect and moves us to disobedience. In this, I believe that Hart is perfectly correct: and he can certainly cite an abundance of examples to support his case. But at the same time, Hart fully recognizes the pervasive influence that ideas regarding the right and the just have exerted on law throughout its history. To a greater or lesser degree and in different variations, all legal systems reflect and embody these ideals; and when they fail to do so, they lose their hold on the allegiance of men.

The critical distinction in Hart's theory—and one that is too often overlooked—is that between the *validity* of specific legal enactments and the *efficacy* of a legal system. For Hart is equally insistent that a legal system cannot flaunt the basic principles of morality and justice and still be efficacious, and he develops this thesis with care and detail in two central chapters (VIII and IX) of *The Concept of Law*. Here he points out that a legal system must meet certain basic substantive and procedural criteria. As regards the former, he says that law must provide for what he calls several "natural necessities" that are inherent in human nature and social life: he identifies these as the protection of persons, property, and promises.[20] The procedural criteria that he cites are such familiar "virtues of justice" as neutrality and impartiality, intelligibility, certainty, and adherence to principles.[21] Hart concludes his discussion with this significant statement:

> What surely is most needed in order to make men clear sighted [sic] in confronting the official abuse of power, is that they should preserve the sense that the certification of something as legally valid is not conclusive of the question of obedience, and that, however great the aura of majesty or authority which the official system may have, its demands must in the end be submitted to a moral scrutiny.[22]

It is not my purpose to follow Hart step by step as he elaborates these ideas. My interest is confined to two points. First, to indicate that Hart,

[20] Hart, *Concept of Law*. See Chapter IX, esp. pp. 194-195, 199.
[21] Ibid. See Chapters VIII and IX, esp. pp. 200, 202.   [22] Ibid., p. 206.

who is certainly the most influential and respected of latter-day positivists, fully recognizes the dependence of the authority of the legal order on these extralegal considerations of justice and morality.[23] His account is thus fully consonant with my insistence on the basic importance of the authority relationship. Second, I want to argue that this positivistic doctrine is not adequate to account for—to establish and maintain—an effective legal system in an actual political society.

It will have been noted even in my very abbreviated account (and the point emerges far more clearly in the cited chapters of *The Concept of Law*) that Hart ties the efficacy of a legal system to only minimal substantive and procedural conditions and demands: these are the "simple truisms"—the "natural necessities" and the "virtues of justice"—previously mentioned. These are all conceived in *general* terms, and they apply to any legal system. Given the focus of Hart's interest, this is an understandable and legitimate way to deal with the issue.

But it is never just "any" legal system that exists. It is always a particular legal system, an instance of this abstract type. And each such system, I would maintain, is tied to quite concrete and specific conditions and demands, as well as to the general ones that Hart describes. That is, every actual legal order is constituted as such by definite expectations regarding the values and purposes it is to serve, the kind of social structure it is to support, the rights it is to recognize, the responsibilities it is to assume, and the powers it is to renounce. In sum, the factors that Hart identifies are *necessary* conditions for the existence of an actual and effective legal system, but they are not *sufficient* conditions. Therefore another indispensable element is needed, and this is to be found in a secure authority relationship, based on a clear and common, if only implicit, understanding between those who exercise authority and those who accept it regarding the uses and limits of law.[24]

It is a mistake to try to derive authority solely from law, for the truth

---

[23] It now begins to seem possible, and even probable, that Hart is going to suffer the same fate that befell Austin: that of having his theory reduced to a single salient idea. This would be the more unjust in Hart's case, for he has expounded quite fully the ideas that flesh out his central doctrine of "secondary rules." Whereas it can be argued that Austin invited his fate—his qualifications of the idea of law as the command of the sovereign were thrown out in a rather casual manner—the same is not true of Hart.

[24] Hart himself seems to recognize this need for a more concrete and specific basis for a legal system. For instance, in speaking of the "simple truisms" that express the conditions that such a system must meet, he says: "They are of vital importance for the understanding of law and morals, and they explain why the definition of the basic forms of these in purely formal terms, without reference to any specific content or social needs, has proved so inadequate." See Hart, *Concept of Law*, p. 194.

lies in just the opposite direction: law is the creature, not the progenitor, of authority. Or to speak more exactly, law is derivative from the authority relationship as a whole. In the movement from primitivism toward high civilization, which we have already traced, significant changes occur in each of the elements of the authority relationship and hence in this relationship itself. Those who exercise supreme authority must delegate many of their functions to subordinate officials. Those subject to authority segregate into factions having special interests that continually have to be compromised and controlled. The purposes that subjects seek and rulers must serve become varied, fluid, and contradictory. As a consequence, the authority relationship becomes looser and weaker, subject to wild fluctuations, uncertain both in its intent and its power. It is to repair these deficiencies that law arises. Through law the participants in the authority relationship make explicit and precise what had been only implicit and ambiguous. They create a language for voices that before were vehement but largely inarticulate. By laying down boundaries and building walls, they make fields of what had been open range. In sum, law is the instrument through which the authority relationship at once formalizes and embodies itself. Authority is now expressed as a body of purposes, principles, rules, and procedures; officials are designated to administer it, with their functions and powers carefully limited; rights and duties, privileges and responsibilities are assigned. And so rulers are transformed into governors, subjects into citizens, and private interests into public policy and the general welfare. Seen from this true perspective, law is best described as the structural framework and operational machinery—the substantive and procedural apparatus—through which the mature authority relationship expresses and asserts itself.

But we should not confuse prominence with power. If we are to deal with the real world, and not simply with a "heaven of concepts," then we must recognize that it is the authority relationship that grounds the legal order, not vice versa. It is commonly said that law defines and distributes authority. But in truth law is the vehicle through which men create both the roles they are to play as governors and citizens and the scripts they are to follow. As the validity of specific legal norms depends upon the efficacy of the legal system, so does this latter depend upon a sound authority relationship. As I have emphasized on other occasions, there is of course ample excuse for our persistent tendency to reverse this connection. A long established and widely accepted legal system does in fact acquire a large measure of internal prestige and stability. It then comes to be acknowledged that authority belongs solely to those legally designated and is to be exercised only in accord with legal norms.

Law then appears as the natural and necessary embodiment of the authority relationship, and it attaches to itself the moral and emotional allegiance, the habit of obedience, and the sense of purpose that constitute the heart of this relationship. Under these conditions, law becomes institutionalized, it takes on a spurious independence, and it can persist even when it is seriously distorting the relationship that originally generated it and of which it is supposedly the agent. Such a system of law can survive incompetent and corrupt rulers, discontented and divided subjects, and the gross subversion of the purposes and values it is intended to serve. History abounds with examples of such "survival of the unfit," and we are amply familiar with them in the present.

But even in the most pervasively legalistic societies there is a limit to this abuse. Indeed, such societies seek to assure their stability by express constitutional provision for controlling the exercise of authority by reference to its intended uses. That is, they explicitly recognize an ideal "higher law" by reference to which the actual practices of legal authority can be criticized and corrected. And this "higher law" is itself an embodiment of the original authority relationship that expresses the nascent social order and founds the legal order.

The full purport of the preceding argument can be made explicit and summed up in brief terms: the authority relationship is prior in time to law, more closely embedded in the social order than law, and capable of superseding law on occasions when these two come into conflict—although this is not to say that it always does so. Two well-known episodes that occurred during the administration of President Franklin Roosevelt confirm this contention so nicely that they are worth recalling.

The first of these is what was referred to at the time as the "court packing" scheme. This was Roosevelt's proposal to appoint several additional justices to the Supreme Court in order to override the then conservative majority that was invalidating much of the New Deal legislation as fast as Congress could enact it. There was nothing in the law of the land to prohibit this: no constitutional provision, statute, or judicial precedent told against it. If Roosevelt had sent up the names of nominees and they had been confirmed by the Senate, the procedure would have been entirely valid: indeed, the numerical composition of the Court is not specified in either the Constitution or elsewhere, and it has in fact varied on several occasions in the past. But the public outcry against the proposal was so immediate, intense, and widespread that it suffered a quick and quiet death. The American people—the Many—had somehow come to regard it as part of their compact with the government—the

One—that there should be nine justices, no more and no less, and that new appointments should be made only when vacancies occurred in the natural course of events. Everyone who had any familiarity with such matters knew perfectly well that all normal appointments to the Court were politically motivated—the president nominated men of his own persuasion. But when Roosevelt proposed to make new and unusual—but not invalid—appointments for frankly political reasons, the people were outraged. The myth that the Supreme Court is apolitical and ideologically neutral—"above all party strife"—had become an essential element in the authority relationship of this country, and when Roosevelt threatened it the people felt betrayed.

This episode takes on added strength when it is remembered that much of the legislation that was being blocked, and for which this proposal was intended to clear the way, was desperately needed to revitalize the economy. This was clearly in the interest of the people, and most of them knew it. But the authority relationship meant more to them than both the law and their own well-being.

The other episode that I have in mind is that known as the "destroyer deal," in which Roosevelt "sold" sixty navy destroyers to Great Britain in return for some bases in the West Indies. This action was blatantly *ultra vires*, altogether beyond Roosevelt's authority, and doubly unconstitutional. Since it was a transaction with a foreign power, it had the substance—if not the form—of a treaty, and so required the "advice and consent" of the Senate. But the Senate was not even officially consulted, must less asked to advise and consent. Furthermore, Article IV, Section 3, of the Constitution provides that *"the Congress* shall have power to dispose of and make all needful rules and regulations regarding the territory and other *property* belonging to the United States" [emphasis added]—the Congress, be it noted, not the President. So this action was in naked violation of the most fundamental law of the land, the very "rule of recognition" itself. But the people applauded it, and very few voices were raised to protest it or even to point out its unconstitutionality. For the people, the defense of the country and its natural allies were an integral part of the authority relationship, so that anything that the president did under that guise was quite acceptable, and the devil take its illegality.

As a final note on this topic, it is interesting to recall that when President Nixon played this same gambit, seeking to justify his actions on the ground that they were necessary to protect the "national security" and "the office" of the presidency, the people rejected the argument. The Supreme Court and the national defense are sacrosanct, but the presidency and the national security were seen as mere fictions, red herrings conjured up to cover a trail. Furthermore, bribery, the "washing" of money by the CIA, and the misuse of the FBI (itself sacrosanct) were clear violations of the rules of the game. In short, Nixon was felt to have betrayed his obligation to both the substantive and the procedural aspects of the authority relationship, and it was this conviction that drove him from office while due process of law was still only snapping at his heels.

This analysis of the complex character of the leader and of the relationship between leadership and authority finds support in the frequent lament that modern leaders are, on the whole, much inferior to those of earlier days. The favorite contrast is that of the Founding Fathers with contemporary political figures. There appears to be virtually universal agreement that men who have held high governmental office for the past several generations compare most unfavorably with the men who signed the Declaration of Independence, drafted the Constitution, and presided over the formative years of this country. Even allowing for the human tendency to glorify the past, I think the general point is sound: considered on a broad scale, the quality of leadership certainly seems to have declined drastically. Granting this, we naturally ask why it has happened. I would suggest that it is because of changes that have occurred in our attitudes toward leadership, in our ideas of the qualities that a leader needs, and—most importantly—in the processes, both formal and informal, through which a leader is selected. These changes have moved constantly in the direction of defining leadership and identifying leaders in strictly legal terms and by purely legal procedures. That is, our behavior has been determined by the illusion that the holding of authority confers a capacity for leadership. We persist in thinking that to place a person in an official position is to make of him a leader.

In earlier times, men became recognized leaders long before they were vested with authority. They achieved positions of leadership through their superior personal qualities of intellect and character; through their ability to reconcile diverse factions, to persuade their colleagues to support a coalition, and to make the compromises that reality demanded; and, finally, through the power they already commanded, and the respect and confidence they received, due to their status in what was still very much a class and class-conscious society. That is, these men became leaders because they possessed to a preeminent degree the qualities that enabled them successfully to fill the roles of dominant male, paramount chief, and anointed king. They did not in sober fact acquire authority by assuming office: rather, their election or appointment to office was little more than the placing of legal stamp upon positions they had already achieved by quite other means. These leaders did not so much run for office as accept it: they became legal officials through a machinery that they themselves had created, and it was largely up to them to determine the exact duties and powers of the offices they occupied, since these were only generally defined. In installing these men in positions of authority, law merely confirmed an effective leadership that they had for long been exercising.

The present situation is vastly different. The various offices of government are already existent, with their duties, powers, and limits closely defined by law. Even more importantly, the manner of acquiring these offices is legally determined. Most of the more important officials (authorities or "leaders") gain their positions through an elaborate system of public primary and general elections. And these follow upon an even more elaborate series of private meetings in which deals are arranged, trades are made, pressures are brought to bear, political IOUs are called in, present support is won by the promise of future favors, and the *quid pro quo* is king.

To survive in this system, the qualities that are most essential to the candidate for office are those of the paramount chief. He must be self-effacing and accessible, a master of compromise, realistic to the point of cynicism, prepared to sacrifice principle to politics when the occasion demands, aware that the image he projects is more important than the results he produces, and attuned more to the influence of the parties he deals with than to the merits of their positions on the issues they present. If this person possesses any of the attributes of the dominant male or the anointed king, he must usually keep these hidden away, exhibiting them only on rare occasions when he can be certain that the great majority of the people will agree with his stand and unite behind him. Only a foreign threat or a domestic crisis—real or manufactured—offers the proper opportunity for the elected official to appear in these more primitive roles. Since we are sovereign, he is our servant, and servants do not give orders. In short, his must be a mind that is more concerned to hold office than to exert leadership.

These accounts are admittedly somewhat exaggerated. I do not doubt that the virtues of the Founding Fathers have been magnified and their shortcomings muted with the passage of time. And it would be foolish as well as churlish to deny that in the past half century we have had men in high office who have exhibited notable qualities of leadership. Furthermore, the people are quite aware that when they elect a president they are also choosing a leader. They make clear their resentment of the

machinations by which their freedom of choice is thwarted and manipulated. Now as always candidates for high office must present themselves
to the people as potential leaders while they make themselves acceptable
to their associates as politicians. I have painted in black and white, while
reality consists of infinite shades of gray.

But I would still maintain that these accounts do reveal two radically
different states of affairs. In making lawful election to legal office the ultimate criterion of leadership—the absolute test that the would-be leader
must pass—we have created an apparatus that tells forcefully against the
emergence to power of men with a real capacity for the role they are
called on to play. The very qualities that a person needs to be an effective
leader make it extremely difficult for him to achieve a position of authority in which he can exercise leadership. Conversely, the habits of mind
and action that equip him admirably for election to office almost automatically make him unfit to be an effective leader. Under these conditions it is inevitable that the quality of leadership should decline.

One thing that is here made clear is that processes do not necessarily
issue in progress. It is a frequent habit of thought to equate these terms
and to assume that the later stages of a process are superior to its earlier
stages. To this there is usually joined another assumption that is far
more dangerous: namely, that the structures and functions that arise in
these later stages altogether supplant and replace those that characterized the earlier stages. That is, we tend to assume that advanced
forms of any process render more primitive forms obsolete.

In the case under consideration, this means that we are led to believe
that once leadership has been given legal dress, its earlier modes become
redundant and the elected official can dispense with the attributes of his
predecessor types. This is a common misconception. It is true that once a
person has assumed such an office as president of the United States he
does not usually have to possess any outstanding capacity for leadership
in order to function satisfactorily and remain securely in office. Whatever deficiencies he may have, members of his entourage will labor to
make good or cover up: like Austin's sovereign, he will receive habitual
obedience; regardless of his shortcomings, the federal bureaucracy will
continue to function; his subordinates and his party will protect him;
the coordinate branches of government will press tolerance to its limits
in order to avoid a confrontation; and the people will accord him the respect they feel for the office he holds. All of this is the gift of legality,
and its value to both governors and citizens is immense, for it protects
them from the vagaries of individual leaders. A president thus does not

often have to rely upon his qualities and status as dominant male, paramount chief, and anointed king: even if he lacks these completely, the office itself will normally sustain him. But the minute leadership and not merely administrative ability is called for, any president is going to need the qualities of the anointed king, the paramount chief, and the dominant male, and his success in meeting great challenges will be measured by the fund of these qualities that he can summon up.

There is a related misconception involved here that is even more serious. This is our assumption that leadership that is defined and secured by law is in all respects superior to its predecessor types and that it in fact represents the total consummation of the quest for an authority that is both effective and responsible. Legal authority does have great advantages, as I have emphasized, and it does represent a distinct advance in certain ways. But it has corresponding weaknesses as compared with its prototypes. Considered as types, both the dominant male and the paramount chief are more responsive to the needs and the expressed goals of those they lead. Indeed they must be, for leaders of these types are not protected by either their sacrosanct status or an assured tenure, so they are readily removed when their leadership falters or proves unsatisfactory. The holder of legal authority, on the other hand, has a guaranteed term of office and a powerful supporting apparatus, so that he is far more insulated from and immune to pressures from either his colleagues or the mass of the people; and he can be removed from office only by a more or less cumbersome process. So we are well advised to measure the price we pay against the advantages we win, and to consider if perhaps there is a better way to balance gain and loss. We touch here on that vague and troublesome area where law and politics meet and overlap, and I shall have more to say on this question in a later chapter.

For the last three chapters I have been discussing the question of the conditions of legal effectiveness. This discussion has raised and considered a cluster of problems. Our thinking about this matter is geared to our familiarity with mature legal systems functioning in stable societies, where there is a close coordination of law with the circumstances and aspirations that it serves. That is, we are accustomed to a symbiosis between the legal order and the actual and ideal orders within which it functions. Under these conditions, law is largely sovereign in fact, and its decrees receive general and almost automatic compliance. So we come to assume that legal validity assures real efficacy. But this assumption very often breaks down in practice, especially where law seeks to innovate social reform on any large scale. In such cases, we are positing through law a new mediating order through which we hope to create new actual and ideal orders. That is, we are seeking to transform the way of life of a people and the values they seek.

As we have seen, these attempts can succeed only if they are guided by a clear understanding of the two key concepts of *value* and *authority*. The reasons for this are simple. Such reforms are obviously intended and undertaken in order to enhance the measure of human value—to increase the happiness and well-being of men. We must therefore understand the nature of value and the conditions of value realization. Furthermore, the attainment of the values sought by reform is sure to be difficult and is often long delayed. If the program of reform is to receive the support it needs, it must be inspired and guided by an authority that has the confidence of the people and the competence that its tasks demand. Thus we must understand the nature of authority and the factors upon which its effective exercise depends. The investigations of this complex of problems led us to explore the nature of intrinsic and extrinsic value, the authority relationship, and finally the concept of leadership.

The final outcome of these discussions, culminating in the analysis of the roles and attributes of the leader, is to reinforce a point that I have insisted upon throughout: that *law is always a supplemental principle of order*. It arises to strengthen and refine earlier principles of order, but it depends equally upon these, and it cannot supplant them. As we have seen most recently, the elected president must be able to assume the roles of anointed king, paramount chief, and even dominant male. If we regard him only in his legal character, we reduce him to a one-dimensional figure, too shallow to carry the part he must play.

The legal order is part and parcel of the larger social order. It has certainly become an increasingly dominant element in the life of society. But just as certainly, it cannot by itself maintain the social order. The power of law as a principle of order is limited: there are things that law can do very effectively, others that it can do much less well, if at all. Since its effectiveness depends upon the presence of other factors, it must respect these and coordinate its efforts with theirs. And it must above all resist the temptation, common to all institutions, to assume that it commands a monopoly of both wisdom and benevolence, and so knows what is best about everything. I think there are now strong signs that law is succumbing to this temptation and that it needs to be brought to realize its limitations and dependence. It is with these matters that I want to deal in my concluding chapters. For I am deeply convinced of the importance of two points: that the sovereignty of law must be maintained, and that this can be accomplished only if law avoids the sin of arrogance. The old saying, whom the gods would destroy they first make mad, is still as relevant as ever. We need only amend it by the recognition that the madness in question is now self-induced.

[CHAPTER XII]

LEGAL OBLIGATION

THE PRECEDING DISCUSSIONS have been carried on primarily from the point of view of those who exercise authority, with those who accept this authority, and the considerations that lead them to do so, being seen largely from that one perspective. It is time now to redress this imbalance and to look at the matter from the point of view of the subjects rather than the sovereign. When we do this, the issue that at once confronts us is the elusive one of *obligation*. Why should and do we on the whole acknowledge the authority of law, obey it, conform our behavior to its dictates, and even accept its penalties? In sum, what is the source of the obligatory character that is everywhere recognized as central to the concept of law?

We can best ease our way into this thorny nest of questions by following the path of the thinkers previously discussed, especially Austin and Hart. Austin finds the essence of this obligatoriness in the notion of a command backed by might. Law is obligatory because a sovereign orders it, threatens sanctions if he is not obeyed, and has the power to enforce his will. As we have seen, Austin later qualifies this overly simplistic account by introducing several subsidiary ideas, such as the habit of obedience and the sovereign's adherence to certain maxims and principles, with the latter of these being conceived as gradually developed during the life of the group and hence as expressive of its fundamental values and purposes. But it is still true that Austin thought that law was obligatory because it could compel those subject to it: we *are obliged* to obey the law because of the pain we face if we do not. The central idea for Austin is that of *coercion*.

It is with an attack on this contention that Hart begins the statement of his own theory. He points out that on this view of the obligatory character of law, the gunman's command, "your money or your life," is a law. And this is manifestly absurd. We all feel a deep difference between the command of the gunman and that of the Internal Revenue Service, although the outcome of obeying might be very little different in the two cases. Hart's search for this "difference" leads him to his central doctrine; his path can be traced in a few steps.

Hart expresses this difference verbally as that between *being* obliged and *having an obligation*. In turn, he regards obligation as being rule-dependent.[1] But not all rules give rise to obligations. For this to occur, the rules in question must have three characteristics. The "primary factor" in effecting this transition is the "importance and seriousness of social pressure" for conformity to the rule.[2] In addition, such rules "are believed to be necessary to the maintainance of social life or of some highly prized feature of it" and "it is generally recognized that the conduct required by these rules may, while benefiting others, conflict with what the person who owes the duty [is under the obligation] may wish to do."[3]

But other rules besides those of law satisfy these conditions and place us under an obligation: many social and moral rules are of this type. So one further step is necessary to arrive at the distinctive nature of legal obligation. This step, of course, is taken with the introduction of Hart's important doctrine of secondary rules, especially the rule of recognition. With this latter rule we arrive at the essence of law. For it identifies any legal enactment (any primary rule of obligation) as being *valid* and hence as representing the legitimate exertion of social pressure. For Hart, we *have an obligation* to obey the law because its rules are the outcome of a procedure that is itself acknowledged to be authoritative. Here the central idea is that of *validity*.

This is a clear advance over Austin's position, even when the latter is broadly enterpreted, as I have suggested that it can and should be. For Hart has spelled out very sharply the conditions of legal validity. However, it is my belief that a further advance is necessary if we are to give a satisfactory account of legal obligation: that is, if we are to explain why we acknowledge the obligatoriness of law, why it has a claim on our obedience, why it is right that we should adhere to its rules. In short, I would maintain that validity is not dispositive of obligation.

Futhermore, it seems altogether clear that Hart himself recognizes this. For he is explicit, and even emphatic, on the point that it is perfectly possible for a law to be valid and yet to be such that men should not obey it. There are further, more basic, demands that law must satisfy if it is properly to claim and effectively to receive our assent and obedience. Hart leaves no doubt about his position on this point, developing it through a succession of statements. He starts with the general assertion that a legal system controlled by his secondary rules is

---

[1] H.L.A. Hart, *The Concept of Law* (Oxford: The Clarendon Press, 1961), pp. 79–88.
[2] Ibid., p. 84.   [3] Ibid., p. 85.

nevertheless "compatible with very great iniquity."[4] Now, Hart is extremely precise in his definition and use of terms: he holds that the primary rules of such a system as this are *valid* and hence legally obligatory. But few people would be willing to maintain that a law that is acknowledgedly iniquitous either places us under an obligation in any fundamental sense or merits our respect and allegiance. Certainly Hart does not maintain this. For he immediately declares that there can be occasions when "we should say: 'This is law; but it is too iniquitous to be applied or obeyed.' "[5] And finally, in a passage already quoted at length, he identifies the ground to which we appeal when we make such a statement. He says that "the certification of something as legally valid is not conclusive of the question of obedience, and . . . its demands must in the end be submitted to a moral scrutiny."[6] And Hart concludes his discussion of this point by saying "that there is something outside the official system, by reference to which in the last resort the individual must solve his problems of obedience."[7]

Now, if we appeal beyond the law in moments of crisis and conflict and when it outrages our moral sense—as we obviously do—then it is at least a reasonable inference that our usual acceptance of the obligatoriness of law also rests upon an extralegal basis. That is, we acknowledge the authority of law and we obey it, not simply because it *is* the law but because of something for which the law stands: something that lies beyond the law, animating and directing it, defining its purposes and procedures, and placing limits upon its reach. The obligation that we recognize and honor is not to the law as an end in itself or final value but to the law as an instrumental value, as a means to the furtherance of goals and values that we hold dear and seek to secure—or, as Hart puts it, to "something outside the official system" that law represents.

But problems persist. What is this "something"? And on what ground does it claim our allegiance? The question that is traditionally posed as critical in this context is usually stated in some such way as this: Why are we obliged to obey the law? Why should we accept the dictates of law as binding upon us? What justifies the obligations that law imposes? Why ought we to be law-abiding?

I think that when the issue is posed in these terms it sets inquiry on the wrong track and after a false scent. In the spirit in which these questions are usually asked, they require that we start with certain factual propositions and then deduce from these the necessary existence of cor-

---

[4] Ibid., p. 202.
[6] Ibid., p. 206.
[5] Ibid., p. 203, and cf. p. 205.
[7] Ibid.

responding axiological conclusions—that is, of certain obligations. We are expected to prove that because some things *are* the case, then other things *should be* the case: logic is charged to carry us from the realm of *facts* to the realm of *values*. In short, these questions ask us to derive an "ought" from an "is."

This is of course impossible. It is also irrelevant. For in this case, as in other similar ones, the "ought" *is* an "is." Our recognition that we are obligated to obey the law—the "ought" that we here feel and acknowledge—is not derived from more basic premises and proved by some process of logical deduction. Rather, it exists as an experienced occasion—a fact—inherent in certain existential situations. This fact functions as a value (an "ought")—as do love, compassion, courage, loyalty, and a horde of other fact-values—when we recognize its worth and accept its demands. But the acknowledgment that we are obligated is not something that permits or eludes logical proof. It is empirically existent or nonexistent, so we can explain when and why people do feel obligated, and we can even understand and control to a large extent the conditions under which they do and do not, will and will not, feel obligated. But we cannot muster a logical argument to prove to the doubtful that they *ought* to feel obligated: we can only put them in situations where as a matter of fact they *will* feel obligated.

These statements are admittedly rather enigmatic and even dogmatic. I will thus attempt to clarify them and render them reasonable with an analogy. The questions just posed amount to this: Why should—do—we accept as authoritative the dictates of law? I would compare this with two other perfectly similar questions: Why should—do—we accept as convincing the conclusion of a logical argument? Why should—do—we accept as persuasive the evidence of our senses? I believe it would be agreed that these two latter questions are meaningless, in the sense that there is nothing we can do to answer the person who asks them. If someone rejects the procedures that they embody, our natural—and only—recourse is to reject him as unreasonable. If a person acknowledges that all A is B, and all B is C, and yet refuses to accept that all A is C, all we can do is break off the argument. Similarly, if a person refuses to believe what he clearly sees or hears, we are helpless to deal with him. Our immediate and intuitive response in either of these situations is to lose our temper, to tell the person he has lost his mind, and then to walk away.[8]

[8] Questions analogous to those just cited (but in different contexts) are: Why is the normal human body temperature 98.6 degrees? Why is the earth's inclination on its axis just what it is? These are simply factual characteristics of the human physiological structure and the solar system, respectively. For a fascinating discussion of the extremely fine

The only proper answer to the question of why we should accept both the conclusion of a logical argument and the evidence of our senses is that we just do as a matter of course. We are simply made that way. We are rational and perceptive creatures, so we believe what our reason and our senses tell us. Of course—and this point is of critical importance—the conditions under which we accept and reject rational arguments and empirical evidence can be specified. Formal logic and scientific method are simply the refined developments of procedures that we all employ quite spontaneously and on the whole effectively: persons with no training in either of these disciplines can detect a spurious argument or an unreliable observation. Being constituted as we are, we use our minds and our senses as naturally as we breathe and walk. We normally accept the ideas and the data that these faculties yield, but sometimes we reject them as sophistical or deceptive. It is probably the case that most people could not tell with any clarity and detail what leads to acceptance or rejection. But these conditions can be specified, and that is precisely what logic does.

What I am suggesting is that the case is exactly similar to this when we consider legal obligation. When it is asked, "Why should and do we acknowledge law as binding upon us?" or "Why should and do we have an obligation to obey the law?," I believe the only answer is that we just do. As in the cases above, we are simply made that way. We are social creatures, so we are responsive to our fellow creatures, we accept the terms of social life, we accommodate ourselves to the provisions that are necessary to preserve the social fabric. In a word, we acknowledge the legitimacy of the obligations that law and the government impose upon us because we recognize that they serve the general interest on which we all depend, even when they impinge on our own immediate private interests. To be thus responsive to the groups we live with is simply an ultimate fact about human nature, just as is our acceptance of the conclusions of logic and the testimony of our senses. But in this present case, as in the others, we can specify the conditions of this acceptance of obligation. To do that is the next and final step in my argument.

I shall first state very baldly and will then elaborate the thesis I seek to establish. This can be put in the form of a brief proposition: *The attitudes and behavior of men toward one another are governed by the sentiment and conviction that relationships that have been mutually es-*

---

correlation between the demands of life and the physical features of the earth, see L. J. Henderson's *The Fitness of the Environment* (New York: Macmillan and Co., 1927). In my analogy I am merely suggesting a similar correlation between the demands of social life and the psychic (emotional, rational, moral, and so forth) characteristics of man.

tablished are not to be unilaterally ruptured or altered. In advancing this thesis, I do not mean to assert that all men are aware of, accept, and consciously adjust their conduct in accord with this proposition. It is not a tenet that men repeat every day, as they might a creed. It intends to advance a sheer fact about human nature. Once we have established a relationship of any sort with other persons—whether as individuals, groups of many sorts and sizes, institutions and organizations in which people combine their interests and efforts—we feel a strong reluctance and we recognize that it is wrong to break off the relationship or to violate its terms by a unilateral act of our own. That is, we *feel obligated*—we know and acknowledge that we ought—to abide by arrangements into which we have voluntarily entered and on the fulfillment of which others have relied.[9]

Two caveats should be briefly entered here. First, to the extent that persons do not have the opportunity to form such relationships, of course they will not experience their influence and will not feel obligated by their terms. That is, they will not recognize and acknowledge the moral duties and obligations that are associated with these relationships. This is to say that all persons *have the capacity* to become moral beings—as they do to become rational, articulate, literate, aesthetically sensitive beings—but they *will in fact become so* only under the proper conditions. It is differences in these lived conditions (along with differences in genetic endowment) that are responsible for the differences in moral sensitivity and steadfastness that we find among persons. Second, people obviously do not always do everything that they feel obligated to do: everyone at times evades or compromises what he still recognizes to be his moral duty or legal obligation. People are moved by other forces and considerations besides the obligations—the bonds—established by these relationships: conflicts occur, and the issue is always in doubt.

The relationships that we form with others are too numerous and various to be counted or classified, but they are so familiar to us that no more need be done than to cite a few examples and call attention to the more important ways in which they differ: experience will supply the rest. Such relationships are formed when we make a promise, borrow a book, become a friend or lover, join a profession, teach a class, accept a client, get married, have a child, make a contract, consult a doctor or

---

[9] The doctrine that moral obligations and duties are created by and rest on relationships among persons was given dramatic treatment by H. A. Prichard in his celebrated article, "Does Moral Philosophy Rest on a Mistake?" See *Mind* 21 (1912). It was developed and argued in detail by W. D. Ross in several works, notably *The Right and The Good* (Oxford: The Clarendon Press, 1930) and *Foundations of Ethics* (Oxford: The Clarendon Press, 1939).

accountant, accept a casual invitation or receive help in a time of serious trouble, visit friends for the weekend or live for years as the citizen of a country. This is but a random sample, but it is sufficient to illustrate the ways in which these relationships are formed and vary. Some are intimate, as within the family; some remote, as with a political party. Some are only implicit and informal, as in friendship; some are explicit and carefully spelled out, as when we make a solemn agreement with someone. Some touch only a small part of our lives and last but briefly; some engage virtually our whole personalities and endure a lifetime. Some we regard as trivial, to be broken on any casual pretext; others we regard as very serious, binding us beyond the reach of any dispensation.

These *lived relationships*, as I shall call them, constitute a significant part of the fabric of our lives; it is only through participation in them that we acquire and express our humanity. It is my central contention that once we enter into and share any such relationship, we feel bound by it and its terms. It establishes a *bond* between us and the other party, and we feel emotionally, recognize rationally, and acknowledge morally that we are obligated by it and that it is wrong for us to break the bond unilaterally.[10]

The simplest example of such a lived relationship is one that is established when we make a promise. A friend lends us some books, and we promise to return them at a certain time, when he has need of them. The

[10] It is interesting to note that Hart makes a suggestion that is virtually identical with the idea just advanced, although he does not elaborate on it or give it any prominent place in his theory. In *The Concept of Law* he speaks of promises as creating obligations, saying: "When we promise, we make use of specified procedures to change our own moral situation by imposing obligations on ourselves and conferring rights on others" (p. 42). And again he refers to "the figure of a *bond* binding the person obligated" and goes on to say: "In this figure, which haunts much legal thought, the social pressure appears as a chain binding those who have obligations so that they are not free to do what they want" (p. 85; emphasis in original). However, Hart is emphatic in his insistence that we must not allow these "figures or metaphors to trap us into a misleading conception of obligation as essentially consisting in some feeling of pressure or compulsion experienced by those who have obligations" (p. 85). He is concerned with the internal and formal conditions that create legal obligations, so that for him the rule of recognition is the independent variable and the ultimate datum. My argument, on the contrary, insists that there is an intimate and necessary connection between recognizing *that one is obligated* and *acknowledging that one has a legal obligation*, and that the former is both prior and necessary to the latter. This argument is fully developed in the immediately following pages.

It might also be pointed out that this concept of the fundamental importance of the "bond" figures prominently in the thought and doctrines of the modern ethologists. Cf., e.g., Konrad Lorenz, *On Aggression*, (Cambridge, Mass.: Harvard University Press, 1974), *passim* but esp. pp. 159, 211, 276-277, 289.

instant we make this promise we feel bound and held by its terms.[11] We have committed ourselves, have pledged ourselves to perform certain actions and assure certain outcomes. In short, we have *assumed an obligation*. And having made the commitment—accepted the obligation—we feel bound to honor it (the two senses, figurative and literal, of the term bound are a nice illustration of my thesis). The point I am making is clearly brought out by our reluctance to break the promise (with the term break lending further support to my argument). If we find it inconvenient or unpleasant to keep the promise, we immediately appeal to the other party and seek to get released from it. If he agrees, then all is well: a relationship that has been mutually established is dissolved by mutual consent. If he does not agree and if the pressure on us is great enough, we will fail to keep the promise: but if we do so, we will certainly do it reluctantly, with the awareness that we are doing what we ought not to do and with a feeling of guilt. There is, of course, one other familiar manner in which we feel released from a promise or other lived relationship: this is if the other party has already violated its terms. But I shall have much to say on this point in a moment.

Applying this argument to the present case, I think that it is this lived relationship that we have with our fellow creatures, and hence with our society, and hence again with the government that is the agent of our society, and hence finally with the legal system that is the instrument of the government, that is the real source of the obligation that we feel and acknowledge to obey the law. We should and do feel and accept this obligation because we have lived on certain terms with our society and so with its government and its legal system.[12] It is this particular lived relationship—this instance of a general type—that constitutes what I have referred to as the authority relationship. Law *imposes* an obligation because of its validity; we *acknowledge* this obligation because of the lived relationship we have had with our society. So where Austin says that we *are obliged*, and Hart says that we *have an obligation*, I say that we *recognize ourselves to be obligated*. For Austin, the central fact is *coercion*; for Hart, it is *validity*; for me, it is the *lived authority relationship*.

That is the heart of my doctrine. But several points require comment

[11] Throughout this discussion I am of course assuming that the promise is not merely verbal or hypocritical but that it is made seriously and with an acceptance of the conditions it imposes. That is, the promise is recognized as creating a lived relationship, and not as only an exchange of words.

[12] Socrates' argument in the *Crito*, explaining and justifying his determination to abide the verdict of the state, is the classic statement of this doctrine. Cf. esp. 49A-53A.

and elaboration. And this will afford me a further occasion to illustrate the practical application of my analysis of the matrix of law in terms of the dimensions of order (Many–One–Process–Pattern) and the regimes of existence (Necessity–Possibility–Purposiveness), for my account of the authority relationship fits naturally into this frame of reference: the One consists of those who exercise authority; the Many consists of those who acknowledge it; and Process and Pattern comprise the terms of the compact, partly explicit and partly implicit, between the two parties. That is, Process and Pattern define the social structure that the One is to serve and the Many to support: its values and purposes, its beliefs and practices, its rights and duties, its procedures, its modes and standards of behavior, the conditions it imposes, and the hopes it holds out. The contents of this "compact" correspond functionally to Austin's "principles or maxims which the sovereign habitually observes" and to Hart's "simple truisms" and "natural necessities" that dictate the "indispensable features" of a legal system: they define the terms of the relationship between sovereign and subject. But there are also significant differences between these concepts and my own.

In the first place, I am thinking of this compact in terms that are very much more concrete and detailed and much less clearly spelled out than were the terms in which Austin and Hart conceived the matter. It would be quite impossible for anyone to delineate fully the rich and complex web of relationships that binds him to his fellows and to his society. This is a lived relationship, not a written convenant or social contract. We participate in it without having consciously entered into it and without having had its terms explained to us. We learn these terms by living them, and as we learn them they become habits that we are hardly aware of. We experience them as obligations, whether owed by us or owing to us, only when their violation is real or threatened. The fundamental obligations that government and the law owe us—the rights they guarantee us—are of course contained in the Constitution, especially the first Ten Amendments. Since we no longer have any ritual of initiation into citizenship (and even prayers and the pledge of allegiance to the flag in schools have been declared unconstitutional), the obligations we owe the government (our duties) are left almost completely unspecified: we know explicitly that we should obey the law and pay our taxes, and that is about it. But no one could possibly suppose that these exhaust the relationships that run between ourselves and the society we live in and the government and law that we live under: they are at best an abstract framework that supports the body politic and social life.

This leads to a second point. The obligations that weigh most heavily upon us are usually the issue of lived relationships that are intimate and richly textured, such as those with family, close friends, professional colleagues, social, artistic, or political groups with which we have worked, institutions we have served, causes that we cherish and have supported. I do not doubt that those whose careers are spent in law and government form a close and concrete relationship with these institutions and feel a strong obligation to support and act in accord with their principles and standards, but this is not the case with most of us. Our direct relationships with law and the government are rare and remote. I think there are actually quite few occasions when we consciously "obey the law" or "acknowledge the sovereignty" of the government: the only instances that come readily to mind are paying taxes and stopping at traffic signals. It is not often that we even become aware of having a legal obligation, much less that we feel it binding us. Which is to say that what we call our legal obligations (and which are in fact just that) are largely felt by us indirectly: they are mediated through other groups or institutions with which we do have close relations and to which we do feel obligated.

Most husbands treat their wives and children in a kindly fashion and provide for their wants out of love, and not because the law imposes this obligation upon them. I slow down in a school zone during recess not because the law says I must but because I care about the children who might dash into the street; if there are neither children nor policemen in sight, I am apt to drive at a normal speed. Many of us worked hard and staked much to integrate our universities not because it was the law of the land but because we felt that it was right to open opportunities to those who had been excluded. And most of us pay our bills on time not because of the threat of legal action but because we realize that the shopkeeper needs his money and we need to maintain our credit ratings. Persons who do not care for their wives, for children, for underprivileged people, or even for their credit ratings do not feel obligated in these ways and they may flout the legal obligations that they indubitably have. Of course, they are not thereby freed of these obligations. Being subject to the law, they are liable to its sanctions: the objective obligations and penalties imposed by the law are there whether or not one feels subjectively obligated by lived relationships to obey them. But it is only the threat of coercion that constrains such persons. Not feeling obligated, they conform—when they do—not out of a sense of responsibility but only because of the liability with which the law charges them. Other examples to this same effect, both serious and casual, could be multipled endlessly.

The law is remote from most of us most of the time. We see here a concrete exemplification of two theses that I have earlier argued at length in theoretical terms. First, law is a supplemental principle of order; it is superimposed upon but does not supersede other more intimate and familiar principles of order: family, friends, church, school, union, profession, and so on. Second, positive law is expository as well as prescriptive and normative. It reflects and supports an actual social order as well as issuing directives designed to secure an ideal order. Much of the time, and in much of our behavior, we act in accord with the law not because it is the law but because this is what is required by lived relationships that we participate in with other more intimate groups, causes, and institutions. We respect the law largely because of our conviction that it supports and serves the compact that is such an essential feature of the authority relationship. Our lives are played out in an elaborate web of social processes and patterns, and we are chiefly conscious of law as a force that pervades this web, reinforcing when necessary bonds that are already and otherwise forged. In short, we *follow* the law without obeying it.[13]

A third point follows as a corollary of the above: the law—the sovereign or government—also has its obligations under the terms of the authority relationship, and when it fails to observe these terms, or acts unilaterally to alter them, it risks losing the allegiance and obedience of the people. For under these conditions, when one party is felt to have violated his obligations, the other party feels freed from his. This, of course, is simply to encounter in different terms the problem that confronts social reform. By definition, this is an effort to change in some way the terms of the authority relationship: it seeks to reformulate the

[13] The views advanced in these paragraphs are very similar to those expressed by Alexander Bickel in *The Morality of Consent* (New Haven: Yale University Press, 1975. Bickel states that:

> The fundamental point was, and remains, that consent and stability are not produced simply by the existence and function of popularly elected institutions, although absolute power may be. Elections, even if they are referenda, do not establish consent, or do not establish it for long. They cannot mean that much. . . . The people begin with "the little platoon we belong to in society," what today we call groups, and they are found in places to which they are attached, in divisions of the country, what we call constituencies, which "have been formed by habit, and not by a sudden jerk of authority." . . . "Public affections," meaning consent to the institutions of government, must begin "in our families . . . pass on to our neighborhoods and our habitual provincial connections," and so on to the nation. No jet age can change that. (Pp. 16-17.)

The internal quotes used by Bickel are from Edmund Burke's *Reflections on the Revolution in France*, without specific citations.

compact that has hitherto been established among all parties and has been embodied in the social order.

In one sense, social reform instigated by legal means in a democracy *cannot* be unilateral, for law is the agent of government, and the government is our agent. So, indirectly, it is we the people who instigate the reforms, who decide that the terms of the authority relationship should and shall be changed. But it is the fact of indirection that is crucial here, for those who oppose the reforms in question, who find them threatening or objectionable, or who simply fear and resent change will reject the suggestion that *they* have in any way agreed to these reforms: they will therefore feel them as a unilateral rupture of the authority relationship. For them, the compact has been altered without their consent; the rules of the game have been changed arbitrarily, and they refuse to support the change and may even actively oppose it. Such confrontations can also be precipitated from exactly the opposite direction. This occurs when some group presses for a change in certain specific terms of the authority relationship, feeling that these are inequitable or oppressive to them and claiming also that they run counter to the fundamental spirit of the relationship.

There is a third prominent cause of such confrontations that is probably the most volatile of all. This comes into play when some group feels that, although the law is paying lip service to the terms of the authority relationship, it is not strongly supporting them but is permitting these groups to be treated in a discriminatory manner and placed in an inferior status. The members of such a group are moved by multiple complaints: they suffer socially and economically, they are frustrated by the failure of law to act by the principles it proclaims, and their sense of justice is outraged.

These confrontations result when there is a significant heightening in the tension between legal validity and the authority relationship. Such tension is unavoidable and ever present. As an imperfect instrument that has to operate in the real world where men pursue their self-interests, law can never perfectly reflect the terms of the social compact, as these are envisaged in ideal terms and need only be dressed in fitting rhetorical garb. And there are other still stronger forces at work creating this tension. For every group inevitably—and often disinterestedly and sincerely—interprets the social compact in terms of its own situation and interests. But law can only embody this compact in *one* form: a single interpretation of the authority relationship must regulate the activities and arrangements of all groups. Society as a whole is permeated by one public structure of Process and Pattern within which each individual and group must pursue its private career. Given these facts, it is inevitable that there should be continual tension and occasional open conflict between the various parties to the authority relationship. Indeed, this is true of all relationships: in even the most intimate and amicable family, quarrels and temporary ruptures occur, as some member gains an advantage, or shirks a task, and others feel put upon. The larger the group and the more divergent the interests of its subgroups—its classes or factions—the more frequent are the occasions for such conflicts and the greater their intensity. And when some group launches a large-scale and organized challenge to the authority relationship as currently embodied in the legally valid, then we have the phenomenon of civil disobedience.

In all of the advanced societies, civil disobedience is now a familiar occurrence in both its violent and nonviolent forms. As such, it has been widely discussed: its merits and demerits, its justification or its lack thereof, have been acrimoniously disputed, and there have been sharply different opinions of the proper response to be made to it by law and government. I will conclude with a brief discussion of this phenomenon, for I think that it is in terms of the foregoing accounts of obligation and of the duality of the legally valid and the authority relationship that we can best understand civil disobedience and the treatment it should be accorded.

Civil disobedience threatens whenever any group does not feel obligated by certain of the obligations that it has under the law. To put the same point in different terms, a group is motivated toward civil disobedience when it becomes persuaded that in some significant area of social life, what is legally valid is in violation of the fundamental tenets of the authority relationship.[14] When this condition persists, the first thing for such a group to do is to try by regular and established legal procedures to get the law changed or to get the government to modify its policy. This attempt will normally be reinforced by a public relations program intended to enlist support and increase the pressure. As these efforts fail, the group becomes steadily more frustrated, until finally it turns to

---

[14] It may of course be certain terms of this relationship itself that are challenged on the ground that they run counter to morality, justice, or the higher law, however this last may be conceived. But this happens far more rarely: in any well-established society, the authority relationship (the Constitution) will have such esteem and will be so deeply respected and even revered that the protesting group will usually argue that its claim is justified by a true interpretation of the terms of the relationship. And as far as my present concern goes, in all events the two cases are essentially identical: in both, it is a change in the law that is sought, whether this be regarded as a sounder interpretation of the authority relationship or as a modification of it. For simplicity's sake, the ensuing discussion is cast in terms of the first case.

other methods to call attention to its plight and its case. The method that has proved the most effective is that of large-scale nonviolent civil disobedience: the group sets out purposely and systematically to break the law in order to make the public—and of course the government—acutely aware of the law that is being broken. In doing this, the group pins its hopes on the conviction that when people are made to see clearly the content and the impact of the law in question, they will recognize that it is unjust, violative of the true spirit if not the letter of the authority relationship, and not deserving of respect or obedience. This in turn should lead to the change that is sought in the law. The substance of the law that was valid will now be declared invalid; and this will be done in accord with due process of law.

There is thus a very real sense in which an act of civil disobedience is a work of art. It is intended to dramatize the oppression and discrimination under which the protesting group suffers, and hence the injustice of the law that is being disobeyed. The familiar marches, sit-ins, and other demonstrations were all devices that were used to present vividly the inequity and persecution that were the outcome of the law as it then stood.[15] The purpose of all this was to persuade the public and the government that the law in question *ought not to be obeyed*. This being the case, it ought to be repealed and changed. In Hart's terms, "This is law; but it is too iniquitous to be applied or obeyed." In nonviolent civil disobedience, which reached its peak of effectiveness under the leadership of Martin Luther King, Jr., large numbers of people systematically violated laws that were then valid and voluntarily accepted the penalty attached to such violation. By this, they hoped to bring home to the country the iniquity of the law and the justice of their own cause. That their hopes were abundantly realized is a matter of history.

The situation and the actions of such groups are, I believe, easily understood in terms of the framework that I have been developing. These protestors do not reject the authority relationship of the society, nor do they usually seek even to change it (although, as noted above, they may occasionally do so). What they challenge are certain parts of the law that supposedly embody and serve specific elements of this relationship; and they do this on the ground that these laws deny them a full participation in this relationship and so violate its fundamental terms. In short, they claim that laws that are indubitably valid under the substantive and procedural provisions of the established and efficacious system of law are

---

[15] The interpretation of art on which this view is based and which regards arts as fundamentally the presentation of particularity was fully developed in my book, *Art and The Human Enterprise* (Cambridge, Mass.: Harvard University Press, 1958).

socially inequitable and morally iniquitous and ought to be declared invalid. When they are successful, as they so properly and spectacularly were in the Civil Rights movement of the 1950s and 1960s, this is precisely what happens. The opprobrious laws are ruled invalid, and new legislative enactments, judicial decisions, and executive orders come into force to bring the *legally valid* into closer accord with what is now perceived as the true spirit and intent of the authority relationship.

Implicit in this discussion have been two assumptions: that the protestors' claims are just, their cause righteous; and that society as a whole immediately recognizes this and willingly grants what is claimed. Neither of these need hold true, and the second in particular is highly improbable. Groups do claim rights that are inherently extravagant and unjustified; more often, what they claim, however reasonable, may be beyond the power or resources of the government to grant. And it is a virtual certainty that any claim advanced by one group will be opposed by some other, since what is at issue in any such case is an alteration of the balance of interests—of rights and duties, benefits and privileges—within the society. So when nonviolent civil disobedience occurs, the government must prepare its response. In doing this, regard must be had for both the merits and the practicality of the claim that is urged. When a decision is reached, it will be couched in legal terms and will initiate legal steps. But both the deliberations that lead to this decision and the measures proposed will be heavily influenced by other moral, social, political, economic, and material considerations. As I have previously argued in detail, I would again suggest that the framework in which these deliberations should be carried on is that of the matrix of positive law developed in my earlier chapters.

Once it has been decided to grant the claim and effect the changes that it requires, the major problem that law faces is that of defining and managing these changes in such a manner that they will be accepted by the groups that initially opposed them. For there will surely be such groups who feel that now the authority relationship as they interpet it and as it has been established and followed has been altered unilaterally and in a manner adverse to their interests. If law is to achieve an effective mediating order—a satisfactory transition—between the present actual order and the envisaged ideal order, it must here take special care to maintain a balance between its expository, prescriptive, and normative elements. Close attention must be paid to the regime of Necessity: to the habits and attitudes of people, to their accustomed arrangements and expectations, as well as to the resources of the society; these must be taken into account, since they place limits on what law can accomplish. The alterations that law proposes in the regime of Purposiveness must be carefully explained and justified, to the end that the people may be convinced that both moral and pragmatic considerations demand these changes and that they represent a truer expression of the society's fundamental authority relationship. Finally, skill must be exercised in exploiting the regime of Possibility: by effecting the changes gradually, persuading the groups benefited not to push their advantage too hard, cushioning any adverse effects that press on other groups, and installing the desired changes with the least possible strain on the social order.

Nonviolent civil disobedience in a just cause can be an extremely effective instrument for social reform—for bringing legal validity into truer accord with the essential terms of the authority relationship. But if it is to be so, law and the government must respond to it in a manner that is at once sensitive to its justified claims, realistic in its appraisal of how and how far these can be granted, and critical of any excessive demands it may advance. And even when all this is done, the issue may hang on the extent to which the changes sought impinge directly upon the daily lives and intimate concerns of people. The play of all of these factors is beautifully illustrated by two contrasting cases: the relative ease with which blacks achieved the right and the power to vote and the great difficulties that have arisen in implementing court-ordered busing to effect school integration.

This discussion can be rounded off with a brief reference to other modes of conduct that are related to but different from nonviolent civil disobedience. The most distantly connected member of this family is revolution. As we have seen, those who engage in nonviolent civil disobedience do not usually challenge the society's authority relationship at all (and certainly not its fundamental principles and values) but merely the interpretations of certain of its terms as these are embodied in the legally valid: they seek to bring the law, and therefore social practice, into closer accord with what they regard as the true meaning and intention of this relationship. On the other hand, the revolutionary denounces the authority relationship totally and vehemently: he rejects its very premises and purposes, and he seeks to create a new society. Seen in this light, it is easy to understand why so few revolutions succeed: if an authority relationship has been indigenous and enduring, it has permeated the structure of the society and the daily lives and habits of its people; to remake all this *de novo* is virtually impossible. The American Revolution was probably so successful because it actually changed so little: touching lightly if at all on the patterns of lived relationships that constitute the substructure of group living, it was little more than a transfer of power. The French Revolution had no such success because it tried to change too much that mattered too rapidly to be tolerated; it disrupted many of the most intimate lived relationships and many of the most important commitments on which people counted, and so it dried up the sources of the sense of obligation itself. Left in such a moral void, people returned to their old faith and ways, and the revolution suffered continual relapses.

Between these types of social conduct are two others of interest. First, there are those groups that turn to violence, disrupting the lives of other people and seeking to impede the operation of law and government. The difference here is primarily one of degree: these groups are more frustrated, less clear about their ultimate goals (they know what they do not want but not what they do want), and more estranged from the body politic. Situated thus, they feel little hope of attracting popular support for their cause; what they cannot win by persuasion they therefore seek to gain by force and intimidation. And if they cannot win, they will at least make sure that others lose. The quarrel of these groups is not with the authority relationship itself but with the government and the legal system, which they feel have perverted this relationship to such an extent that they have proved themselves incapable of truly interpreting and implementing it.

Second, there is the type that is usually described as "a-social" or "anti-social" and that has recently attracted the widest attention and given rise to the deepest perplexity. Since it lacks all cohesion or organization, this is not truly a group but simply a faceless mass of individuals who engage in apparently meaningless and random violence: they assault and kill people with no apparent motive; they destroy property with no hope of gain; they steal and loot even from their own kind. In short, their actions appear to be totally unreasonable and inexplicable— instances of sheer viciousness. But in terms of my earlier analysis, I think that these persons and their behavior can be readily understood. These are people who have had extremely limited opportunities (if any at all) to establish meaningful lived relationships with others: with parents, siblings, friends, schoolmates, church members, fellow workers, social clubs, and least of all with those remote entities, society, law, and government. Consequently, they feel no obligations to anyone or anything at all. These persons have suffered deprivation in the most elemental sense, for they have never had the occasion to make common cause with other persons. The world in general becomes not an enemy but something far more formless and meaningless: a stranger. The stranger is to all intents and purposes a nonperson, a mere accidental existence without character or value. It is before persons who have been thus deprived that the law, the government, and other social agencies are the most helpless. There is simply no way to get a grip on them. In contrast, those who are committed to civil disobedience and even revolution can be reasoned with: since they have known lived relationships, and even very intense ones, there are persons they respect, principles they believe in, causes to which they are dedicated. So they feel obligations. And this being the case, it is at least possible to persuade them that the authority relationship that they challenge can respond to the obligations they already acknowledge and that the content of the legally valid can be changed to accommodate the reforms they seek. Similarly, as I have previously argued, for most of us most of the time, the authority relationship is experienced and accepted as a force that permeates and supports a mass of more intimate and familiar relationships: we respect it because it reflects them. But for persons who have never experienced even the most natural and spontaneous lived relationships, the authority relationship is an empty abstraction and the legal system is an alien order. Such persons seek to change neither the law nor the compact on which it is based. For the alienated, neither of these has any significance nor merits obedience: they are not seen as having value in themselves or as serving values that are in the reach of these people. The authority relationship and especially the legal system are simply obdurate facts that one must expect to encounter and must guard against, like rain, cold, inflation, and hardhearted landlords. To try to change them is as pointless as trying to change the weather. And the only sort of respect that they merit is that which is paid to any physical phenomenon, such as a tornado or a speeding car, because of its power to harm. Law is meaningless to the alienated because it serves nothing that has meaning for them.

I would not maintain that this analysis, based on a theory of obligation, solves all of the problems of civil disobedience and so lays the issue to rest. I would merely claim that it furnishes a framework within which actual cases, infinitely various, can be resolved. As we have seen, when the government prepares its response to civil disobedience, it must consider both what should be done and what can be done to satisfy the claim that is urged; and each of these questions is complex. In this case, as in others discussed earlier, no theory can dictate a "correct" answer to a concrete problem: it can only supply the terms by reference to which a decision is to be made. In discussing this same issue of civil disobedience, Alexander Bickel comes to a conclusion very similar to that which I have advanced. He summarizes his view in this way:

Society is to judge, and the legal order does judge, formally or informally, whether the moral claim is plausible. And the response of the legal order to genuine acts of conscience, and even to widespread ones, varies: there is a calculus into which the moral intensity of the objector, the moral weight of his objection, and the moral foundation of the law all enter.[16]

I would like to think that the foregoing theory of legal obligation would be acceptable to both of those broad movements of thought known as positivism and idealism and that it would bridge the gap—if there is one—between them. It accepts the fundamental positivist thesis that the validity of law is an internal or formal question, quite distinct from its morality: invalidity and iniquity are different matters. On the other hand, this theory agrees with the idealists in their insistence that if law is to deserve our respect and win our allegiance, it must reflect our moral beliefs and commitments and must be faithful to the basic terms of the authority relationship that it serves.[17]

If my earlier account of Hart represents a correct reading, then he could perfectly accept the analysis of obligation that I have given—although whether he would is of course another question. I would also think that Fuller, who is commonly regarded as both the leading exponent of legal idealism and as Hart's doctrinal opposite, could accept my doctrine. The thrust of Fuller's latest major work is to clarify what he calls the "inner morality" of law, the procedural principles that a legal order must observe: and this analysis can best be understood as a further elucidation of Hart's rule of recognition.[18] And Fuller, of course, is principally known for his insistence that law is a "purposeful enterprise" that supports goals and values that lie beyond itself. Finally, Fuller lays great stress on the fact that our respect for law depends on our belief that it adheres to standards and serves ends of which we approve on other grounds. On this point, he says: "There is no doubt that a legal system derives its ultimate support from a sense of its being 'right'; and this sense itself derives from 'tacit expectations and acceptances.' "[19]

But certainly the contemporary thinker with whose views my own have the closest affinity is Alexander Bickel. In Bickel's final statement

[16] Bickel, *The Morality of Consent*, p. 104.

[17] As my earlier account suggests, I think that the positivists would themselves agree with this view. Indeed, I find it rather difficult to understand just what it is that the positivists and idealists are arguing about, unless it is words.

[18] Lon L. Fuller, *The Morality of Law* (New Haven: Yale University Press, 1964), Chapter II.

[19] Ibid., p. 138.

of his doctrine, the weight of the argument rests on the twin concepts of the "consent" of the governed and the "responsiveness" of the government to their "needs and interests." The people respect and accept law only if it meets the conditions expressed in these concepts; and when law does not meet them and the people reject its enactments, it is threatened with breakdown and needs to reconsider its position. Bickel's views of these matters can be briefly presented in his own words:

> What is above all important is consent—not a presumed theoretical consent but a continuous actual one, born of continual responsiveness. . . . To be responsive and to enjoy consent, government must register numerous expressions of need and interest. . . . Enactment and enforcement of law are sometimes only episodes, even if the single most important ones, in a long and varied process by which society, working through a number of institutions, manages to realize a given purpose. . . . Whenever a minority is sufficiently large or determined or, in the case of *Brown*, strategically placed, we do not quite have law. We must then generate a greater measure of consent, or reconsider our stance on the minority's position. We must, in such circumstances, resort to methods other than coercive law, methods of persuasion and inducement, appeal to reason and shared values, appeal to interest, and not only material but political interest.[20]

I believe that the essential similarity between this doctrine and that which I have embodied in the concepts of obligation and the authority relationship is close and obvious.

In conclusion, I would summarize this long discussion in these terms. It is my belief that the views of these thinkers and my own are in accord on two fundamental points: first, that the validity of any legal enactment, given an efficacious legal system, is an internal question, formal and procedural; second, that law can win public support and be effectively enforced only if it is perceived to support certain standards and purposes to which the people feel a strong antecedent attachment and allegiance. These extralegal factors are Austin's "principles or maxims," Hart's "simple truisms" and "natural necessities," Fuller's "expectations and acceptances," Bickel's "consent" and "needs and interests." It is the origin, status, and significance of these "factors" that I have hoped to clarify with my theory of obligation as based on lived relationships.

[20] Bickel, *The Morality of Consent*, pp. 100, 106, 110.

The principal contemporary figure whose views would seem to diverge from those just summarized is Professor Ronald Dworkin. I purposely say "would seem" because Dworkin's major work, *Taking Rights Seriously*, consists largely of essays written over a period of years and addressed to various issues.[21] The same ideas and doctrines are applied throughout, but due to the shift in contexts and emphasis one is not completely confident of interpreting them correctly. Dworkin would certainly accept the second of the preceding propositions. Indeed, he stresses this point so strongly that it conflicts with the first point and seems to entail its rejection. There are passages and arguments in these essays that clearly imply this, if they do not state it quite explicitly. Thus, in the title essay of his book, Dworkin says: "In our society a man does sometimes have the right, in the strong sense, to disobey a law" (p. 192); and again he says: "It (the government) must dispense with the claim that citizens never have the right to break its law" (p. 204). The meaning conveyed by these statements seems at best confused, if not contradictory. I presume that the law in question—whether of legislative, judicial, or executive origin—is legally valid: that it has been enacted in full accord with due process and established rules. Any such law, one would think, is assumed to be valid until it has been declared invalid, as a man is assumed to be innocent until he is proved guilty. Accepting this argument, Dworkin's position amounts to this: the government has the right to make the law in question, but then, since citizens have the right to break it, the government has the correlative duty not to enforce the law it has made. This seems a strange doctrine, one that would reduce many government acts to so many exercises in futility.

In the essay entitled "Civil Disobedience," Dworkin develops this doctrine a step further. Here he says: "In the United States, at least, almost any law which a significant number of people would be tempted to disobey on moral grounds would be doubtful—if not clearly invalid—on constitutional grounds as well. The Constitution makes our conventional political morality relevant to the question of validity" (p. 208). This statement contains at least two terms—"moral" and "our"—that are so ambiguous that it is difficult to construe the passage with any certainty. I presume that "moral" means at least strong convictions about what it is right and wrong, proper and improper, for government to do.

---

[21] Ronald Dworkin, *Taking Rights Seriously* (Cambridge, Mass.: Harvard University Press, 1977). All subsequent references to this source will appear in parentheses in the text.

"Our" poses greater problems: it implies a common set of moral beliefs and standards across all classes and regions of the country, and that is palpably contrary to fact. But waiving these difficulties, the doctrine enunciated here leads to some startling conclusions. To begin with, the Eighteenth Amendment to the Constitution, adopted and ratified through procedures set out in the Constitution, must have been "invalid" from the start, since millions of people disobeyed it on the unimpeachable moral ground that it was an unjustified invasion of privacy. But even more startling consequences follow. For this doctrine tells us that the same act in law will be "valid" in one part of the country and "invalid" in another at one and the same time. The original responses in the South and the North to the school desegregation decision in *Brown* are merely a striking example of a familiar phenomenon. In this same context, it is ironic (and heart warming to a Southerner!) that the busing orders that have followed on *Brown* are now "valid" in the South, which has largely accepted school integration, and altogether "invalid" in such a liberal Northern stronghold as Boston, where Judge Garrity's orders have invited disobedience, violence, and total disruption. I thoroughly agree with Dworkin—and so I am sure would the men whom I have previously discussed—that a law that is clearly morally evil does not merit respect or obedience and should be resisted. I further agree that a person is *morally* justified in breaking a law that outrages his conscience, although in making a statement of this latter type there is always the hidden assumption that the law in question is iniquitous and the man's conscience is sound, and neither of these need be the case. This is not a matter about which sweeping generalizations are very safe. Furthermore, the specific cases that Dworkin analyzes in developing these doctrines—freedom of speech, rights of minorities, the Vietnam draft evaders—are such as to win the sympathy of the reader and so to render the doctrine itself more persuasive: it is all too easy for a laudable end to trap us into adopting a dubious means to achieve it. But if I read Dworkin correctly, he is reintroducing the confusion between what the law is and what the law ought to be. Further, he is saying that when a "significant number" of people agree on this latter point, then the law that "is" is invalid. In short, Dworkin appears to be making legal validity a function of conformity to "our" views on "morality." And this seems to me to do nothing but muddy the waters that so many thinkers have labored long and hard to clear up.

CHAPTER XIII

LAW AS SOCIAL ENGINEERING

FROM ITS INCEPTION, law has been at work shaping and reshaping the social order. The manner and degree of this legal intervention have varied with time, place, and circumstance. But, as I have previously argued in Chapter VIII, when we survey the whole panorama of legal history we can clearly detect a general movement composed of three successive phases. These phases I have identified as conservative, liberalizing, and constructive. In the first phase, law is primarily concerned to protect and reinforce an established order that is threatened by disputes among individuals and by defiance of group rules and decisions. That is, law is largely preoccupied with what has been called the "trouble case." In the second phase, the emphasis shifts to law as an instrument of change. The social order becomes more complex and fluid, individuals assert themselves, and new forces seek new outlets. Law is now seen as providing the general rules and framework within which men are to be free to manage their own affairs and make their own arrangements. In its final phase, law assumes a positive and creative role. When private interests are left too much to themselves, initiative issues in exploitation, with injustice and disorder the result. So the task of law now becomes that of regulating the forces at play in society and organizing the social effort toward clearly defined goals. That is, law becomes an instrument for achieving a new social order.

This account is admittedly too clear-cut to be true to history, and as such it requires two qualifications in particular. This movement of the law has been irregular and cyclical, rather than steady and linear. In different societies at different times, and even in different fields in the same society at the same time, emphasis will be placed on one or the other of these legal functions. The law is continually correcting its own exaggerations, like a sailboat beating against the wind toward its destination. Further, as law enters its later phases and assumes new functions, it does not escape its old ones: it always has the three tasks of preserving continuity with the established order, providing for the emergence of new forces and purposes, and directing the passage toward a future order. As I have more than sufficiently emphasized, the being of law is always three dimensional, as it seeks to achieve a balance between the regimes of Necessity, Possibility, and Purposiveness.

But underlying these shifts and reversals, the general movement of the law has been toward an increasingly active role in the life of society. The principle of the sovereignty of law has long been established: law is recognized as the final locus of authority, handing down decisions that permit no appeal and supervising all other institutions and activities, subject only to rules and standards of its own making. But it is only recently that law is beginning to assert, and men are coming to accept, the more sweeping claim of omnicompetence.[1] Law is now intervening in areas that it has hitherto steered clear of; it is imposing its opinions and principles upon other social bodies; it is settling questions that were formerly thought of as being political, economic, or moral, rather than legal, in nature; and it is issuing detailed directives about the ordering of various aspects of society and social life. From being ultimate but relatively unobtrusive, law has become pervasive.

This is a familiar story that has attracted a large literature. I have touched upon it in general terms in several earlier chapters. Although it is not my intention—and it is not within my competence—to discuss the details of this process of legal proliferation, there are two developments that are particularly striking and important that I do want to examine. One of these is the movement known as "social engineering," which proposes to treat law as a practical science and to employ the legal apparatus, in close association with other sciences, to organize and direct systematic programs of social reform on a large scale. The other is the significant extension that the courts have recently given to the content and reach of the concept of legal rights. Many of the problems that confront the first of these developments have been anticipated in the discussions of Chapters IX and X, so I will deal with this development rather briefly. The second has not received the attention it deserves, so I will examine it closely and at some length in the next two chapters.

Seen in historical perspective, there is nothing radically novel in the present close association of the legal and scientific communities, nor in the proposal to apply scientific methods in effecting social reform. Those charged with the administration of law and the governance of the realm have always sought help and guidance from whatever source offered any promise, whether this was the gods, oracles, auguries, or experts. The

---

[1] It might be fairer and more accurate to say that this role is being forced upon legal institutions against their will and by forces beyond their control. I will examine this issue carefully in my final chapters.

king's council in England, like its analogues elsewhere, was the primary instrument through which policies were formulated and power exerted; and it was largely composed of men who were knowledgeable in the fields that mattered then, expecially war, finance, and religion. Consequent upon the dislocations caused by the Black Death, as early as the middle of the fourteenth century there were legal efforts to control wages, prices, and the movement of labor. Parliament and the courts were engaged with these same problems during the Elizabethan era, using what power and skill they had to solve them. The economic, social, and political reformers of more recent times, from the Mercantilists through the Utilitarians to Marx and Engels and the Fabian Society, all thought of their proposals as the application of sound scientific theories and practices—however different their interpretations of these may have been. This intention received a fresh impetus and even more detailed programs from the adherents of sociological jurisprudence, the jurisprudence of interests, and legal realism in Europe and America in the early twentieth century, under the leadership of such men as Ehrlich, Duguit, Pound, and others.

But the impact of these schools has so far been rather fragmentary and episodic, moving in diverse directions and disjointed efforts. The only plausible exception is the Communist experiment, and it is a questionable one. Thus it is only in strictly contemporary times, and even more emphatically with reference to the future, that we find it being seriously proposed that we should plan and execute social reforms on the model of scientific and technological enterprises. Such phrases as "social engineering," "science in the service of society," "the technological revolution," and "the planned society" have been very much in the air. The intent of these phrases can be stated in either of two ways: the legal apparatus should take advantage of scientific knowledge and technological efficiency to effect desired social reforms, or scientific and technical experts should employ law as an instrument through which to realize their blueprint of the good society. Which meaning is intended will depend of course on whether one belongs to the legal or scientific community, and the change of emphasis is obviously important, as it determines who acts as principal and who as agent.

Three factors have operated in unplanned conjunction to bring this movement of thought toward its climax in action. One of these has been the high refinement of what is widely familiar, even if not widely understood, as "scientific method"—the techniques of enquiry, explanation, and application through which man has vastly extended his theoretical and practical mastery of the world. Science has achieved such spectacular successes in so many different areas that it has bewitched our minds, and we come to feel that its methods are of universal relevance and can be applied in any context whatsoever. If the scientist can solve so many problems and overcome such diverse difficulties, it seems only natural and proper to call on him to cure our social ills.

The second of these factors has been the steady extension of the scope and effectiveness of law. As law assumes its normative and constructive functions with increasing self-consciousness and confidence, it emerges as the dominant principle of social order. As this occurs, the legal apparatus grows in size and power, becomes more highly centralized, and acquires a large measure of independence: rather than passively waiting for other social groups and forces to act upon it to effect their purposes, it projects goals that it deems desirable and establishes programs to achieve them. Legislative, executive, and judicial bodies now vie with one another in initiating and implementing social policies. As a result, the legal apparatus appears to be available as an instrument that can move society as it wills.

The third factor in this situation is of course the acceleration of the reform movement itself. This exhibits itself as an intense effort to make the material advantages of the technologically and politically advanced societies available to all men, where now they are the privilege of a favored few. The workings of this aspiration in established societies are various and familiar: the civil rights movement; equal opportunity and fair employment legislation designed to improve and protect the economic position of women, blacks, and other minority groups; action to extend the availability of medical care and mental health facilities; such poverty programs as public housing and food stamps; the successes and accomplishments of Labor, Socialist, and Communist parties in many European countries; and all of this culminating in the concept of the state itself as a gigantic welfare agency. This aspiration asserts itself even more dramatically in the so-called "newly emergent" and "underdeveloped" nations of the Third World, since there the process of reform has further to go and less to work with.

Commencing their development largely independently, these three movements have mutually fueled one another and have finally come to exert their forces in the same direction. As scientists extend their knowledge and mastery of the world, simple curiosity (the passion for understanding) gives way to more worldly concerns. Theoretical interests and advances certainly continue, but the practical impulse now moves to the fore. Knowledge, after all, is power: and when the power that is generated by scientific knowledge becomes so vast, it is natural that the men who have unleashed it should want a voice in determining the uses to which it is put. The achievements of the scientist give him foresight and confidence: he feels that he can anticipate the problems we are preparing for ourselves, as well as the difficulties in which we are involved; and he is sure of his ability to overcome the latter and prevent the former. Given these attitudes, then, as attention shifts from the conquest of nature to the mastery of man and his affairs, a vast array of technological experts is ready with advice about the regulation of all aspects of human behavior and the social order.

The legal community has undergone a similar experience. Those who are in any way concerned with the law, whether as legislators, judges, private attorneys, or staff members of administrative agencies, have seen a great increase in the uses to which the legal apparatus can be put and the power that it can exert. Like their counterparts in science, these men of the law have supreme confidence in the institutions they command and stand ready to undertake any task that commends itself to them.

Enter now our third factor. As the reform movement intensifies and proliferates, it seeks the means to achieve its ends. It must find allies and instruments that can transform its dreams into realities. Commanding the powerful tools of the legal apparatus and the scientific method, the men of law and science seem perfectly cast for this role. In principle and on paper, the terms of this alliance are perfectly simple and straightforward: the reform movement—more exactly, the different reform groups with their different concerns and purposes—would define the goals of social action; appropriate scientific experts would examine these proposals, weigh them against the technical and material resources available, and recommend the measures best calculated to achieve them; the relevant legal bodies would hear these requests and counsels, pass judgment on their substantive validity and procedural practicality, prescribe the necessary arrangements and courses of action, and see that these edicts were enforced. In sum, reform would propose, science would plan, and law would dispose.

In practice, and amid the welter of the social scene, things are rarely this simple. All too often quarrels erupt among the partners to this alliance, both within and between the parties. What one element in a group wants, another element opposes: minorities seek privileged access to jobs, while unions seek to protect the economic position of their members; biologists recommend environmental measures that economists assert to be disastrous; and to support programs of reform, Congress appropriates funds that the president promptly impounds.

As each seeks to assert its dominance, there are even more confrontations between these major participants. Supported by the doctrine of the sovereignty of law, the legal apparatus is supreme in theory; and it can always have the last word in fact if it can muster the confidence and courage to assert itself. But this theoretical supremacy is continually threatened by the pressure of reform groups and the prestige of scientists. Those who seek particular reforms and who are persuaded of the justice of their cause do not hesitate to appeal to massive protests and demonstrations, strikes, publicity campaigns, civil disobedience, and finally violence, if they feel that law is unresponsive to their claims. Intimidated by this show of force and by the disruption that it threatens, the legal apparatus will succumb and acquiesce against its own best judgment.

It is in a more subtle fashion that the sovereignty of law is eroded by the prestige of science. Scientists are far too civilized and sophisticated to show disrespect for the law, much less to defy it. But the sheer mass of their knowledge, their proved ability to explain and control events, and the assurance with which they speak carry tremendous weight. So when scientists predict catastrophe from certain courses of action—or from inaction—and recommend other courses, men of the law are easily overawed. The most extreme and familiar case of this phenomenon is the surrender of legal independence when faced with the testimony of the military technologists. But biologists, economists, sociologists, psychologists, criminologists, demographers, and even educators can exert an impressive influence on legal decisions. When scientists promise desired results, or predict dire consequences, the legal apparatus lends an attentive ear. By those who must make final decisions, few things are more to be feared than an expert's "I told you so."

Given such powerful forces as those of law, science, and reform, it is inevitable that disputes should occur over the issue of who is master and who is man. Indeed, it is the spirit of amity and the intention to cooperate that exist among these three that is surprising. This spirit and intention have been steadily on the rise and are now approaching flood tide. More specifically, the conviction is growing that it is only ignorance that has hitherto frustrated the efforts of social reform through law: if we only knew enough about the workings of human nature and the social order, we could control and fashion these as we wanted. The various sciences can now afford us the knowledge and power to repair our deficiencies. So all we need to do is to apply scientific and technological methods, and through law we will be able to achieve the social reforms that we seek.

It is this conviction, fostered in this way, that lies behind such phrases as "social engineering" and "the planned society." And this conviction merits careful consideration: it is certainly reasonably grounded, both in principle and in fact. The modern temper is unabashedly naturalistic: man is a part of nature, and nature is all of a piece. Accepting this view, there should in principle be no limitation to the power of science to understand, and of technology to control, the course of events throughout nature. The human context is no exception. The phenomena here are more complex, particularly as regards the causal factors involved. But that is to be regarded as a difference of degree, not of kind. Further, the actual accomplishments of science and technology in recent years do much to confirm this principle. The knowledge garnered by the theoretician has been translated into the power of the technologist, and this in turn has been used to bring about radical changes in such diverse and important areas of human concern as agricultural methods, the production and sale of goods, the regulation of wages and prices, medical care, mental health, the determination of criminal guilt and the treatment of criminals, the learning process, human motivation, and the control of behavior and even of emotional states. Success has varied from case to case, and whether the changes are also improvements is sometimes debatable. But practice has followed hard on the footsteps of principle. What is science fiction at one moment is in a short while scientific fact. It would thus be foolish to maintain that there are certain areas that science cannot reach or to propose that it should be disbarred from these areas even if it could reach them.

But it would be just as foolish to commit ourselves wholeheartedly to science and the technique of "social engineering" without a clear realization of what we are doing. The very familiarity of the term science can easily disguise a large unfamiliarity with the thing itself. As in many other cases, we reify and personify instead of thinking concretely. Science becomes for us the clean-cut young man in the spotless white jacket working away in a gleaming metalic and ceramic laboratory, just as law becomes the blindfolded figure of Justice holding her scales in even balance. We substitute symbol for reality and delude ourselves. The achievements of science breed the belief that it is an instrument of knowledge and control that is unlimited and unchallengeable: we come to think that through it we can know and do anything and that there are no other reputable ways of knowing and doing things. Similarly, as I have already indicated, we are coming to regard law as not only sovereign but also omnicompetent. These views are dangerously simplistic. As we have seen, law is in fact an elaborate substantive and procedural apparatus, administered by fallible men and facing stringent limitations upon its effectiveness. In the same way, science is in fact an intricate conceptual and methodological apparatus, created and operated by fallible men and having its own built-in limitations. So in using science, we limit ourselves to investigating and knowing only those phenomena that conform to its assumptions. And we can control these phenomena only to the extent that they can be manipulated in definite ways. Like any instruments, science and technology set the conditions of their use. What we need to do is to expose these conditions and the degree to which programs of social reform through law can satisfy them.

Such phrases as "social engineering" and "the planned society" at once suggest an analogy with the procedures of the applied sciences. Certain goals and accomplishments are put forward as desirable by various reform groups. Appropriate scientific and technical experts are called in to recommend plans to achieve these reforms. After due deliberation, the legal apparatus, through its legislative, judicial, executive, and administrative elements, takes the steps to implement these plans and realize these purposes insofar as it deems them good and reasonable. Thus, the NAACP and other organizations press hard for improved educational opportunities for minority groups; psychologists and sociologists urge that the only way to achieve this goal is by integration of the schools; the courts accept this argument and issue the requisite orders. Almost everyone is anxious to control inflation—though always with the proviso that the sources of his own income be excepted; violent debate ensues, but those economists supporting wage and price controls win out; Congress listens, and legislation is enacted. There is widespread recognition that population growth must be slowed, and women add the argument that they have the right to determine the uses to which their bodies will be put; medical experts give advice regarding the efficacy and dangers of contraception and abortion; the law acts to liberalize and regulate these practices. These examples could be multiplied endlessly.[2]

All of this seems strikingly analogous to the ways in which the scientist and technologist master nature for man's benefit. The agronomist tells us: "If you will plant these hybrid seeds, and use these fertilizers

---

[2] Herbert Spencer cites the case (I have no idea with what accuracy) of a government that faced a similar problem: poor families were having too many children for whom they could not care. The government sought to solve the problem by the more primitive method of declaring that a couple could not be married until they had an assured minimum income. Spencer gloats over the outcome: there were as many indigent children as ever, but now they were also illegitimate.

and insecticides, then you will increase your yield of grain." We follow his advice and eat better. The public health officer tells us: "If you will follow these dietary and sanitary directions, your health will improve." We do as he says and feel better. The chemical engineer tells us: "If you will make clothes of these synthetic fibers, both their appearance and their durability will be improved." We do so and dress better. Along comes the social reformer, accompanied by his scientific entourage, urging the law to accept his goals and implement his proposals. And he says: "If you will reorder society along these lines, regulate human relations in these ways, establish these new arrangements, and permit and prohibit certain modes of behavior, then the quality of life will be improved."

This analogy is obvious and tempting. But although it may seem to be a gift horse, affording us a tested and accredited technique of reform, we need to examine it more closely. For the scientific method has internal demands and limitations that determine both its reach and its results, and it behooves us to be well aware of these, and to take careful account of them, in applying this analogy to the implementation of programs of social action. To this end, it is necessary to look briefly at certain of the more critical conditions that must be met if the scientist and technologist are to be able to apply themselves successfully to the solution of our social problems. These conditions overlap and intermingle to a considerable extent, so I will discuss them serially before turning to the crucial question of how well the law as "social engineer" can meet them.

Probably the most obvious requirement of sound scientific work is that we have a clear idea of the terms we employ, as regards both their connotation and denotation. We must be able to define our concepts and identify their referents—the actual things, relations, events, and situations with which we are attempting to deal. The agronomist can tell us exactly what seeds to plant, where to plant them, what fertilizers to use, and how much water and sun are needed; and he can then predict quite closely what our yield will be. The chemical or civil engineer, the nuclear physicist, the medical geneticist, the computer expert, and the public health officer can do the same for their respective fields. These efforts vary in their degree of exactitude and their margin of error, and even the best of them sometimes misfire egregiously. But if the scientist and technologist are to function effectively, they must know with considerable precision and detail what factors they are dealing with and what they are trying to accomplish.

A second equally important requirement is the ability to control the elements and situations with which one is concerned. The great advantage of the laboratory—and of such rough equivalents as the testing ground, the agricultural experimental station, and the isolated population—is that it permits the scientist to carry out his work in an artificially closed environment where he can regulate at will the various factors and processes that are involved. It is only in this way that causal factors can be disentangled, that they can be studied separately and in different conjunctions, and that their relative significance can be determined. And until this is known, one cannot predict, much less control, the course of events.

There is a third consideration that is closely related to the preceding. If scientific techniques are to be successfully applied to the clarification and solution of social problems, it is highly important that we be able to make a clear-cut distinction between ends and means. Wanting more and better food, we take pains to ensure a proper employment of seeds, soil, water, and human effort. Seeking to eliminate certain endemic diseases, we see that everyone is inoculated against them. Wishing to save human lives and expedite travel, we build carefully engineered super highways. Science can work wonders when ends are clear and compelling and the necessary means are readily procured and manipulated. And it is the essence of straightforward engineering practice that we employ materials to the fate of which we are indifferent and that we exploit these for purposes that are obvious and unchallenged.

The preceding account clearly is not (as it is not intended to be) an exhaustive catalogue of the conditions of successful scientific work; but as it touches essential matters, it is sufficient for my present purposes. And this brings us to the critical question: To what extent can law conceived as social engineering meet these conditions? Before broaching this, it is only fair to point out that no engineering project conforms perfectly to this paradigm: there are always discrepancies between our sharply and arbitrarily defined concepts and actual things and events; when translated into action, the most careful experiments and studies turn up unanticipated causes and consequences; and what the engineer wants to treat as a means, to be manipulated as he wills, turns out to be an end in itself for some of the people affected. A bridge changes the flow of traffic, agricultural machinery threatens the family farm, and inoculation impinges on religious convictions. These uncertainties and surprises are inevitable, for no matter how physical may be the material the engineer manipulates and the product he creates, the final intention of his work is its human utilization. To change the physical world is to change man's lived world; and to change this is to change man. In this important sense, *all* engineering is "social" engineering.

So social engineering in the restricted sense, as the employment of law to create the planned society, is not a unique case; it differs only in degree, not in kind, from the traditional and familiar kinds of engineering that operate more directly upon the material world and only indirectly upon human behavior and relations. But this difference of degree is more than great enough to raise serious questions and problems. To see this, we need but measure the extent to which social engineering through law can satisfy the conditions set by scientific method. As we examine these in order, I think it becomes clear that the lawyer-engineer has progressively greater difficulty in meeting them. I will trace this course quite briefly, as we here tread on ground that was covered very fully in Chapters IX and X.

Difficulties appear at the very start of this enterprise, when the attempt is made to define and identify the factors to be dealt with: the forces and interests at issue, established relationships and the changes sought in them, the various needs to be considered, the ends to be sought and the means at hand, competing claims and available resources. The human and social actualities with which we seek to come to grips are complex and elusive, and the concepts through which we hope to grasp them are vague and ambiguous, with the same words carrying quite different meanings for different persons. We feel very intensely the defects of the present: its difficulties and problems, its inequities and deprivations, the oppression of some and the powerlessness of others. And we long with an equal intensity for the cure of these ills: for peace, security, happiness, and justice. But we are largely unable to specify any of these elements with satisfactory precision and clarity. It was in 1954 that the Supreme Court ruled that school "desegregation" must proceed with "all deliberate speed." Both of these critical terms certainly had some meaning in the minds of the justices: they articulated intentions that were meant to be implemented by school boards under the supervision of lower courts. But the intervening twenty years have not settled the effective meanings of these goals, still less specified the ways to achieve them. Is busing required? If so, over what distances and across what political divisions? When is segregation de facto and when de jure? Must student and teacher assignments reflect a "balance" of racial groups? And while Secretary Weinberger seemed to think that he knew the difference between "justified opposition" and "bigoted defiance," no one else does, and the evidence strongly suggests that for him the difference was defined partly by the Mason and Dixon Line and partly by the political power of various cities. To take a more recent case, the proposed Equal Rights for Women Amendment seems at first blush to be simple, innocuous, and eminently just, but as its implications are drawn out, and its impact considered, numerous uncertainties and problems arise.

And this is not the end of the matter. For when we do discover what we mean—when we specify present ills and future cures—we encounter disagreement and opposition from every quarter. Indeed, the more closely we spell out actual defects, desirable goals, and alternative courses, the more acrimonious become the disputes. As long as we confine ourselves to the rhetoric of generalities and abstractions, we all agree that things are bad and something must be done. But as soon as we begin to translate these discontents and their remedies into the concrete terms that action in the real world demands, agreement ceases. Everyone is for "integration"—until they realize that this means the busing of their children, a different complexion to their neighborhoods, and increased competition for employment. Everyone wants to curb "inflation"—until they are asked to lower their standard of living. Everyone is for "equality"—until they are told to forfeit the places that they have earned to others who are less qualified but have been underprivileged. Everyone is for "clean air and water"—until their jobs or profits are threatened.

One cause of these contradictions is the simple fact of human egoism. People are voluble in their support of those abstract goals, "the common good" and "the general welfare," until they discover that the promotion of these impinges upon that far more concrete goal, their own "pursuit of happiness." Then reasons cancel out, intentions counter one another, people become confused and unsettled, and emotion easily takes over. But even more troublesome than this is the inscrutability of both social interaction and human purposes. The terms we use to identify the deficiencies we feel and the reforms we propose are loose and slippery. Take such words as alienation and amnesty; discrimination and integration; recession, unemployment, and wage and price controls; underprivileged, equal protection, and compensatory justice; clean air standards and adequate health care. We know what these mean, in the sense that we can give conceptual definitions of them. But the minute we try to translate these concepts into action—to cure the ills and bring about the situations that they seem to depict so clearly—these meanings evaporate. *Alienation* and *underprivileged* refer to human conditions that are deeply felt and resented. *Amnesty* and *compensatory justice* name moral ideals that have a wide appeal. But when we set out to correct these conditions and realize these ideals, it turns out that they entail consequences and side effects that people did not anticipate and do not want. What reform achieves is often very different from what it intended. And what people desire often proves undesirable when it is achieved. We have all laughed at the man who, goaded beyond endurance, blurted out, "How can I know what I mean until I say it?" But this seeming absurdity becomes literally true when applied to many of our projects for social reform. For in this context we do not really know what we mean until we do it, and then we are often surprised and even shocked by what we have done.

These uncertainties make it very difficult to control the course and outcome of social reforms. Even when the law can formulate its intention in detailed programs, these are often frustrated by the recalcitrance of men and the intractability of social institutions. The problems that arise in this effort have been discussed at length in Chapters IX and X, so I will here touch on them only lightly. Part of the trouble arises from the sheer multiplicity, complexity, and elusiveness of the variables that are involved—the elements with which reform must deal. These are intermingled in such intricate ways that they defy our best efforts to disentangle them and measure their relative causal importance. Economics is the most sophisticated of the social sciences, with its pretensions to exactitude expressed in tables, graphs, and computer print-outs. Yet when a score of economists are gathered together, they cannot even agree in their estimation of the present situation, still less on what should be done to correct it. When accord is reached on a course of action, further troubles arise: the necessary physical resources may not be available; if they are, their use for the proposed reform may divert them from other desirable efforts; and institutions that feel threatened by the reform will erect obstacles against it. In short, as it was put before, the legal apparatus finds that it has at best a tenuous control of the instrumental values that are conditions for achieving the final values that it has in view.

But these difficulties pale before those that are created by the people affected by reform. Men may not have the intellectual and moral qualities that are needed to achieve the proposed reform and to profit from it. The temper of their minds and characters may be corrupted under the new conditions: liberty offers as many challenges as it does opportunities, and security may release energy or encourage sloth. People may be unwilling to make the effort that the reform demands: they ask for the fruits of reform, not for its disciplines and duties. Even when the reform is established, it may disappoint the high expectations it has aroused; and it is very apt to entail the loss of other goods and enjoyments. As we have seen, the attainment of value entails a corresponding sacrifice of value. For all of these reasons, there is a constant threat that people will withdraw from active participation in the reform movement or that they will begin to resist it; and since the human population is by far the most important factor in any program of reform, the leaders of the reform are continually losing their grip on the processes they are trying to control. The movement then gets out of hand and either relapses or goes off on a tangent.

We are thus brought to recognize that it is extremely difficult to know in advance either what reform will actually issue in or what people really want. We find that we cannot identify with any real precision the ends that reform seeks, nor can we adequately master the means that we employ toward these ends. And just when we think that we have repaired these deficiencies and have achieved the requisite clarity and control, we come upon the culminating paradox. For now we discover that these ends and means merge into and interfere with one another. The factors that we distinguish in our planning as ends and means—as intrinsic and extrinsic values—turn out in fact to be indistinguishable. The practices and possessions, the principles and positions that those engaged in the reform movement regard simply as a means, and that they want the people to surrender or modify in order to enhance the quality of social life, reveal themselves as constituting for these people vital elements in the good life as they conceive it and pursue it as their final end.

The major source of such conflicts lies in the different points of view of those who are promoting the reform and those who are affected by it. The former analyze the situation objectively; the latter live it subjectively. To the men of science and the law, there is a problem of "social engineering" to be solved. To the people involved, the "solution" constitutes a radical change in their lived world and so in their mode of life. What the first treat as a neutral value and seek to use as the means to some further end, the second view as a positive and immediate value, a source of rich and complex satisfactions. To a federal district court, a local school may appear simply as a convenient site to integrate the races and thus to promote racial equality and harmony. But to the parents and their children, this same school is a focal point of their neighborhood and their community activities—its local character is an inherent value. Similarly, to various federal agencies, farms are merely producers of abundant food supplies and hence sources of a favorable balance of trade, while to very many families, these same farms are integral and essential elements in a way of life that they deeply cherish.

What is here brought out very sharply is that we cannot break up human existence into separate elements and episodes, we cannot deal with one aspect of individual or social life without affecting other aspects, and we cannot subordinate some of life's activities and pursuits to others as means to ends. What frustrates all such efforts is the integrity and cohesiveness of life itself, which rejects any sharp separation of ends and means, of form and content, of purposes to be achieved and programs of reform to achieve these purposes. This is to say that the happiness men seek is not a pot of gold that lies at the end of their efforts; it is an accompaniment of these efforts themselves. As Aristotle put it long ago, happiness is not a state or condition: it consists in activity. And all of the activities in which we engage, and hence all of the varied supports on which these activities rely, are shot through with both intrinsic and instrumental values: they are sources of immediate enjoyment, and at the same time they serve purposes beyond themselves. Finally, these two modes of value are not distinct elements, or constituents, of the activities in which they inhere: rather, they are facets or aspects that these activities exhibit, depending on the perspective from which we view them.

With regard to these issues, it is interesting to look back to the attitude of Roscoe Pound when, some fifty odd years ago, he introduced the concept of social engineering to a prominent place in legal thought. When we now read what Pound then wrote, it strikes us as singularly optimistic and almost simplistic. All of Pound's emphasis is on elucidating and extolling the power of law as a tool that the social engineer can use in his task of satisfying human wants and interests. When questions arise of conflicts among these interests and of the difficulties that these conflicts create for jurists, Pound brushes them aside in a cursory manner. Conceived as social engineering, the methods and criteria of legal action are defined in pragmatic terms; theoretical issues are dismissed as hypothetical, or at worst as looming only in the distant future, and so are regarded with impatience. The jurist as social engineer has immediate practical problems to solve, and he cannot be distracted by subtle philosophical disputes.

This attitude comes through very clearly in Pound's Storrs Lectures of 1921-1922. He writes:

> For present purposes I am content to see in legal history the record of a continually wider recognizing and satisfying of human wants or claims or desires through social control; a more embracing and more effective securing of social interests; a continually more complete and effective elimination of waste and precluding of friction in human enjoyment of the goods of existence—in short, a continually more efficacious social engineering.

Difficulties arise chiefly in connection with criteria of value. If we say that interests are to be catalogued or inventoried, that they are then to be valued, that those which are found to be of requisite value are to be recognized legally and given effect within limits determined by the valuation, so far as inherent difficulties in effective legal securing of interests will permit, the question arises at once, How shall we do this work of valuing? Philosophers have devoted much ingenuity to the discovery of some method of getting at the intrinsic importance of various interests, so that an absolute formula may be reached in accordance wherewith it may be assured that the weightier interests intrinsically shall prevail. But I am skeptical as to the possibility of an absolute judgment. We are confronted at this point by a fundamental question of social and political philosophy. I do not believe the jurist has to do more than recognize the problem and perceive that it is presented to him as one of securing all social interest so far as he may, of maintaining a balance or harmony among them that is compatible with the securing of all of them.[3]

This casual optimism contrasts sharply with the powerful soul-searching and bitter divisiveness that present-day jurists experience in trying to settle these same conflicts of interest. Social engineering through law is indeed a fairly simple enterprise as long as conditions are stable and a dominant class has effective control of the legal apparatus and the social order. This class settles disputes among its members by its own internal procedures, reaches agreement about its paramount interests, and calls upon law merely to implement the policies that it sets. Under these circumstances, the demands set by scientific methodology can be met quite satisfactorily. The dominant class has a clear idea of the conditions it wants to promote, the relations it needs to maintain with other groups and forces, the patterns of behavior that must be maintained, and the distribution of goods and benefits—the division of the spoils—that it needs to make if peace and order are to be secured. Further, since this dominant class has great economic and political power and since it largely controls the media of communication, it is able to exert a pervasive influence throughout the social order and to gain the acquiescence of other groups, whether through force, persuasion, or ap-

---

[3] Roscoe Pound, *An Introduction to the Philosophy of Law* (New Haven: Yale University Press, 1922). The first paragraph is found on p. 99 of Pound's text; the remainder of the passage is from pp. 95-96.

peasement. Finally, there is here no problem in distinguishing means and ends or in subordinating the one to the other: the interests of the dominant class define the ends to be sought, and the human and physical resources of the society are treated as means to be used in the attainment of these ends.

I think that this is a passably accurate picture of the social situation and the psychological atmosphere at the time when Pound was writing. And his casual dismissal of the difficulties that the jurist faces in making value decisions reflects these conditions. Given the actual state of society and Pound's own position in the social order, it was neither naive nor callous of him to assume that interests could be balanced and wants harmonized without the need for conflict or sacrifice. From where he stood, and what he saw, it was quite reasonable to draw three important conclusions: that the ends men sought—their wants, desires, claims, and demands—could be clearly defined and distinguished; that the available means were adequate to secure these ends without disproportionate sacrifice of any of them; and, most importantly, that the legal apparatus is capable of indefinite development to meet any demands imposed upon it. Situated as Pound was, it was natural for him to be impatient of theoretical quibbles: the jurist as social engineer had pressing concrete problems to solve and the tools with which to solve them, and he could not wait for final answers to ultimate questions—which he did not need anyway.

But in a time of social ferment, with power more evenly distributed, with the spread of egalitarian ideas, and with factions at odds with one another, the present situation is radically different. The theoretical chickens have now come home to roost, and they are making a shambles of our comfortable pragmatic farmyard. Different reform groups attach different meanings to the same term, so that what appear verbally to be common interests and shared values turn out in fact to be conflicting purposes and contradictory claims; what the social engineer proposes to treat as a means, the people affected regard as an end in itself; and the legal apparatus finds it difficult to disentangle the mesh of causes and effects with which it must deal and even more difficult to enlist the popular support that it needs.

As these conditions intensify, social engineering through law falls more and more under the sway of the law of diminishing returns. The demands set by scientific methodology become increasingly difficult to meet, and in its efforts to meet them the legal apparatus gets caught in a vicious circle. In the attempt to define its goals and policies with adequate precision, it continually falls into the fallacies of simple and single cause. Due to this narrowing of its view, unanticipated consequences and undesirable side-effects occur with mounting frequency. In trying to mitigate these, law is led into fields and up against problems with which it is not prepared to cope. Legal activity thus becomes steadily more frenetic in its input and more uncertain in its outcome.

While recognizing that there are limits to what law can successfully undertake, Pound nevertheless felt that these limits were indefinitely expansible as law developed improved tools and techniques. In summing up his views, he says this: "Better legal machinery extends the field of legal effectiveness as better machinery extends the field of industrial effectiveness."[4] But I think this is the wrong approach; or perhaps more accurately, it is by itself an inadequate solution to the problem. In the years since Pound wrote, the arsenal of the law has been greatly increased and strengthened. We have seen such developments as administrative law, arbitration and mediation procedures, a proliferation of government bureaus, vast improvements in legislative committee staffs, and class action suits, to name but a few. But still the difficulties multiply and the results disappoint.

I believe that the solution lies in a different direction. It is not—or not only—more and better legal machinery that we need. Rather, it is more effective action by other social forces and institutions, directed toward assuring a stable and coherent social order in which there is a sense of shared values and purposes, agreement on the priority to be assigned to various social goals and needs, accepted standards of behavior, and an acknowledgment by all of the duties that go with the rights that are claimed. That is, what is required is thorough preparatory work by other social agencies that are more basic than law. As I have argued throughout, law is only a supplemental principle of order. Its success depends upon the successful efforts of other principles of order. As matters now stand, the legal apparatus is being asked to do too much with too little support: because other institutions, such as the family, the church, and the school, are not functioning as they once did to develop character and define conduct, law is having to deal with a social substance that approaches the condition of Aristotle's prime matter, without form or limits. This is to impose an impossible task. Contemporary democratic societies are becoming so torn by internal differences and strife that their domestic legal systems are confronted with a situation that approximates that faced by international law. Such a situation can have but two outcomes: law becomes either repressive or ineffectual. For law can operate effectively only within a community—it cannot by itself create one. So

[4] Ibid., p. 97.

it is not so much internal improvement of the "machinery" of law that is needed as an improved performance by other pieces of social machinery. And, along with this, law must recognize its own limitations, and it must exhibit a willingness to let these other institutions do their own work in their own way. If law is to secure the competent assistance that it so badly needs, it must cease to assert its own omnicompetence. There is fault on both sides in this matter, and it is as important for law to moderate its claims as for other institutions to increase their contribution. This is a theme to which I shall return more fully in my final chapter, but now I want to consider a quite different issue that is raised by the idea of law as social engineering.[5]

I have heretofore been dealing with the obstacles that human nature and the social order present to scientific treatment and to programs of social engineering through law. I now want to turn my attention to the converse of this issue and to consider the danger we run when we set out to treat men and societies—the human and social undertakings—in scientific terms. The essence of this danger is, quite simply, that we may permit our adherence to the methodology of science to control our substantive view of the entities and processes that we seek to understand and reform. So, having examined the *methodological conditions* that science sets, I now want to examine the *substantive commitments* that science demands.

It is a truism that science imposes its own terms upon any subject matter with which it deals. When we approach any facts and problems with the scientific intention, the first thing we must do is interpret or translate these things in terms that are congenial to the scientific manner of thinking and doing. It is neither appropriate nor necessary to my present purpose to engage in a careful analysis of the conceptual apparatus of science: all that is required is a citation of the more prominent and agreed-upon items in this catalogue. With that reservation, I think it can safely be said that the scientific creed includes the following significant tenets: it regards all things as manifestations of mass-energy, as having a precise space-time location, as being closely bound together by a causal nexus, as consisting of elements within an antecedent pattern of order and connection or system of relationships, and as leading existences that

---

[5] Among contemporary legal writers, Alexander Bickel and Roberto Unger in particular have stressed the importance of community as the necessary milieu and support of law. See Bickel, *The Morality of Consent* (New Haven: Yale University Press, 1975), Chapter I; and Unger, *Knowledge and Politics* (New York: Free Press, 1975) and *Law in Modern Society* (New York: Free Press, 1976), *passim*, with references in the indices.

are strict functions of their essences and their situations. That is, science describes a world that is already complete and determinate, in which individual things are engulfed by their surroundings, in which present and future merely unroll the past, and from which effective initiative and origination are excluded.

This brief account is admittedly a simplification: in the hands of its best advocates, science is a great deal more subtle and sophisticated than this rehearsal allows. But I think it is nevertheless the case that when we approach any subject matter with the intention of dealing with it scientifically, we do tend to interpret it in the terms outlined above. This is the conceptual schema that served as the original foundation on which the spectacular development of the physical (or natural) sciences was built, so it was adopted as the master model when the social and human disciplines set out to become sciences. And since social scientists and reformers, jurists, and politicians usually have only a distant acquaintance with contemporary refinements of these concepts, they tend to adopt this schema in a highly literal manner.

It remains only to ask what happens to men and societies and to their undertakings when they are interpreted in this manner. The answer hardly needs to be spelled out. Many of the aspects of human existence that assert themselves as most significant are denied or impoverished by the vocabulary of science. The enjoyments, affections, aspirations, and ideals that loom so large in our lives are simply not describable in terms of mass and energy. The purposes we project, the commitments we undertake, and the feelings that unite us with others refuse to be localized in space and time. Our sense of engaging in activities, of exercising initiative, of being blessed and cursed with freedom denies the bonds of an external causation. Our obvious ability to find our own situation in society and to make private arrangements with other persons refutes the notion that we are caught in a web of preestablished relations, and the fact that we feel ourselves as perpetually incomplete, as continually thrusting toward the future, rejects the idea that we merely become what we already were.

In more concrete terms, what all of this emphasizes is the point I insisted upon earlier in this enquiry (particularly in Chapter III), that human existence spans the regimes of Necessity, Possibility, and Purposiveness. Man is certainly subject to many natural necessities: physical and biological forces, instinct, conditioned reflex, imitation, habit, psychological factors, lived experiences, community pressure, inculcated moral and religious beliefs—all of these act on him and within him to fashion his character and conduct. To the extent that these various influences put their stamp on man, his behavior is the effect of assignable causes; and the corresponding patterns of behavior can be expressed in the form of laws that are predominantly expository, as I identified these in Chapters V and VI. Many of man's most vital interests are supported by processes and activities that are largely devoid of either volition or forethought.

But man's nature and career are totally misunderstood unless we make room in our interpretations for the possibility and purposiveness that loom so large in other contexts of his life. It is a compelling experiential fact—even if also a theoretical mystery—that many of man's most significant undertakings are the result of deliberation and decision. This experienced fact is at once a function and a witness of that most basic and pervasive feature of human existence, its plasticity: man is above all the being who is potentially capable of becoming many things; who, since he is finite, can actualize only a limited range of his potentialities; who must, therefore, choose which of the possibilities open to him he is to transform into purposes; and who must, finally, exercise discipline and cultivation if these purposes are to be realized.

This plasticity characterizes social activities and organization just as thoroughly as it does our individual lives. All societies face certain common problems and must satisfy certain basic human needs, drives, and interests. But both the relative values to be placed on various purposes and the methods to be adopted in reaching these are open questions. They can be settled in any number of ways, and different societies settle them in different ways: cultural relativism, national differences, and competing political systems are monuments to these facts.

As I argued at length in Chapters V through VIII, it is exactly these facts of human nature and existence that call into being positive law, with its prominent normative and prescriptive elements. There comes a time in natural evolution and human history when more primitive mechanisms for defining behavior require supplementation: instinct, imitation, custom, and so forth prove inadequate to the tasks of identifying purposes and choosing among possibilities. These simpler principles of order cannot cope with the complexity and volatility that characterize civilized men and societies. Plasticity creates situations and poses problems that require more sophisticated and versatile principles of order. It is to satisfy this need that positive law emerges and develops. In this sense, positive law is just as truly an adaptive device as are the opposable thumb, the big brain, and the taboo on endogamous marriage.

What I am here identifying as "plasticity" is of course no more than the genetic and biological equivalent and basis of what, in the more familiar language of morality and politics, we call freedom. Man is by nature free precisely because, and just to the extent that, his nature is plastic. We insist that law must respect man's freedom, and we take elaborate precautions to ensure that it will. The immediate psychological source of this demand is our intense desire to preserve our privacy, to be safe against undue intrusion, and to be allowed to express ourselves and to go our own ways unmolested. But the much deeper biological ground of the value we set on freedom lies in the fact that it preserves plasticity and hence the diversity, novelty, imagination, and initiative that are the issue of plasticity. If we too much abridge freedom, if we too closely regulate human behavior by compressing it into a closed and rigid schema, we commit two serious errors and prepare for ourselves a double failure. First, and more superficially, this coercion arouses a deep resentment and invites eventual rebellion. Second, and at a more basic level, it stifles effort in the present and closes the door to origination and creativity for the future. In short, positive law is called to respect freedom because freedom is itself a reflection and an instrument of plasticity. Law arises as the principle of an open order, and it denies itself and its raison d'être if it seeks to impose a closed order.

It is just for this reason that we need to be cautious in our commitment to social engineering through law. To do this is to treat law as a science. But the model of a science is for us the natural sciences, especially physics and chemistry. The only modes of law that these sciences recognize are expository: they presuppose an order—a state of affairs—corresponding closely to the regime of Necessity. So in becoming a science, law directs its efforts toward reproducing the conditions of Necessity, on the assumption that these express the true character of the human and social phenomena with which it deals. But this denies the significance of the regimes of Possibility and Purposiveness and eventually issues in a serious distortion of human nature and human well-being. What we are threatened with here is another of those too frequent cases in which, in the effort to correct certain evils and achieve certain purposes, we bring upon ourselves greater evils and sacrifice more important purposes. In short, to vary an old figure, we kill the baby by bathing it in scalding water.[6]

[6] In his *Law, Legislation, and Liberty: Vol. I, Rules and Order* (Chicago: Chicago University Press, 1973), F. A. Hayek develops a similar position. He argues that the proper function of the "organizations" through which law and government operate is to maintain a stable but open social environment in which the "self-generating orders" through which the real work of the society is carried on can function in accord with their own internal rules and so can adapt readily to changing circumstances. See esp. Chapter II.

In brief conclusion of this discussion, I want to guard against serious misunderstandings that it might invite, for what I have said could be taken as a diatribe against science and a disavowal of its usefulness in the melioration of the social situation and the human condition. Any such contention is as distant from my intentions as it would be absurd in itself. As I have insisted—sincerely if perhaps too cursorily—science has abundantly proved the contributions it can make to our efforts in these directions. By enhancing our understanding of the fundamental structures and processes that support individual and group life, it has enabled us to improve considerably man's management of both his personal and public affairs. I have merely intended to warn against the difficulties and dangers that lie in ambush for law if it tries to transform itself into the science of social engineering. These can be quickly summarized: law assumes that social goals are clear and coherent, whereas they are in fact confused and conflicting, and so it imposes upon men values and patterns of behavior that are uncongenial and unsatisfactory to them; law exaggerates its power of control over human and social processes, so its efforts often issue in frustration; law makes an unwarranted disjunction of ends and means, and in its pursuit of what it thinks people ought to have it deprives them of what they really want; and, finally, law is led to a distorted image of man that diminishes his nature and confines his field of action. In short, in following this course law is very apt to defeat both its own good intentions and man's pursuit of his own purposes.

None of these things has to happen. To avoid them, all that is required is that those who serve the law not allow themselves to be led astray by the passions of overzealous reformers or the pretensions of overconfident scientists. Law should certainly be attentive to the demands voiced by the former and solicitous of the help that can be offered by the latter. But law must not allow either of these, or both of them in alliance, to dominate its counsels and to dictate its decisions.

At the conclusion of this discussion we thus confront the issue that arose at its inception: Within this triumvirate, who is to be master and who man? But now it can be answered unequivocally. Law must be master in its own house, for its house is that of government, and government is of, by, and for the people. And it is only law that can be responsive to the whole of the people and to the whole range of their purposes and desires. Reformers inevitably represent special interests with limited ends in view: they are therefore prone to neglect some groups and to sacrifice some values in the pursuit of their special goals. The commitment of scientists to their substantive and methodological apparatus is apt to blind them to the true temper of the people and to the real forces at work in society. It is the unique quality of law that it has the capacity to be responsive to all the desires and demands of all the people it serves and yet to impose upon these an order of its own devising. Law can be sensitive without becoming servile. It is incumbent upon law to exercise its sovereignty, while at the same time recognizing, as I have emphasized before and will again, that sovereignty is not synonymous with omnicompetence. For if law interprets itself as the science of social engineering at the service of social reform, it abdicates its responsibilities and gives them into the hands of those who are not equipped to discharge them.

But this is not the end or the worst of what such a development threatens, for if law acknowledges the supremacy of science and subordinates its principles and procedures to the doctrines and methods of science, it destroys itself. This would be to assert the universal sway of determinism—of the regime of Necessity. And if that were the true state of affairs, then there are other ways to fashion human character and control human behavior that are—at least in theory—far more effective than positive law. These "ways" are those of the sciences, and we are familiar with them by name and vague description: brain operation, electrode implants and chemotherapy to control emotional states and attitudes, indoctrination through subliminal perception, positive and negative reinforcers, and so on. These and other procedures are summarized in the concept of operant conditioning made famous by B. F. Skinner and his school. If this view is correct and determinism holds, then law is merely a stopgap measure that will whither away as science extends its reach. The term social engineering is all very well as a metaphor, but it cannot be taken literally. For if it is, law is destroyed as a principle of a distinctive type of order, and man is reduced from a person to a thing.

The present situation can perhaps be illuminated by a glance at the past. History affords many familiar occasions on which law has been the bulwark of human freedom and an open society when these have been threatened by other forces and institutions. What has not been sufficiently noted is that these other forces and institutions have often, if not always, been necessary adjuncts of social life, beneficent in their original intentions and effects and responsive to the special needs of their times. They abuse the power they have rightly acquired and become repressive only when they seek to extend this power beyond its proper use and to impose their views and values upon all segments of society and all areas of life. This has happened with the church, the military, the feudal barons and their successors, the landed aristocracy, the economic establishment, labor unions, and the revolutionary hero turned despot. Each of these serves important purposes and has a legitimate sphere of influence. But it often happens that, not content with this limited role, each in its turn tries to make itself supreme and to dominate its society. This drive toward supremacy is often fired from two sources: on the one hand, there is the sincere conviction of each group that its interests coincide with those of society and that it is the sole supplier of the leadership that is needed; and on the other hand, there is the sheer greed and the lust for power that move men and groups, often unbeknownst even to themselves.

All of these cases exhibit one feature in common: the institution or faction that is seeking dominance makes an immediate effort to gain control of the legal apparatus and to subordinate this to its own purposes. The usurper gains two great advantages from this: he clothes himself with the mantle of legitimacy, and he can use law as a public instrument through which to exert, while yet hiding, his private will. These efforts often meet with a temporary success. But it is the glory of law—of legal institutions and the men who serve them—that it succumbs only in appearance and that it ends by imposing its forms and norms upon those who sought to subordinate it to their purposes. This is the endless task of the law: to domesticate these forces and institutions and to hold them to their proper tasks.

I think that the present situation represents simply a new recurrence of this old pattern. And I would suggest, as farfetched as it might seem, that the present threat to law and the social order comes from the presence of an indefinite number of reform groups, each with its own demands to press and with a coterie of scientists (more broadly, "experts") who support its cause and devise its programs. There are differences of detail in the present case, to be sure. And there is one difference that is of major significance. In the past, the threat to law and freedom has come from one class or institution or organized group that has been able to concentrate power in its hands, to gain control of the legal apparatus, and to impose its will upon society, whether through force, fear, or persuasion. Consequently, law had a known even if unacknowledged enemy. Furthermore, it had at least the covert, and often the active, support of those who felt repressed: that is, it had allies, even if they had to lie low.

In the present situation, these advantages are lost. Law has no visible enemies. There is no group that is powerful enough to dominate it and to use it as an instrument of repression. Indeed, there is almost surely no group that even wants to do this. As a result, law has no allies who value it for itself, cherish its principles and procedures, and see in it the constitutive and formative principle of the society.

Instead of enemies and allies, law is now besieged by a horde of suppliants. Each of these has some special purpose to further, some particular cause to plead, some private grievance to urge, some specific complaint to make, some public concern to express, some social need to support. Each of these suppliants brings in its train a group of scientists, who, at the proper moment, step forward with a detailed plan of the reforms that must be instituted in order to achieve what its clients propose. And all come demanding that law, whose sovereignty they acknowledge, take steps to implement their proposals. In short, as I put it earlier, the reformers propose the ends, the scientists plan the means, and the men of the law are asked only to make the necessary dispositions.

It is this proliferation of separate social action groups and scientific programs of reform that poses such difficulties for law.[7] For now the law finds itself confronted with a plethora of very specific social engineering projects that it is supposed to carry out. If this demand is taken seriously, if what is proposed is to be accomplished, then law will have to impose a tight regulation over all aspects of individual and social life. To put the matter very briefly, limited resources will have to be allocated, the uses of property controlled, the distribution of wealth regulated, the conditions of life defined, and human personnel mobilized, trained for particular roles, and assigned to special tasks. We speak very glibly of launching "wars" on poverty, disease, hunger, illiteracy, discrimination, and a horde of other social evils. Under the urgings of social reformers and scientific planners we seem ready to remove these "wars" from their quotation marks and to prosecute them literally as such. Given the complexity of contemporary society and the dislocations from which it is suffering, this may be our only recourse.

But if we take this step, we should at least do so with our eyes open to its consequences. For war is "social engineering" with a vengeance: in

[7] This tendency is now (1979) making itself felt intensely and deleteriously in the political life of this country in the form of what has come to be known as the "single issue" voter. Those in public life complain that they are besieged by voters whose interest is narrowly and passionately focused on one particular issue, to the neglect of all else, and who judge them solely by their stand on this issue. Those who are for or against abortion, or nuclear energy, or the Equal Rights Amendment, or SALT II ignore a candidate's program as a whole, insisting only that he support their *idée fixe*. The complaint is that these numerous and divergent "single issue" voters are making a shambles of the political process, as they create a climate in which compromise and the achievement of a consensus are impossible.

the pursuit of its goal—victory—it is ruthless of all that stands in its way and relentless in the uses it makes of human and physical resources. If law is really to wage war on all of the ills of which men complain, then it is going to have to mobilize human efforts solely to these public ends with no regard for private preferences. To state the matter in another way, if all of the claims that are now being advanced as human rights are to be recognized by law and transformed into legal rights, then it seems clear that traditional individual rights will have to be seriously curtailed.[8]

This again may be the inevitable wave of the future. If it is, it will demand a radical change both in our conception of law and in the structure of our legal systems. The new dispensation would require that law as the science of social engineering become an instrument that would rigidly control human conduct in all of its aspects, while hitherto law has been premised on the faith that men can be governed but that they cannot and should not be moulded like raw material, driven like machines, or herded like beasts.

---

[8] This problem is discussed and its occurrence illustrated in the following two chapters, where the nature of rights and their recent proliferation are examined in detail.

[CHAPTER XIV]

THE CONCEPT OF RIGHTS

I ARGUED in the previous Chapter that in recent years law has come both to assert itself and to be accepted not only as sovereign but also as omnicompetent. I further suggested that two developments have played particularly important roles in encouraging this process of legal proliferation and pervasiveness. One of these, the notion of law as social engineering, has already been discussed. I now want to turn to the other: the significant extension that is currently being given to the content and reach of the concept of legal rights.

Any discussion of the concept of rights is confused from the start because the meanings attached to the concept and the uses made of it spread through several different and often conflicting dimensions. When people speak of or appeal to rights, they may be talking in any one—or several—of the following contexts: metaphysical, moral, political, legal, social, or rhetorical. A good deal of this discussion is concerned with the problems of assuring the status and defining the contents of rights by rooting them in some more ultimate metaphysical ground, whether this be God, nature, human nature, or the structure of political society. Again, there is a strong moral overtone, which often becomes dominant, in all talk of rights: legislative and judicial acts are recommended or enjoined according to whether they further or hinder the realization of ethical values, and individual citizens are told that respect of the rights of others is a moral duty. Those who are interested in either bringing about social change or preserving the status quo appeal to the doctrine of rights to justify their efforts. The political organization and administration of any society are largely determined by the rights that are respectively granted to citizens and reserved to the government. Legally, the recognition that certain persons have a certain right has two immediate and important consequences: it imposes corresponding duties on other persons, and it enlists the state in the protection of these rights. Last, but by no means least, the doctrine of rights is a powerful rhetorical tool. Since it has great emotional power and persuasive value, every individual and group voicing any appeal at all clothes this in the language of rights, maintaining that its most extravagant demands are really claims of right. Given these multiple universes of discourse and the special interests of the various parties, it is small wonder that discussion gets bogged down in acrimonious disputes about what a right is and what things are rights. However, I think that these two questions can be dealt with in a manner that bypasses these disputes.

Obviously the basic issue is that of the status of rights—of what a right is—for on this hinges the identification of rights. Without becoming superficial or simplistic, I believe it is fair to say that disputes about this issue have centered on two broad views. One of these holds that rights have a real metaphysical and moral status: they are extra- and supralegal. Rights derive directly from God or Nature—from the ultimate structure of things—and they belong to man as part of his intrinsic nature, as much as do his body, his mind, and his various powers. Law merely recognizes these rights and enforces respect for them. This is the classical view, as expressed in the doctrines of natural law and natural rights, and it was the dominant influence for centuries.

The other view holds that rights are strictly legal entities or notions. They owe their being and their nature exclusively to law—to the substantive and procedural apparatus of a legal system—whose creatures they are. Law literally creates rights: the legislative or judicial act accords certain privileges and protections to some persons and imposes corresponding duties on other persons, and it is this act that brings the right into being and constitutes its content. This is the view made famous by Holmes and Gray, and it is associated with the schools of legal positivism, formalism, and analytical jurisprudence.

These statements are admittedly so general as to seem almost a caricature of the labyrinthine arguments that have been spun out in support of the different theories of rights. But I think that these broad interpretations constitute the only real and fundamental alternatives. Regarded substantively, rights are either legal or metalegal. They are either conceived and created by law, or they exist as aspects of reality prior to their legal annunciation and are merely recognized by law. However sophisticated and exotic legal theory may become, it must adopt one or the other of these substantive views.

Furthermore, and most importantly, the functional role and the psychological force of rights are the same on both of these views. In either case, rights are means to ends to which men feel they are entitled. Men are "endowed" with rights—by God, Nature, or law—in order to serve certain purposes that lie beyond these rights themselves. The claims, privileges, liberties, and immunities that make up the body of rights are all so many particular means to the general end of human well-being.

Their role is to secure to men the things and conditions that they need and that are owed them if they are to have the opportunity to develop to their full potential—though there have been and still are strong disagreements regarding the catalogue of these "things and conditions" to which men are entitled.

Divorced from technicalities and reduced to the primitive terms in which they are felt and asserted, rights express demands for things and conditions that men insist are due them. In their original occurrence and long before there is any machinery for their enforcement or even recognition of their legitimacy, rights already carry the double weight of *need* and *title*. It is exactly this that gives the assertion of a right its emotional force and its practical urgency. When men declare that they have a right to something, they are voicing the conviction that what they are demanding is both legitimate and necessary: it belongs to them as human beings, and it is requisite to their human well-being.

The essential characteristics of a right are thus *obligatoriness* and *instrumentality* ; alternatively, and with no shift in meaning, these can be identified respectively as the *deontological* and the *pragmatic* dimensions of rights. Rights are obligatory in the sense that they declare that they "ought" to be recognized and respected. To assert something as a right is to insist upon its legitimacy and binding power. This is made explicit in the case of legal rights, which impose duties and threaten sanctions. But this is true of all claims of right, long before their recognition and embodiment in law. When we assert our right to something— as distinct from saying that we want or desire or require or intend to have something—we feel and mean that our demand is justified and that others are obligated to acknowledge and accord it. Rights are instrumental in the sense that they function as means to ends. When men claim as rights certain freedoms and protections, they do so because these are felt to be necessary to secure their integrity as human beings and to assure them the opportunity to exercise and develop their human capacities. Men assert as rights those conditions and benefits (such as freedom of expression and assembly, education, a minimum wage) that they deem indispensable to their well-being. Thus rights are rooted in the various needs and deprivations, the threats and insecurities, that weigh upon men: they designate the guarantees and the contributions that the individual requires if he is to realize his essential purposes and values.

The primary locus of rights might thus be said to lie in the sense of injustice. Rights have their origin in the effort to redress what is experienced as an undeserved harm; that is, as a wrong. The purpose of a right is thus to right a wrong. As with everything else that men pursue, rights are felt and fought for well before they are enunciated and catalogued, much less justified. They are seized by force and only later supported by argument.

But when men set out upon this second task—when they seek to legitimate possession and make it secure—they soon realize that they face a twofold challenge. They must justify the claim to rights in general, and they must identify the specific rights that they are claiming. In other words, they are called upon to establish both the ground and the content of the rights they assert. Of course these efforts go on concurrently, but it is upon the former that attention is first centered. And this is as we would expect: since men feel compellingly, if not too clearly, their pressing needs and the measures that would repair them, they take all of this for granted and assume that these needs—the content of the rights they claim—are self-evident. The deficiencies of the present are always so obvious and their ideal solutions so appealing that they impose themselves without argument. The content of rights therefore seems to need only to be proclaimed.

The case is quite otherwise with the ground of rights. To claim something as a right is different in every way—psychologically, legally, socially, and even philosophically—from clamoring for it as a desirable relief, benefit, redressment, or adjustment. Men bargain for better wages, they petition for improved schools or roads, they protest high prices, and they demonstrate for everything from lower taxes to disengagement in Viet Nam. But they do not claim any of these things as "rights"—or if they do, it is the result of an injudicious mixture of rhetoric and belligerency. However desirable and reasonable these things may be, they are not normally regarded as rights. It is extraordinarily difficult—perhaps even impossible—to circumscribe with precision the field of rights and to explain satisfactorily why some things do and others do not fall within this field. But at least the foundation on which this distinction rests can be discerned: it lies in the intense feeling of men that some things (those claimed as rights) belong to them and are due to them in the very nature of the world and society. It is simply felt that rights are somehow man's just and primal desert: rights may have to be won, but they do not have to be earned or merited.

This conviction gives rise to three problems; or, to state it differently, it initiates three lines of inquiry directed toward achieving what it claims: the conviction must be justified, its proper reach delimited, and its grasp made secure. That is, a doctrine is needed to clarify the ground and the content of rights, and an apparatus is needed to provide and protect these rights. The journey toward these goals has been long and complex, and it is by no means over. I do not intend to retrace the ups and downs of this path. Rather, it is my concern first to recapitulate its principal moments, or stages, in order to expose the complexity that lies at the heart of the seemingly simple notion of rights and second to examine very carefully the present state of the doctrine of rights, the direction in which this is moving, and the problems to which this movement points.

My first task can best be approached by focusing attention on the various terms that have been employed to qualify rights: natural, legal, human, personal, constitutional, civil, individual, political, religious, women's, and so on. Each such qualifier signifies a special interest in the ground, the content, or the apparatus of rights. And when one qualifier supplants another in the current vocabulary of "rights" talk, this signifies a shift of concern from one set of problems and grievances to another.

A good many of these qualifiers indicate a concentration of attention either on the rights of certain groups or on a certain range of rights: this is obviously the case with civil and religious rights, women's rights, the right to work, and other similar terms. But three of these types of rights have a larger reference and indicate broader and more basic approaches to the subject. I have in mind the concepts of natural rights, legal rights, and human rights. As these refer to large-scale shifts of focus and to important phases in the history of rights, they deserve to be examined in some detail.

The concept of rights first appeared prominently on the stage of thought in the guise of natural rights. The thrust of this doctrine was primarily toward justifying the claim of rights in principle, with relatively little attention to detailing the rights that were claimed. As was indicated above, this latter point appeared so compellingly obvious that it was largely taken for granted. Such philosophers as Hobbes, Locke, and Rousseau, and such acute political thinkers as the leaders of the American and French Revolutions, each had a clear, if not always identical, conception of the rights (that is, the conditions and guarantees) that must be assured to men if they were to live with any security and decency. Life, liberty, equality, property, the right to bear arms and to assemble and petition, the guarantee of due process and trial by jury, protection against arbitrary governmental action and self-incrimination—all of these represent such transparent needs and values that they seem to require only enumeration, not clarification. This latter challenge will appear later.

Thus the doctrine of natural rights was concerned with the ground of rights rather than their content: it sought to justify the needs and demands that men were voicing and so to transform these into claims. To this end, it marshalled the various arguments that have become familiar: the appeal to the state of nature, to the social contract, to the inherent nature of man, to the designs of the Creator, to history, to tradition and the Golden Age. The aim of all of these arguments was to establish that rights belonged to the individual in his naked condition, prior to any form of social or political organization, and so must be respected by all men and all governments.

But the doctrine of natural rights had a side effect that may have been unintended but was nonetheless important. In the very fact of designating these rights as "natural" and grounding them in the aboriginal and solitary status of man, a check was put on what this claim would cover. Rights were tied very closely to what were regarded as man's essential and indispensable functional needs, where these last two words must be read with strict literalness and equal emphasis. What men could claim as rights were only those conditions and protections that were necessary for them to function as men. The traditional rights contained in the classic declarations and likewise the more detailed list in the first ten amendments to the United States Constitution are almost entirely prohibitions against interference with the individual. The same is true of the common law rights that had been gradually formulated in terms of such concepts as trespass, tort, negligence, and liability. Man was conceived as an active and self-directing agent, living in an environment that offered him ample resources to satisfy his needs. What he could claim under the guise of rights was the opportunity to exercise his talents and enjoy the fruits of his efforts. Natural rights were thus conceived as functional rather than substantive; they were designed to afford opportunities, not to assure outcomes. It is in this way that the ground alleged to justify rights controlled the content of these rights. To speak of natural rights is inevitably to think of man in a state of nature. And this is to conceive him as a self-dependent being, needing only to be guaranteed his independence.

The doctrine of natural rights had served its primary purpose when it had aroused and justified men in their struggle against various forms of oppression that had themselves been grounded in political, religious, military, or proprietary facts and claims. Attention now shifts to the task of establishing an apparatus to secure and administer the rights that have been won. The concept of natural rights is then supplanted by that of legal rights, and the former gradually drops from sight, to be invoked less and less frequently and only on occasions of special significance. The fate of natural rights is very similar to that of a mother and father from a simple, provincial background who become wealthy, give to their sons and daughters every advantage that they themselves lacked, and then find that they are rejected by their children, who are ashamed of their parents' lack of manners and culture and embarrassed to present them to their new friends. The doctrine of natural rights achieves a magnificent practical success, but it is theoretically suspect from the start, it never attains intellectual respectability, and it is incapable of exploiting the ground it has won. So the lawyers take over from the revolutionaries and set about consolidating and distributing the fruits of victory.

The transformation of natural rights into legal rights is a twofold process. First, there is the analytical task of refining the concept of legal rights in general and establishing the catalogue of specific legal rights. Second, there is the constructive task of developing a substantive and procedural apparatus that can protect the exercise of these rights and remedy their violation. These efforts of course go forward concurrently and in close relationship with one another, and their history is too familiar to require detailing. But a few remarks about the broad course of this process, and particularly about its contemporary culmination, are needed if we are to have a full view of this legal dimension of rights talk.

The traditional doctrine of analytical jurisprudence recognizes four principal elements of a legal right: 1) there is the holder, or subject, of the right—the person, real or legal, in whom the right inheres; 2) there is the res that the right governs—the object (in the widest sense of the term) of the right; 3) there is the act or forebearance commanded by the right; 4) there are the persons (definite or indefinite) on whom specific duties are imposed. Legal realism soon placed explicit emphasis upon another element that had all along been effectively present even if unrecognized as such: this consisted in 5) the legal procedures and remedies by which the right is protected and sanctioned.

If we think in terms of aetiology rather than analysis—of function rather than structure—then this last element has pride of place. For it is the elaborate substantive and procedural apparatus of law, supported by the authority of the state, that makes rights really secure. Natural rights are merely claims, regardless of the intellectual justification and emotional fervor with which they are pressed. Legal rights give title, backed by force.

Indeed, this apparatus of enforcement does more than merely ground legal rights: it plays a very significant part in determining their content. The range of the protection and remedies that law provides does much to define the other four elements of a right. As a matter of logic and principle, it might seem that we would first settle these other more substantive aspects of a right and then devise the rules and procedures that would secure it; but as the slightest perusal of legal history makes clear, movement has been largely in the other direction. The right begins its career as a broad claim, only loosely localized as regards its holders, its *res*, the acts it demands or prohibits, and the duties it imposes: the rights to equality, liberty, due process, property, reputation, and so on are acknowledged, but no one knows at all precisely what they mean. That is made clear only slowly and gradually in the course of time, through a long line of judicial decisions and—especially more recently—statutory enactments. These basic rights are never fully delineated and stabilized. There accretes around each of them a huge, complex, and recondite body of doctrine. This body of doctrine arose in response to the needs that men felt and the values they cherished. As it took shape, it defined these needs and values more closely, it tailored them to the limitations of what was actual and possible, it reconciled their competing claims, and it transformed them from dreams into realities. All of this is an achievement of the first order, but it is also an achievement that exacts a price. For finally, this body of doctrine *becomes* the right.

This is to say that in the course of this process of legalization the right-as-defined-by-law is largely isolated from the needs that initiated it and the values that it envisaged. As the mass of substantive and procedural law concerned with rights accumulates, it comes to be regarded as internally complete and self-sufficient. So when new claims of right are made, or questions about rights arise, the tendency is to subject them to only doctrinal analysis. The reach of rights is extended or retracted, their content is changed, additional duties are imposed on additional parties, and fresh protections and remedies are given to the exercise of rights: and all these conclusions are reached and justified by almost exclusively legal arguments, without due regard to the physical, social, and moral environment of which law is a part. Since law has become the effective ground of rights, it is easy to assume that the content and meaning of these rights also have their source in law and so can be logically derived from the relevant constitutional provisions, statutes, and judicial precedents.

I do not, of course, mean to suggest that the judicial process and those who administer it are altogether removed from human concerns and worldly influences and that they are thus isolated in a domain of pure law. That would be absurd in principle and obviously false in fact. Judges and lawyers are just as much susceptible to prejudice, emotion, and parochialism, and are just as much subject to outside pressures and interests, as any other men: when they come to the bench and bar, they bring with them their full freight as human beings. The perspectives they adopt, the causes they respect, and the decisions they render are all influenced by their moral, social, and political views. The trouble lies in the fact that this influence is exerted in a thoroughly haphazard, unconscious, and uncritical manner. It is not the opinions, values, and predilections of these men that are isolated in a realm of pure law but only their mode of legal reasoning. When it is held that the meaning of a particular right is exhaustively given by the relevant body of legal doctrine, then argument is confined to this doctrinal apparatus, while the decisions that are reached are strongly influenced by these extrinsic and unacknowledged considerations. Under this dispensation, legal reasoning becomes an unhappy mixture of formalism and personalism. The content and exercise of rights are enmeshed within an obsolescent body of law, which in turn is interpreted in the light of convictions and commitments whose influence is exerted in an erratic and unexamined manner.

When this attitude prevails—and it may do so in some fields of law and not in others during the same period of time—law loses touch with the needs and aspirations of people. Persuaded that the questions that society poses in the present can be answered by reference to legal concepts and doctrines developed in the past, law hews to a strict logical line interspersed with capricious emotional impulses. To the extent that law is responsive only to its own inner logic and the individual consciences of judges, it ceases to be sensitive to the conditions and the mood of the time. I do not mean to denigrate the quality of this logic and these consciences, but there is no guarantee that they will be contemporary or representative. When they are not, legal doctrine moves at a tangent to social reality. This appears to me to be what happened in each of the following cases: the history of the concepts of due process and equal protection between the Civil War and the 1920s; the application of the "full faith and credit" clause of the Constitution to the issue of migratory divorce; the aberrations and divagations in the interpretation of obscenity; the recent extremely rapid extension of the protection afforded the accused in criminal cases; and, perhaps the most striking instance, our insistence upon exporting our doctrine of rights to newly-emergent states that are in no way adapted to appreciate or implement this doctrine. These examples illustrate in their various ways what eventuates when legal rights are absolutized.

Among other things, this outcome stringently inhibits and distorts the recognition of new claims of right or the extension of recognized rights to new claimants. When this situation is generally realized, men become concerned to correct it. They thus seek a fresh ground from which to attack the established conception of legal rights, with the intent of broadening this and making it more sensitive and flexible in its response to hitherto unfilled needs and neglected values. It is in the pursuit of this end that human rights are advanced to a leading role.

The conception of human rights first emerged at the end of the eighteenth century in the series of Declaration of Rights with which the French justified and consecrated their Revolution. It fell quickly into abeyance, pushed aside by the rapid development of legal rights, and it remained in the background for a century and a half. It was introduced prominently into the vocabulary of rights talk toward the end of World War II. It was officially invested as the sovereign principle of this realm on 10 December 1948, when the General Assembly of the United Nations adopted the Universal Declaration of Human Rights. Shocked by the experiences through which they had passed and thus made vividly aware of the abject conditions under which millions of men lived and the abuses to which they were subjected, the nations of the world disavowed the past and proclaimed their determination to create a brighter future. Human rights are the vehicle they chose to delineate the contours of this future and to spell out its most important features.

The interest taken in human rights during the past twenty years has been overwhelmingly practical in both its origin and its intent. It is only very lately—almost yesterday—that any serious attention has been paid to the philosophical problems that arise when we talk of human rights. And the theoretical content of the concept is not so much obscure or confused as simply nonexistent. The appeal to human rights has been employed as a stimulant to men's emotions and as a lever to move them to action, but such abstract issues as the status, basis, justification, and cataloging of such rights were ignored or dismissed as irrelevant. Human rights must be real and legitimate because they are so desperately needed to guide and moderate the behavior of governments. And the list of these rights was easily derived from the atrocities, abuses, and privations to which men had been subjected by despots and conquerors.

The origin of human rights is thus quite similar to that of natural rights: each is born of desperation and dedicated to action. But there are also important differences that will have important consequences. The doctrine of human rights appeals chiefly to the feelings of men, while that of natural rights spoke more seriously to their minds (though it must be acknowledged that this voice might have been softened by time and have sounded very differently to men of the seventeenth and the eighteenth centuries). This can be put differently by saying that the doctrine of human rights marks a return to that of natural rights but without the metaphysical foundation of the latter. Discussion of human rights—as distinct from action based on them—is uncertain and uneasy in tone, lacking both clarity and conviction. Thinkers who now talk of human rights exhibit a strong nostalgia for the rational and moral self-assurance of the earlier adherents of natural rights, but they are altogether unwilling to make the ontological commitment that is necessary to give them this assurance. The writings of these moderns have exactly the tone of Virginia's famous letter to the newspaper, begging to be reassured that there really is a Santa Claus. But so far there has been no reply from an editor that could dispel their doubts. These men pay extravagant homage to the ethical and social significance of human rights; they regard them as invaluable safeguards for individuals and as strong controls on government. They would dearly love to believe that these rights really exist. But they cannot. They sniff the intellectual atmosphere, and their nerve fails them. Victims of the positivistic and analytical temper of the times, they could be convinced of the existence of human rights only if they could see them fixed to a pin-board and put under a microscope. Thus, human rights are left in an intellectual limbo.[1]

But this theoretical poverty has not prevented the idea of human rights from having a strong, and on the whole beneficent, practical effect. Indeed, it might be argued that this lack of a coherent theory has been a positive advantage: where social ills are urgent and their cure is both obvious and available, swift action is more needed and fruitful than careful thought, which is apt to provide distractions and delays. The need for a sound theory will appear only later. But it will appear, as we shall see.

The introduction of the concept of human rights into the universe of rights talk has several significant consequences. First, and most obviously, it opens up the field of rights for fresh consideration: it allows for the recognition of new claimants, it leads men to examine the effectiveness with which established legal rights are doing the jobs for which they are intended, and so it prepares the way for improved procedures. In sum, the emphasis on human rights serves to renovate the consideration of rights in general and to insure that it will be relevant to contemporary conditions.

Second, and most importantly, the idea of human rights refocuses at-

---

[1] This mood of regretful skepticism that pervades the current literature on rights can be seen in a concentrated form in the excellent and revealing articles in the issue of *The Monist* devoted to human rights (vol. 57, no. 4; October 1968).

tention on the fact that rights are instruments for the achievement of purposes and values that lie beyond them: that is, it reminds us that rights are means, not ends in themselves. When we think of rights as natural or legal, we easily fall into the habit of regarding them as somehow ultimate and autonomous, needing no justification beyond their own intrinsic rightness. Rights then tend to become their own excuse for being, without regard to their actual consequences. When we think of rights as human, we are forcefully reminded that they are "ours" and are of value only through the benefits that they make available to us. The reason for the existence of a right now comes to reside in the fact that it is regarded as an indispensable condition or constituent of human well-being. The idea of human rights stresses an element that is always present but often forgotten: namely, the end or purpose for the sake of which the right is conferred. In short, this doctrine insists that the ultimate correlative of a right is a good.

Unfortunately, but not surprisingly, the doctrine of human rights has other consequences that are potentially undesirable and even malicious. The doctrine is inherently dangerous just because it is at once emotionally appealing and intellectually vacuous. It leaves both the ground and the content of human rights undefined and hence undisciplined, thus arousing enthusiastic support devoid of any guidance or control. No limit is placed on what men may claim as a right, and there is no reason in theory why there should be any such limit. Every good or value, every benefit and support and satisfaction that can be brought under the rubric human, can now in principle be regarded as a right. If rights are human, then man is their measure. And it is not long before every special group identifies itself with man and asserts that its particular needs and interests constitute rights. When it is said that men have a right to have all of their essential wants satisfied, it is only natural that they should transfer the meaning of *want* from *need* to *desire*: the potential range of rights is thus extended indefinitely. We now find the most exaggerated hopes and extravagant claims advanced as rights. This movement has reached what must be its ultimate travesty with the demand of dissident students of the "right to amnesty." This outcome was certainly not intended by those who proclaimed human rights: it is another case of an idea that escapes its author, enters into the stream of thought, and undergoes surprising transformation. But the outcome might nevertheless have been anticipated. It has often been pointed out that the natural and legal rights of classical doctrines were conceived primarily—though not exclusively—in negative terms. Their chief function was to assure freedom *from* various intrusions and oppressions. Men sought the rights of liberty, property, equality, security, assembly, due process, and so forth in order to be protected against arbitrary power, whether this was political, religious, military, or economic. For much the greater part, such rights required only that other parties—particularly the government—refrain from interfering with the holders of the rights.

The case is very different with human rights. These are far more positive in their content and intention. Human rights tend to take the form of claims *to* or *for* something. Their function is to assure to people certain goods, benefits, and supports for which they experience an urgent need, to which they feel entitled, and which they are unable to procure by their individual efforts. Men seek rights to low-cost housing, a food allowance, minimum income, education, medical assistance, useful employment, and so forth on the ground that these are due them as human beings and so are owed them by society. Human rights embody claims for positive social and political action in support of the purposes and values that these rights represent. They require that government plan and administer society in a manner that assures men a standard of living and a way of life that will afford them a satisfactory existence.

There is much in the doctrine of human rights that deserves the sympathy and support of all men. There is so much unnecessary human suffering and deprivation, so much wanton abuse and neglect of men in need, that a doctrine that cries out against these conditions and demands their correction merits both our thanks and our attention. Furthermore, there can be little doubt that something like the contemporary human rights movement was necessary to revitalize the whole subject of rights, place it in a new perspective, and direct it toward wider horizons than those envisaged by established legal rights.

There is also much in this doctrine that seems unsound and unbalanced, arousing doubts and reservations in the minds of many. This is due in part to its sheer novelty, but it is due far more largely to the fact just noted that the doctrine seems altogether devoid of internal restraints and controls. It is a dangerous doctrine because it advances no criteria, whether theoretical, empirical, or practical, for determining its reach. It grounds rights in humanity and then leaves this notion undefined; the content of rights is thus indefinite and indeterminate.

Regarded in retrospect, this long passage from natural to legal to human rights has the profile of a ride on a seesaw, with its succession of ups and downs. Somewhat more exactly, this passage has been a series of expansions and contractions. There is the assertion of certain claims as natural rights, then the effort to secure these as legal rights, and then the assertion of fresh claims as human rights. And there have of course been numerous smaller cycles within these larger ones. The meaning of natural and legal rights was continually being redefined, their reach extended here and withdrawn there, their emphasis shifted, and their content modified. This steady slow movement is marked by the phrases that have enjoyed momentary prominence: corporate rights, shareholders' rights, and student rights; the right to picket, the right to privacy, and the right to attend an integrated school; voting rights, women's rights, and civil rights.

We are now at the height of this latest cycle of expansion. The proclamation of human rights is the exuberant cry of the child who finds himself at the top of the seesaw, with the world spread out at his feet. It is at this moment that we—child and man—discover the riches and beauty of the world and are moved to make them our own. We stake out our claim and gleefully tell our parent, who sits on the bottom of the seesaw with a limited vista but in secure possession, that we are the lords of creation. But to make good our claim, we must come back to earth and work it. To speak more literally, this means that the task of the near future will be to take a true assessment of the claims advanced as human rights and then to implement those that pass muster as legitimate and possible.

As we set about this task, it is of the highest importance that we bear in mind all of the dimensions of rights as they have been exposed by the successive doctrines of natural, legal, and human rights. These movements embody a gradual exploration and clarification of the field of rights; together they expose the principal types of problems that are encountered in the quest for rights and the broad lines along which solutions to these problems must be sought. In concluding this survey, it should therefore be instructive to extract and summarize the lessons of these different doctrines.

The concept of natural rights teaches us that any doctrine of rights must have a firm theoretical basis. Since rights are means to the achievement of human good, a correct catalogue of rights depends upon a sound theory of human nature and the human situation. Without such a theory, the determination of what claims constitute rights becomes a purely subjective and haphazard operation; all we can then do is attend to the manifold demands that men voice, estimate the extent of their support, and try to satisfy those that are the most widely and vociferously urged. This is obviously a hit and miss procedure, substituting clamor (if not violence) for reason and discontent for justification.

The doctrine of legal rights teaches us that declarations of rights are vain without an effective apparatus to implement them. This is a familiar teaching, but two of its more important lessons are often overlooked. One of these concerns the need for a constant renovation of the legal apparatus itself, to keep it responsive to changes in social circumstances and human expectations. The other reminds us that we must take steps to ensure that all men are able to invoke these rights when they stand in need of them. Legal rights cannot be truly established until everyone has equal access to, and standing before, the legal apparatus.[2] The generality of men must therefore be informed of the rights that are theirs in theory and of the procedures through which they can secure these rights in fact.

When we turn to the doctrine of human rights, we find that there is not so much that we can learn from it as a vast amount that we must teach ourselves. This doctrine is so novel and its growth has been so rapid that there has been insufficient time to accumulate experience of its effects or to develop theories for its control. Human rights have become accomplished facts overnight, almost before our eyes and well before their claims have been justified or their consequences anticipated. This sudden explosion of the concept of rights gives rise to serious problems. So I will now turn from a survey of the past to a scrutiny of the present and a contemplation of the future.

During recent years, a radically new content has been steadily pouring into the concept of rights. Partly through legislative acts and partly through the accumulation of judicial decisions, men have been accorded rights that as lately as two generations ago were altogether undreamed of: it would never have occurred to men to claim them, and if such claims had been advanced governments would have scoffed at them. But we are now so accustomed to this extension of the reach of rights that we accept it as both natural and necessary, and we fail to see that it has carried us almost unconsciously into social regions that are vast, novel, and largely unexplored. We are even more blind to the further implications that are inherent in the momentum of this process. As a result, we find ourselves forced by the logic of this movement to accept situations for which experience has not prepared us and which we find emotionally disturbing and sometimes even morally perverse. The disputes that currently rage around such issues as Medicare and Medicaid, busing, welfare, public housing, and legal services to the poor are familiar

---

[2] This requirement has been recognized (in an extreme form, it might be argued) in several of the majority opinions in the so-called "death penalty" cases, Furman v. Georgia, 403 U.S. 952, 92 S.Ct. 2726 (1972).

symptoms of the unrest and uncertainty that are aroused by government programs initiated in support of these new rights.

The essence of the present crisis is this: men find that their commitment to law is leading them in directions that do violence to many of their most settled habits and convictions, and to dismiss these as mere bigotry and prejudice (as many do) does not lessen their force. This is evidently a dangerous and debilitating state of affairs; and its threat to the future is becoming immensely greater as the pace of change and the pressure of events sweep us on. In such a situation, it is advisable to pause and take one's bearings—to get a sense of the ground that has been traversed and especially of the future that portends if our present course is maintained. In attempting such an overview, there are three points in particular that I want to consider: the character of these newly created rights; the role of the courts in their development; and the ultimate outcome to which they point.

The first and most obvious point to be noticed is the radically novel character of the current breed of rights, such as health care, guaranteed income, housing, welfare, food allowance, education. These rights differ in kind and not merely in degree from those that have been so intimately associated with the liberal-democratic movement. Traditional rights, such as are embodied in the Bill of Rights and the Fourteenth and Fifteenth Amendments to the Constitution—freedom of speech and religion; the rights to assemble, petition, and bear arms; the guarantees of due process of law and of security of person and property—have very little in common with these newly emergent rights. To regard the latter as the direct lineal descendants of the former is as farfetched as to expect that a mouse would labor and bring forth a mountain.

Traditional legal rights are primarily protective: they guarantee citizens certain basic freedoms and immunities, and they protect them against intrusion or arbitrary action by the state. These rights do not bestow any positive benefits upon people. They do not promise to provide arms, an enlightened press, churches, places to assemble, legal fees, or houses and other property: they merely assure the citizen that the state will not interfere with his pursuit of these goods nor deprive him of what he has won by his efforts. If traditional rights are to bear fruit, they must be exercised by those who hold them, since by themselves they merely give assurance of an open field and fair play (at least within the rules of the game).

The duties correlative with these rights have a similarly restricted reach, being largely prohibitions: they enjoin the state from doing certain things. These duties therefore impose relatively light responsibilities on government and society: they rarely require any positive action by the state, but merely demand that it shall refrain from interfering with the free activities of the citizens and from discriminating arbitrarily among them. In this regard it is interesting to note that the language of the Bill of Rights and of the Fourteenth and Fifteenth Amendments is preponderantly negative in character. Every one of them except the Sixth Amendment (which defines the rights of persons accused of crime) is controlled by a negative verb—a "no" or a "not." Each of them forbids the state to "prohibit," "abridge," "infringe," "violate," "deny," "deprive," or "disparage" some specific rights held by the citizens. The philosophy that underlies this language is clear: these traditional rights are not conferred on citizens by the state; rather, the people hold these rights prior to and independently of the state, which is merely enjoined to respect them and to assure their free exercise.

The new rights have quite another character, and their reach and impact are of a different order. These rights are beneficial rather than protective. They embody the claim that men are entitled to certain benefits and services, such as food, housing, minimum income, and health care. These rights do not require to be exercised but are simply to be enjoyed. The essence of what is happening here is that the concept of "right" is being enlarged to include not only means but also ends. What men are now claiming as a right is not merely that they be left unhindered in their pursuit of values but that these values be bestowed upon them. These new rights go far beyond guaranteeing men certain basic liberties and immunities—they promise to endow men with a wide range of positive goods.

These enlarged rights obviously impose similarly enlarged duties, which are positive and stringent in character. The state is now charged with the obligation to provide for many of men's needs—food, housing, income, health care—whenever men are for any reason unable or unwilling to secure these for themselves. If men have rights to these benefits and services, then corresponding duties must lie somewhere, and this "somewhere" can only be the state. Where before the state was merely charged not to "prohibit," "infringe," "abridge," or "violate" its citizens exercise of their rights, it now bears the far more onerous responsibility of providing for their enjoyment of the world's goods. Finally, a wholly new philosophy of rights is emerging, for these rights conceived as benefits clearly cannot be regarded as forming part of man's original baggage but are conferred and bestowed exclusively by the state.

Not even the most chauvinistic advocate of the state of nature has ever maintained that the environment owed man a dry cave, a sharp flint, and a beast waiting with bent neck.

There is a second significant difference between the old family of rights and the new: constitutional rights inhere in the people generally, with all entitled to and none excluded from their protection, while most—if not all—human rights attach to special groups and classes, with only some entitled to and many excluded from the benefits they confer. The rights set forth in the Bill of Rights and in the Fourteenth and Fifteenth Amendments are, as the Supreme Court has repeatedly emphasized, *personal* rights: they apply to individuals strictly as such, with no one being able to claim them and no one being denied them because of membership in a class or group. On the other hand, human rights embody claims for special consideration and treatment: this is notably true of such rights as those to privileged admission and preferential employment, which are now the subject of extensive debate and judicial soul-searching; but it is also true, if less obviously, of other human rights. Because of these characteristics, human rights hold the potential for generating tension and divisiveness within society, leading to fragmentation and conflict. These matters will be fully argued and illustrated in the next chapter.

This is the change in the doctrine of rights that has been taking place and is now virtually accomplished. It received the official sanction of the United Nations in the extraordinarily fulsome form of the Universal Declaration of Human Rights. It has since been paid equally universal lip service as the ideal to be pursued, and, as the previous account indicates, we in this country have been busy putting the doctrine into practice. Waiving for the moment any consideration of the merits of this change, its sheer extent is enough to give us pause—to make us marvel just how we could have moved so far so fast and to wonder whether the vehicle of this movement is to be trusted for the future. That is the question I will now examine.

This extension of the doctrine of rights has been the work of all three branches of government. In several areas, the necessary foundation was laid by explicit legislation, as in the case of Medicare and Medicaid, the food stamp program, and the various enactments having to do with fair employment and public housing. Executive orders and administrative bureaus have also made important contributions to this movement. But the courts have taken a central part in defining more precisely and assuring the extension of the concept of rights, and in many areas they have played the major role. The "Warren Court" has become a byword for judicial involvement in social, political, and economic affairs, with some praising and others condemning it for seeming to subordinate strictly legal considerations to its own sense of social justice and human rights. The impetus of the decisions of the Warren years is far from spent, with almost every week bringing fresh court actions that extend the reach and content of rights. However much we may approve the accomplishments of this judicial movement, it is still possible to question whether judges are the proper agents of such social change and to be alert for dangers that may lie hidden in this process of judicial "right making." There are three characteristics of the judiciary and the judicial process that particularly threaten the social order and thus call for special attention. These can be briefly identified as internal momentum, elitism, and irresponsibility. I will discuss them in that order.

Those twin pillars of the American legal tradition, judicial supremacy and *stare decisis*, are so enshrined in our hearts and minds that it is virtual heresy to express even the slightest doubt concerning them. The technique of developing a body of law through single cases, the reliance upon precedents, and the use of analogy do have very great advantages: they allow society to move along a certain line step by step, to experiment with solutions to problems without committing itself, to keep various options open, and to change course when experience proves it advisable. But there is a concomitant danger in this method. It is easy to move by almost imperceptible steps from one position to another that is radically different if not diametrically opposite. The principles laid down in the Constitution, in Supreme Court decisions, and in legislative acts are usually couched in language that is so general as to be systematically ambiguous: they allow various interpretations, all of which are equally defensible. Under these conditions, a particular line of decisions can soon acquire a momentum that is overpowering in its force and rate of acceleration. With the reach of a principle extended in this way and with so much left to judicial discretion, a society can find itself in a new world before it even becomes aware of the change. Whether this new world is better or worse, it is at any rate quite different from anything that the members of the society originally intended or for which they are prepared. Once granted, legal rights tend to be both irrevocable and uncontrollable: they cling to men as tenaciously as their skin and bones, and they grow like tumors, spreading far beyond their point of origin and assuming unintended and unpredictable guises, sometimes benign but also sometimes malignant. I believe that this has already occurred in such areas as the busing of children to achieve racial integration, the protection of those accused of crime, and the establishment of residency requirements for voting. In these and other instances a line of decisions has taken on a life of its own, determining its own path and tempo of development altogether independently of the rest of society. As a result, this technique of right making based on judicial supremacy and *stare decisis* often becomes powerfully cumulative, moving at an exponential rate and overriding all resistance.

There is a second feature of the judicial process that further strengthens this tendency toward autonomy and internal inertia. This is the fact that the judiciary itself—and especially the federal judiciary—is a small, closed, and highly self-conscious group. The moment a person becomes a federal judge, he enters a community that is largely isolated from society at large and intensely dedicated to its own particular creed and customs. This community embraces more than only judges: it includes the more prestigious law schools and legal scholars, eminent practitioners of the proper bent, many of the larger foundations, and public figures who support approved social causes. If a judge is to be accepted into this community and enjoy the respect of his fellows, he must acknowledge its dogmas and follow its practices.

This is simply to note the obvious fact that the federal judiciary is an elite group. And the members of this elite, like those of any other, tend to be far more sensitive to their colleagues than to the outside world. Judges naturally seek approval from their fellow judges (especially those of a higher court), from the notes in the more famous law reviews and the articles of accredited legal scholars, and from those groups that are caught up in, and are even largely supplying, the same momentum as the current line of decisions. To say this is not to criticize or condemn judges. It is merely to recognize that they *do* constitute an elite. And it is the inherent nature of any elite to be closed in upon itself: to be dedicated to its own principles and values, assured of its own rectitude, and confident that it represents the true conscience and best intelligence of its society. This self-certainty is at once the strength and the weakness of all elites: it gives them the vitality, cohesion, and continuity that are necessary to define and execute a policy, but at the same time it breeds a certain arrogance, and it closes their eyes to facts, values, and possibilities that do not fall within their creed.

As a result, once this judicial extension of the reach and the content of rights has been accepted, it spreads and accelerates at a steadily increasing rate. Each fresh decision establishes the doctrine more securely and invites its application in other areas and to other issues. Both principle and prudence—both professional commitment to the creed of the elite and personal desire for its approval—dictate to judges that they ride with the tide. Thus the momentum of the movement is fed not only by the theory of legal precedent but also by the facts of human nature.

There is yet a third factor that greatly facilitates this development— the fact that judges are not responsible for the implementation of the decisions they hand down. Once a judge has ruled, the duty of transforming this ruling from the law reports to social reality falls largely on other officials. And in the case of the new rights, this duty can be extremely onerous. I do not mean to belittle the heavy responsibilities that do weigh upon the judiciary: its members must be learned in the law, sensitive to delicate shadings of fact and value, and steadfast in their respect for the legal order. Having ruled, a judge may even keep a case within his jurisdiction and under his supervision in order to see that his dictates are carried out. But the hard task of actually carrying out his ruling passes to others. Having ordered massive busing to achieve racial balance, a judge does not have to find the needed funds, purchase the buses, plan the new pupil alignment, transfer teachers and students, and face the wrath of parents and taxpayers. Nor does a judge who has established standards for the care of patients committed to state mental hospitals have to find the doctors, nurses, and physical facilities that his order requires.

For this reason, it is all too easy for judges to be unaware of or insensitive to the social strains and dislocations that their decisions may cause. The judge's attention and concern are focused on the particular case before him, and he issues specific orders to support the right that he finds denied or abridged. But these orders have repercussions that reach out far beyond the instant facts and issues: they may disrupt the economy of the region in question, undermine its financial position, change the balance of political power, overburden its schools, its transportation, or its health facilities, erode its tax base while increasing its welfare rolls. Yet the judge may not even be aware of these consequences; and if he is, he may dismiss them as irrelevant, on the ground that his duty is to protect the right that is threatened in the case before him. It is the business of others to deal with these further problems, and they had better stop hectoring him and set about the task. *Fiat justitia ruat coelum* is a comforting maxim, especially when the heavens are going to fall on someone else.[3]

These strictures on judicial right making are to be taken as expressing a reservation, not a condemnation. I am well aware that in recent years

---

[3] In Chapter X we have seen this tendency manifesting itself in actual practice in the discussion of the *Wyatt* orders and their impact. Another instance will be more fully examined in the following chapter.

the cause of social justice and the realization of individual rights have been notably advanced in several areas by the strong affirmative action of the courts. But the fact that a certain procedure has achieved positive results in particular circumstances and with regard to particular issues does not certify it as a sound general policy. The three characteristics of the judiciary and the judicial process to which I have called attention are not figments of my imagination. On the other hand, I do not mean to add them to the list of deadly vices or to suggest that they are new aspects of original sin. They are quite simply built-in features of the judge's lot and life: a line of decisions does acquire a vast momentum, judges are members of an elite, and since judges are not responsible for the implementation of their rulings, they do become insensitive to the full impact of these rulings upon society.

When these three features are all present to a marked degree, they form an extremely volatile mix, and that is clearly the present situation regarding judicial right making. This process is already weaving a new pattern into the social and political fabric of the country, and its dynamism is by no means spent: indeed, it seems to be gaining strength, with new claims of human right being constantly advanced and acknowledged. It is still too early to foretell with any confidence or detail what the ultimate outcome of these developments will be. The uncertainty and discontent that they have aroused in the minds of many, the strain they have placed on various public services, the organized opposition in some quarters, the inexorable demands and limitations of the real world—all of these may combine to brake the movement. But if its momentum holds, if more and more sectors of life are brought within the ambit of the concept of right, then we will be able to extrapolate quite confidently the general pattern of the future that is being prepared by the decisions of the present.

If we try to express briefly the abiding dream of men of good will, there is no better way than in the celebrated formula of Marx: "From each according to his ability, to each according to his need." This dream has been embodied in various maxims, there have been innumerable interpretations of "ability" and "need" and as many proposals for measuring these intangibles, various forms of government have been suggested as the best means to this end, and emphasis has been placed now on one of the clauses, now on the other. It is the last point that presently interests me, for I think that it affords an effective way to characterize the present drift of events.

This drift has two aspects, or moments. On the one hand—and this is the aspect that I have been discussing throughout this chapter—we have been rapidly extending the reach and the content of the concept of rights. In doing this, we are declaring that more and more of the needs of men constitute legitimate claims that must be satisfied. That is, the state is held to be under a duty to supply the goods and services that these needs require. If men have a right to health, education, food, employment, housing, and so forth, then the state must make them available. In a word, the expansion of the concept of human rights places enormous emphasis on the second clause of the Marxist formula—"to each according to his needs."

But, on the other hand, we insist as strongly as ever on the traditional rights that grew up through the common law and are recognized in the Constitution. These have as their purpose to guarantee the liberty and privacy of the individual and to protect him against interference by the state. That is, these rights enjoin the state from intruding into the private lives of the citizens, abridging their freedom of action, dictating their role and function in life, or demanding service from them. The practical impact of the traditional doctrine of rights is virtually to deny the first clause of the formula—"from each according to his ability."

The gist of the present situation, then, would seem to me to be this. Like all men of good will, we honor the formula—whether in these words or others—"From each according to his ability, to each according to his needs." But both our attitudes toward the two injunctions and the steps we take to carry them out are utterly different. Under the impetus of a steadily expanding concept of the new human rights, we are mobilizing an immense political and social effort to satisfy the needs of men. But at the same time, under the influence of the traditional doctrine of individual rights, we reject any proposal that would require men to contribute to society to the measure of their ability (the sole important exceptions are the ineffective ones of taxation and the military draft). We are placing the state under a legal duty to make good all of the basic needs of all men, but we are placing men under no duties of discipline, responsibility, and service to support the effort made in their behalf.

As the rights that men assert become more positive, as they take the form of claims to or for certain benefits and conditions rather than from certain intrusions and oppressions, we are evidently going to have to measure carefully the resources that are available to satisfy these claims. The more "goods" that we accord as "rights," the more stringently will we be forced toward some mode of rationing: housing, schools, teachers, doctors, jobs, and now even money are all in short supply. Indeed, the only thing that seems to be unlimited is credit: and our extravagant indulgence in this luxury is evidence of our desire to will our problems to the future instead of dealing with them ourselves. I do not doubt that a more equitable distribution of these goods could and should be achieved. But it is equally certain that to transform them into rights will require radical changes in human attitudes and social organization. Tolerance for differences, respect for individual integrity apart from personal merit, a willingness to share with others beyond what they earn, sympathy without charity, and discrimination without invidious distinctions— these will be indispensable virtues, with the need for them far exceeding any present supply. And even then they will be able to make themselves effective only through programs that are planned and administered in detail. To cite but one example, we will have to find some way of fruitfully employing the huge excess of human time and energy that is now available: we must prevent leisure from degenerating into unemployment.

Springing immediately from this problem is that of creating new institutions to serve these new rights. Our usual instrument for the enforcement of rights has been law. But law is inadequate by itself to enforce these rights. Indeed, even to speak of "enforcement" in these contexts is absurd. Many of the rights that men now seek cannot be enforced. At the most, they can be promoted or furthered. It is a healthy sign that men should want to become well educated, to lead meaningful lives, to engage in relevant activities, to achieve a higher cultural level, to participate effectively in their communities, and so forth. But the power of law to secure these claims is strictly limited. Many of the institutions that have hitherto served these purposes, such as the family, the church, the small community, and an indigenous tradition, are in a serious state of decline. If they cannot be revived—and it seems improbable that they can—we will have to develop new institutions, for law has a very limited effectiveness in these areas. As rights take on a more than legal meaning, they will require more than legal support.

As I have said before, I am not concerned to pass value judgments on the extension being given on the reach and content of rights. But I think that it requires only the simplest logical judgment to recognize that our present behavior is contradictory. You cannot possibly grant men the liberty to do what they want—including nothing at all—with their lives and at the same time assure them that all their needs will be satisfied. If society and the state were real entities with resources and energies of their own, this might be a sound doctrine in principle. So long as the needs that must be satisfied gratuitously are not excessive and a country is sufficiently rich and productive, the doctrine can even work tolerably well in practice. Under these conditions we can delude ourselves into thinking that society is a real entity and that the state is its real agent. These conditions are fast failing in this country. The demands being made on many public services—schools, hospitals, transportation systems, day-care centers, police, courts, and so on—far outweigh the real contribution of time and energy that individuals give to the support of these services. We are thus learning that society and the state are fictions: society is merely all of us, and we are all the state can call upon. As people demand more and more and contribute less and less, whether through their own fault or as victims of circumstance, the system breaks down. We see the evidence for this in two familiar and closely related facts: the serious decline in the quality of public services, and the steady refusal of people to accept higher taxes to bolster them.

Put in more legal terms, the outcome of this discussion is simple. I do not see how the traditional doctrine of individual rights and the new doctrine of human rights can possibly coexist in their present forms, for the conditions that they are respectively intended to promote are quite irreconcilable. In guaranteeing the liberty and privacy of persons, the doctrine of individual rights requires that the state not interfere in the lives of its citizens but leave them free to live how and where they choose; conversely, it requires that individuals bear the risk of their own decisions and actions. In guaranteeing to satisfy men's needs, the doctrine of human rights requires that the state supply positive goods and services to its citizens and protect them against their mistakes and misfortunes; conversely, it requires that individuals accept the high degree of mobilization and regulation, of state control and direction, that are demanded if the state is to be able to discharge these duties.

The effort to adhere to both of these doctrines involves us in a series of contradictions. The state is obligated to organize and administer the national effort in order to satisfy men's needs, and yet it is enjoined from mobilizing and regulating the lives of individuals. Men are assured of their freedom of action, and yet they are guaranteed against not only the blows of misfortune but also against the consequences of their own delinquency, irresponsibility, and incompetence. The services to be supplied by the state are compulsory; the cooperation of citizens in staffing the services is voluntary. Put baldly, this means that the state must direct the efforts of all of us without being able to direct the efforts of any of us. A doctrine composed of such incompatible elements as these cannot hold together. If health care, education, decent food and housing, and the other necessities and amenities of life are declared to be human rights to which people are entitled, then a complex machinery of public services must be instituted to furnish these benefits. It is futile to hold that this duty falls upon the state and then to hold that men also have individual rights which the state cannot violate or abridge. These latter rights prevent the state from obtaining from its citizens the performance of the tasks that are necessary to support these services, for the state has nowhere else to turn. In sum, we cannot continue to place onerous duties upon the state, as the agent of society, while refusing to place duties upon individual persons, who are the only substance of society. Thus, if these contradictions are to be resolved, we are going to have to modify either the traditional doctrine of individual rights or the new doctrine of human rights—or, more probably and preferably, both. Although it is possible that we will opt for one of the extreme procedures, it is unlikely, since both "rugged individualism" and "the welfare state" are now pejorative terms.

The real threat, then, is that individual rights will be steadily eroded and finally engulfed by the movement that is so rapidly transforming claimed human rights into recognized legal rights. This movement is still very young, but it is already beginning to be clear that the duties of care that it imposes upon the state must necessarily elicit a double response. First, the state will need to intervene in the lives of people at a very early age, or even before their birth, in order to protect itself against the multiplication of the types that cause such a drain upon its resources: children who are unwanted and uncared for; drug addicts; people with no training or skills; youthful delinquents and habitual criminals. From this intervention in the breeding and rearing of its citizens, it is but a step for the state to assert the need to control the uses they make of their lives. If the state is to discharge its new duties, it will need not only to assure itself of a sound citizen body but it will also need to draft, train, and assign people to specific roles.

I presume that most persons would hold this vision to be as implausible as it is undesirable. We acknowledge that you cannot make bricks without straw, that you can't eat your cake and have it too, that he who dances must pay the piper, and that having made your bed you must lie in it. We somehow persist, however, in believing that you can confer rights without imposing duties—or at least without having these duties fall on anyone. But we will inevitably learn that you cannot, for sooner or later, to cite another proverb, the chickens will come home to roost.

It is just for this reason that we should move ahead with great circumspection in acknowledging the claims of human rights. It is one thing for a society to assert that its public policy, adopted for both humanitarian and practical reasons, will be to do whatever its resources permit to provide its members the health care, education, decent housing, and so forth that they need, for then the extent to which these benefits and services are made available will be determined by representative and responsible bodies, largely regional and local rather than national in scope, that are in close touch with the needs and resources of their communities. It is quite another thing for a society to declare that people have a claim of right to these benefits and services, for once something is recognized as a legal right, it largely escapes from popular and political control and becomes subject only to judicial determination. Indeed, because of the momentum, elitism, and insulation that characterize the judiciary, one can say that rights even escape the grasp of judges and so altogether elude human control. They go their way ruthlessly, impelled by an inner logic of their own, sweeping aside all objections and obstacles until they have run their course. One does not have to accept the jeremiads of those who cry out against judicial autocracy and tyranny to recognize that this tendency is always present and has often surfaced in our legal history. Thus, if the doctrine of human rights becomes established in the legal system, there is a high probability that it will gradually subordinate and finally destroy the doctrine of individual rights. That may be the best, or only, solution to the welter of problems that currently beset the "advanced industrial societies," although I see no evidence that even the most fervent advocates of human rights and the new liberalism either desire or anticipate such an outcome. But if this is the path we are to follow, we should at least rid ourselves of the belief that we can secure the new rights without encroaching upon the old. For if the above argument is sound, that belief is a delusion. The dilemma in which we find ourselves is simple and inescapable: the recognition of human rights imposes duties upon the state; the adequate performance of these duties entails corresponding powers; but the effective exercise of these powers is thwarted by the doctrine of individual rights.

The conclusion to which this discussion points can be put very briefly. While this dilemma is inescapable once entered, there is a way to avoid it altogether: the claims advanced under the guise of human rights should be accepted as social goals rather than acknowledged as legal rights.

[CHAPTER XV]

HUMAN RIGHTS AND
THEIR IMPLEMENTATION

I HAVE BEEN TREATING of human rights in general, but have examined none closely. And I have argued that the implementation of these rights is apt to intrude upon individual rights and to disrupt the social order, but I have not documented this thesis with a careful examination of any actual instance. Although the detailed discussion of *Wyatt* v. *Stickney*[1] addresses these points (particularly the latter), that analysis was carried on from a different perspective and with a different purpose. It will therefore be well to present a case study that deals directly with these issues. This will have the added advantage of affording me another opportunity to apply my abstract matrix of law to the treatment of a concrete problem.

The human right I shall focus on is the right to privileged admission.[2] This is an extremely prickly and even dangerous subject. But it has compensating advantages: the issue is close and critical, posing the question of human rights in sharp terms; there are important court decisions in which the majority and dissenting opinions argue the question persuasively, so that both parties are ably represented; and finally, the arguments that are advanced to justify privileged admission—legally, morally, and socially—exhibit in a glaring light the ultimate consequences that can follow from the defense and implementation of a human right.

The subject is dangerous because it is heavily charged with emotion. This being the case, it is best to explain at once the conclusion to which my analysis will lead me. It is my belief that the programs that have been instituted to implement the right to privileged admission are defeating their own purpose. Although they are intended to promote equality among races and to create a unified society, they are in fact issuing in a doctrine and in practices that threaten to perpetuate the present

---

[1] See Chapter X.

[2] Marshall Cohen, Thomas Nagel, and Thomas Scanlon, eds., *Equality and Preferential Treatment* (Princeton: Princeton University Press, 1977), contains an interesting series of essays on this issue and on the closely related one of preferential employment.

inequalities and to destroy social cohesion. My argument will focus on the rationales that are advanced to justify programs of privileged admission. In the course of the chapter, I shall trace the movement of these rationales from their inception with the doctrine of "compelling state interest" to their climax in the theory of the "cultural bias" of admission tests, and I shall contend that this climactic rationale contains the bitter seeds of a pluralism and divisiveness that will frustrate the individual programs' intentions.

The two leading cases dealing with this issue are *DeFunis* v. *Odegaard*,[3] which involved a privileged admission program at the University of Washington Law School, and *Bakke* v. *Regents of the University of California*,[4] which involved a similar program at the medical school of the Davis campus of that university. The Washington Supreme Court held that the law school's privileged admission program was constitutional and valid, while the California Supreme Court held to the contrary regarding the Davis Medical School program; the two programs were identical in all essential respects. When the United States Supreme Court held *DeFunis* moot, Justice Douglas wrote a strong dissenting opinion in which the arguments both for and against privileged admission were set out in a very revealing manner.[5] It is upon the rationales developed in the majority and dissenting opinions in these cases that my argument will rely.

This argument is very apt to invite misunderstanding, for it questions both the legitimacy and the effectiveness of privileged admission as a means to the end it seeks, and this is all too easily misinterpreted as a rejection of the end itself. That is not at all my position nor intention. I agree that our society has an obligation to eliminate the racial discrimination that has prevailed in the past and to erase the harm that it has done, I support the goal of equal opportunity for all, and I share the vision of a society in which racial considerations will cease to have any legal or political significance. However, it is my belief and contention that programs designed to implement the right to privileged admission will subvert these goals instead of serving them. This—and only this—is what my argument seeks to establish.

[3] 507 P. 2d 1169 (1973).

[4] 533 P. 2d 1152 (1976). The ensuing discussion of privileged admission was written prior to the Supreme Court's decision in Regents of the University of California v. Bakke, 438 U.S. 265, 98 S. Ct. 2733 (1978). But that ruling does nothing to challenge the argument that I am about to develop; indeed, I think it strengthens its force. The decision will be analyzed and this contention supported in the second section of this chapter (see pp. 286-301).

[5] DeFunis v. Odegaard, 416 U.S. 312 (1974) at 320-348.

The purpose of these programs is explicit and laudable: they are meant to increase the representation of minority groups in professional schools and hence in the professions themselves, thus furthering the process of integration. To achieve this purpose, they incorporate four significant features. First, certain numbers or percentages of places ("quotas" in fact if not in name) are reserved to members of minority groups. Second, applications of these minority members are set apart to be considered by a special committee and special procedures. Third, the standards applied to minority members are less stringent than those that majority members must meet. Fourth, these programs are restricted to members of designated minority races; no member of the majority white race is eligible to be judged by these more lenient standards. The result is that most of the minority members admitted under the programs at the Universities of Washington and California-Davis had considerably lower marks in college and on the admission tests than did DeFunis, Bakke, and other whites who were denied admission. These programs clearly discriminated against these men solely on the basis of their race: DeFunis and Bakke were placed at a disadvantage—they were treated unequally—not through any shortcoming or wrongdoing of their own but simply because they were members of the majority white race. All of this was admitted by the defendant universities.[6]

Due to this racial classification and this discriminatory impact, privileged admission appears to entail a denial of the rights to due process and equal protection, which is violative of the Fifth and Fourteenth Amendments and hence unconstitutional. That these basic rights extend to public education was unequivocally affirmed in the landmark case of Brown v. Board of Education, where the Supreme Court, noting the importance of education in contemporary society, declared that access to education "is a right which must be made available to all on equal terms."[7] In his dissent in DeFunis, Justice Douglas echoed this note, saying that, whatever his race may be, DeFunis "had a constitutional right to have his application considered on its individual merits in a racially neutral manner."[8]

The newly claimed right to privileged admission thus comes into direct conflict with the traditional constitutional right to equal protection. Thus, if admission policies based on a racial classification are to be jus-

[6] On the character and impact of these programs, cf. DeFunis, supra, n. 3 at 1191, 1174, 1182; Bakke, supra. n. 4 at 1156, 1159, 1163, 1179; DeFunis, supra, n. 5 at 331-334.

[7] 347 U.S. 483, 493 (1954).

[8] 416 U.S. 312, 334 (1974). Emphasis added. As we shall see shortly, the phrase "racially neutral manner" is to play a decisive role in the debate over privileged admission.

tified, it must be established that the former right takes precedence over the latter. Given the explicit injunction of the Fourteenth Amendment, that no state shall "deny to any person within its jurisdiction the equal protection of the laws," and the central position that the right to equal protection has come to occupy in American legal theory and practice, this is an arduous task. The burden of proof that it imposes has been defined by the Washington Supreme Court with admirable brevity and precision: "The burden is upon the law school to show that its consideration of race in admitting students is *necessary* to the accomplishment of *a compelling state interest*."[9]

The rationale advanced to meet this challenge constitutes the first line of defense of privileged admission: it is simple and straightforward, proceeding through three steps. The first of these identifies, the "compelling state interest" in question as that of making good the deprivation that minority groups have suffered in the past and thus promoting equality among the races. The second step holds that an essential ingredient of this "interest" is the securing of more minority professionals—doctors, lawyers, and so forth—who are in turn needed to serve the members of their respective races. The third step argues that privileged admission is "necessary" to achieve this purpose: all other possible means have been tried and have proved fruitless.

This appears to be a strong case. But it is met with an even stronger rebuttal, challenging both the effectiveness and the legitimacy of privileged admission as a means to the end it purports to serve. As regards the first point, the courts have pointed out that there is no empirical evidence whatsoever to support the supposition that these minority group professionals will put aside their own interests and careers and dedicate themselves to the service of underprivileged races. To make matters worse, the contention that they, and only they, will do so rests on the invidious assumption that, as the California Supreme Court put it, "one race is more selflessly socially oriented or by contrast that another is more selfishly acquisitive."[10] As regards the second point, it is doubtful if this purpose of creating an array of minority group lawyers and doctors to serve their respective races is even a proper one. Justice Douglas, who certainly has impeccable credentials as a friend of minorities, has made this point in strong terms. In his words: "The Equal Protection Clause commands the elimination of racial barriers, not their creation in order to satisfy our theory as to how society ought to be organized. The purpose of the University of Washington cannot be to

---

[9] DeFunis, supra, n. 3 at 1182. Emphasis added.   [10] Bakke, supra, n. 4 at 1167.

produce black lawyers for blacks, Polish lawyers for Poles, Jewish lawyers for Jews, Irish lawyers for Irish. It should be to produce good lawyers for Americans and not to place First Amendment barriers against anyone."[11] In sum, the best that this "compelling state interest" argument can yield is the rather weak claim that privileged admission is a dubiously effective means of furthering a constitutionally questionable end.

These programs, then, would seem to be fatally flawed by the fact that they are based on a rigid racial classification that discriminates against members of one race without regard to their individual merits or demerits and for no other reason than their racial membership. But the advocates of privileged admission have other positions to fall back upon, for there are two conditions under which courts have sanctioned such practices. One of these hangs on the distinction between "invidious" and "benign" racial classifications: the former are intended to stigmatize one race and put it in a disadvantaged position; the latter are intended to repair the effects of past discrimination and to promote integration of the races. However, this distinction is fictional rather than factual, ideal rather than practical, since it is virtually impossible to grant privileges to one race without imposing burdens upon another. This requires the difficult trick of not letting either of your hands know what the other is doing. And it is clearly impossible in the case of privileged admission, for everyone concerned admits that these programs are not "benign" as regards DeFunis, Bakke, and other whites. Whatever the intention of these programs—and that point is unquestioned—their impact is discriminatory and violative of the Fourteenth Amendment's equal protection clause.

The second condition under which courts have sanctioned racial classifications that favor one race to the detriment of another is in those cases where this has been found necessary to repair past discrimination by the defendant now called to make amends. But this doctrine is of no help in the present instance. For amid all of the confusion and conflict surrounding the DeFunis and Bakke cases, the one thing that is clear and upon which everyone is agreed is that the schools concerned had not discriminated against the minority races they now seek to favor. To the contrary, they had made varied and determined efforts to recruit minority members, and it was the failure of these efforts that led them to institute programs of privileged admission as a measure of last resort.

The impact of these facts upon the equal protection clause would seem

[11] DeFunis, supra, n. 5 at 342.

to ring the death knell over privileged admissions. But the outcome is otherwise, for the advocates of these programs now shift to a radically different line of argument, and one that raises critically serious issues and poses far-reaching consequences. This argument holds that the two universities have all along been guilty of de facto discrimination, albeit unknowingly and unintentionally, because the admission tests they have employed are such as to place minority members at a grave disadvantage. This is the famous thesis of the "cultural bias" of all tests designed by the white majority and used to choose among candidates for admission to professional schools, for employment, and for promotion. All such tests, it is charged, have a built-in bias, whether intended or not, against minority races, depriving them of an equal opportunity to compete fairly and on even terms with the white majority.

This general charge is supported by two specific complaints. The first of these maintains that success on these tests requires a certain level of educational and cultural experience, so that those whose exposure to education and culture have been inferior or meager cannot be expected to do as well on them as others who are better prepared. The second complaint—and this is the crux of the matter—holds that the cultural backgrounds (the experiences and aspirations, the intellectual attitudes and habits) of minority races are quite different from that of the majority white race; hence, tests designed by the latter group, based on its own linguistic usage, methods of training, lived experiences and expectations, conceptual models, and modes of thought are unfair and inappropriate to minority members because they are incapable of reaching and measuring the innate capacities and competences of these members. Finally, this argument has a codicil that assumes that *all* members of minority races suffer from this deprivation and difference and that *no* member of the majority race does.

This thesis is beyond challenge regarding the facts it asserts, although its codicil is more than suspect.[12] To the extent that any persons of any race and for any reason are inadequately informed and trained—if they read slowly and with imperfect comprehension, if they cannot express themselves with sufficient clarity and exactness, if they lack rudimentary skills in mathematics and logical reasoning, if they have English as a

---

[12] All three of the court opinions dealing with the *DeFunis* and *Bakke* cases have pointed out that this assumption is unsupported by any empirical evidence and that it is quite obviously contrary to fact. And both of the professional schools concerned acknowledged that they had made no serious effort to determine the economic, educational, and cultural backgrounds of the minority members who were admitted under their privileged admission programs.

second language or choose to speak some dialect of their own, and if they are largely ignorant of the history and traditions of Western civilization—then they are going to do badly on tests that assume these accomplishments. No one would dispute this.

But the significant question remains: Does this fact render such tests "culturally biased" and de facto discriminatory? When the white majority identifies certain levels of verbal and analytical competence, familiarity with certain bodies of knowledge, and the acquirement of certain skills as prerequisites to gaining access to various programs and employments, are the resulting tests prejudiced in themselves, irrelevant to their purported ends, and biased against minorities whose backgrounds, experiences, and training are different from those of the majority? Or do such tests define standards that must be met, a training that must be acquired, and conditions that must be satisfied if the necessary social tasks are to be effectively performed and the society itself to be a coherent whole?[13]

Advocates of privileged admission contend that the correct answer to the first question is "yes"; to the second, "no." The argument in support of this contention is laid out by Justice Douglas with classic simplicity and directness. He begins with a bow to the Equal Protection clause: "There is no constitutional right for any race to be preferred."[14] To the contrary, the whole purpose of the Fourteenth Amendment is to eliminate racial discrimination. And it is Douglas's argument that this can be accomplished only if "cultural standards of a diverse rather than a homogeneous society are taken into account. . . . The key to the problem is the consideration of each applicant *in a racially neutral way*. Since the LSAT reflects questions touching on cultural backgrounds, the Admissions Committee acted properly in my view in setting minority applicants apart for separate processing."[15] Douglas then points out that there are innumerable minority groups in the United States, including poor whites, who "come from such disparate backgrounds that a test sensitively tuned to most applicants would be wide of the mark for many minorities."[16] And so to the conclusion: "My reaction is that the pres-

---

[13] In practice, of course, this question can be answered only by examining each such test to determine whether it is appropriate to the selective process for which it is employed and whether it adequately predicts competence and success. When a test is challenged on these grounds, it is subject to rigid scrutiny by the courts. I am here discussing the matter in general and theoretical terms only. And I am assuming (what courts will decide) that the tests are relevant and unbiased. This issue will shortly be discussed in more detail.

[14] DeFunis, supra, n. 5 at 336.

[15] Ibid. at 334. Emphasis in original.   [16] Ibid.

ence of an LSAT is sufficient warrant for a school to put racial minorities into a separate class in order to better probe their capacities and potentials."[17]

No one would deny that tests that reflect the characteristics and standards of the majority white race will pose difficulties for persons of any race whose educational and cultural backgrounds are notably different in content or quality from the majority norm. But to argue from this fact to the conclusion that such tests are de facto biased and unconstitutional requires two covert assumptions.

The first of these is purely legal, and I shall deal with it very briefly. It maintains that the mere fact that minorities do less well than majority members on a test is enough by itself, and without even searching the content and intention of the test, to stigmatize it as biased and unfair. This claim has not figured prominently in *DeFunis* or *Bakke*, and so it has not been ruled on in the context of privileged admissions. But it has been the central issue in numerous suits challenging the tests used to determine employment and promotion, and the Supreme Court has recently handed down a firm decision on the question.[18]

This case arose when some blacks filed suit against the District of Columbia Police Department, claiming that the test used to select recruits discriminated against them. The test in question was Civil Service Test 21, which is widely used to ascertain whether applicants for various government positions have the required level of verbal skill. The test was held to be neutral on its face, and there was no evidence of a discriminatory intent;[19] the only argument to support the charge of discriminatory impact was the fact that many more blacks than whites failed it.

The district court ruled against the plaintiff blacks.[20] The court of appeals did not question the neutrality of the test or the recruiting efforts of the police department, but it nevertheless reversed in an opinion that advances the "cultural bias" thesis in an extreme form. As summarized in the Supreme Court opinion, this argument held that "lack of dis-

---

[17] Ibid. at 335. It is interesting to note that Justice Douglas is not altogether happy with the conclusion to which his argument leads. At several points in his opinion he suggests that it would be possible and desirable to open these special admission programs to members of all races (including whites) on the basis of economic, educational, and cultural deprivation rather than racial membership. Justice Douglas is torn between his sympathy for minorities and his respect for the Fourteenth Amendment. Cf. also ibid. at 332, 334, 339.

[18] Washington v. Davis, 426 U.S. 229 (1976).

[19] To the contrary, the police department submitted convincing evidence (accepted by all of the courts that have heard the case) of its strenuous and successful efforts to recruit and promote more blacks.

[20] Washington v. Davis, 348 F. Supp. 15 (1972).

criminatory intent in designing and administering Test 21 was irrelevant; the critical fact was rather that a far greater proportion of blacks—four times as many—failed the test as did whites. This disproportionate impact, standing alone and without regard to whether it indicated a discriminatory purpose, was held sufficient to establish a constitutional violation."[21]

The Supreme Court rejected this argument and reversed the appeals court in a strongly worded opinion that carried the sting of rebuke. It stated:

> As an initial matter, we have difficulty understanding how a law establishing a racially neutral qualification for employment is nevertheless racially discriminatory and denies "any person . . . equal protection of the laws" simply because a greater proportion of Negroes fail to qualify than members of other racial or ethnic groups. . . . it is untenable that the Constitution prevents the government from seeking modestly to upgrade the communicative abilities of its employees rather than be satisfied with some lower level of comprehension. . . . Respondents, as Negroes, could no more successfully claim that the test denied them equal protection than could white applicants who also failed.[22]

This opinion established two significant points. First, it asserts that a test cannot be held to be discriminatory simply on the ground that members of one race fail it more often than do members of another race. Second, it asserts that mere membership in a race does not entitle persons to be judged by different or more lenient standards than those applied to other races.

Although this decision would seem to close the door on the cultural bias thesis and on programs of privileged admission, it does not. For there now enters the second assumption that is employed to challenge the validity of LSAT and other similar tests. This advances a particular view of the proper character and function of "racially neutral" tests; and underlying this view, and of far greater significance, is a particular vision of human nature and the social order. On both of these points, this assumption directly challenges the Supreme Court interpretation as expressed in the opinion in *Washington* v. *Davis*.

According to the Court, a "racially neutral" test is one that measures

---

[21] Ibid., 426 U.S. 229 (1976) at 237. It is significant to note the manner in which the court of appeals interprets a differential outcome as necessarily discriminatory. See ibid., 512 F. 2d 956 (1975).

[22] Ibid., 426 U.S. 229 (1976) at 245-246.

skills and talents that are presumed to be the human heritage of all races, judges these against a common standard, and sets what society regards as reasonable attainments for entrance into its various programs and positions. To be "racially neutral" a test must treat all races alike, offering no special advantages, imposing no special handicaps, and making no special allowances to any race because of traits or circumstances that are peculiar to it. The Supreme Court is assuming that a society can be viable only if all of its members share certain basic similarities and attainments, acknowledge common values and standards, and accept the responsibility of conforming to rules and norms that apply equally to all.

The assumption that supports the cultural bias thesis interprets these matters in a radically different manner. This is brought out clearly by Justice Douglas in explaining why, despite the explicit injunction of the Fourteenth Amendment, he thinks that privileged admission programs are necessary, proper, and constitutional. He argues in this way: "The reason is that professional persons, particularly lawyers, are not selected for life in a computerized society. The Indian who walks to the beat of Chief Seattle of the Muckleshoot Tribe in Washington has a different culture from examiners at law schools. . . . Many Eskimos, American Indians, Filipinos, Chicanos, Asian Americans, Burmese, and Africans come from such disparate backgrounds that a test sensitively tuned for most applicants would be wide of the mark for many minorities." These tests make race "a subtle force in eliminating minority members because of cultural differences," whereas ideally these members "should be chosen on talent and character alone, not on cultural orientation or leanings. The melting pot is not designed to homogenize people, making them uniform in consistency. . . . Insofar as LSAT's reflect the dimensions and orientation of the Organization Man they do a disservice to minorities." And so to the conclusion: "The case, in my view, should be remanded for a new trial to consider, *inter alia*, whether the established LSAT's should be eliminated so far as racial minorities are concerned."[23]

We can now see quite clearly what Justice Douglas and the adherents of privileged admission mean by a racially neutral test: it is one that in its design and administration is adjusted to the particular educational and cultural backgrounds of each minority race, making allowances for the ways in which their several life styles diverge from that of the majority.

[23] DeFunis, supra, n. 5 at 334, 335, 336. It is worth noting how heavily Justice Douglas's opinion rests on sheerly *ad hominem* arguments. Chief Seattle is evidently intended to portray Rousseau's noble savage; the Organization Man, to epitomize the worst of Madison Avenue hucksterism. This is an appeal to emotional stereotypes rather than rational concepts.

To escape the taint of cultural bias, a test must be "sensitively tuned" to the distinctive language habits, modes of thought, patterns of behavior, levels of attainment in basic intellectual skills, and standards of achievement of each race, must respect the right of each race to be itself, and must acknowledge the equal legitimacy of each of them.

Furthermore, we can now extrapolate and see equally clearly the sort of society that the cultural bias thesis envisages and that programs of privileged admission would promote. It would seem that this society must be to a high degree heterogeneous, relativistic, and egalitarian: it would harbor numerous extremely diverse groups; it would demand from them no conformity to a common set of standards and would judge them against no common norms; and it would accept each of these groups on its own terms, treating all of them as though they had equal merits and claims. In such a society, each racial and national minority would have the right to retain its own modes and norms of life, and society would have the duty to grant all of them equal access to roles and positions, accommodating the requirements and performance of these to the particular background and attainment of each minority.

Justice Douglas and the advocates of the cultural bias thesis do not, of course, carry their argument this far. They might—indeed, they probably would—reject this conclusion as logically sophistical and practically unrealistic. But if the preceding analysis is sound, then this is the clear implication of the rationale that is employed to justify privileged admission. And certain recent developments, which I will discuss shortly, foreshadow a society of precisely this kind. However, it is neither my intention nor my present purpose to argue the merits and demerits of this vision of the social order. This raises the delicate issue of how wide a diversity a society can permit—or how close a uniformity it must demand—if it is to be viable. Certainly a society need not, and should not, be monolithic and inflexible: it should allow for differences and movement within it and for change through time. But it is generally held that a society must have a basic coherence, built around a framework of common values, beliefs, expectations, and conventions. Tolerance with regard to these matters is a very great virtue, but it is not an absolute virtue. For tolerance can flouish only where certain patterns and standards of thought and action are commonly acknowledged and adhered to. Here, as in so many other cases, Aristotle's doctrine of the mean speaks compellingly.

Be that as it may, my present concern with the right to privileged admission has a narrower focus than this large social issue. I began this discussion by hypothesizing that the arguments devised to validate the right to privileged admission and the programs instituted to implement this right would defeat their own purpose. They are intended to promote equality among races and to create a truly integrated and unified society. But if my reading of the rationale and impact of these programs is correct, they will perpetuate and magnify the present inequalities and they will foster intense divisiveness and hostility among the races. Each group now requires of all of the others that they make allowance for any inherent and situational characteristics peculiar to it and that they accept and judge it on the basis of these characteristics rather than against a common standard. Every group now rejects any attempt by any other group—and especially by one pretending to speak through the law as an agent of the society—to impose upon it any other norms than its own, for this would constitute enforced submission to an alien regime and so would be impugned as an invasion of privacy, an abridgment of freedom of expression, and a denial of equal protection. This is a recipe for inequality and enmity.[24]

If the theses of cultural bias and racial neutrality were appealed to only for the purpose of justifying privileged admission to professional schools, the preceding argument might be dismissed as nothing more than an academic exercise, having little or no practical significance. These programs would affect, favorably and adversely, only a very small number of persons, and their social impact would be modest. We might then look through our fingers at their legal and moral flaws and accept them as a placatory gesture that might have some utilitarian value. But, like any others, these ideas cannot be confined. As was just mentioned, this rationale has already been widely used to challenge the validity of numerous tests administered to screen applicants for employment in a wide variety of fields. In this context it would obviously have a very much greater impact, as it would touch a vital interest of large numbers of persons, and it could, as courts have pointed out, have an adverse effect upon the quality of both public services and private interests.[25]

[24] In *The Morality of Consent* (New Haven: Yale University Press, 1975), Alexander Bickel argues to this same effect. After deploring the manner in which universities have given ground to privileged admission by "yield [ing] to pressure simply to relax standards" and after deriding the manner in which the plea for equality has been transformed into the demand to be treated more than equally, he says: "The history of the racial quota is a history of subjugation, not beneficence. Its evil lies not in its name but in its effect: a quota is a divider of society, a creator of castes, and it is all the worse for its racial base, especially in a society desperately striving for an equality that will make race irrelevant" (pp. 132-133).

[25] Cf. cases cited in Washington v. Davis, supra, n. 18. Bickel stresses this same danger in *The Morality of Consent*, pp. 133-134.

This rationale continues to gain momentum, and in two recent cases it has been extended to a context that is of even greater significance to society: this is the field of general public education, which touches the lives of everyone and has a determining influence on the quality of these lives and on the caliber of society. In these instances, the cultural bias thesis has been carried in actual practice to extremes that one would have hesitated to suggest even as logical possibilities.

One of these cases evolved out of the new practice of "proficiency testing" of high-school students prior to and as a condition of graduation. Such a program was recently instituted in Florida, and in high schools with predominantly black or Hispanic student bodies failure rates ran over 75 percent. As a result, the Florida NAACP has signified its intention to file suit for a restraining order to enjoin such testing on the ground that the tests are "culturally biased" and discriminatory. Mr. Charles Cherry, president of the Florida NAACP, had this to say about the test: "There were items on that test dealing with check books and interest rates. The average black kid has no knowledge of that whatsoever, while the white kids are taught it at home."[26]

The test in question—known as a "functional literacy" test—is "secure" and hence not open to public inspection. But I have been able to examine a similar test designed by the Dade County (Florida) School Board,[27] and sample questions from other such tests have been widely published since interest in this subject became acute. The questions on these tests would seem to satisfy the two essential criteria of validity: to meet a rigid court scrutiny for "neutrality" and to be relevant to their purpose, which is to ascertain whether students are competent to deal with the kinds of practical situations and demands that they will face in everyday life in society. They require nothing more than fundamental verbal and mathematical skills, and they are concerned with such matters as reading bus and plane schedules, making change, interpreting graphs and charts, filling out job application forms, and the use of such basic sources of information as dictionaries, telephone books, catalogues, and maps. Finally, as regards the test challenged in Florida, the Department of Education has taken pains to ensure that it should be "racially neutral" and not discriminatory. "The Department conducts several different checks for bias *including test review by minorities*. No bias has

---

[26] *Newsweek*, 9 January 1978, p. 65.

[27] I owe this information and the copy of the Dade County test to the courtesy of a private communication from Dr. Thomas H. Fisher of the Assessment Section of the Florida Department of Education.

been detected in the items thus far, but, in court, I suspect the burden of proof will be on the State, not the NAACP."[28]

Minority group objections to these tests clearly exhibit the paradoxical consequences of the cultural bias thesis. In the first place, they assume that parents have no responsibility to teach and train their children or to initiate them into the ways of the society they are going to enter and in which they must compete. This becomes exclusively the duty of the state. But then, when the state assumes this function and devises tests to measure and improve its performance, it is charged with invidious racial discrimination. Second, and more importantly, these complainants seem to be prepared to have minority students graduated from high school and placed on the labor market so unprepared and ill-equipped that they can fill only the most menial jobs, if any at all.

In this context, then, the cultural bias thesis leads to the result that apparently sincere and well-intentioned efforts on the part of the state to improve the education of its future citizens and to ensure that they are able to cope with society as it now exists are unfair and discriminatory regarding minorities. This goes to the heart of the educational process—which is itself crucial to the life of society—challenging the right of the state to employ "proficiency" or "functional literacy" tests as a means to detect and correct deficiencies in the students' preparation and to see that high-school graduates do have certain basic skills and competences.

As I have acknowledged, the neutrality and relevance of any such test must be—and is—determined by a rigid scrutiny by the courts. But given the sensitiveness of our society to minority claims, the dependence

---

[28] Personal communication from Dr. Fisher, supra, n. 27. Emphasis added. The expectation voiced in the final clause indicates the rigid scrutiny to which these tests are subjected, virtually amounting to the assumption that the defendant is guilty until he is proved innocent.

The other case previously mentioned that deals with this issue challenged South Carolina's use of the National Teacher Examinations as a factor in certification and promotion of teachers. The United States Department of Justice brought suit against the state, charging bias in the test. The district court ruled in favor of the state (Civil Action No. 75-1610, April 1977) and the Supreme Court affirmed (Civil Action Nos. 77-122 and 77-543, decided 16 January 1978). Both courts were satisfied that there was no discriminatory intention, though there was a strong discriminatory impact—the 1976 revision of the test-score requirements will disqualify 83 percent of black applicants but only 17.5 percent of white applicants. The courts also held that the test was appropriate to the state's interest and purpose in employing it. This latter ruling involved the complex and elusive legal issue (not relevant to the present discussion) of whether a test must be validated as predictive of job capability and performance or whether it need only be shown to ascertain whether applicants have certain competences and knowledge.

of all public school systems upon federal monies, the safeguards erected by the Florida Department of Education, and the Supreme Court's validation of the South Carolina program, I presume that these tests are neutral, meaning to discriminate against no racial or national minority because of its cultural background but seeking rather to make good the disadvantages that any persons of any race have suffered because of earlier educational and cultural deprivation. Granting (stipulating, if one will) the sincerity of this intention and the neutrality of these tests, for any minority to protest programs of this sort would appear to be clearly detrimental to the good of society and, even more certainly, to be suicidal as regards the minorities themselves.

This brings my argument full circle and should go far to substantiate the charge with which I started: that the rationales employed to justify the right to privileged admission would eventually subvert the end in view. For it is difficult to imagine a more effective way to perpetuate the inequalities that the cultural bias doctrine seeks to correct than by undermining the effort to improve the education and enhance the skills of all students, particularly underprivileged minorities. Indeed, with these long-range consequences exposed, it is cynics among the white majority who might be expected to espouse with enthusiasm the cultural bias rationale, while minorities should eschew it as though it were the serpent offering Eve the apple.

Which brings us to the question, why should a policy instituted by sophisticated and well-intentioned institutions have led to such a paradoxical result? To understand this outcome, we need to place this course of events in a more systematic context. For this purpose, I shall again employ my analysis of order and the matrix of law in which this found expression, seeking thereby to indicate just where and why the argument for privileged admission goes astray and misses its goal.

The fundamental mistake, I would argue, is the same as that made by Judge Johnson in his orders in *Wyatt* v. *Stickney*: atttention is closely focused on only a narrow range of the elements of order with a neglect of the others. As a result, quite obvious repercussions and reactions are not foreseen (or they are brushed aside as incidental and unimportant), and it is this that has led to the unintended anticlimax. Furthermore, this mistake is not only generically but even specifically the same in the two cases: regard is had for only a small segment—or population—of the Many, and programs are designed with an eye solely for a single desired outcome in the regime of Purposiveness. The other populations that compose the Many, the other legitimate concerns of society, the limits set by Necessity and the options offered by Possibility, and all of the other elements of order are simply lost sight of. As we saw in considering the *Wyatt* case and the right to treatment, this procedure created problems and aroused opposition that could have been anticipated and minimized if a larger view had been taken at the start. The same thing is occurring with the programs instituted to implement the right to privileged admission.[29]

This identity of mistake and outcome may seem to be merely coincidental, but it is not. Rather, it is inherent in the very nature of human rights that the response to them should be of this kind and should fall into this error. A human right is always claimed by some particular group or class of persons who complain that they are in some way abused, exploited, or discriminated against, and who seek relief and redress. When this claim is argued by its adherents, and when a court accords it legal recognition and seeks to secure its enforcement, it is all but inevitable that attention should center on only two elements: the wronged group and the steps that must be taken (the changes that must be effected) if the wrong is to be righted. It is precisely this characteristic of human rights that, besides constituting the term a woeful misnomer, makes them so questionable and creates so many difficulties in their implementation. Traditional constitutional rights inhere in the people generally, and their enforcement in the interest of one person does not normally touch the rights of others. Human rights inhere in special groups or classes that are specially circumstanced, and their enforcement is apt to impinge on the rights of others and to strain the social fabric in various ways. Total absorption in repairing the wrongs of one group—however laudable it may be—cannot but result in a partial view and an unbalanced treatment of the problem with which one is dealing.

I have already discussed in detail the troubled path and dubious outcome of privileged admission. It remains only to indicate, quite briefly, how these mistakes could have been foreseen and guarded against if

[29] It is particularly difficult to understand how a law school, versed in constitutional law and familiar with Supreme Court decisions, could have installed a program that baldly relied on racial classifications and quotas. Given the wide discretion of deans and admission committees in selecting applicants and the variety of criteria to which they can appeal to justify their decisions the desired result could have been achieved with greater effectiveness and fairness by a series of admissions based on a scrutiny of the records and traits of individual students. DeFunis and Bakke would then have had to challenge the judgment of the dean and committee in each case, instead of being able to claim a quite obvious denial of equal protection. This would have imposed a burden of proof that would have been difficult to sustain. Justice Douglas also suggested this as the preferred method of increasing minority representation and meeting constitutional requirements. Justice Powell's opinion in *Bakke*, announcing the ruling of the Supreme Court, recommends a procedure quite similar to this, with race to be considered as one factor among others in an admissions policy designed to procure a diverse student body. This decision is analyzed on pp. 293-296 of this chapter.

these programs had been drafted in the context and with full consciousness of a systematic analysis and matrix of law.

The most immediate and apparent effect of this narrow focus of attention manifests itself in the dimension of the Many: it consists in the adverse impact of privileged admission on all those who are both excluded from the reach of the right and are disadvantaged when it is exercised by others. Since the places available in any professional school are limited, this discriminatory result could not be avoided; but its psychological impact on those who are disadvantaged by it could have been cushioned, and its legal justification eased, if the acceptance of minority members had been based, at least ostensibly, on special individual traits rather than on class membership. Intent on the right they sought to secure, the planners of these programs did not measure the wrong they wrought: they appear to have acted in the simple hope that this wrong could be casually dismissed as too slight to be significant. When this hope was disappointed (as it had to be, since the right to equal protection is personal), they launched the line of argument just traced, starting with the "compelling state interest" rationale, then introducing the "benign" racial classification doctrine, and finally relying on the "cultural bias" thesis.

The arguments and programs that are mustered to further the implementation of privileged admission have immediate repercussions in the dimension of Pattern: they segregate society into innumerable castes, with each caste voicing its own demand for special concessions and with caste membership rather than personal characteristics becoming the decisive factor in determining the treatment to be accorded to individuals. This explicit and arbitrarily defined diversity of groups has several harmful effects: it fosters divisiveness among these groups, which are transformed into hostile and competing factions; it treats real inequalities as though they did not exist or as though they were merely qualitatively neutral differences; and it imposes artificial conditions and relationships that hinder individuals from being themselves and that prohibit society from operating effectively.

The impact of privileged admission in the dimension of Process is at least as serious and more insidious, for the rationales that were developed to justify this right have been taken over and used to attack any tests or programs in which minorities do less well than the majority whites. The paradoxical and deplorable effect of this is to undermine all efforts to correct the very deprivations and deficiencies that are responsible for these differential results. In the field of employment, this penalizes the skilled and competent as well as the employers who seek these, treating these acquirements as though they were irrelevant and even suspect. What is even worse, because more basic, this practice threatens to reduce the educational process to little more than a diploma-and degree-granting function.[30]

It is in the dimension of the One that the impact of privileged admission is at once the least conspicuous immediately and the most critical ultimately, for the outcome of the arguments designed to justify these programs and of the attitudes that these in turn engender is to threaten the integrity of the social order. As we have seen, the cultural bias thesis points toward the elimination of all general standards of competence and achievement, since these are stigmatized as arbitrary and discriminatory. Instead of individuals being called on to meet common requirements for admission to various programs and positions, it is now demanded that such requirements be tailored to the "cultural and educational background" of each minority group. Until only yesterday, any such suggestion would not have been taken seriously enough to be rejected but would simply have been laughed at: even such a social rebel and intellectual iconoclast as Hutchins clothed his prophecy in the modest apparel of irony. But the previously discussed cases, dealing with proficiency testing and conditions of employment, make it clear that what the imagination boggles at, moral fervor married to logic takes in its stride. When United States courts of appeal declare that a test, neutral on its face and with no showing of a discriminatory intent, is invalidated by the mere fact that members of one race fail it more often than do members of another; and when the NAACP seeks to prevent states from employing tests—again held to be neutral and nondiscriminatory—to assure that its high-school graduates are equipped to function successfully in today's society—when sober and responsible bodies take such steps as these, then fantasy has become fact and the situation must indeed be taken seriously. For now the very right of society to define its character and to defend its integrity is being denied.

The effort to establish the validity of privileged admission is having a similar effect on the legal system. These programs are handicapped from the start by their direct confrontation with the due process and equal protection provisions of the Constitution and with a long line of

---

[30] It is worth recalling that the late Robert Hutchins prophesied some forty years ago that this would be the end result of the "educational egalitarianism" that he felt to be nascent even then. As an antidote, he suggested that on reaching his majority every person be awarded whatever degree his heart desired; then those with the taste and talent for it could set out to acquire an education. If the cultural bias thesis wins the field, what Hutchins proposed with tongue in cheek will become, under a thin disguise, the guiding principle of our educational system—with the notable difference that now there will be no place to pursue an education.

Supreme Court decisions. There is thus a very real sense in which the rationales mustered in their defense are so many exercises in constitutional evasion. The Constitution has for long stood as not only the fundamental law of the land but also as the embodiment of a definite vision of the social order and the social good. Furthermore, the Constitution provides for changes in itself to reflect changes in this vision. But the procedure it establishes for this purpose is carefully designed to assure that this re-vision is clearly spelled out and widely accepted, thereby protecting against sudden changes fed by momentary passions or engineered by narrow interests. Seen in this light, privileged admission is a dramatic example of a movement that has been gaining momentum, the purpose of which is to stretch and bend the Constitution in order to have it accommodate the claims of pressure groups or to serve special social purposes. In his dissent in *DeFunis*, Justice Douglas took note of this practice and pointed out its danger: "The Equal Protection Clause commands the elimination of racial barriers, not their creation in order to satisfy our theory as to how society ought to be organized. . . . If discrimination based on race is constitutionally permissible when those who hold the reins can come up with 'compelling' reasons to justify it, then constitutional guarantees acquire an accordionlike quality."[31] The fact that Justice Douglas himself then came up with a "compelling" reason to give the accordion a further stretch merely underlines the importance of his strictures.

This contention that the arguments that are advanced and the rationales that are developed in the effort to validate privileged admissions have a disruptive impact on the legal system—and indeed on all of the elements and dimensions of order—can be illustrated and strengthened by an examination of two important treatments of the subject. One of these is the recent Supreme Court decision in the *Bakke* case;[32] the other is a much cited article by Professor Ronald Dworkin.[33] I shall discuss these in turn.

[31] DeFunis v. Odegaard, 416 U.S. 312 (1974) at 342, 343.

[32] Regents of the University of California v. Bakke, 438 U.S. 265, 98 S. Ct. 2733 (1978). Citation is to the latter report. All subsequent references to this case will appear in the text in parentheses following the quoted material.

[33] "Reverse Discrimination," in Ronald Dworkin's *Taking Rights Seriously* (Cambridge, Mass.: Harvard University Press, 1977). The article originally appeared in the *New York Review of Books* in 1976: citation is to the former source. There is also a more recent article by Dworkin that deals with the same issue. "Why Bakke Has No Case," *New York Review of Books* 24, no. 18 (Nov. 1977): 11-15.

The Bakke decision again presents us with the picture of a court whose members are sharply divided in their views and even, it would appear, bitterly at odds: there are two different rulings, each with a five to four division and with the members of one of these majorities disagreeing among themselves as to the meaning of their ruling; there are strong dissenting opinions by each of the minorities; and three justices filed separate opinions to expound their individual views of the issue and the outcome. The decision leaves a good deal unsettled and uncertain, and to foresee its effect on future developments is hardly a respectable prophecy and certainly not a prediction.

Justice Powell, who delivered the judgment of the Court, was the hinge on which each majority swung. His majority opinion ruled that the Davis program was illegal and that Bakke must be admitted fo the medical school: Justice Powell held that the program violated the Equal Protection clause of the Fourteenth Amendment, while the Chief Justice and Justices Stewart, Rehnquist, and Stevens did not think it necessary to reach the constitutional question, holding the program to be in violation of Section 601 of Title VI of the Civil Rights Act of 1964 (42 U.S.C. 2000d et seq.). Justice Brennan, joined by Justices White, Marshall, and Blackmun, dissented vigorously on both of these rulings. Justice Powell joined with the four preceding in the opinion that race may be considered as one factor in framing an admissions program; but it is important to note (and this point will be developed later) that there is radical disagreement between Justice Powell and the other four regarding the permissible purpose of such racial consideration and how much weight it can carry. Finally, Justice Stevens, joined by the Chief Justice and Justices Stewart and Rehnquist, argued that the "question whether race can ever be used as a factor in an admission decision is not an issue in this case, and that discussion of that issue is inappropriate." (2810; footnote omitted)

It is presumably the opinion announced by Justice Powell that will set the framework for public and scholarly discussions and judicial decisions for at least the immediate future, so we must begin with that. In *Bakke*, the crucial point around which the debates among the justices are woven and on which the final rulings hang is that of the proper interpretation of Section 601. But before trying to unravel that knotty problem it will be well to look more briefly at the other headings of Justice Powell's opinion. After describing the pertinent features of the Davis program, after rehearsing the earlier history of the case, and after disposing of various legal niceties (that need not here concern us), Justice Powell turns his attention to a consideration and rebuttal of the various rationales that have been advanced to justify such a program as that at Davis, with its reservation of a specified number of places for members of selected minority races.

The centerpiece of Justice Powell's opinion is his analysis of the "compelling state interest" argument, and the final rulings are the result of a very precise and narrow interpretation of one of the counts in this argument as it was advanced by the university. He introduces his discussion of this argument by citing the principal reasons urged by the university to justify the program at Davis:

> The special admissions program purports to serve the purposes of: (i) "reducing the historic deficit of traditionally disfavored minorities in medical schools and the medical profession," Brief for Petitioner 32; (ii) countering the effects of societal discrimination; (iii) increasing the number of physicians who will practice in communities currently underserved; and (iv) obtaining the educational benefits that flow from an ethnically diverse student body. (2757; footnote omitted)

Several other subgoals are also identified: to compensate members of minority races for the harm done them by past discrimination; to enable these members to attain the economic level they would have enjoyed except for such discrimination; to provide role models for other members of these races to emulate; and, finally, to assure "fair appraisal of each individual's academic promise in the light of some cultural bias in grading or testing procedures" (2757, note 43). Justice Powell then concludes: "It is necessary to decide which, if any, of these purposes is substantial enough to support the use of a suspect classification" (2757).

The first of these purposes is rejected as prima facie invalid. "Preferring members of any one group for no reason other than race or ethnic origin is discrimination for its own sake. This the Constitution forbids" (2757). The second purpose is flawed by the fact that the Supreme Court has "never approved a classification that aids persons perceived as members of relatively victimized groups at the expense of other innocent individuals in the absence of judicial, legislative, or administrative findings of constitutional or statutory violations" (2757-2758); and, as we have seen, the university has certainly not engaged in any past discriminatory practices against the races it now seeks to favor. The third purpose is dismissed on the ground, first, that it is based on pejorative and untested assumptions about the relative social consciences of different races, and second, that no evidence whatever is advanced to establish that the program would even promote its goal. As for most of the subgoals just mentioned, Justice Powell sees no need to give them separate consideration. But the cultural bias thesis does apparently touch a sensitive nerve, for he speaks directly to it:

> Nothing in this record, however, suggests either that any of the quantitative factors considered by the Medical School were culturally biased or that petitioner's special admissions program was formulated to correct for such biases. Furthermore, if race or ethnic background were used solely to arrive at an unbiased prediction of academic success, the reservation of fixed numbers of seats would be inexplicable. (2757, note 43)

This leaves the fourth major purpose advanced by the university to justify the Davis program: this is the securing of an "ethnically diverse" student body. The university's argument in support of this claim has two points: first, that this is a proper and substantial goal of any educational program; second, that a program such as that at Davis, with its rigid and exclusive racial classification, is a necessary and legitimate means of reaching this goal. Justice Powell readily grants the first point, and his reasons for doing so will be discussed later in tracing the argument by which he reaches his own conclusion. But he rejects the second claim, substituting for it a much qualified doctrine of the extent to which race can be considered in framing an admission policy. This doctrine now constitutes the official Supreme Court position—the law of the land—on this thorny issue; it is therefore critically important to understand its content and the argument by which it is reached. And this raises the crucial point of the proper interpretation of Section 601 of the Civil Rights Act of 1964. The Court divides very sharply on this point, with three positions being marked out: one is that of justice Brennan, joined by Justices White, Marshall, and Blackmun; at the other extreme is the opinion of Justice Stevens, joined by the Chief Justice and Justices Stewart and Rehnquist; and finally there is the intermediate view of Justice Powell, which—though only he holds it!—becomes somehow the holding of the Court.

Section 601, which is the center of this debate, provides as follows:

> No person in the United States shall, on the ground of race, color, or national origin, be excluded from participation in, be denied the benefits of, or be subjected to discrimination under any program or activity receiving Federal financial assistance.

The most straightforward reading of this provision is that of Justice Stevens and the justices who join with him. They take the statute quite literally, maintaining that it must mean what it clearly says, which is that *no person* is to be excluded, denied, or disadvantaged because of race, color, or national origin. These justices do not reach the constitutional question, they do not consider whether the program can be justified by some compelling interest, and they do not weigh the measure of judicial scrutiny that is required: they do not acknowledge the need to explore any of these questions, for they hold—and the natural meaning of words certainly supports them—that the most casual scrutiny of the Davis program, which excludes whites and a good many other minorities from consideration for 16 out of 100 places in the entering class of the medical school, reveals that it is a flagrant violation of the statute. In sum, these justices insist that the wording of Title VI clearly requires "a colorblind standard on the part of government" (2813). In further support of their position, they cite the House Report on Title VI and numerous remarks made by senators and representatives in the course of the debates on the act (2811-2814; with footnotes).[34]

As opposed to this straightforward semantic procedure, Justice Brennan and the justices who join him give to Section 601 what can best be called a contextual or historical reading. They go behind the wording of the statute to the legislative intent that motivated it, seeking this intent in the situation that led to the introduction of the statute—the evil it was intended to correct—and in the congressional hearings and debates that preceded the enactment of Title VI.

The argument that Justice Brennan derives from this perusal of history and policy is essentially quite simple. It holds that what Congress had in mind—what it was acutely aware of—was the then still prevalent discrimination against negroes. In many federally funded programs and services, negroes were treated unequally and were excluded from the full benefits that were available to the members of the majority white race. This was true in hospitals, colleges, vocational training programs, access to financial relief, the distribution of surplus food to the needy, and in many other areas. In enacting Title VI, Congress meant to end this discriminatory treatment. Justice Brennan summarizes the matter in this way:

> The history of Title VI . . . reveals one fixed purpose: to give the Executive Branch of Government clear authority to terminate federal funding of private programs that use race as a means of disad-

---

[34] It should be noted, and will be commented on later, that all three opinions make this same appeal in their support, frequently citing the same speakers.

vantaging minorities in a manner that would be prohibited by the Constitution if engaged in by government. (2768)

No one challenges this conclusion—although it should be noted, and the point is to become of crucial importance, that the wording of Section 601 extends this protection to all persons, not merely to minorities. All nine of the justices are fully agreed that Title VI means to, and does, *proscribe* discrimination based on race, color, or national origin. The debate centers on what Title VI *permits*: all are in accord that Congress meant to *prohibit* action against any person because of race; but did Congress also mean to *allow* action in favor of persons because of race? And if so, what sorts of preferential treatment are permitted, to what groups of persons, and under what conditions? Most particularly, did Congress mean to permit such preferential treatment of one race when it entailed exclusion and disadvantage for innocent members of other races? It is around these questions that debate rages, arguments abound, replication follows upon rebuttal, and citations are hurled back and forth in barrages.

As we have seen, Justice Stevens and his brothers adopt a strict and narrow stance on these questions: they hold that the Davis program obviously violates Section 601, and they maintain that the broader question of "whether race can ever be used as a factor in an admissions decision is not an issue in this case" (2810). Justice Brennan and his brothers take exactly the opposite position, saying:

The threshold question we must decide is whether Title VI of the Civil Rights Act of 1964 bars recipients of federal funds from giving preferential consideration to disadvantaged members of racial minorities as part of a program designed to enable such individuals to surmount the obstacles imposed by racial discrimination. (2768; footnote omitted, quoting Section 601)

And Justice Brennan at once answers the question:

In our view, Title VI . . . does not bar the preferential treatment of racial minorities as a means of remedying past societal discrimination to the extent that such action is consistent with the Fourteenth Amendment. The legislative history of Title VI, administrative regulations interpreting the statute, subsequent congressional and executive action, and the prior decisions of this Court compel this conclusion. None of these sources lends support to the proposition that Congress intended to bar all race conscious [sic] efforts to extend the benefits of federally financed programs to minorities who have been historically excluded from the full benefits of American life. (2768; footnote omitted, quoting Section 601)

Having asserted this broad interpretation of Title VI, Justice Brennan must now answer the subsidiary questions: What sorts of preferential treatment are permitted, to whom, and when? The kernel of the answers to these questions is contained in the statement just quoted, and it can be extracted briefly.

Justice Brennan takes his point of departure from the undeniable and unchallenged fact of past discrimination and its harmful effects. It is equally clear and agreed that Congress meant to end this: the legislation it has enacted, as well as the federal court decisions interpreting and implementing such enactments, are intended to put a stop to all such discrimination. But, Justice Brennan argues—and it is here that he parts company with five of his brothers—Congress has meant to do more than this. Beyond this negative step, it has meant to approve and encourage positive steps that give preferential treatment and special benefits to those groups hitherto discriminated against. That is, according to this argument, congressional enactments such as Title VI permit certain racial classifications and "race conscious programs" that are designed to have this effect and further this end.

The argument now moves to its conclusion by explicating the circumstances under which, and the groups for which, such race conscious programs are permissible. To justify such treatment, two conditions are held to be necessary and sufficient. In the first place, such programs must be for the benefit of definite and identifiable minority groups— "discrete and nuclear" minorities—that have suffered under past discrimination. Justice Brennan states the case in this way:

> Properly construed, therefore, our prior cases unequivocally show that a state government may adopt race-conscious programs if the purpose of such programs is to remove the disparate racial impact its actions might otherwise have and if there is reason to believe that the disparate impact is itself the product of past discrimination, whether its own or that of society at large. (2789)

In the second place, the racial classification on which such a program is based must be "benign," intended only to help certain groups, devoid of any purpose to disadvantage or disparage others, casting no "stigma" upon any groups or individuals affected by it. In conclusion, Justice Brennan holds that the racial classifications employed by such programs as that at Davis abundantly satisfy both of these conditions: they are exclusively benevolent in their intention, purposing only to remedy past discrimination and to help persecuted minorities to improve their lot. In both respects they differ totally from the racial classifications and policies that were long prevalent and were intended to perpetuate discrimination and deprivation. In short, "benign" racial classifications are necessary and justified in order to correct the evils wrought by earlier "malign" classifications.

These are the two extreme readings—the literal and the contextual—of Section 601 of Title VI, both of which Justice Powell rejects. We can now examine the grounds on which he bases these rejections and the way in which he threads his way between them to reach the position that becomes the Court's ruling. Since Justice Stevens's opinion did not reach the question of "whether race can ever be used as a factor in an admissions decision" (though there are strong indications that the answer would be in the negative), Justice Powell does not discuss it: he agrees with its holdings that the Davis program is invalid and that Bakke must be admitted to the medical school; then he decides to take the further step and face the issue. On the other hand, his rebuttal of Justice Brennan's opinion is careful and detailed.

Justice Powell discusses and rejects in turn the various points in Justice Brennan's argument. The "benign" racial classification thesis is dismissed on the ground that it is certainly not benign regarding those whom it excludes. The "discrete and insular" minority contention is discredited by the fact that there is nothing in Title VI or the Fourteenth Amendment to justify it: on the contrary, both of these sources are emphatic in asserting that the protection they afford is personal and covers everyone. The claim that "disparate impact" by itself is sufficient to establish past "societal" discrimination and hence to justify preferential treatment is rejected for similar reasons: such treatment requires a finding of past discrimination by the defendant presently called to answer, and even then every effort is made to ensure that innocent parties will not suffer. Finally, the contention that but for such past societal discrimination minorities would have qualified for admission to Davis under the regular program and filled up its places (with the result that Bakke would have failed to be admitted even if there had been no special program) is characterized by Justice Powell as an hypothesis of "unprecedented" breadth, involving a "speculative leap" unsupported by either evidence or argument (2751-2752, note 36).

Having renounced and refuted these extreme positions, Justice Powell launches the positive argument by which he reaches his own outcome. He takes his point of departure from the fourth goal asserted by the university to justify the Davis program: this is "the attainment of a diverse student body" (2760). He maintains that this "clearly is a constitutionally permissible goal for an institution of higher education" (2760). Courts have long held that academic freedom enjoys the protection of the First Amendment: it is a species of the freedom of speech guaranteed by that amendment. And one important aspect of that freedom is the right of a university to determine the type of student body that it deems desirable and hence to establish admission standards designed to procure such a student body. Furthermore, a university can advance persuasive reasons why a diverse student body is eminently desirable and even essential: it fosters an "atmosphere of 'speculation, experiment, and creation' " (2760), and it exposes students to the ideas, mores, and attitudes of groups with different cultural backgrounds (2761). Consequently, when a university establishes an admissions program that is reasonably designed to provide such a student body, it "invokes a countervailing constitutional interest, that of the First Amendment," in support of its case (2761). The question of the legitimacy of the Davis program's racial classification must therefore be faced and decided. Two constitutional rights, the freedom of speech of the First Amendment and the equal protection of the Fourteenth, now confront one another, and it must be determined which is to prevail and why.

With the critical issue thus posed, Justice Powell moves quickly to the conclusion of his argument. He holds that programs such as that at Davis, with their rigid and exclusive racial classifications, are impermissible. He bases this holding on two grounds. First, the fact that the Davis program excludes and disadvantages innocent persons simply because of their race or color, in the absence of any past discrimination by the university, is clearly a denial of individual rights and of equal protection and hence is highly suspect as violative of the Fourteenth Amendment (2764). Second, when the university seeks to counter this obstacle with its "compelling state interest" claim, Justice Powell holds that it altogether fails. For, he says, such a program would actually hinder rather than further its avowed purpose because it is too narrow and specialized in the diversity at which it aims. It is not a simple ethnic diversity that is desirable but one that takes into account all attributes of the persons considered for admission. Justice Powell summarizes the matter in this way: "[the] petitioner's argument that this is the only effective means of serving the interest of diversity is seriously flawed. In a most fundamental sense the argument misconceives the nature of the state interest that would justify consideration of race or ethnic background. It is not an interest in simple ethnic diversity. . . . The diversity that furthers a compelling state interest encompasses a far broader array of qualifications and characteristics of which racial or ethnic origin is but a single though important element" (2761). In sum, there is a compelling state interest here, but the means chosen to serve this interest is not necessary, and in fact does it a disservice. And so the critical issue arises: Is there some other type of admissions program in which race or ethnic origin can serve as a necessary and effective means to secure a desirably diverse student body?

Justice Powell's answer to this question is implicit in his preceding remarks, and he comes at once to his final and crucial ruling, which holds that race may be taken into consideration as one factor among others in framing an admissions program and choosing among applicants for the purpose of achieving a diverse student body. A person's race may weigh in his favor as one element in a galaxy of items, including academic record, geographic origin, economic status, special intellectual or artistic interests, and such other qualities as "exceptional personal talents, unique work or service experience, leadership potential, maturity, demonstrated compassion, a history of overcoming disadvantage, ability to communicate with the poor, or other qualifications deemed important" (2763). Justice Powell summarizes the characteristics and advantages of a policy of this kind and justifies its validity in the following terms:

> In short, an admissions program operated in this way is flexible enough to consider all pertinent elements of diversity in light of the particular qualifications of each applicant, and to place them on the same footing for consideration, although not necessarily according them the same weight. . . .
>
> This kind of program treats each applicant as an individual in the admissions process. The applicant who loses out on the last available seat to another candidate receiving a "plus" on the basis of ethnic background will not have been foreclosed from all consideration because he was not the right color or had the wrong surname. It would mean only that his combined qualifications, which may have included similar nonobjective factors, did not outweigh those of the other applicant. His qualifications would have been weighed fairly and competitively, and he would have no basis to complain of unequal treatment under the Fourteenth Amendment. (2763; footnote omitted)

On the basis of this argument, Justice Powell concludes that "the state has a substantial interest that legitimately may be served by a properly devised admissions program involving the *competitive consideration of race and ethnic origin*" (2764; emphasis added). Thus the judgment in the California Supreme Court that "enjoins petitioner from any consideration of the race of any applicant must be reversed" (2764).

There are two extremely significant differences between the Davis type admissions program, supported by Justice Brennan, and the type here approved by Justice Powell and now carrying the sanction of the Supreme Court: one of these concerns the permitted *purpose* that such programs may serve; the other concerns the permitted *method* by which applicants may be selected. As regards the former, Justice Powell is explicit and emphatic in holding that this legitimate purpose is only that of securing a diverse student body. The purpose of giving preferential treatment to members of certain races and of repairing the harm done by past "societal" discrimination is rejected. As concerns method, this must count race or ethnic origin as only one factor on the same footing as others. The policy of reserving some places to applicants solely on the basis of race is declared invalid. These differences are of crucial importance, and the purpose and method of such "competitive consideration of race" will control decisions in this field for the immediate future at least.

This examination of the *Bakke* case was not undertaken simply for its own sake. As I stated at the outset, I am interested in the opinions and the decision as illustrating the stress and strain that can be placed on the judicial process and on the body of the law by efforts to construct arguments and rationales that can validate the new human rights, in this particular case the claimed right to privileged admission. The foregoing account of the diverse conclusions reached by different justices, of the sometimes specious arguments advanced, of the contradictory interpretations of prior decisions, of the citations to the same case to support conflicting views, and of the sharp exchanges among the justices—all of this should have amply substantiated my contention. In conclusion, I shall discuss only briefly what seem to be some of the more undesirable, and even dangerous, stratagems that have been employed to justify a preferred outcome.

Certainly the most serious instance of this kind is found in the opinion of Justice Brennan and his brothers, for this opinion seriously misrepresents Justice Powell on two counts. The most extreme—one is tempted to say, egregious—case of this misrepresentation occurs when these justices pretend to announce the real meaning and thrust of the Court's ruling. After referring to the difficulty of the issue presented by the case and to the diversity of opinions that it has elicited, they summarize as follows:

But this should not and must not mask the central meaning of to-day's opinions: Government may take race into account, when it acts not to demean or insult any racial group, but to remedy disadvantages cast on minorities by past racial prejudice, at least when appropriate findings have been made by judicial, legislative, or administrative bodies with competence to act in this area. (2766)

Justice Powell, of course, does not espouse any such central meaning as this—and certainly Justice Stevens and his brothers for whom he speaks do not. Quite to the contrary, he categorically denies that government can do this—except, perhaps, where there has been past explicit discrimination by the present party, and that is an issue that has never arisen in any of the special program cases. Instead, he differs radically regarding both the purpose and the method that are permissible in framing such programs, holding only that race may be taken into consideration as one factor among others in order to provide a diverse student body.

The other less open and obvious misrepresentation occurs when Justice Brennan asserts that the decision reverses "the judgment below in so far as it prohibits the University from establishing race-conscious programs in the future" (2767). The critical point here is the meaning to be attached to the term race-conscious, for the type of program approved by Justice Powell in announcing the judgment of the court is "race-conscious" in only an attenuated sense of the term and emphatically not with the meaning that Justice Brennan and his brothers wish it to have. The latter mean programs explicitly based on strict racial classifications and intended to afford preferential treatment to certain races, whereas Justice Powell means only programs that take account of race as one factor to be weighed along with numerous others to provide a diverse student body. These misrepresentations can easily give the appearance of being a deliberate attempt by Justice Brennan and his brothers to distort the opinion and outcome of Justice Powell in order to give to the judgment of the Court the result and the thrust that they think desirable. This is clearly the view of Justice Stevens, joined by the Chief Justice and Justices Stewart and Rehnquist, for at the very outset of Justice Stevens's opinion he rejects the suggestion that this is the central meaning of the court's ruling and rebukes the effort to establish it as such. He says:

Four Members of the Court have undertaken to announce the legal and constitutional effect of this Court's judgment. See opinion of Justices BRENNAN, WHITE, MARSHALL, and BLACKMUN, *ante*, at 2766-2777. It is hardly necessary to state that only a majority can speak for the Court or determine what is the "central meaning" of any judgment of the Court. (2809, note 1)

Of a quite different order, but almost equally serious in its potential impact, is the willingness of Justice Stevens and his brothers to avoid the significant issue posed by *Bakke* and hence to postpone its settlement. It is of course impossible to determine what was in the minds of the justices who joined in this opinion, what motives and intentions moved them. An adverse view would hold that they were simply reluctant to confront the issue. But, on the other hand, these justices could argue that their course is the best: to invalidate on a narrow ground such explicitly racially-based programs as that at Davis and then to leave universities to devise more satisfactory admissions programs, rather than having the Court assume this function for them, is an appealing solution to the problem. In fact, such a position would have a good deal of merit and would be in line with frequent Supreme Court practice in similar situations: it minimizes judicial intrusion and leaves decisions to those who have more experience and expertise. And yet again, and in support of Justice Powell's position, it would seem wiser to explicitly sanction some consideration of race, thus authorizing and even encouraging universities to devise admission programs conformable to the broad standards laid down in the announced judgment of the Court.

There is, I think, much to applaud in the moderate and reasonable opinion of Justice Powell announcing the judgment of the Court. This avoids the extreme positions of Justice Brennan and Justice Stevens: it proscribes strict racial classifications that exclude innocent members of one race in order to repair "societal" discrimination of another race, but at the same time it allows for race to be taken into consideration as one factor in framing an admissions program. And it is interesting to note that Justice Powell's solution of this issue—the now official judgment of the Court—is very similar to that proposed by Justice Douglas in his *De-Funis* dissent[35] before he disavowed his own argument and adopted the cultural bias and disparate impact theses. This ruling thus marks a broad channel and leaves universities leeway to chart the courses they think best within the limits set by these markings.

But there is little to applaud, and much to deplore, in the manner in which the Court reached this judgment, in the arguments and stratagems employed, in the sharp divisions in the Court that are here exposed, and in the legal status quo that the judgment creates and leaves

[35] DeFunis v. Odegaard, 416 U.S. 312 (1974) at 331-334, 340-343.

behind it. With regard to these matters, three points in particular merit a brief mention.

In the first place (and this is a point I have earlier argued at length in general terms), when some claimed human right (some social goal or desirable policy) is embodied as a legal right, its meaning, enforcement, and implementation are issues to be settled in court hearings and decisions. When the right and these issues that it raises are brought before a court for settlement, they immediately become the subject of adversarial proceedings: the issues are defined in terms of harsh dichotomies of black and white, pro and con, right and wrong. The adversarial atmosphere of the courtroom breeds conflict, issuing in victory and defeat. This is virtually fatal to a satisfactory settlement of the problems that are raised by human rights, for these problems demand above all to be treated in a spirit of compromise and conciliation. It is the great merit of Justice Powell's opinion that it achieved such a compromise—though it clearly did not succeed in achieving conciliation. And it won as much as it did despite the judicial process rather than through it.

This leads directly to a second point. There is a sense in which it seems doubtful if there even is any real decision or central meaning to be found in the *Bakke* judgment, for there is no doctrine or holding that is accepted by any five justices that is sufficiently specific to offer guidance for the future. A majority of five does agree that an admissions program can take race into consideration: but there is radical disagreement within this majority as to what this phrase means—what it permits, prohibits, and requires. Justice Powell announces the judgment of the Court: but he is the only justice who holds the view embodied in this judgment. Four justices adopt a far broader interpretation of the import of the judgment, and another four justices hold that nothing whatever of general import has been decided on this issue. Indeed, if Justice Stevens's dictum that "only a majority can speak for the Court" is sound doctrine, then it is perfectly clear that the Court's judgment has no "central meaning" at all.

One can imagine two competing lines of argument being advanced in the future, each seeking to establish a different central meaning in the judgment. There are two important questions that the decision in *Bakke* should have answered. First, can race ever be used in framing an admissions program? Second, if so, for what purpose and by what method? One argument would hold that the Chief Justice and Justices Stewart, Rehnquist, and Stevens have refused even to face these questions, holding that they are not at issue in the case. That leaves the five Justices, Brennan, White, Marshall, Blackmun, and Powell to answer them. All five say "yes" to the first question, but they disagree on the second; and Justice Brennan and those who join him constitute a majority of four to one over Justice Powell. Thus their broad interpretation of "race-conscious" should be regarded as the central meaning of the Court's judgment. The other argument would run as follows. When these questions arise again in a case where they must be faced and decided, the Chief Justice and Justices Stewart, Rehnquist, and Stevens can reasonably be expected to accept Justice Powell's view and answer "yes" to the first question. And they would very certainly agree with Justice Powell's holding as regards the permitted purpose and method for taking race into consideration in an admissions program. This would give a majority of five to four for a narrow interpretation of "race-conscious" and make it the central meaning of the judgment.

The final and ironic confusion coiled at the heart of this judgment is found in the fact that Justice Powell constitutes a majority—if indeed there is one—with Justice Brennan and his brothers, but his position is far closer to that of Justice Stevens and his brothers. For he emphatically rejects the view of the former that admissions programs can give preferential treatment to members of certain races to repair past "societal" discrimination simply on a finding of "disparate impact" and with harm done to innocent parties, while his position is perfectly described in the statement of Justice Stevens that such programs must "focus on fairness to individuals rather than fairness to classes."[36] It therefore seems all but certain that in the years ahead the Supreme Court chamber will echo with these and other more recondite arguments.

A final point that is emphasized by the *Bakke* case is the extent to which decisions on issues raised by human rights have the air of depending less on the body of the law than on the beliefs, attitudes, and purposes of the several justices—on their various views "as to how society ought to be organized," to borrow the phrase of Justice Douglas. Of course, the personality and persuasions of any judge will impinge to some extent upon every interpretation of the law that he renders. But in one instance after another in human rights cases, it appears to be the personality and persuasions that control the decision, with the law not being interpreted but rather being employed to justify and implement an outcome otherwise arrived at. To put the matter in perhaps extreme terms, this tendency, as expressed in the opinions in *Bakke*, confronts us

---

[36] Bakke v. Regents of the University of California, 98 S. Ct. 2733 at 2813, n. 19. Quoting City of Los Angeles Dept. of Power and Water v. Manhart, 98 S. Ct. 1370 at 1376 (1978).

with the fact that future developments on this critical issue hang entirely on the convictions and predilections of the next appointee to the Supreme Court. For when this event occurs, as it must, it raises the distinct possibility that one of the present four member minorities, representing extreme positions, will become the majority. And such a contingency as this makes a travesty of our proud boast that we are a government "not of men, but of laws."

These are the stresses and strains that the judicial process and the body of the law undergo when they seek to come to grips with privileged admissions. I now want to look at what happens when a legal theorist makes a similar attempt. And I shall argue that the outcome is the same: the framework of his theory is severely stretched, and some of its leading principles are either ignored or violated. For this purpose, I shall examine Professor Ronald Dworkin's defense of privileged admissions.

In launching his discussion, Dworkin poses the problem in the strongest possible terms by comparing the 1945 action of the University of Texas Law School in refusing admission to Sweatt because he was black with the 1971 action of the University of Washington Law School in refusing to consider DeFunis for its special admission program because he was white.[37] Dworkin denounces the former of these actions as morally, socially, and legally wrong; he approves the latter as right in all of these respects. The problem is to explain and justify these contradictory judgments, since both of these actions are based on rigid racial classifications that exclude and disadvantage innocent parties for no reason other than their race. Why is discrimination to be condemned in the one case and condoned in the other?

The argument that is developed to justify this distinction is essentially pragmatic; but it is not strictly utilitarian, for Dworkin does not accept the "greatest happiness of the greatest number" as the goal and criterion of government action. Instead, he substitutes for this the thesis that the end to be sought by government is a society that is "better off in an ideal sense" (p. 232). And what Dworkin has in mind as an "ideal society" is at once made clear: it is one that is dedicated to equality. This equating of the ideal with the equal is a postulate of Dworkin's thought. Thus, at one point he says that "a more equal society is a better society" (p. 239); and again he refers to a community as being "more equal and therefore more just" (p. 232). In Chapter XII of his book, he states his position

---

[37] Dworkin, *Taking Rights Seriously*, pp. 223-225, 239. Hereafter all subsequent page references will appear in parentheses in the text.

explicitly: "The central concept of my argument will be the concept not of liberty but of equality"(p. 272). The entire weight of his further argument then rests on the contention that programs such as that at Washington will "make the community more equal overall"(p. 228). And this contention is in turn supported by appeal to the various ways in which these programs will further the goal of equality: they will provide more black lawyers to serve the black community; they will "decrease the difference in wealth and power that now exists between different racial groups" (p. 228); and the black students will both broaden the social horizon of white students and serve as role models to those of their own race. These are the familiar claims that are advanced by the proponents of privileged admission.[38] Dworkin then summarizes and concludes his argument: "It is, as I said, controversial whether a preferential admission program will in fact promote these various policies, but it cannot be said to be implausible that it will. The disadvantage to applicants such as DeFunis is, on that hypothesis, a cost that must be paid for a greater gain" (p. 228).

This is a brief résumé of what Dworkin argues at much greater length, but I think that it is fair and that it captures the gist of his argument. The Texas policy—the discrimination that Sweatt suffered—is rejected because it intends to and does perpetuate inequality. The Washington program—the discrimination that DeFunis suffered—is acceptable because it intends to and may very well promote equality. I am willing to stipulate Dworkin's hypothesis that these programs based on a rigid racial classification will promote equality, although, as I have previously argued at length, I have grave doubts on the point. And I am prepared to grant his equating of the "ideal society" with one that furthers equality, although I have equally grave doubts about this thesis and even more about Dworkin's apparent equating of an "equal" society with an "egalitarian" one. Since these issues are extraneous to my present purpose, suffice it to point out that an "ideal" society obviously comprises other values besides equality: to mention but a random few, it should certainly provide liberty, fairness, safety, opportunity, and the absence of arbitrariness. But my present interest lies in arguing that Dworkin's defense of the Washington program and his willingness to deprive DeFunis of his Fourteenth Amendment right to equal protection violate several of his own fundamental principles and doctrines as these are developed elsewhere in *Taking Rights Seriously*.

---

[38] See the discussion on pp. 271-272 of this chapter. And cf. the discussion of Justice Powell in his opinion in *Bakke*, 98 S.Ct. 2733 at 2757-2760.

As this title itself indicates, Dworkin holds a very strong view of rights. He denies that this view rests on any "ontological assumptions," such as that men have rights in the same sense in which they have tonsils (p. 139). But he clearly regards rights as having a status that is, in the language I used at the beginning of this chapter, extralegal and supralegal: law and government do not create rights but merely recognize and enforce them. Thus, at one point Dworkin says: "In the United States citizens are supposed to have certain fundamental rights against their government, certain moral rights made into legal rights by the Constitution" (p. 190); and again he says: "Our constitutional system rests on a particular moral theory, namely, that men have moral rights against the state" (p. 147). For Dworkin, then, rights are clearly metalegal. He nowhere makes clear what their status is, contenting himself with the modest position that "a claim of right is a special, in the sense of a restricted, sort of judgment about what it is right or wrong for governments to do" (p. 139). They might be said to be elements in an implicit commitment between a government and its citizens; or, if Dworkin were to accept the concept, they could be seen as grounded in the authority relationship, as I analyzed this in Chapter XI. These rights are then made explicit and at least somewhat specific in the Constitution. Since Dworkin holds that rights have no ontological basis, it is only by reference to the relevant provisions of the Constitution that claims of right can be legally justified; so the character and content that are ascribed to rights by these provisions are obviously of vital significance. This fact is of importance in evaluating Dworkin's further argument for the Washington program and against DeFunis.

Among these fundamental rights, the right to equality has pride of place: "The central concept in my argument will be the concept not of liberty but of equality" (p. 272). It is on this right, specifically on the right to equal protection guaranteed by the Fourteenth Amendment, that DeFunis's case rests. This claim of right must therefore be turned if privileged admission programs are to be justified. Dworkin's argument to this end is based on a distinction that he draws between two different senses of the right to equality. One of these is the right to *equal treatment*—"to an equal distribution of some opportunity or resource or burden" (p. 227); the other is the right to *treatment as an equal*—"to be treated with the same respect and concern as anyone else" (p. 277). Furthermore, Dworkin holds that "the right to treatment as an equal is fundamental, and the right to equal treatment, derivative" (p. 227; cf. also pp. 199, 273). Finally, Dworkin argues that this right to treatment as an equal is a right in what he calls the "strong sense," meaning that the government would do wrong if it were to impede someone in the exercise of such a right.[39]

I believe it is correct to say that this doctrine of the "right to treatment as an equal" is the central theme of Dworkin's work: it certainly is the basis of his defense of privileged admissions. He asserts its importance emphatically and repeatedly, insisting that it is the keystone of a democratic and liberal society; it is a right that must not be abridged even when to do so would presumably be in the public interest or when its assurance to an individual is counter to this interest. Dworkin makes this point most briefly and sharply when he says that government "must not define citizens' rights so that these are cut off for supposed reasons of the general good" (p. 204), and he elaborates this thesis more fully when he states:

> I shall say that an individual has a *right* to a particular political act, within a political theory, if the failure to provide that act, when he calls for it, would be unjustified within that theory even if the goals of the theory would, on the balance, be disserviced by that act. (P. 169)

Finally, in a passage that is most relevant to programs of privileged admission, Dworkin asserts:

> Government must not only treat people with concern and respect, but with equal concern and respect. It must not distribute goods or opportunities unequally on the ground that some citizens are entitled to more because they are worthy of more concern. (Pp. 272-273)

I stated at the outset of this discussion that my primary intention in examining Dworkin's treatment of privileged admission was to establish that his defense of such a program involved him in a contradiction of his own most basic principles. The first count in my argument has now come to its climax and conclusion, for, as the above citations should make abundantly clear, Dworkin attaches supreme importance to the right to be treated as an equal. People must be treated with "equal con-

---

[39] It is worth noting that there is nothing in the Constitution that speaks to a "right to equality" in either of these senses. What the Fourteenth Amendement guarantees is the equal protection of the laws. It says nothing whatever about the "equal distribution" of anything at all, whether it be benefits or burdens. And it certainly has no traffic with such elusive concepts as "concern" and "respect." Throughout his argument, Dworkin seems to treat rights as primarily beneficial; but the rights embodied in the Constitution are protective.

cern and respect," and this right is not to be "cut off" for reasons of the "general good" or even when this good is "disserviced" by protecting the right.

But—and this is of course the crux of the matter—Dworkin is quite prepared to have DeFunis, an altogether innocent party, suffer in all of these ways in order to promote a society that is supposedly "better" and "more just" because more "equal." DeFunis's right to be treated as an equal is "cut off" in order to serve this hoped for goal. His fundamental and background right is denied him because government thinks it would be a "disservice" to enforce it in this case. And he is treated as though he were "worthy" of less concern and respect than members of selected minorities. If fundamental moral rights are to suffer this fate whenever government thinks it convenient, then it is understandable that Dworkin is unwilling to ascribe to them any "ontological basis," for they are based on quicksand.

The other two counts in my argument can be covered more briefly. A second doctrine that is prominent in Dworkin's work revolves around the distinction between arguments of policy and those of principle. Arguments of policy are based on the ground of furthering or protecting some collective social goal. Those of principle are based on the appeal to some individual or group right. Dworkin argues very strongly that "hard cases"—those which "cannot be brought under a clear rule of law" that is already established and in which judges therefore have some discretion—"should be generated by principle not policy" (pp. 81, 84). *DeFunis* and *Bakke* would certainly appear to be hard cases. But Dworkin's argument in support of the Washington program and his more recent article on the *Bakke* case are both based entirely on an appeal to policy. He insists that equality—in his sense of the term—is a legitimate and even vital goal of the society, and so he argues that DeFunis's and Bakke's rights "to be treated as equals" can properly be sacrificed in the pursuit of this goal. Dworkin seeks to escape this contradiction by treating the *policy* of privileged admission as though it served and were subservient to the *principle* of equal treatment. Thus he says: "the fairness—and constitutionality—of any admission program . . . is justified if it serves a proper policy that respects the right of all members of the community to be treated as equals, but not otherwise"(p. 239). But this only compounds the contradiction. For not only is a decision in a hard case being based explicitly on policy rather than principle but the policy being served is one that cuts off DeFunis's and Bakke's rights to be treated as equals, holding that simply because of their race they are less worthy of concern and respect.

A third doctrine to which Dworkin attaches much importance is that of "political responsibility" or "articulate consistency." This holds

> that political officials must make only such political decisions as they can justify within a political theory that also justifies the other decisions they propose to make. . . . It condemns the practice of making decisions that seem right in isolation, but cannot be brought within some comprehensive theory of general principles and policies that is consistent with other decisions also thought right. (P. 87)

It certainly appears that a result upholding the Washington and Davis programs of special admission would be a clear violation of this doctrine. These programs are based on rigid racial classifications that exclude and disadvantage innocent persons for no reason other than their race. To validate such programs would be to make "decisions that seem right in isolation" in flagrant disregard of the Fourteenth Amendment and of the even more explicit injunction of Section 601 of the Civil Rights Act of 1964. And I presume that Professor Dworkin would agree that the Constitution and Title VI are integral and even essential elements of the "comprehensive theory of general principles" that political officials in this country are pledged to observe. If generally followed, the practice that Dworkin recommends in this instance would give the Constitution more than Justice Douglas's famous "accordionlike quality": it would reduce the Constitution to total ambiguity, a carte blanche to make whatever decision happens to "seem right" to a particular court on a particular occasion. Such a Constitution would be writ in flowing water.

This may seem an unduly harsh critique of an acute and important legal thinker. I would therefore like to balance it with some extenuating considerations, which will also serve to place the issue of privileged admission in a broader framework. There are three perspectives from which this issue can be regarded. The issue spreads through three dimensions, and there are three criteria that can be appealed to in seeking to defend a decision concerning it: these are the moral, the social, and the legal. (I omit a fourth possible dimension, the political. Insofar as this is distinct from the three above, it reduces simply to questions of expediency.)

From the moral point of view, Dworkin is entirely correct in finding a sharp and important difference between the Texas program that excluded Sweatt and the Washington program that excluded DeFunis. The two programs have completely opposite outlooks and intentions: the Texas policy rests on the doctrine that the negro is inherently inferior, and it intends to keep negroes in an underprivileged and disadvantaged position; the Washington policy rests on the doctrine of racial equality, and it seeks to assist negroes and other minorities to achieve a position where they will be equal in fact. Morally, the treatment of Sweatt by Texas is to be condemned; the treatment of minorities by Washington is, at least in its motivating intention, to be praised. But even here two caveats must be entered. The discriminatory treatment of DeFunis is not easily condoned, even if it is an unintended side effect. About the only excuse in justification that can be offered here is to argue that in this case two wrongs do make a right. Like the doctrine that the end justifies the means, this is an extremely dangerous gambit that invites abuse and the persecution of the innocent. It would appear sounder to develop programs that can eliminate the one wrong without committing the other. It is also debatable whether such programs as these are the most effective means to promote the end they seek or whether they actually work to defeat this end.

This latter point translates the issue into social terms. Are programs such as those at Washington and Davis really going to meliorate racial relations, further racial equality, and promote a social order in which race ceases to be a meaningful consideration? This is an open question, with the outcome uncertain, and Dworkin himself acknowledges this with admirable candor. At the outset of his argument in support of privileged admissions he says that "it is far too early, as wise critics concede, to decide whether preferential treatment does more harm than good"(p. 224). And at the conclusion of an argument based exclusively on this pragmatic consideration he concedes the possibility "that preferential admission programs will not, in fact, make a more equal society, because they may not have the effects their advocates believe they will"(p. 239). Judging the issue from this perspective, Dworkin hopes that these programs will ease the friction between races, will raise the educational and economic levels of minorities, and will help to create a society that is "more equal overall." On the other hand, it is my fear that these programs, and especially the disparate impact and cultural bias theses that are now receiving such prominence, will have exactly the opposite effect: they will exacerbate the tension between races, lead to both a general lowering of standards and a proliferation of special standards for various minorities with different "cultural backgrounds," and elevate "color-consciousness" into a constitutional principle. But along with Dworkin, I admit that the issue lies in the womb of time and the laps of the gods.

This leaves the legal dimension. It is here that the issue is posed in the most critical terms and also settled most decisively. I presume that, if pressed, Dworkin would acknowledge that we need to take law at least as seriously as we do rights, for law is the first and best bulwark of defense of these rights. To the extent that the integrity and coherence of the legal order are diluted, our rights are undermined: their content becomes ambiguous and variable, they are enforced selectively and erratically, and even their existence is threatened. Consequently, it is a matter of the highest seriousness to ignore or distort an established legal principle—and especially an explicit constitutional provision—in order to reach a particular outcome, however much this may be desired and however desirable it may appear. Indeed, Dworkin himself argues this point strongly and persuasively, as I have previously indicated: it is explicit both in his insistence that "hard cases" should be generated by principle rather than policy and in his doctrine of "articulate consistency." Yet it appears to me self-evident that programs such as those at Washington and Davis, based as they are on rigid and discriminatory racial classifications, can be justified only if we close our eyes to the clear and unequivocal proscription of the Fourteenth Amendment and to the innumerable legislative enactments and judicial decisions that have implemented and strengthened its protections.

One can understand and sympathize with the explicit and limited intention that animates Dworkin. But ad hoc decisions such as those that he recommends in *DeFunis* and *Bakke* are extremely dangerous expedients. Mill and de Tocqueville warned eloquently of the danger that democracy would lead to the tyranny of the majority, and this fear has permeated American thought, especially that strand that has appropriated the term "liberal." Law comes to be regarded as a device to protect those who are fewer and less powerful, those who swim against the stream, those who dissent and protest. This preconception stands out clearly and influentially in the work of Dworkin himself, for on numerous occasions he speaks of rights, and especially of the right to equality, as though their only function were to protect such individuals and groups against the oppression of the majority. Thus he says that the "idea of political equality" means that "the weaker members of a political community are entitled to the same concern and respect of their government as the more powerful members have secured for themselves" (pp. 198-199). And at another point he is even more explicit: "The institution of rights is therefore crucial, because it represents the majority's promise to the minorities that their dignity and equality will be respected" (p. 205).

To think in these terms is to seriously distort both the facts of life and the meaning of the Constitution. It invokes a picture of DeFunis and

Bakke as rich and powerful individuals seeking to secure for themselves positions to which they are in no way entitled and to exclude others who have a far stronger claim: it implies opprobrium—even if unintended— and it appeals for sympathy—which is clearly intended.

The Constitution has a far broader and more impartial sweep than this. There is no place in the law and the rights that the law guarantees for weaker and stronger, poorer and richer, minorities and majorities. These rights (to make the point once again) are *personal*: they are held by persons as individuals, not as members of special groups or classes. Law is a guardian not only against the tyranny of the majority but against that which can come from minorities, pressure groups, disciples of violence and disruption, special interests, momentarily popular policies, and the power of an *idée fixe*.

It is of the essence of law to provide a stable framework for the social order and to keep a tight rein on the political process. It is far from unknown—indeed, it is quite usual—for us as a people to sacrifice socially desirable goals or to tolerate socially undesirable conditions in order to maintain the integrity of law against discrete passions or purposes. Thus, it is at least arguable that the moral tone of our society would be improved and the traditional virtues and values—if they are still regarded as such!—would be strengthened if there were a closer control of magazines, cinema, and television. It is quite certain that we would all be safer from random violence and organized crime if the procedural safeguards afforded those who are suspected or accused in criminal cases were relaxed. And finally—to refer again to an example cited earlier—the economic recovery of the country would have been hastened if President Roosevelt had had his way and appointed more members to the Supreme Court. Yet none of these steps have been taken. What these refusals manifest is a deep, if largely inarticulate, commitment to the rule of law as our best guardian against not only the tyranny of others but also against that of our own transient good intentions.

It is this characteristic and function of law that tells powerfully against the argument that *DeFunis* and *Bakke* present an issue with respect to which courts should exercise judicial restraint and deference. This is not a line of argument that one often finds in the writings of those who support such causes as privileged admission, since they tend to be judicial activists. And Dworkin does no more than hint at it in the work that I have been considering. But in his more recent article, "Why Bakke Has No Case,"[40] he advances it explicitly, summarizing the position in this way: "The Court has no business substituting its speculative judgment

<hr />

[40] The *New York Review of Books* 24, no. 18: 11-15.

about the probable consequences of educational policies for the judgment of professional educators."[41]

To state the matter thus is to seriously distort what is at issue and what the Supreme Court is doing in *Bakke*. The Court is not expressing a "speculative judgment" about "educational policies." Rather, it is handing down a judicial ruling on constitutional principles. And this certainly is its business. This is made perfectly clear in Justice Powell's opinion, when he stresses the First Amendment right of the university to decide on reasonable educational goals and policies and then rules that the particular program in question is invalid because it is violative of Bakke's Fourteenth Amendment right to equal protection.

The point at issue here is who is to be restrained. Dworkin argues that the Court should restrain itself and allow the university to make its own decision about how to promote what it regards as equality. I would argue that the Court should restrain the university from following a course that in the Court's opinion is clearly unconstitutional—and this is surely a question on which the justices are the professionals.

In conclusion, and to return to my original point, I would suggest that this discussion emphasizes once again the importance of considering discrete legal and social issues by explicit reference to a systematic framework and body of theory, such as my matrix of law. When we fail to do this, when our attention is focused too closely on only certain of the elements of order, our decisions reverberate disastrously, if inadvertently, through other regions, disrupting the social order and undermining the legal order. If I have read Dworkin correctly, this is precisely the trap into which he falls. The fact that such an acute legal thinker as he can argue for a result that flies in the face of his own most fundamental principles should serve as a stunning illustration of this danger.

One can be very sure that the professional schools that initiated programs of privileged admission and the legal scholars who devised the rationales to justify these programs neither anticipated nor intended, and certainly would not welcome, these theoretical and practical outcomes in which their efforts are culminating. The history of privileged admission is a textbook study of what can happen when the single-minded pursuit of a particular goal—no matter how worthwhile this may be—blinds us to the larger context in which this pursuit must take place and to the further consequences it inevitably entails. The more passionate and narrowly focused is this pursuit of a particular goal, the more vital it is to

[41] Ibid., p. 12.

have clearly in mind a view of the full field of legal action. Without some such matrix of law to temper and guide our efforts, the harm we ultimately cause is almost certain to outweigh the good we temporarily achieve, for then, inattentive to everything beyond our immediate purview, we ignore the limitations imposed by the regime of Necessity, the options offered by the regime of Possibility, and the range of goals comprised in the regime of Purposiveness.

The history of privileged admission stands as a model and a warning of these dangerous tendencies that are inherent in human rights. I think that it is beyond dispute that most, though not all, of the pleas that are urged in this guise are reasonable and justified: they are voiced by groups of persons who suffer under conditions that are both insupportable and inexcusable, and they impose upon society the obligation to correct them. The claims advanced as human rights should thus be acknowledged and pursued as social goals. But they should not be recognized as legal rights, for to give them this status threatens to defeat the claims themselves by undermining the social structure on which their realization depends.

[CHAPTER XVI]

LAW AND
THE IMAGE OF MAN

IN THESE CONCLUDING CHAPTERS I want to draw together the several lines of my earlier discussions, thereby placing positive law in true perspective and assigning it to its proper niche in the human and social panorama. My efforts up to this point have been twofold. First, I have sought to develop a general theory that views positive law as a supplemental principle of order that arises in the human context because of the special characteristics of man and the situation he faces. Here I was particularly concerned to analyze the conditions that gave rise to law, to identify the basic tasks of law as determined by these conditions, to trace the relation of positive law to other modes of law and principles of order, and to expose the complex nature of positive law as a synthesis of expository, normative, and prescriptive elements. Second, I sought to exhibit positive law in action as an instrument of order. This effort in turn centered on two themes: the conditions of legal effectiveness, with special reference to the concepts of value and authority; and the dangers that are present in the recent tendency of positive law to assert not only its sovereignty but also its omnicompetence, particularly through the doctrine of social engineering and the radical extension given to the concept of legal rights.

Within this broad framework, I now want to examine more closely the question of the role and function of law. A good many issues are involved in such an inquiry: the nature of man as an individual being, his status as a social creature, the relation of law to other social institutions, the tasks properly to be assigned to law, the peculiar characteristics of the legal apparatus, the limits of legal effectiveness—this list is neither exhaustive nor systematic. These issues constitute various decisions and adjustments that legal systems must make in one way or another and that other systems must deal with in their own respective ways. The stand that a legal system takes on these issues—its views on these matters—are often unconsidered and almost unconscious. Any legal system inevitably embodies a philosophy of man, society, and law, but this is apt to have been adopted without being critically examined and to function without being acknowledged: that is, the legal system will have answered these questions and resolved these issues implicitly without ever having really faced them. It is therefore important that the issues be brought out into the open, in order that the problems they pose and the alternatives they offer can be clearly understood, for it is only then that intelligent choices can be made.

As I have previously remarked, the legal order is part and parcel of the larger social order. Law is but one participant in the undertaking of human culture as a whole—the conscious and directed effort through which man seeks to develop his own powers, to master the resources of the world, and so to arrange his multiple affairs successfully. This effort spawns a great many institutions: family, morality, religion, science, technology, economic and industrial organizations, positive law, and others. As each such institution separates from a primitive synthesis, it tends to be primarily concerned with some particular area of human affairs, to have a specific purpose and a sphere of special competence, and to develop techniques and procedures that are peculiarly its own. But these institutions overlap in their functions, they depend upon one another, and the relations among them exhibit a constant tension between cooperation and competition. Finally, every such institution has an inner dynamism that inclines it to extend its reach and influence beyond its original purposes and wherever it finds room for expansion.

Law has certainly become the dominant element in this complex of institutions—the major factor in arranging the life of society. But just as certainly, law cannot by itself maintain the social order. The power of law as an instrument of order is limited by the very nature of the legal apparatus: this apparatus is admirably adapted to some tasks and functions, much less so if at all to others. The effectiveness of law depends heavily upon the contributions of these other institutions: so law must respect their integrity and coordinate its efforts with theirs. More particularly, law must inhibit the tendency, which is now running strong, to obtrude itself into the operations of its partners, forcing its standards upon them and challenging their authority in their own domains. When this happens, what should be a partnership becomes a rivalry, with interference and resistance aggravating one another in a mounting spiral.

Consequently, if we are to clarify the issues raised at the beginning of this chapter and determine the true reach and limits of legal effectiveness, there are three distinct but closely related matters that demand attention. The success with which any legal system functions as a principle of order and the quality of the relations that it sustains with other elements in the social structure depend largely on the soundness of its views on these matters. First, we need to reach an understanding—to come to some settled conclusions—regarding human nature and the human situation. Every legal system rests, consciously or unconsciously, upon a theory of law; and every theory of law rests similarly upon a theory of man. In both cases (and especially the latter), the underlying theory is apt to be present only implicitly. But this does not lessen its influence: in fact, it probably enhances it, for then the theory, being hidden, goes unquestioned and its consequences go unchallenged. What is at issue here is the kind of creature man is, his inherent potentialities and limitations, and the conditions of his well-being. This is, in brief, the question of the human career—of man's goals and capacities. Second, there is the question of the ideal conditions that society, through its various institutions, should strive to provide for its members, given their inherent characteristics. This speaks to the nature and structure of the just society. And finally there is the question of the role of positive law in this enterprise. This refers to the division of responsibility between law and other institutions.

If law is to do its own job effectively and to cooperate properly in the social enterprise, it is essential that these questions be separated and that each of them be carefully investigated. The fact that certain things and situations are desired does not establish that they are possible, much less that they embody sound and legitimate purposes. The conviction that men should enjoy certain goods and attain certain ends does not mean that through its institutions society either owes them to or can bestow them upon its members. Finally, the knowledge that organized efforts are required to achieve certain values does not entail that this effort devolves upon or is within the reach of law. In brief, to hold that law is an instrument for the achievement of human values is not to urge that law must acknowledge as values all of the claims asserted by men, or that law can promote all of the values that it acknowledges, or that these acknowledged values can be promoted only—or most effectively—by law. Yet these theoretical conclusions are frequently drawn, to the serious detriment of practical results. The threefold inquiry just outlined is therefore necessary if mistakes and exaggerations are to be avoided and the proper tasks of the law delimited.

Unfortunately, there are no established or agreed-upon answers to the questions posed by these inquiries. Indeed, there can be no definitive answers to them. Human nature is so complex and plastic and the human situation is so volatile that they defy reduction to any simple set of categories: the possibilities that men envisage and the outcomes they pursue are too variable to accept any final settlement, so there will always be different interpretations both of what man is and in what his well-being consists. These represent emphases upon different aspects of the human character and potential: all are true, and only time will tell—if anything can—where the proper balance lies. As regards the second and third questions, final answers are made impossible by differences in social structure, the fluidity of the social order, the shifting balance of power among factions, and the rise and fall of institutions. As changes occur in the aspirations men voice and the satisfactions they seek, societies can move in various ways to accommodate these new demands.

Thus these issues cannot be settled or these problems solved. The most that can be hoped for is to clarify them: to expose the complexity that lies at their heart, the alternative ways of dealing with them, and the values that these ways will differently realize and sacrifice. In this context, all answers and solutions are provisional; but even provisional settlements can be more or less well adapted to the circumstances they confront. With these limitations well in mind, I will discuss these questions in order.

This is not the place to engage in any large-scale theorizing about the nature of man. My intentions are more modest. I want to uncover and examine the views of man that can be found underlying different schools and systems of law, and thus to exhibit the issues and alternatives that law encounters at this basic level. The most direct way to open up this subject is by making explicit the particular views of man that are implicit, even if unintended, in the three concepts of rights—natural, legal, and human—that have played such a large part in fashioning contemporary legal theory and practice, for I think it is clear that each of these doctrines presupposes a particular interpretation of human nature and the human situation. Bringing these interpretations into the open should clarify the stresses and strains that the legal order is presently undergoing and that it must somehow resolve.

Before taking up these various doctrines of rights, there is an earlier theory of law, with its own implicit theory of man, that must be considered. I refer, of course, to that view of man and his place in the world and in society—or rather, that family of views—that is known as natural law. This theory endured for long periods of time, it adapted itself to different philosophical and cultural milieus, and in this process it underwent numerous and often radical metamorphoses. Because we are really dealing with a tradition rather than a theory, it is difficult to summarize this save in the most general terms. But the effort must be made, for natural law and the view of man that it embodies serve as the background and foil to the doctrine of natural rights and so to the whole modern development of the concept of rights.

There is one theme that dominates all natural law doctrines: this maintains that there is a single pattern of order and connection that pervades the universe, impressing itself upon all existent things. The uniformities of character, regularities of behavior, and constancies of relationship that hold among things and compose this pattern of order are inherent in the structure of nature or reality; they express themselves as the laws of nature's being, and they bind all things. As Montesquieu put it, "all things have their laws": these laws determine the character of things, define their places in the natural order, incline them toward their proper goods and ends, and establish the relations that hold among them. The laws are simply impressed upon or embedded in the characters of most existent things (roughly the realms of matter and life), which then "follow" them quite spontaneously and unconsciously. But because man has reason, he can discern these laws and know that he should follow them; and because he is free, he can and often does act contrary to their dictates.

It is the recognition of these two facts that gives rise to the doctrine of natural law. Put very simply, natural law is man's formulation of the ends he should pursue, the rules he should adhere to, and the duties he should acknowledge in his dealings with his fellows. The content of natural law—what it ordains—is rooted in man's nature: its formulation is the work of reason; its enforcement is the task of government.

The exact metaphysical status of natural law and its relation to the human and social orders have been differently interpreted by different schools of thought. The classical views on these matters—those of the stoic philosophers and, perhaps to a lesser degree, of the Roman jurists—were thoroughly synthetic: these thinkers held that natural law depicts an ideal order, ordains this as a rule, and inclines men toward it. In the language that I used earlier, natural law is at once normative, prescriptive, and expository. But in the course of time this synthesis is disrupted, and its expository and prescriptive elements are gradually stripped away. Already Aquinas and the scholastics conceived natural law as reason's grasp ("participation") of God's eternal law. Later thinkers with deistic tendencies were content to locate it vaguely in the heavens, where it subsisted as a "higher law," manifesting itself as the principles of natural justice. Thus the mode of being of natural law becomes steadily thinner and less substantial, until finally it is reduced to Mr. Justice Holmes's "brooding omnipresence in the sky."[1] But this is to anticipate; and I am here concerned only with the interpretation of natural law that was developed by medieval philosophy and inherited by modern thought.

Under this interpretation, natural law serves as the acknowledged model upon which the social order is to be patterned: it impinges very directly upon human affairs and the governance of man, and it projects a regime under which the characters and careers of men are closely conditioned by their positions in the social order. The social order is itself a part of the divine scheme of things; it is ordained by God as the proper habitat of men, in which their needs can be satisfied, their willfulness controlled, and their lives directed toward salvation. The governance of society is similarly ordained: authority is vested in the rulers, to whom all others owe obedience. The doctrine thus exhibits a fundamental ambivalence: society serves the good of men, but how this good is to be served is determined by the ruler, acting as the agent of a greater sovereign, God. Under this dispensation, there is great emphasis on status and duties, very little on freedom or rights. The primary obligation that presses on all men, whether king or commoner, is to discharge faithfully the functions of the positions to which they are called—which means to which they are born. So far as rights are recognized, they attach directly to the degree and position that a person occupies, not to the individual person as such.

Both the problem that natural law faces here and its solution can be brought out by reference to the ambiguity that is inherent in such terms as "subject" and "member." In one sense, a subject is thought of as an independent entity, a self-determining being and an end in himself; but in another sense, he is subjected to the control of another. Similarly, members participate in and enjoy the benefits of the groups of which they are members; but on the other hand they are subordinate parts of the wholes to which they belong—in much the same way as we speak of our arms and legs as being members of our bodies. This duality is of course rooted inextricably in the human condition, and we are still struggling with the tensions that it creates.

Thought of in these terms, natural law doctrine is simply one way of trying to resolve this tension: it throws the emphasis on the second of

---

[1] Southern Pacific Co. v. Jensen, 244 U.S. 205, 221 (1917). In this case Holmes was actually referring to the Fourteenth Amendment, but the phrase perfectly expresses his—and his contemporaries'—attitude toward natural law and toward legal idealism in general.

these meanings that lie uneasily together in the terms subject and member. Individuals are viewed from the perspective of society, the human person is largely reduced to his social role, and the meaning of life is said to lie in the performance of service rather than the pursuit of happiness. In the terms of my earlier analysis (see Chapter VIII), natural law exhibits law in its conservative phase: highly conscious of the dangers of disorder, it is anxious to preserve the social fabric against the threat of individual self-assertion, to establish public authority above private quarrels, and to assure that men discharge the duties and tasks assigned to them by their degrees and positions.

The image of man that is projected by natural law is that of a weak and wayward creature. He is regarded as totally dependent upon the support of the social order and the guidance of his social superiors; so he owes total conformity to the former and total obedience to the latter. His course through life, his duties and rights, his relations with others, and his standing before law are all determined by his place in the social scale. Through conformity, obedience, and service men can have happy and peaceful lives in this world and can assure themselves salvation in the world to come. Left to their own devices, men will inevitably go astray, to the disruption of society and the destruction of themselves. The core of this doctrine might be put by saying that man's social essence altogether precedes his individual existence: in the eyes of the church, man, as a child of God, is an immortal soul; in the eyes of positive (or human) law, man, as a social member, is a status holder.

This account of natural law and its image of man might seem to be both harsh and distorted. In the sense that it is incomplete, it is admittedly distorted, but it is not intended to be harsh. As I have made abundantly clear in earlier chapters (especially Chapter VI), I hold firmly to the principle of the continuity of law. Thus on this very basic point I am in thorough accord with natural law doctrine, although I would reject the idea that positive law derives from a prior body of higher law that is already complete and permanent. Furthermore, I believe that there is much truth in the teachings of natural law regarding man's character and his position in and duties toward the social order: this is a sound but partial interpretation of these complex issues. Finally, the preceding account certainly expresses the views of those legal and political innovators who repudiated natural law and set modern thought on its course. It is against the background of such a doctrine, conceived in far more grotesquely exaggerated terms, that the modern concept of rights is launched on its meteoric career. And from the point of view of historical influence, this is what counts: it is what contemporaries think of their intellectual inheritance, not what this actually is, that determines their response to it.

The doctrine of natural rights is the direct antithesis of the doctrine of natural law. It effects a truly Copernican revolution in its shifting of the human individual to the center of concern and in its pushing of society into the background. From now on we will hear a great deal of freedom, equality, and rights as tangible possessions that inhere in the individual; we will hear very little, if anything at all, of order, status, and duties as necessary features of social existence. The new emphasis is on what society owes to its members, and the idea that these members may have reciprocal obligations to their societies is simply ignored: more exactly, given the natural law heritage and modes of thought, it is assumed that men do have and recognize these obligations and that society will take care to see that men discharge them. This aspect of the matter is so obvious that there is no need to expatiate on it. What is needed is a full exposure of the other side of the coin: the rights that men hold, with the consequent obligations that the state must acknowledge and the limitations that it must observe. There now commences a long movement toward a new synthesis, which, like all others, will prove only temporary. I have traced this movement in some detail in Chapter XIV; my present concern is merely to draw out the ideas of man that are implicit in the doctrines that constitute its major stages: that is, in the concepts of natural, legal, and human rights.

Taken literally, the doctrine of natural rights assumes men whose essential attributes are independence and self-sufficiency. These men originally existed in a state of nature, where each was a law unto himself, acknowledging no obligations and taking what he needed and could seize from the environment and from others. Such men were thoroughly human but altogether asocial. When circumstances and convenience led them to group life, they accepted this reluctantly and made the fewest possible concessions to its demands. They drew up a social contract in which all agreed to surrender certain powers and to abide by certain rules, and all that they requested of government was the assurance of peace abroad and security at home. The only rights that they were deemed to want were liberty of action, equality of treatment, and acknowledgment of property: all else they would take for themselves as they could. In short, the holder of natural rights is conceived as a finite god.

The doctrine of legal rights assumes men who are prudent and self-seeking. They welcome social organization but not necessarily the society of their fellows. That is, they support political power and the legal system because these define and enforce the rules that every man can then employ in the pursuit of his own purposes. The social contract has now grown into a constitution that lays down the general principles in accord with which men are to arrange their affairs and carry on their transactions with one another. This doctrine assumes that men are adequately endowed by nature and circumstances to know their own best interests and to secure these through the apparatus that law puts at their disposal. In sum, the holder of legal rights is a rational egoist.

The doctrine of human rights assumes men whose individual efforts cannot possibly prevail against the complexity and inequity of the economic system. Despite what their capacities and energies may be, they do not have the opportunity to exert these effectively in their own behalf. The masses of men are now seen as bewildered and overwhelmed by a world and a social order that they can hardly understand and cannot at all master. It is not that men are incompetent or indolent and so bring these troubles on themselves. It is not even the oppression of the many by the few with vested interests, or the discrimination against minority groups, or the corruption of the agencies of government that defeat the best efforts of the common man, although these certainly aggravate the situation. Rather, it is the sheer size and intricacy of the social order, the interdependence of economic factors, the tangled webs of cause and effect, and the pressure of numbers that render men helpless. That is, the fault is seen as lying in the artificial world that man has created, in the very economic, political, and scientific organizations on which he had pinned his hopes. And since it is "the system" that has crowded men to the wall, it is up to the system to rescue them from this condition. To this end, the constitution is now transformed into a blueprint for the "good society," for it is only under these conditions that men can be protected against misfortune and assured of a decent existence. In short, the holder of human rights is a hapless victim.

The above accounts are admittedly simplifications, but they are not caricatures, distortions, or depictions of men of straw. Rather, they make manifest the unexpressed views of man that underlie these various doctrines: that is, the rights that these doctrines regard as necessary and sufficient make sense only if this is, in each case, the kind of creature that man is, the kind of existence to which he aspires, and the kind of support that he requires.

Furthermore, it is obvious that these several doctrines all manifest partial truths. Each of them calls attention to a real and important aspect of human nature and the human condition; but if any of them is taken as adequate and complete in itself, it issues in a travesty of man. Each of us at different times feels himself to be, and conducts himself as, a status holder, a finite god, a rational egoist, and a hapless victim. But none of us would ever admit that any one of these categories exhausts his nature and position. Whenever some one of these doctrines gains too great an ascendancy over thought and begins to imprint its exclusive image of man upon society, men cry out against this as an abuse. They feel instinctively that their natures are being restricted and their lives confined, and they demand recognition for those of their characteristics and needs that the ascendant doctrine neglects; for these concepts of man and his situation are complementary, not contradictory, so that each needs to be supported and balanced by all of the others.

The mutual interdependence of these views of man is exemplified in the movement of thought that I have just traced that runs from the doctrine of natural law, through the concepts of natural and legal rights, to finally culminate in the concept of human rights. Two features of this process are especially worthy of note. First, and quite obviously, there is the manner in which each of these doctrines in turn solicits the next as its corrective. Second, and more significantly, there is the manner in which the final moment of this process, the concept of human rights, represents a return to its point of departure, the doctrine of natural law. For the view of man as a hapless victim is closely similar in its essential content, and especially in its practical consequences, to the view of man as a status holder. There is of course a distinct shift in emphasis and perspective: the hapless victim is the focus of concern, and society and government are seen as obligated to support his claims and supply his needs, whereas the status holder is viewed as subordinate to the social order, within which he must accept his place and discharge his allotted functions. In short, the former asserts rights while the latter acknowledges duties.

But the difference in outcome is very slight, if it even exists at all. In both cases, men are seen as totally dependent upon society: acting by and for himself, the individual cannot prevail. It is only through the social structure, which musters and organizes the efforts of all men, that the needs of each man can be assured. To be sure, natural law emphasizes the common good and summons men to submerge their private interests in order to secure the public weal. The doctrine of human rights emphasizes the inalienable rights of the individual and calls upon the social order to provide for these. The doctrines thus stress different values, and appear to aim at different goals, but the final outcomes to which they point coincide very closely. A society governed by the doctrines of natural law must win the allegiance of men and secure to them the necessities of life if they are to be able to perform the services defined by their positions. Conversely, as I argued in Chapter XIV, a society dominated by the concept of human rights will quite surely have to control and organize the efforts of men—to assign them to roles and functions—if it is to be able to make good all of the claims that it acknowledges. In short, the situations envisaged by these seemingly opposed doctrines turn out to be mirror images of one another: the features and relations are the same, and it is only their positions that are reversed. One doctrine imposes duties; the other protects rights: but both submerge the individual in the social order and treat the human person as an abstraction upon which duties and rights are to be hung at the will of the state.

Thus the long journey from natural law to human rights appears to be leading us back to our starting point: we find once again that *plus ça change, plus c'est la même chose*, for change has certainly occurred, even though the pattern is repeating itself. And if we can learn the lessons of this three-hundred year journey of thought, it will not have been in vain: for then we can preserve what we have won in the process and we can achieve a better synthesis, even if it is one that will again prove only temporary.

The obvious lesson of this doctrinal development is that there can be no single best or final answer to the question of man's nature—this is too complex and too plastic to be pinned down and labeled. Consequently, as I have already argued, no one of the solutions represented by the various views of man as status holder, finite god, rational egoist, or hapless victim can possibly impose itself exclusively upon a society. Men being what they are, they will demand to be treated in all of these ways. As individuals, they will press claims for what they regard as their natural, their legal, and their human rights; as members of particular groups with specific functions and responsibilities, they will demand special privileges and protection. But these various claims run counter to one another. If natural rights are given free play, human rights will be compromised; if human rights are to be satisfied, natural rights must be stringently limited; the compromise that legal rights seek to effect is always crumbling under pressure from the two extremes; and the privileges claimed by some groups as due to their stations clash with those of other groups.

To state this matter from the other side, the duties that are respectively coordinate with these various rights are contradictory to one another; so when society, through law, seeks to impose the duties (whether of performance or forbearance) that are necessary to secure certain of these rights, it finds itself checked by the vehement assertion of other rights. And it is not simply a question of different groups and interests claiming different rights, thus requiring arbitration by the state as a superior power, but of every man, at different times, in different moods, under different circumstances, seeking to be treated as a status holder, a finite god, a rational egoist, and a hapless victim.

Since this is the human condition, all that the legal order can do is to try to maintain a stable but flexible balance among these various doctrines and the claims that they assert, as these represent different aspects of man's social nature and situation, each of which demands expression. What is therefore required is an institutional structure—a plot of the human and social drama—that will allow men to shift among these different roles. This brings me to the other questions just posed: What are the ideal conditions that society, through its various institutions, should strive to provide for its members? And what is the exact role of law—its functions and responsibilities—in this enterprise? These two matters will be discussed in successive chapters.

CHAPTER XVII

JUSTICE AS IDEAL
AND IDEOLOGY

IT IS EVIDENT that views on these matters will largely derive from and vary with the different views of man that have just been discussed, and like other issues that I have previously considered, they permit of no final and "correct" answers. The doctrines that dispute these issues are complementary rather than contradictory; and each one, no matter where it grounds itself, finds it necessary to make concessions to its rivals in order to embrace their legitimate claims. Furthermore, opinions concerning both the good society and the role of law in securing it are complicated by an additional factor: they depend not only upon abstract theories of the nature of man but also upon the actual circumstances out of which they arise and with which they seek to deal. Thus, as societies find themselves differently situated, they will give different responses.

The central point on which these problems and disputes turn is, of course, that of the nature and conditions of justice. With this recognition, we are at once warned that we are treading on ground that is mined with confusions and conflicts, for the idea of justice is even more contentious than that of rights. In broaching this discussion, the first necessity is to differentiate between two distinct senses in which the term "justice" is used—two distinct ideals or goals that it sets before our eyes. These can be identified as material or substantive on the one hand and formal or procedural on the other.

In the first usage, justice is a depiction of the good society, the ideal state of affairs, the consummation of man's hopes and dreams, the heaven on earth that we should seek to achieve. Here, the "just" society—and so derivatively the "just" legal order—is that which most fully affords men a milieu in which they can realize their potentials and lead decent and satisfying lives. In more homely terms, the just society is one that secures to men such familiar but elusive values as freedom, equality, security, and opportunity: it gives them the public support and protection that they need to make good their inadequacies, and it also allows them the room to exercise initiative and direct their private lives. Taken in this sense, one's views on the just society and the manner in which this is to be achieved will obviously vary with the image of man that one accepts.

In the second usage, justice identifies the standards to which society and the legal apparatus should adhere in their dealings with citizens. Here, justice refers not to the goals to be pursued but to the procedures to be followed. In this sense, the dictates of justice are familiar and widely acknowledged: there is little disagreement about the ideal to be aimed at, even though there is wide divergence in actual practice. The laws should be certain, known, and impartially administered; men are to be regarded as equal before the law and are to be treated with fairness; no man is to be judge in his own cause, and there should be no room for arbitrariness; enforcement must be effective and evenhanded.[1] In American jurisprudence, these demands of formal justice are largely summarized in the twin doctrines of due process and equal protection, and in this regard, three points are worthy of comment. First, I think it is correct to say that the determination and furtherance of substantive justice—the good society—would usually and historically have been regarded as the concern of legislative bodies, with the judicial function confined to assuring procedural justice. Second, it is certainly correct to say that this is not the present state of affairs in this country. Rather, the courts are now taking a leading part in defining the good society and overseeing its creation. Finally, the courts are doing this by radically extending the guarantees of equal protection and due process to a whole new spectrum of human rights. This is a matter that I have already discussed in Chapters XIV and XV and to which I shall return.

The substantive and procedural ideas of justice cannot of course be altogether disentangled, and especially not when we consider their issue in practice: the ideal ends that are envisaged for the law will obviously in-

---

[1] These broad outlines of the requirements of procedural justice were laid down by Aristotle and have undergone little change since then. Details have been added to extend and refine the original doctrine, and the dictum that "equals are to be treated equally, unequals unequally" has stirred much discussion directed toward determining what factors are relevant in identifying equals and unequals. There is a cogent and concise discussion of this aspect of justice in H.L.A. Hart, *The Concept of Law* (Oxford: The Clarendon Press, 1961), Chapter VIII, especially pages 153-163. The most elaborate philosophical treatment of the issue is that of John Rawls in a succession of articles and more recently in his book, *Theory of Justice* (Cambridge, Mass.: Harvard University Press, 1971). From the strictly legal point of view, a most illuminating analysis is that of Lon L. Fuller in *The Morality of Law* (New Haven: Yale University Press, 1964). Fuller distinguishes eight conditions that a legal system must satisfy if it is to achieve its formal purpose of administering justice. I think that the title of the book is most unfortunate, and this seems to have misled many reviewers into overlooking its virtues while criticizing it for failing to accomplish what it never pretended to undertake.

fluence the manner in which an actual legal system is structured and administered; conversely, once a legal system and apparatus are established, they play a large part in determining those values that law will promote and those that it will neglect. But taken strictly as ideals, the purposes and conditions that law is intended to further can be distinguished from the procedural standards it is expected to adhere to: this distinction is clearly marked in everyday speech by the two phrases, "social justice" and "legal justice."

The relation between these modes of justice can be epitomized by saying that the former depicts the justice that law serves, the latter the justice that it renders. My interest here is centered on the first of these. Regarding it, three points require attention: first, the nature of social justice as the ideal that law pursues; second, the extent to which we can expect to depict a single universally acceptable and applicable interpretation of social justice and, conversely, the degree of relativity that we must admit into this ideal; finally, the role and efficacy of law as an instrument to promote social justice and realize its conditions.

My present treatment of the first of these matters will be brief, as I have already discussed the issues at length, even though in different terms and from a different point of view. This was done particularly in Chapters III and IV. In the former, I examined in detail the changes that occur in time in the human and social situation, calling positive law into being as a supplemental principle of order and defining the tasks that it must undertake: this culminated in a systematic presentation of the complex problem that law confronts and the mission with which it is charged. In Chapter IV, I translated this abstract analysis into more concrete and dynamic terms, depicting the field of real legal action and the law at work in trying to solve its problems.

This earlier investigation was carried on in purely functional and genetic—or historical—terms. I was concerned to expose the situation that gives rise to law and the tasks that are committed to it. Such terms as justice, values, ends, and ideals were never mentioned. The analysis attempted to be strictly empirical and realistic, eschewing all speculative and moral considerations. It was based upon the fundamental idea that *law is before and above all a principle of order*. It sought to determine with great precision the bearing of this principle: to discover what order means, why it poses a problem to man alone among creatures, and what tasks it imposes.

But this analysis that was carried on from the point of view of beginnings can be transposed directly into the language of ends. Indeed, it demands such translation and closely controls its terms, although, as we shall see, it does not define these exhaustively or in a manner to exclude alternative interpretations. To speak of the tasks of the law is already to posit their performance, and to depict these tasks systematically and in detail, as I have done, is to describe the achievements that they envisage, the consequent condition to which they point.

Thus to my first postulate—law is a principle of order—we can now add a second: *Justice is the Completion of Law*. That is, justice represents the ideal form of the order that man seeks to create both through law and through the whole complex of his social institutions. Conceived as the outcomes that lie at the end of law, the structure and substance of justice have already been exposed by my earlier analyses that wrought into a single framework the dimensions of order—Many, One, Process, and Pattern—and the regimes of becoming—Necessity, Possibility, and Purposiveness. It would be pointless to repeat these detailed accounts, so I will first summarize their findings, and then present in diagramatic form this complex pattern that I have called the matrix of positive law.

The regime of Necessity constitutes the substratum—the fabric and framework—of human existence: it comprises men who share a common nature and situation, who are sensitive to their fellows and responsive to group pressure, whose reactions and behavior follow set courses, and whose roles and functions are defined by a pervasive web of relationships. The regime of Possibility ushers in the conditions that are distinctive to the human situation: it is composed of highly differentiated individuals, participating actively in group decisions and affairs, who have a large power of self-determination, and whose private and joint undertakings require a flexible social milieu. Finally, the regime of Purposiveness announces men's recognition, whether vague or clear, tentative or decisive, of the tasks with which these conditions challenge them: it requires the cultivation of human potentialities, the establishment and control of authority, the inculcation and acceptance of responsibility, and the assurance of continuity within the social whole. These are the tasks of law and the goals of justice.

DIMENSIONS OF ORDER	REGIMES OF BECOMING		
	Necessity	*Possibility*	*Purposiveness*
Many	Similarity	Differentiation	Cultivation
One	Domination-Subordination	Participation	Authority
Process	Action-Reaction	Self-determination	Responsibility
Pattern	Rigidity	Flexibility	Continuity

The matrix can be conveniently summarized as follows: this compact presentation, serving as a reminder of the detailed discussions of Chapters II-IV, should be a helpful frame of reference as I now go on to examine first, the extent to which any particular interpretation of these goals—any single conception of substantive justice—can claim universal relevance and the extent to which it must admit variant but equally legitimate interpretations; and second, the role and efficacy of positive law in securing these conditions of social justice. In short, how sound an ideal is this, and how effectively can law promote it?

My argument up to this point can be briefly summarized. Justice is the form of the order that man seeks to create through law. This form is composed around the four poles of cultivation, authority, responsibility, and continuity. The contents of these aspects, or goals, of justice are closely controlled by the antecedent course of events that has given rise to them—by the problems to which they are the envisaged solutions. It is this complex but tightly interrelated set of conditions that defines justice as a substantive concept, constitutive of the good society and regulative of legal and political institutions. The quest for justice *through*—as distinct from *under*—law is the quest for a state of affairs where these four conditions would be perfectly realized.

At this point an inevitable question arises. To what extent can this conception of justice claim to be both generally relevant and practically useful? It is a familiar charge against all theories of substantive justice that the terms in which they are couched are either too general to offer guidance in concrete cases or too specific to be accepted as universal and absolute. All such theories, it is claimed, are caught in a dilemma on one or the other of whose horns they must eventually be impaled. If they try to maintain their position as truly neutral and objective principles, valid under all conditions and categorical for all decisions, then they must be expressed in formulas that are so abstract and imprecise as to be practically useless. If they try to define in detail the ideal conditions that they mean to realize and to embody themselves in exact norms and rules that will promote this realization, then they inevitably become partisan political creeds, based on preference and expedience as much as reason and therefore provincial rather than cosmopolitan in their relevance. The history of the theory of justice is in large measure the effort to turn the thrust of this corrosive either/or.

It is the gist of this charge that the concept of justice does not have and cannot be given sufficient intrinsic structure and content to control the logical inferences and the practical directives that are drawn from it: that is, it does not generate a body of doctrine that serves to amplify and apply it. It is a sterile concept, in the sense that nothing definite follows from it. Rather, it stands as an empty and formless receptacle that must receive its shape and substance from elsewhere and is ready to take on the lineaments of any doctrine proposed to it. Consequently, it is held that justice is continually degenerating toward either a congeries of merely honorific precepts or toward a series of competing action programs. Finally, these two retrogressive movements hasten their tragic climax by mutually supporting each other. Action programs supply the precepts of justice with the content that their ambiguity requires; in their turn, these precepts lend to action programs the aura of ideality that they need to win the allegiance of men.

There is a large measure of historical truth in these charges. In its appearances in legal-political speculation and debate, justice has often worn the guise of either vacuous generality or partisan specificity. When challenged to decision, the justice that philosophy and jurisprudence urge on us as the guide and rule of life has the habit of dissolving into pious truisms and logical tautologies. The "eternal justice" to which political manifestoes ask us to dedicate our resources of mind and spirit soon puts on the clothes of a sectarian ideology that wants only the blank check of our emotional commitment.

The concept of justice has suffered under both of these mistreatments: it has been debased by uncritical minds and betrayed by unscrupulous wills. There is nothing unusual in this fate. Sins beyond counting have been perpetrated and protected under the names of liberty, equality, patriotism, democracy, morality, the will of God, due process of law, the public interest, and other such convenient verbal shields. We have even come to accept it as an unfortunate but unavoidable fact that most of the ideas that figure prominently in the direction of our individual and group lives are to a high degree friable and volatile; they tend to crumble if we press them too hard or to undergo metamorphosis if we scrutinize them too closely. Furthermore, exactly this fate often befalls the concepts of the natural sciences, which we tend to regard as having a content so fully determinate and so objectively grounded that it renders them inviolate. Such concepts as evolution, relativity, Heisenbergian indeterminism, the second law of thermodynamics, and many others have been similarly exploited by those who wanted to use them either to explain everything or to justify a *parti pris*.

And so the question repeats itself: Is the theory of justice that is here advanced able to turn the thrust of this critical either/or? Can it defend itself against the twin charges of vacuous generality and partisan specificity? I believe the answer is "yes," but at the same time I know that it is a qualified "yes." While this analysis does yield a comprehensive understanding of the essential conditions and values that must be secured by any social and legal order that is to qualify as just, it is evident that it cannot by itself yield a detailed picture of the "good society" to which all actual societies should conform: a determination of what constitutes the "best" social and legal order in any particular case cannot be logically derived solely from this doctrine but also depends on other considerations. This is to say that any such determination is a decision, not a deduction. This conception of justice claims to enunciate principles that are objective and neutral and thus to posit goals that hold true for all men at all times; but it is admittedly a general conception that requires to be filled out by specific interpretations before it can be implemented. In short, any effective doctrine of substantive justice must be both an ideal and an ideology. These two aspects of justice need brief elaboration.

Much of the confusion surrounding this matter springs from a misunderstanding of what we can legitimately expect an ideal to be and to do. We tend to think of ideals as definite and concrete models, or precise standards, by reference to which we can make exact comparisons and evaluations of actual instances. But this is to ask both for what is far too much and for what is not very important. The demand for such ideals has two sources. One of these is the contemporary obsession with measurement: we suffer under a terrible compulsion to reduce all things to points on a scale and to describe them exclusively and exhaustively in numerical terms. The other source of this demand is our apparent inability to accept the fact that things can very well be different without at all being better or worse. These tendencies are not only futile but vicious. With respect to justice—as with respect to health, happiness, morality, beauty, and many other traits—it is of vital significance that we be able to distinguish the licit and illicit, the real and the illusory, the honest and the deceptive. But it is impossible and unimportant to arrange things and situations on an exact scale as regards these traits. Ignorance alone would prevent us from doing this. And even with perfect knowledge we could not do it, simply because there are too many differences that are legitimate and neutral: the situations and conditions that people seek to realize, the purposes and values they pursue, often differ without our being able to say that some are better and others worse. When we delude ourselves into thinking that we can attain ideals that will yield us this certainty and exactitude regarding moral, social, and political decisions, then we are well on our way to dogmatism, intolerance, and finally persecution. And these are hardly functions that ideals are intended to serve.

What we can validly ask of an ideal is that it illuminate our present encounters and guide our future dealings with actuality. By their completeness and coherence, ideals can alert us to the richness and complexity of reality, they can help us to a rounded and balanced consideration of things, and they can prevent us from being blinded to some aspects of situations by the urgency that we feel for the other aspects. Here, ideals function much as conceptual models do for scientists. Furthermore, ideals can animate and guide our efforts as these move toward the future. They can make us aware of the total consequences of courses where we would otherwise be engrossed in their immediate outcomes. They can indicate which paths are apt to be fruitful—to lead toward development and progress. Ideals cannot define perfection, but they can identify mistakes. They can both sharpen our insight into our present surroundings and refine our vision of future goals. In a word, by illuminating the possibilities that we face, ideals can improve our uses of Purposiveness.

Within these limits of reasonable expectation, I believe that the present account of substantive justice constitutes a legitimate and fruitful ideal. Its analyses have not intended to depict any ultimate and utopian state of affairs. They have sought only to decipher the general course of man's development, to elicit the opportunity and the challenge that are inherent in the human situation, and to indicate the broad contours of the good society. This theory of justice maintains that cultivation, authority, responsibility, and continuity—as these terms have been systematically derived and analyzed—are at once the continuing tasks and the final goals of society and of law. These four conditions, and the tasks and goals they summarize, are rooted in the nature of man's being and well-being. They function as an ideal (as a matrix or model) by reference to which we can reach a sound assessment of the ends we propose and the means we adopt in our social, political, and legal efforts. Perhaps above all, this conception of justice can remind us of the complexity of this effort and thus protect us against neglect of any of its facets. If a social and legal order deviates too much from the tasks and goals set by this ideal, or if it too much distorts or misconstrues them, then we can safely say that it is unjust, for these are goals that man cannot reject and tasks that he cannot refuse without renouncing his own nature. This conception thus defines with at least some precision and coherence the conditions that any legal order must secure and the values that it must promote if it is to serve the cause of justice. To this extent, it embodies an ideal that is objectively grounded, systematically articulated, and universally relevant.

But this conception of justice as an ideal still requires further specification before it can be implemented, for it does not yield any complete and detailed delineation of the conditions it posits as the substance of justice: the goals that it sets and the tasks that it imposes are general rather than specific. This is necessarily the case, for these are matters that do not permit of any absolute predetermination that can claim to hold good for all peoples, times, and circumstances. Justice is the ideal form of order, but it is a form that is itself flexible and will accept various contents. This means that the concepts of cultivation, authority, responsibility, and continuity designate goals and tasks that require a more precise and concrete interpretation before they can function as guidelines to legal and political action. Any such interpretation constitutes an ideology. And these interpretations, and the ideologies they compose, will vary quite legitimately along three major axes.

First, there will be differences in the exact meaning and content given to these concepts that together define substantive justice. I believe that there would be universal agreement—certainly verbal assent—that the conditions I here described under the rubrics cultivation, authority, responsibility, and continuity represent the essential goals toward which political and legal efforts should be directed: if we could perfectly realize these conditions, we would indeed have created the good society. But it is equally certain that these conditions do not appear in the same guise to all men at all times and places. Unless one society is to claim for its ideology a monopoly of virtue, then it must be acknowledged that different groups have, with equal sincerity, placed different interpretations upon these concepts. Every society—every legal order—would certainly insist that it is dedicated to promoting the cultivation of its members: to affording them the material support and protection, the education, and the opportunities that will allow them to realize their potentialities. But. there are honest and legitimate differences of opinion as to what constitutes such proper fulfillment and how it can most effectively be furthered. We find a striking illustration of this within a relatively coherent and continuous culture in the various images of man that I canvassed in the previous chapter: to cite but one striking case, the rational egoist (the rugged individualist) who was so conspicuous only a couple of generations ago has become virtually extinct, to be replaced by the hapless victim (the underprivileged minority). Depending partly upon how the nature of man is construed and partly upon circumstances, societies will seek the ideal of cultivation along different paths. The same is true of the other concepts at issue. In each of the dimensions of order, the goal sought and the task imposed are so complex that some of their aspects will inevitably need to be subordinated, if not altogether sacrificed. Various peoples will therefore make choices that differ without being better or worse.

Of particular significance in this regard is the question of how the movement of Purposiveness is to strike a balance between the regimes of Necessity and Possibility. If law is to serve the cause of justice, the stability that is afforded by the conditions of Necessity—similarity, subordination, action-reaction, and rigidity—must be preserved. But at the same time law must keep the way open for the changes and innovations that are continually being generated through the conditions of Possibility—individuation, participation, self-determination, and flexibility. The ideal resolution of the tension between these regimes is one in which the benefits of each are secured, their shortcomings are mitigated, and the two are fused in a coherent manner. Cultivation, authority, responsibility, and community represent these envisaged syntheses. But we have clearly not achieved such syntheses, and we never will: we can depict them in utopias, which are static, but we cannot achieve them in life, which is dynamic. So in all of these cases our efforts are reduced to effecting some sort of compromise and conciliation, and there is no best or permanent way of doing this. Different societies differently circumstanced will with equal justice strike the balance in different ways. And no matter how it is struck, it soon becomes unbalanced and requires a new adjustment. This is more than familiar to us in the antinomies that haunt our legal and political efforts: stability and change, liberty and equality, private rights and the public interest, free enterprise and a planned economy, individual initiative and the general welfare, personal privacy and the public police power—these are but a sample of the poles between which societies oscillate in the quest for justice. All societies are continually seeking the broad goals of cultivation, authority, responsibility, and continuity, but the precise terms in which these goals present themselves will vary with the concerns that men feel and the circumstances in which they find themselves.

The other axes along which differences of interpretation occur can be treated together and more briefly. In the first place, opinions will differ as to the relative importance of these conditions that together compose justice. Secondly, views will vary regarding the proper means to be adopted to effect these common ends; even where there is close agreement on goals, the tasks of achieving them may be undertaken in quite different but equally justifiable ways. Given the double complexity of the ideal of justice itself and of the actual circumstances in which it must be realized, these differences are understandable and acceptable. As the moral, physical, and cultural situations of societies change, these goals will present themselves in differing terms and with varying degrees of urgency. Furthermore, the quest for justice does not take place under abstract and artificially simplified conditions but within a definite natural and social milieu that imposes demands and limits of its own. Thus, even when there is agreement upon general goals, judgment may still render differing verdicts regarding both the evaluation of specific ends and the selection of appropriate means.[2]

Law is a principle of order, and justice is the completion of law. These are general and abstract statements from which I have tried to derive an objective and neutral meaning of justice. But any particular legal system is the principle (instrument) of a concrete and determinate social order, and this requires an equally concrete and determinate completion. As the ideal form of order, justice must therefore take on a similarly specific guise of it is to be effectively embodied in an actual setting.

It is for these reasons that any working idea of justice must always have an ideological as well as an ideal component. Ideals as such are indispensable as directing and controlling elements in the life of the law; but they are by themselves inadequate to this task. They are necessary but not sufficient conditions. To function effectively, the general and abstract idea of justice must associate itself with a specific and concrete body of doctrine. That is, the ideal must be supplemented by an ideology.

This is often regretted on the ground that in this process the ideal loses its most significant features, namely, its objective basis and its universal relevance. But this is a partial view of the matter, for what happens here is gain as well as loss: without renouncing its intrinsic nature, the ideal acquires a richer meaning by assuming the guise of a definite and detailed interpretation of its own provisions. When the ideal is transformed into an ideology, it does indeed surrender its objectivity and universality; for any ideology is subjective and local, being a set of fallible decisions made in shifting circumstances.

---

[2] The influence of these differences of emphasis and interpretation is forcefully illustrated by the tensions and misconceptions that characterize the relations between the United States and Russia. The *confrontations* of these countries occur because two extremely powerful states fear one another, with each seeking to achieve a superiority of strength. But the misconceptions between them occur because the two peoples have different ideologies, deriving from different visions of the ideal of justice and from the different actual circumstances in which their societies have originated and grown to maturity. The Russians cannot understand our obsession with human rights and civil liberty and our apparent equanimity before public disorder and the idleness that accompanies high unemployment. We cannot understand the Russians' obsessive fear of dissent and social disruption and their apparent indifference to individual freedom and social tolerance. Alexander Solzhenitsyn perfectly epitomizes the difficulty of even an acutely sensitive writer in comprehending an alien ideology and culture. His 1978 Harvard commencement address makes it clear that he instinctively judges us in terms of his Russian ideology: he therefore has a somewhat exaggerated view of our faults, and he seems totally incapable of appreciating our virtues—and of seeing that our faults are largely correlative with our virtues.

And it is here that the gain accrues. Now there is enunciated a concrete and particular conception of order—of the good society—and a definite meaning is given to the goals and tasks of cultivation, authority, responsibility, and continuity. Institutions develop to perform these tasks and secure these goals, and these engender a detailed action program. It is in this way that the ideal becomes a moving force: transformed into an ideology, it initiates a dynamic chain of events. The implicit meanings of the ideology are elicited and elaborated, instruments are created to realize these meanings, and, finally, they are made effective in society and their impact on human life is exposed.

Once transformed into an ideology, the ideal of justice in turn transforms the human world. The various ideologies that are spawned by this single ideal represent so many explorations of the potentialities of human development: they are experimental probings of the nature of the good society and the way to secure it. They can correct and supplement one another. We can even expect that they will gradually bracket their target. But they will certainly never hit it, for the very good reason that it does not exist. The ideal as such is never embodied: it remains always an abstract concept, defining only the general condition of man's being and well-being. It rests with men to give it a concrete meaning, accommodating it to their circumstances and concerns. As long as knowledge is incomplete, and the future uncertain, these interpretations can only be tentative, awaiting the verdict of their outcomes. The ideologies that men proclaim thus have a double obligation: they must be faithful to both the ideal they represent and the actualities they confront. As the justice we achieve is less than that which we seek, so is the latter an imperfect vision of the ideal laid up in heaven. To bring the ideal within our reach, we must catch it in an ideology. As in any capture, the prey is somewhat harmed. But the gain to us offsets the loss, for an ideology is the ideal tamed, domesticated, and put to human use.

CHAPTER XVIII

SOCIAL JUSTICE AND
LEGAL JUSTICE

THE PRECEDING DISCUSSIONS lead directly to a final question: What is the role of law in the enterprise of justice? How much can law contribute to the realization of these substantive goals, and how much should be left to other forces and institutions or to the free play of individual choice and effort? Again there can be no single correct answer to these questions. Too much depends on the prevalent image of man, on current ideas regarding the nature of social justice and the good society, and on the institutional structure that is available. It is self-evident that the rational egoist and the hapless victim will demand—and get—quite different services from the legal order. Similarly, as societies conceive their four basic goals in different terms (as, for instance, they feel the need to strengthen or relax the grip of authority), so will they call on the legal apparatus for different tasks. Finally, the role of law will vary with the relative influence and effectiveness of other social institutions, such as morality, religion, education, and so forth.

We are dealing here with issues that we can at best hope to clarify but certainly not to resolve. In this chapter I want to explore in general terms the aptness of the legal apparatus for the tasks of substantive justice—for securing the values of cultivation, authority, responsibility, and continuity. In this context I shall be especially concerned to examine one particular aspect of the problem that stands out as singularly important and provocative: namely, the manner in which law seems inevitably to transform these goals of justice in seeking to secure them.

As regards the general issue of the conditions and the limits of legal effectiveness, the ground has been carefully mapped in Chapters IX-XIII. So we need only recall the lessons of those inquiries and then apply them to the specific question of the role of law in furthering the goals of justice. The discussions of those chapters can best be characterized as a detailed explication of the fundamental point that I have insisted on throughout: positive law is a *supplemental* principle of order. In its original occurrence, law supervenes upon an established social order that is expressed and supported by an array of institutions. This institutional structure is the constant and indispensable milieu within which law operates. As such, the qualifying term "supplemental" must be strictly construed: law supplements but does not supersede these other institutions. It is called into being to support and complete their efforts; but it is not intended to, nor can it, supplant them.

This is to say that law is a necessary but not a sufficient cause—or instrument—of order. As human groups become sufficiently large, complex, and diversified, they suffer an erosion of the cohesion and stability that they formerly had. Patterns of behavior become uncertain and insecure. Men find themselves in novel situations and relationships that are not covered by common usage. Private interests diverge and conflict. In short, to borrow Bagehot's phrase, the cake of custom crumbles. As this occurs, the apparatus of positive law is created—gradually, and hesitantly, and often against the grain of inertia and opposition—to make good what has been lost.

The essential features of a legal system are determined by these deficiencies in the social order that it is called on to repair. There are three demands in particular that law must satisfy, but these are so intimately interrelated and are so closely dependent upon one another that it is impossible for them to exist altogether separately and difficult even to describe them individually. For one thing (I purposely do not say "in the first place"), provision must be made for establishing norms of behavior: for prescribing and prohibiting certain modes of conduct, for defining personal and property rights, for establishing general rules under which people are to carry on their day-to-day relations and make their private arrangements, and for allocating social duties, functions, and privileges. In short, at least a rudimentary body of civil, criminal, and public law is needed. Further, there must be provision for applying this body of law in a way to settle disputes and secure compliance: this requires techniques for ascertaining the relevant facts in cases at issue, for determining the applicable rules, and for imposing and enforcing sanctions. Finally, provision must be made to reassert the threatened unity of the group: as the agent of the whole society—of what will later be called the state—law must be given a position of preeminence, such that it can adjudicate all differences, exercise supervision of other institutions and forces, and have its decisions acknowledged as final and binding.

All of this is achieved only slowly and circuitously, with rebuffs and false starts. It is doubtful if these goals are even recognized until they are more than half accomplished. The movement toward them is impelled by necessity more than it is guided by clear purposes. But as it continues it acquires both momentum and direction, and when it is finished it has issued in positive law with its three distinctive features: official sovereignty and the monopoly of force, an explicit and detailed body of substantive law, and a highly formalized body of procedural law.

All of this is familiar matter; it has been explored in depth and analyzed in detail many times over.[1] Indeed, as I have argued before, the final outcome of this movement—the fully developed legal system closely merged with its national state—is so familiar to us that we tend to regard it as an eternal object, without beginning, end, or limitation. That is, we think of positive law as both self-sufficient and omnicompetent. But this is to forget the circumstances that initiated the quest for law, the conditions that presided over its development, and the pressing needs it was called on to satisfy. In the context of my present concern (the adequacy of law to the enterprise of justice), this forgetfulness takes two particularly serious forms. First, we forget those other institutions that have always been present alongside of law, serving different aspects of the same general purposes and lending significant support to the work of law. Second, we forget the extent to which the very nature of the legal apparatus, which has been explicitly fashioned to repair specific deficiencies and to secure specific results, must limit its reach and effectiveness in other directions. With regard to both of these points, a brief discussion should serve to remind us of what habit and familiarity make us overlook.

The slightest reflection will make clear how rarely positive law impinges directly and explicitly upon the ordering of our lives and affairs. We need only bring to mind a normal week—or month or even year—out of the past and then ask ourselves: How often during this period have I been conscious of law and what it requires? How often have I looked to the law in making a decision? To what extent have my character and conduct—my feelings, thoughts, and actions—been influenced by the legal apparatus? The answers to all of these questions can be summed up in a phrase: very little and very rarely. A day in the life of "Everyman" will reveal that what he is and what he does are overwhelmingly the function of other than legal considerations and influences. My guess would be that the only legal figures with whom the or-

---

[1] Closely reasoned and interesting discussions of the deficiencies that law is called upon to repair, the purposes it is intended to serve, and the form it takes to fit it for these tasks are to be found in H.L.A. Hart, The Concept of Law (Oxford: The Clarendon Press, 1961), Chapters V and VI; and Lon L. Fuller, The Morality of Law (New Haven: Yale University Press, 1964), Chapter II.

dinary citizen has any direct dealings are the traffic officer and the tax collector. And now even these have been replaced by those more impersonal factors, traffic lights and Form 1040, so that the legal apparatus recedes more and more into the background.

If we now ask ourselves how it is that we have become what we are and why it is that we act as we do, the answer is harder to come by. But when we look more closely, we begin to discern shapes looming through this fog of becoming. And with patience we can identify the factors and forces that have set us on our course and still serve us as guides— although even then it is impossible for us to see how it is that they have done this. We can pick out the apparatus and the outcome, but the mode of operation largely escapes us.

This apparatus consists of the numerous institutions, organizations, and systems that pervade society. The most basic and least accessible of these is the mechanism of genetic inheritance: this is what first makes us human, endowing us with specific instincts, powers, and tendencies and with individual characteristics and capacities. Until just yesterday, this mechanism was so secret and intricate—-and hence so mysterious—that there was no thought of interfering with its operation or outcome: we talked much of blue blood and of good and bad blood, but we took what heredity gave us. Now all of that is changing so rapidly that yesterday's ignorance becomes tomorrow's mastery. Once we know with precision what it is that makes us human, we are well on the way to being able to create and eliminate types of human beings through the processes of selective breeding and "genetic engineering." This may sound like fantasy, but when we have at our disposal such a powerful tool for fashioning human character and controlling human behavior (which, after all, is what all institutions seek to accomplish in one way or another and with varying degrees of success), it is hard to believe that it will not be used. And it must be remembered that the agencies that will exploit this tool are already available in scientific and medical organizations.

The most basic factor in determining what men are to become is the genotype: it programs us for general courses and patterns of development. Supervening immediately upon this is the body of custom and common morality under whose influence a person grows up: this composes what can best be called the way of life that is transmitted to every person by his particular social environment. This way of life has a wide content. Its most explicit element is the moral code that one is taught: the catalogue of rights and wrongs, do's and don't's, duties and obligations, rules and norms. But these represent only the tip of an iceberg: they are the codified directives that it is hoped men will follow when

they stop to think of what they are about to do. Of far greater significance is the hidden body of the iceberg, which largely controls behavior
because, prior to any deliberation, it determines the attitudes with which
men confront the world and the responses that they make to lived situations. This hidden body of the way of life is heterogeneous in makeup.
Its most pervasive feature is the mass of habits that we begin to acquire
from earliest childhood. And here it must be emphasized that the term
"habit" is to be taken in a broad sense. We usually think of it as referring to overt patterns of behavior, and it does include these. But
far more important are our habits of perception, feeling, thought, and
judgment: what we call stereotypes or prejudices. These habits are so
many screens through which the world is filtered to consciousness: they
determine the way in which we see things and events, our emotional
responses to them, the manner in which we interpret and evaluate them.
And they are all the more influential because we are not conscious of
their working. What peoples our consciousness is precisely what our
habits project, so that only the most violent collisions of expectation
with experience will elicit these preconceptions and expose them to criticism, making us aware of the difference between appearance and reality.

Above the threshold of consciousness we find a motley array of items
that do much to define the behavior of people. Among these are the
hopes and aspirations that men nourish, the values and ideals to which
they hold, and the purposes that they envisage. Less often verbalized
than these, but probably more influential, are the terms in which men
picture success and the way to achieve it: these constitute their image of
the good life, with its status, possessions, privileges, and accomplishments.

This cultural inheritance becomes for us a second nature, closely
grafted upon our biological heredity. It is transmitted by a variety of institutions, the social analogues of genes and chromosomes. Traditionally, the most conspicuous and important of these institutions have been
the triumvirate of family, education, and religion. It has been largely
through the ministrations of these three that the raw material of human
nature has been transformed into successive generations of mature persons, individually developed and socially adapted. As has often been remarked, the adult human being and social member is at least as much a
work of art as of nature: and the primary artists in this case have been
the home, the school, and the church.

But other forces and agencies have also contributed their share. Of
particular importance has been the neighborhood, that relatively small,
coherent, and clearly demarcated region of social space that spreads out-

ward from the home as its nucleus. To grow up in a neighborhood is to know and to be known by everyone, to have always before one's eyes a model of social structure and the lived world, and to be under a constant pressure to conform to established rules and norms of behavior.

Pervading a neighborhood, but also extending far beyond it, are two other social features of prime importance: these are the class structure that characterizes the society and the economic system under which it operates. These exert a powerful if largely unformalized influence upon the attitudes and the behavior of people: they instill in varying proportions the antithetical notions of status and opportunity, of duty and right; they establish relationships among individuals and groups, defining the terms on which they meet and the ways in which they treat one another; and they set the conditions that must be satisfied and the courses that must be followed if people are to achieve the positions and benefits that they seek.

The class structure and economic system of a society find expression and exert their influence through a multitude of professional and trade associations, labor unions, and other special interest groups. These institutions speak for their members to the outside world—and especially the government—representing and protecting their private concerns. At the same time, they stamp their mold upon their members, instilling in them attitudes, patterns of behavior, standards of conduct, and a sense of allegiance to the group and its purposes. Doctors, lawyers, bankers, industrialists, auto workers, coal miners, school teachers—all of these bear the stamp of their trade, reflecting its outlook and intentions, so that a person is a lawyer or a miner just as truly as he is John Doe or Richard Roe.

This is not intended to be an exhaustive catalogue of social institutions, much less a thorough account of the manifold ways in which they fashion human character and conduct. I merely want to call to mind the influence exerted by these institutions and the extent to which the effective operation of law depends upon their prior effectiveness. When it is functioning properly, what this institutional structure collectively does is to provide law with a relatively finished human and social product. Law is then able to deal with men who have already been domesticated: imbued with common habits, attitudes, and modes of behavior, and trained to live together peacefully and to work together in cooperation. In short, the legal apparatus has at its disposal the two invaluable ingredients of a body of *citizens* who already constitute a *community*. Given these materials, it is but a short and easy step to those familiar figures of jurisprudence: the *legal person*, with his rights and duties clearly spelled out; and the *state*, with its powers and responsibilities sharply defined. Conversely, to the extent that this institutional foundation is weakened, the legal framework is at once subjected to intolerable stresses and strains. Law then has to work with the raw material of human nature, which eludes its grasp and confronts it with tasks for which it is ill-equipped.

With regard to these matters, it is interesting to contrast Dean Pound's position in the Storrs lectures of 1922 (which I quoted earlier)[2] with the views he expressed some twenty years later in the Mahlon Powell lectures.[3] In the earlier work, Pound had been supremely confident, and even complacent, of the power of law to refine and extend its apparatus in a way that could deal with any social problems whatsoever. Law was social engineering, and all that needed to be done was to create new machinery to perform new tasks as they arose. This was what the civil and mechanical and electrical engineer did, and there seemed to be no reason why the social engineer, with law as his tool, should not do the same. Pound's view at that time was summed up in a sentence: "Better legal machinery extends the field of legal effectiveness as better machinery extends the field of industrial effectiveness."[4]

But a great deal had happened between 1922 and 1942! Various institutions and systems that had been working to secure a satisfactory measure of order—if not always of justice—began to break down. As this happened, a social vacuum was created: law was confronted with novel situations and unanticipated problems, and the legal machinery was called upon to intervene in matters with which it was unfamiliar and to do things for which it had never been designed,[5] so that those charged with the administration of law were made aware of the extent to which they had depended upon other social institutions that were now effectively absent. It is the significance of this absence that Pound now recognizes. He begins by stressing again the principle and the fact of legal sovereignty:

> Since the sixteenth century political organization of society has become paramount. It has, or claims to have and on the whole maintains, a monopoly of force. All other agencies of social control are

[2] See Chapter XIII.

[3] Roscoe Pound, *Social Control through Law* (New Haven: Yale University Press, 1942). Subsequent references to this source will appear in parentheses in the text.

[4] Pound, *An Introduction to the Philosophy of Law* (New Haven: Yale University Press, 1922), p. 97.

[5] It hardly needs mentioning that the changes and challenges that have arisen between 1942 and 1975 quite overshadow those that arose between 1927 and 1942.

held to exercise disciplinary authority subject to the law and within bounds fixed by law. . . . The household, the church, the associations which serve to some extent to organize morals in contemporary society, all operate within legally prescribed limits and subject to the scrutiny of the courts. Today social control is primarily the function of the state and is exercised through law. Its ultimate effectiveness depends upon the application of force exercised by bodies and agencies and officials set up or chosen for that purpose. It operates chiefly through law, that is, through the systematic and orderly application of force by the appointed agents. (Pp. 24-25)

But this conventional insistence upon the supremacy of law is now immediately followed by the more novel recognition that the legal apparatus is neither self-sufficient nor omnicompetent. And Pound goes on to say:

It would be a mistake, however, to assume that politically organized society and the law by which it brings pressure to bear upon individuals are self-sufficient for the task of social control in the complex society of the time. The law must function on a background of other less direct but no less important agencies, the home and home training, religion, and education. If these have done their work properly and well much that otherwise would fall to the law will have been done in advance. Anti-social conduct calling for regulation and ill-adjusted relations with neighbors will have been obviated by bringing up and training and teaching, leading to life measured by reason. (Pp. 25-26)

Pound then goes on to comment on the decline of many of these social agencies, such as religion and the neighborhood, and on the secularization of education. The outcome of this process, he notes, is a serious lapse in the inculcation and support of moral rules. And he concludes in these terms: "The problem of enforcing its [society's moral] precepts has become acute as law takes the whole field of social control for its province" (p. 26).[6]

It is among the most typical of human traits to take things for granted when they are going well. As long as health, career, bank balance, and

---

[6] This same point was emphasized in an address by Edward Levi, former United States Attorney General, at the dedication of a new law school building at the University of Nebraska. Levi said: "Law is not everything in society. Law is one of a number of institutions through which we express ourselves and which in turn influence us, maintain our customs and change our habits. Thus, law takes a place along with family structures, religious beliefs, the expressions of art and the explanations of science."

family life are in good shape, we do not scrutinize them to see what keeps them so. It is only when things go wrong that we become concerned and ask ourselves what has been done, or left undone, that is causing the trouble. It is this situation and this response that are reflected in the remarks of Dean Pound and Attorney General Levi, who speak from the realization that in their times law is missing the support that it previously took for granted and is finding itself faced with tasks that had hitherto been undertaken by others.

This discussion leads directly to the other point that is often overlooked: namely, the extent to which the legal apparatus, taking shape as it did under certain conditions and to serve limited purposes, is apt to find itself overtaxed when it faces new and diverse conditions and is asked to serve larger purposes. This raises the time-honored question of the limits of legal effectiveness. If this question were to be explored in any depth and from a strictly legal point of view, it would soon involve technicalities that are beyond the scope of this book. In Chapters IX-XVI, I have already discussed the larger social and philosophical issues. Since my primary concern in this chapter is to examine the specific issue of the relative adequacy of law for the goals of substantive justice, I shall consider only briefly and superficially the general question of the limits of legal effectiveness.

The question at issue here can be briefly stated: To what extent does the essential procedural apparatus of law limit its ability to deal with matters of substance—to solve social problems and promote social goals? With regard to this question, it is again interesting to consider the change in Dean Pound's attitude in the twenty years between the Storrs and Mahlon Powell lectures. In 1922, Pound expressed unbounded confidence in the power of law to extend and refine its techniques in a way to deal successfully with whatever new challenges it might face. He took the analogy with engineering quite seriously, and he appeared to believe that the "machinery" of law was susceptible to indefinite expansion: there were no limits in principle to what the legal apparatus could do. By 1942 this attitude had undergone considerable change. Pound now recognizes definite and even stringent limits to the reach of law. He introduces his discussion of the issue in this way:

> When we have got so far we must pause to inquire how far, after all, the law in any of its senses can achieve this purpose (of harmonizing human demands, maintaining a social order, and furthering the course of civilization). We must ask how far social control through politically organized society, operating in an orderly and

systematic way by a judicial and administrative process applying authoritative grounds of or guides to decision by an authoritative technique, can stand by itself as self-sufficient and equal by itself to the maintaining and furthering of civilization. Thus we are brought to consider the limits of effective legal action, the practical limitations which preclude our doing by means of law everything which ethical considerations or social ideals move us to attempt. (P. 54)

Following upon this general statement, Pound proceeds to cite five "sets of limitations" that set bounds to effective legal action. These are discussed in a somewhat casual manner: they give the appearance of being intended as illustrations rather than as constituting an exhaustive or systematic account. I think that a closer analysis reveals that they fall into three major types of limitations, concerned respectively with the initiation of legal proceedings, the application of the law to the facts of cases at issue, and the inability of the legal apparatus to protect certain rights and correct certain wrongs even when these have been recognized as such.

As regards the first point, legal action is limited by "the necessity of appealing to individuals to set the law in motion"(p. 60). This "ultraindividualism of the common law" is of course not absolute: the state takes responsibility for the operation of the criminal law and intervenes frequently in other areas of broad public concern. But the Anglo-American legal tradition is opposed in principle to such "administrative enforcement" of the law, seeing it as a threat to individual freedom. The extent to which rights are protected and redress obtained thus depends largely on the will and the power of private persons to initiate and sustain legal actions.

A second set of limitations arises from the difficulty of ascertaining the facts at issue. In its quest for certainty and precision, its insistence upon rules and forms, and its laudable determination to protect against incrimination by rumor and hearsay, the law has established rigid standards that exclude a good deal of available and often relevant testimony. Much that is common knowledge will not be judicially recognized and accepted in evidence. To the legal outsider—the man in the street—this gives the impression that those who administer the law are more anxious to protect themselves against the slightest chance of the most trivial mistake than they are to protect him against obvious wrongs and harms.

The third set of limitations concerns the frequent inability of the legal apparatus to enforce duties, protect rights, and secure redress even in cases that clearly fall within its purview. Pound discusses this limitation under three headings, but these are obviously so closely related as to be examples of the same general type. He calls attention first to "the intangibleness of many duties which morally are of great moment but defy legal enforcement" (p. 55). Cases in point are gratitude, benevolence, disinterestedness in one serving as a trustee or company director, and the obligation to help those in distress. Closely related to this problem is the fact that private interests and rights are often infringed in ways that are so subtle and difficult to establish that the law cannot protect against them: tale-bearing, alienation of affection, and various invasions of privacy fall under this heading. Finally, in this regard, limits are set by "the inapplicability of the legal machinery of rule and remedy to many phases of human conduct, to many important human relations, and to some serious wrongs" (pp. 56-57). These three sorts of limitations are obviously variations on the familiar theme that "you cannot legislate morality." They recognize that there are many traits of character, modes of conduct, and forms of mutuality that are morally and socially desirable but that law is largely helpless to impose. And Pound is explicit on the reason for this: "Law secures interests by punishment, by prevention, by specific redress, and by substitutional redress; and the wit of man has discovered no further possibilities of judicial action" (p. 58).

In the years since Pound wrote this, the machinery available to the law has been vastly increased, and the will to use this machinery for various social purposes has been greatly intensified. But I believe that Pound's general analysis still holds true and that these five limitations do operate, as he puts it, to "preclude our doing by means of law everything which ethical considerations or social ideals move us to attempt."

There are two obvious but important corollaries to this proposition. In the first place, those things that are necessary to social order and justice, but that law cannot do, must be done by other means. We have to rely upon other institutions and agencies—the family, morality, religion, education, professional and economic organizations—to instill in men the habits and attitudes, the modes of behavior, and the mutual respect and cooperation that are indispensable to a decent social life. Secondly, from this it follows that it very much behooves the law to recognize its limitations and so to protect and nourish these other agencies whose support it so badly needs. Law must accept these other institutions and professions as allies in a common enterprise; it should therefore allow them to go about their tasks in their own ways, assuming their integrity and competence until there is strong evidence to the contrary.

The force of these corollaries should become clear as I now turn to measure more closely the limits of legal effectiveness by examining the relative adequacy—the success and the failure—of law with regard to the goals of substantive justice.

In introducing the discussions of this chapter, I suggested that law seems inevitably to transform the goals of substantive justice in seeking to secure them. I want now to explore this suggestion, to see if the facts confirm it, and if so, what this means for the place of law in the social order. I will first state my view of the situation in general terms, and I will then develop this in detail.

There can be no question that, under present conditions, law is an indispensable instrument of social justice, making a distinctive contribution to this effort. But it does appear to be the case that the actual outcomes in which legal action issues—the social conditions and human relationships that it is able to secure—are not identical with the ideal goals of justice. Law achieves something of real value, but it does not achieve the moral and social aims that are set before it and which it claims as its own. Further—and this point is of particular importance—it is not simply that law achieves less than it aims at: this is the common fate of all human efforts. Rather, the actual results in which legal action issues are different in character from the ideal outcomes that justice seeks. When law, relying solely upon its own powers, sets out to secure the goals of social justice, these undergo a distinct metamorphosis; for law must then translate these goals into the terms of its own conceptual and procedural apparatus, since it is only in this way that it can get a grip on them. What we find here is thus a difference of kind, not merely of degree.

We are at once prompted to ask why this should be the case. What is responsible for these limitations on legal effectiveness? I believe that at least a large part of the answer to this question follows from Dean Pound's analysis. The law's proper insistence upon formal or procedural justice limits its effectiveness as an agent of material or substantive justice. The apparatus and the sanctions available to law do not equip it to promote the conditions of cultivation, authority, responsibility, and continuity, as I described these earlier, so that in pursuing these goals, law unavoidably modifies them, unconsciously replacing these ideal realizations with more limited conditions that do lie within its power.

Given the principle of legal sovereignty, this situation contains the seeds of a double danger. In the first place, there is the risk that those charged with the administration of law will identify what they can accomplish with what they set out to achieve. Overlooking the limitations of their apparatus, they will assume that the conditions that law promotes constitute social justice. In the second place, and as a consequence of the above, there is the risk that the men of the law will intrude too much into the affairs of other agencies and professions, asserting a close control of their decisions and operations. The result of this would be the imposition of legal standards and procedures upon the entire institutional life of the society.

I will return later to a consideration of these matters, with the aim of determining whether these dangers are real and threatening or only theoretical. But before attempting to settle the extent and immediacy of these dangers, it is important to understand their nature. To this end, we must deal with two critical questions. First, in just what ways—by means of what legal concepts and doctrines—does law transform the goals of social justice? That is, what are the conditions that legal action does in fact promote? Second, what are the foreseeable outcomes if for any reason these conditions that law promotes supplant the original goals of social justice and come to dominate the life of society? That is, what would a thoroughly legalistic society be like? To answer these questions, we must watch the law at work in pursuit of the four goals of social justice, thus spelling out the difference between what law seeks and what it can secure.

In Chapter IV, I have already had a good deal to say about the manner in which law, in all of the dimensions of order (Many, One, Process, and Pattern), seeks at once to preserve the beneficial features of the regimes of Necessity and Possibility, to avert the dangers inherent in them, and to achieve, insofar as it can, a synthesis of these regimes that will yield the ideal conditions of Purposiveness. And in Chapter XI, I examined this problem in detail with regard to the effort to secure by legal means a sound and effective authority. There is no need to repeat those discussions, so I will here confine my attention to the manner in which legal action necessarily transforms the goals of cultivation, authority, responsibility, and continuity in transposing them into the terms of its conceptual and procedural apparatus.

The idea of cultivation—more concretely, of a cultivated person—is made up of both social and individual elements. This twofoldness springs from a duality that is deeply rooted in the human situation, for every human being is at once a unique individual and a social member. The process that we call cultivation—or socialization—is necessarily directed toward both of these dimensions of the person: it must form the character and conduct of people in such a way that they will conform to the mores of the group and fit into the social order, and it must respect and foster the particular potentialities—the traits and talents—of each individual.[7]

A society can remain sound and stable only by maintaining certain basic similarities among its members. Among the more important of these are a common language, tradition, and culture, generally acknowledged moral standards and practices, well-established customs and habits, a general belief in the fairness of the social system, a recognition that different social positions require different skills, impose different responsibilities, and offer different rewards. If a society is to be healthy, it must take care to instill in its new members—its youth—an acceptance of its beliefs, values, and practices, and to prepare them to serve in some useful role. In other words, the members of each new generation must be initiated into the society's way of life and integrated into its functional systems.

But society must be equally solicitous of the differentiations that are so characteristic of human nature. People feel their individuality very strongly: they value their own particular tastes and talents, they seek to develop these, they insist on the opportunity to express and assert themselves. Furthermore, society is dependent upon these individual skills and energies for its own well-being: it must seek out and train human capabilities for the more and more varied and specialized tasks that are essential to its smooth functioning.

Cultivation thus has a double purpose: it seeks to make the human person at once an acceptable social member and a fully developed individual. As we have seen, the work of cultivation is very largely carried

[7] The tension between these two aspects of human nature and the human situation is one of the central themes in the work of Roberto Unger. He regards this tension and the efforts to resolve it as posing one of the basic problems for social theory and for legal and political doctrines. In *Law in Modern Society* (New York: Free Press, 1976), he summarizes his views in these terms:

Each of the two main variants of social life, together with the doctrine or order that describes it, draws its vitality from a basic aspect of human nature: in one case the individuality, in the other the sociability, of persons. The ultimate reason why no society can resolve its problem of order by leaning exclusively on one of these two features of personality is that neither of these two attributes of humanity allows itself to be completely supressed. A society resolves the crisis of order insofar as it manages to reconcile individual freedom with community cohesion. (P. 264)

I would suggest (although this is not the place to pursue the matter) that this problem is becoming steadily more acute and more difficult to resolve because, under the conditions of contemporary life, the human person is becoming at once more and more highly individuated and more and more intricately socialized.

on by other institutions than positive law. I now want to consider more carefully how law fits into the picture. I will be concerned with such questions as these: What is the proper role of law in this enterprise? Through what concepts and procedures does law operate in this context? In what way, into what other terms, does law transform the twin goals of cultivation—similarity and differentiation—in seeking to promote them? What is the proper relationship of law to the other institutions engaged in the same effort? What changes ensue if law, purposely or inadvertently, assumes too commanding a role in this enterprise, substituting its limited purposes and special procedures for the larger goals and more varied processes of the social whole? We shall then need to ask these same questions with regard to each of the other goals of justice.

There is not a great deal that law can do directly to assure the similarities or promote the differentiations that cultivation envisages. The legal apparatus is poorly adapted to the tasks of raising and nurturing children, inculcating morality, instilling habits of conformity and obedience, or fashioning the attitudes, expectations, and ideals that do so much to bind a people together. This apparatus is at least as ill equipped to educate people, to foster their talents and refine their taste, to give them the training and discipline they need if they are to fulfill themselves and realize their hopes. In short, law is not an effective instrument for the formation of human character or the development of human potentialities. It has a very limited power to make men into acceptable social members or to help them become accomplished individuals.

There is, however, a great deal that law can do indirectly to promote these goals. Stated generally, it can keep a watchful eye on the entire institutional structure of society to see that its several elements properly discharge their various responsibilities, performing equitably and conscientiously the tasks they have assumed. The legal apparatus can be particularly effective in assuring that the essential services and benefits of society are made available to all people on a fair and reasonable basis. Law intervenes to correct any form of exclusion, discrimination, and exploitation whenever it suspects that they are being practiced. There are supports that people must have, needs that must be satisfied, if their lives are to be even minimally rewarding and if the public order and the general welfare are to be secured: adequate diet, housing, and health care; a general education and some form of special training; employment under decent conditions; access to the political process; leisure and the means to put it to use. And although the legal apparatus is ill equipped to supply these services and make good these wants, or even to determine in any detail by what means and in what measure they are to be furnished to people, it is quite well equipped to guarantee that whatever is done and offered in these respects is made available to all alike in an equitable manner: none are to be arbitrarily deprived and none are to receive special favors. Furthermore, law can set minimum standards and define broad guidelines to assure that institutions do in fact provide the services and promote the purposes for which they acknowledge obligation and claim credit. Though law cannot secure the essential similarities that are necessary to a sound society, it can eliminate gross dissimilarities among individuals and groups, and it can prevent serious nonfeasance or misfeasance on the part of other institutions.

Law is in a similar situation with respect to the human differentiations that seek expression in such diverse ways. Here again its function is essentially protective rather than constructive. The legal apparatus is employed to secure the lives and affairs of men against undue harassment or intrusion by other institutions, and even by the law itself. Steps are taken to guarantee such basic freedoms as those of speech, assembly, movement, choice of career, and the use one is to make of his resources, thus providing for the integrity and privacy of the individual. Law can do very little to assure men of success in their undertakings or satisfaction in their lives, but it can do a good deal to guarantee them the opportunity, within broad limits, to pursue these as they see fit. Law makes men free to order their lives as they choose, so long as their choices do not obviously disrupt the social order itself.

We can now epitomize the changes that law effects when it translates the goals of cultivation into its own lexicon. Cultivation envisages an outcome in which essential human similarities are preserved and individual differentiations are shaped in accord with established norms and models. The machinery that law commands cannot directly further such an outcome. Instead, the legal apparatus transforms these goals into conditions that it can effectively promote. It does this by translating "similarities" as *equality* and "differentiations" as *freedom*. The shift that this brings about in interpretation and intention is quite radical and can be quickly summarized: the similarities and differentiations that cultivation aims at are conceived in terms of human character and conduct; the equalities and freedoms that law aims at are couched in terms of social conditions and treatment. Law envisages an outcome in which equals will be treated equally and personal freedom will be protected.

The goals of equality and freedom find legal expression in the constitutional concepts of equal protection and personal rights, with both of these being implemented by the requirements of due process. These doctrines are at first construed in quite narrow terms: equal protection applies only to the formal standing of the parties, with no pretense of putting them on the same material footing; legally recognized rights are few in number and protective, or prohibitive, in character; and the standards of due process are limited to strictly procedural matters, with no reference to substantive issues. In the course of time, this picture changes radically. The original legal meaning of equal protection acquires a wide spectrum of social, political, and economic overtones; law becomes more and more receptive in its acknowledgment of claims of right; and due process comes to require not merely that formal justice be done but also that the outcomes satisfy the court's sense of material or social justice.

As we would expect, the original role of law in the task of cultivation (its relationship to other social institutions) is that of a supplemental principle of order. Law supervenes upon a social order in which similarities are being preserved and differentiations are being fostered by an array of established institutions. But this order exhibits inequities of two sorts: the services and benefits of society are being distributed unequally, with a good deal of discrimination and exploitation; and only certain approved differentiations are permitted, with many forms of individual expression being suppressed. Equipped with its constitutional doctrines of equal protection, personal rights, and due process, the legal apparatus takes steps to remove these inequities and restrictions. Law requires that all persons be treated in the same manner and have the same access to the services and benefits of society unless good reasons can be advanced to justify differential treatment. And it requires that people be allowed to speak, act, and live as they choose, except when there is persuasive evidence that certain forms of expression and behavior are opposed to the public interest. The achievements of law in both of these respects have been very great.

There remains a final question. What is apt to be the outcome if, for any reason, the legal concepts of equality and freedom come to supplant rather than supplement the social goals of similarity and differentiation? What can we logically anticipate in this context, if law asserts its omnicompetence as well as its sovereignty?

Where class discrimination and individual repression are prominent features of a society, the legal doctrines of equal protection and personal rights work very effectively as correctives. Further, these doctrines then work hand in glove, mutually implementing one another: arbitrary inequities are removed, throwing open the doors of opportunity to all alike, and the pressure to conform is relaxed, leaving more options to exploit. But as the concepts of equality and freedom cease to be weapons directed against an established order and come themselves to define the goals of a new order, the outcome is very different. Equality comes to mean that all be put on the same footing, and freedom comes to mean that each be allowed to express himself and order his life as he chooses; equality becomes a duty imposed on society—the state—to supply to all alike the services and benefits that they need, while freedom becomes a right inherent in individuals to make what use they will of these. The logical outcome of this is that society becomes solely the bearer of duties, with no right to impose conditions on or to make demands of its members, and individuals become solely the holders of rights, with no duty to conform or contribute. Under such a dispensation, society would no longer be able to secure essential similarities or to discriminate among differentiations, since everyone could equally claim the support of society in his freely chosen courses. The result to which this tends is chaos, not order. But this is only logic, and there is no necessity—only the possibility and the danger—that fact will follow in its footsteps.[8]

[8] This has been presented as a merely hypothetical account of what *might* happen *if* the legal concepts of equality and freedom were to gain too great an ascendancy over the social and moral concepts of similarity and differentiation. But the writings of two outstanding contemporary constitutional scholars, Archibald Cox and the late Alexander Bickel, bear witness that the law has in fact been following this course and leading toward this outcome. It is worthy of note that these men agree entirely in their interpretation of the direction that events have been taking and of the importance of this movement, although they disagree sharply in their attitudes toward this, with Bickel deploring and Cox approving. Both ascribe primary responsibility—blame or praise—for this movement to the Supreme Court under Chief Justice Warren; and their analyses of the intentions and consequences of the "Warren Court" correspond virtually point by point. Thus, Bickel identifies three principal goals and themes of the Warren period: 1) progress toward an egalitarian society, 2) enlargement of the dominion of law, and 3) centralization in national institutions of the law-giving function (see *The Supreme Court and the Idea of Progress* [New Haven: Yale University Press, 1978], passim and especially pp. 13, 103). Cox in turn cites these "forces" and "factors" that have been most influential in "shaping current constitutional decisions": 1) egalitarianism, 2) emphasis on the affirmative duty of government to secure racial justice, human rights, and personal liberty and privacy, 3) "expansion of federal judicial power at the expense of the States" (see *The Warren Court* [Cambridge, Mass.: Harvard University Press, 1968], passim but specifically pp. 5-8, 13). I have merged three of Cox's points in the second category.

Bickel is unequivocal in his denunciation of these developments as a constitutionally unwarranted usurpation of power by the Supreme Court and the federal judiciary in general and in his view that they are having disastrous effects on social order and justice. Cox is somewhat more restrained in his approval: he praises the steps so far taken under the leadership of the Warren Court, he warns of the extreme results to which this movement could lead, and he expresses confidence that the courts and Congress will show a proper restraint and deference for traditional values and canons of interpretation (see *The Warren*

With this general pattern in mind, the role of law in securing the other goals of justice can be discussed more briefly. The matter of authority and the law was examined in depth in Chapter XI, so here a summary will suffice. I there argued that in any real and effective sense, authority is a relationship, not a property. Further, this relationship is triadic: authority is vested in some men, it is acknowledged by other men, and it is directed to definite purposes. If authority is to be established and maintained, all of these elements must be present and they must be in tune with one another: there must be officials who can exercise it competently and responsibly, subjects who will accept its decisions, and common purposes that direct and delimit its uses. The relationship is weakened to the extent that any of these elements is absent or discordant.

The authority relationship is essentially a bond. It may be explicit or implicit in varying degrees, but if it is to be vital, it must be a real bond: governors must have the qualities of leadership and a concern for the welfare of the people; subjects must have faith in the integrity and ability of those who govern; and there must be a shared, even if unexpressed, commitment to certain values and purposes, a conviction of the high importance of these, and a confidence of success in achieving them. It is impossible to say with any precision, or in a manner that is true of all cases, just how this bond is established. Certain significant factors can be identified: the character and mood of the people, the personal characteristics of those who emerge as leaders, circumstances of the moment, the pressure of a harsh environment or a hostile country, the pursuit of a great adventure, the belief in a common destiny—various of these factors contribute in different proportions on different occasions. This bond expresses itself through such sentiments as loyalty, patriotism, mutual trust among men, and each man's sense of derived benefit. The bond is inculcated by family, church, and schools, and it is made vivid by appeal to national heroes and holidays. Generalities cannot explain much here, and even explanations of particular cases are uncertain, but one thing is clear: law does not create this bond, nor can it by itself maintain it. Rather, it is concern, confidence, and mutuality that cement the authority relationship and make of it a bond.[9]

Court, pp. 7-8, 59-60, 67-68, 90-91). In the ten years since Cox's book was published, many of the developments that he suggested as possible, but hoped and thought would not become actual, are now parts of history. Cox's warnings were sound but his optimism was misplaced. As I argued in Chapter XIV, human rights easily acquire a momentum that virtually defies all control.

[9] I have discussed this issue at length in the analysis of obligation in Chapter XII.

As we saw in Chapter XI, the role of law is to formalize this relationship: to define its terms more precisely, to make its arrangements explicit, and thus to render it both stable and elastic, capable of change but only in settled ways. The elements in the relationship and the footing on which they stand are now expressed by constitutional principles, legal procedures, powers and limitations, rights and duties. The outcome of this is that rulers are transformed into governors and subjects into citizens, leaders turn into officials, and shared purposes become the general welfare. Something of the spontaneity and vividness of the bond is undoubtedly lost in this process of legal formalization, but a great deal is also gained: the terms of the authority relationship are spelled out, mechanisms for its administration are established, the positions of the parties are made clear, and guarantees against abuse are provided. In all of these respects, the law of the constitution is similar to the law of marriage, and what legal formalization does for society is exactly analogous to what it does for the family. Law serves the same purposes and makes the same important contribution in both cases, but in neither case can law by itself sustain the relationship.

It remains to ask what outcome could logically be expected if the factors that created and sustained the original bond were somehow seriously weakened, so that the authority relationship became largely formal, dependent on its legal framework and apparatus for its maintenance. It is of the essence of a vital authority relationship that it transforms a multiplicity of individuals, each with his own concerns and goals, into a real unity, able to count on the cooperation of its members and to act in their name. If the spirit that cements this relationship is poisoned or diluted, its elements segregate and revert toward their purely private status. Governors become that anonymous entity, ''the government,'' which then appears to be an independent and nonhuman fact that stands apart from the people and is all but unapproachable. Officials become bureaucrats, remote from their constituents and more interested in strengthening their positions than in performing any services: the bureaucracy becomes an end in itself, occupied chiefly with its own internal affairs. Concurrently, and inevitably, an estranged people turn in upon themselves, think only of protecting and furthering their private interests, constitute factions, and regard an alien government solely as something to be propitiated or exploited: that is, citizens become suppliants and scavengers. Under the pressure of such factionalism, the concept of the general welfare becomes merely a cover for the struggle of class against class, region against region, and interest against interest. In sum, the bond is degraded into a bargain that each party seeks to interpret in its favor and to use to its advantage. Again, this is but logic, and the facts will fit it only if we let them.

An analogous outcome threatens in the dimension of Process. A sense of responsibility is indispensable if men are to live and work together. As human behavior escapes the grip of Necessity (of action-reaction), human nature becomes more plastic and man exercises a greater degree of self-determination. Individuals now have a larger voice in deciding what their actions are to be: they directly influence the course of events, and what they decide has repercussions for others as well as for themselves. Men mutually rely upon one another's commitments in making their plans, and each counts upon the others not to harm or interfere with him. This being the case, men must adhere to their declared intentions, show respect for their fellows, and be concerned about the difference they make. Man becomes a responsible agent to the degree that he takes pains that his actions should issue in good, not evil. In short, to be responsible is to care and to take care.

Responsibility is a moral virtue, a trait of character, a habit of attitude and action. As such, there is very little that law can do directly to inculcate it. This is primarily the task of other forces and institutions, notably the family, the church, the schools, the neighborhood, and morality. But although law cannot do much to lead men to care about the differences they make, it can very effectively hold them accountable for these differences: that is, it can bring them to task for the consequences of their actions. Law does this through the law of torts and the criminal law, which create duties, proscribe certain forms of conduct, and establish penalties for any breach of these. Law enforces its edicts with fines, imprisonment, damages, reparation, and other forms of punishment. While the legal apparatus cannot instill in men a spirit of benevolence and concern, it can induce them to act with forethought and caution.

Law thus transforms responsibility into liability. It decrees an artificial order of antecedents and consequents with which to minimize and repair the harm men do when they violate the natural order of mutual respect and care. This is a necessary but second-best solution to the problem: it does not make men good but can only inhibit them from being bad. If it is to achieve even this much, other social institutions must be working effectively to inculcate a sense of responsibility, so that the majority of men will abide by and support the social order and only the few delinquent or vicious will need to be brought to book for civil or criminal liability. Here as elsewhere law is only a supplemental principle of order.

Suppose now that two things happen. First, those institutions that

have hitherto done the most to inculcate a sense of responsibility—
especially the family, the school, and the church—begin to lose their effectiveness. Their hold on the minds and hearts of men and their own
sense of mission are greatly weakened. They find it difficult to adapt to
changed social conditions and human attitudes. As the current phrase
puts it, they cease to be relevant. In its commitment to individual freedom, the law itself restricts the field of action of these institutions and
frustrates their efforts to shape men's characters. As a result, people no
longer grow up in an environment that instills responsibility as a moral
virtue and demands responsible behavior. So the sense of concern and
the habit of care are seriously eroded, with a consequent increase in actions that fall under *dolus* and *culpa*.

Secondly, and at the same time, law creates such mechanisms of protection against civil liability that there is no reason for men to exercise
responsibility, or even forethought and caution. Insurance, the doctrine
of society as the ultimate bearer of risks, the concept of the welfare state,
and other developments all combine to insulate men against the consequences of mistake and failure, whether these result from misfortune or
their own fault. The same devices spare men from having to make rec-
ompense for the harm they do to others. Then, since one will not himself be made to suffer for his carelessness, negligence, incompetence, and
wastefulness, there is no need for him to care or take care for the difference he makes and the future he prepares. In short, the sense of responsibility becomes redundant. Again, this is mere hypothesis. But if the
antecedent should become real, the consequent will surely follow.

If the work of society is to be done, individual effort and group cooperation are necessary. There are various ways in which the conjunction
of these two can be procured. Where societies are small, simple, and
underdeveloped—primitive, as we call them—performance and coordination are more or less spontaneous: tasks are dictated by the environment, and roles are determined by such basic human factors as age and
sex. What people are and do (their status and function) appear as natural, necessary, and proper, and conditions making for discontent and
conflict are at a minimum.

As societies grow larger and more complex, the variety of tasks and
hence the differentiations of role and status multiply, individual self-
consciousness intensifies, and distinct classes or ranks emerge within the
hitherto unified group. Artificial measures to ensure social cohesion and
continuity must now be introduced to supplement the natural forces that
are no longer adequate. Among the earliest of these are such indigenous
and uncontrived developments as custom, heritage, and tradition. These

work effectively to ensure that there will be a constant supply of people to step unasked into various roles and perform the tasks assigned them, and they have played a major, if not dominant, part right up to the immediate past. Even now it is easy for us to overlook the influence that they exert: since they have no explicit organization and staff—no visible body, so to speak—we are not conscious of them.

When these measures prove inadequate to the increasingly complex task of organizing the work of the society, more explicit institutions arise: a caste system, often in conjunction with slavery; feudal arrangements; paternalism, whether of a landed aristocracy or an industrial oligarchy. Along with these there appear guilds of artisans, professional associations, trade unions, commercial, financial, and industrial combines, and schools of various sorts to provide trained personnel. These levels of institutional development cannot be clearly distinguished, nor can their chronology be traced with any exactitude: the earlier generate (or partially transform themselves into) the later, and they do not altogether disappear in the process. At least traces of all of them persist, and most of them still exert an appreciable influence on the life of even the most advanced societies, although this will be disguised and unacknowledged. Children still tend to follow in their parents' footsteps; the rich and the dispossessed form virtually self-perpetuating castes; and there are many social contexts in which the relation of superior to subordinates—employer to employee, patron to clients, leaders to their retinues—has something distinctly feudal about it.

Law has of course been on the scene from the early stages of this process. But for the greater part of the time it has remained in the background, with the task of organizing the social effort left largely to these other forces and institutions. Throughout, legal action has exhibited an ambivalence that reflects the tension between the social whole and its parts—between centripetal and centrifugal forces. As an instrument of the state, law seeks to maintain the integrity of the social order and to prevent the pursuit of private interests from becoming disruptive. But as a distinct and autonomous entity, the state is a fiction: in fact, every special group is continually trying to influence the state organization and personnel and to bend them to its particular uses. As a major implement of state policy, the legal apparatus stands at the center of these conflicting pressures. Finally, as the legal system gains in strength and prestige, those who serve it become more and more independent, dedicated to those principles and values that have come to constitute the idea of law itself. Now the legal apparatus tries to stand above a struggle in which it is inevitably deeply involved and to serve both the general welfare and the array of competing private interests. That is, it seeks to assure a social order that will be both stable and flexible, both organized and open.

For a long while the conflicts that this duality threatens are cushioned by the social forces and institutions just mentioned. These exercise restraint in two ways. In the first place, one class, or a close alliance of classes, is able to establish its dominance, control the political and legal machinery of the state, and keep other classes in a subservient position. At the same time, these forces and institutions serve to moderate the self-seeking tendencies of individuals and classes. Custom, tradition, and the schools instill in all people a sense of belonging and obligation, and the associations through which groups and special interests organize themselves have a genuine concern for their public functions as well as for the private interests of their members: they preach the ideal of service with the same sincerity that they promise benefits. Under these conditions, the struggles that are incipient in this situation are at once smothered and mitigated.

But as differentiations of role and status proceed apace and competition becomes more intense and more balanced, all aspects of this situation change. The conservative and unifying forces of custom and tradition are diluted by the size and heterogeneity, the mobility and anonymity, of the population. People become increasingly absorbed in their special functions and relative standings in the social order. The social whole grows remote, so that the individuals' sense of belonging to it and his feeling of allegiance with other groups than his own are countered by class consciousness. Reflecting these changes, associations become primarily pressure groups, intent on strengthening their positions and procuring better conditions for their members. Within each individual and each group, the conflicts between egoism and altruism, self-interest and the sense of service, the profit motive and professional pride become steadily sharper, with the former sentiments more and more submerging the latter.

The projected outcome of this movement follows the path we have already traced in considering the role of law in the other tasks of social justice. As other institutions and associations cease to function as unifying agents, two things happen. First, the tension between centrifugal and centripetal forces increases enormously: different classes, regions, and interests become more strongly entrenched and assert their demands more vociferously, and this requires an intensified effort on the part of the state to control their activities and prevent the social whole from falling apart. At the same time, law loses its status as merely a supplemental principle of order and becomes the dominant, if not the only effective, instrument of social cohesion and continuity. Left in this isolated position and pulled violently in two contradictory directions, law can hope to achieve at best only a series of increasingly strained compromises. Organized private interests have more and more of their claims recognized as rights, and they are given a continually freer hand in pushing their demands and bargaining for position. But at the same time there is a corresponding increase in both the power of the state and the machinery available to it to intervene in their affairs and regulate their activities. Both parties thus become theoretically stronger because backed by law, but practically weaker because so much of their effort is wasted as friction.

Law cannot create the spirit of cooperation and the sense of community that are envisaged by social justice. What law can do is establish and enforce a body of rules that will serve the dual purpose of regularizing the competition among private interests and enabling the government to assert itself on behalf of the public interest. Here as elsewhere the legal apparatus transforms the goals of justice: the spirit of cooperation is replaced by the law of contract, and the sense of community is vested in a multitude of regulatory agencies. What should ideally be a cooperative enterprise, with all working for the same end, becomes a welter of contractual arrangements in which each party is primarily concerned to improve its own position; and what should be a community of feeling and purpose becomes a struggle in which private groups try desperately to evade regulations that innumerable government agencies are trying equally hard to enforce. This conclusion follows logically, but it is within our power to falsify the premises.

This discussion of the difference between and the relationship of social justice and legal justice, as well as the earlier analyses of validity, obligation, and authority (Chapter XI), can be illustrated by a brief examination of an issue that is frequently raised in legal arguments. This concerns the status of a legal system that not merely contains certain "iniquitous" laws but that is based in its entirety on general policies that are discriminatory and oppressive. For a long time the familiar example has been Nazi Germany, but the case that is now usually cited is South Africa, with its explicit policy of racial apartheid. With respect to such cases, it is asked if these seeming "legal" systems do in fact qualify for this status: Do they satisfy the criteria for admission to this class? Are they really legal systems?

To understand and deal satisfactorily with this issue requires that we make a triple distinction between the legal, moral, and practical aspects of the problem. The legal and the moral aspects pose no difficulties of principle: the first is settled simply by definition, and the second is resolved by appeal to standards that are taken for granted in contemporary Western societies. The practical problem is another matter, and it is to an analysis of this that I shall devote my major attention.

As I have suggested, the legal aspect of this issue is largely a question of semantics: How are we to define the term "legal system"? If we accept the teachings of Hart, Kelsen, and others, the South African body of law clearly is a proper legal system. It has its explicit "basic norm" or set of "secondary rules" in the form of the Republican Constitution of 1961. Through this constitution, the legal system administers and supports an established social order: it has comprehensive bodies of substantive and procedural rules and a fully developed legislative, executive, and judicial apparatus. It is efficacious, receiving official adherence and habitual obedience—however forced and unwilling this latter may be on the part of a large majority of the population. Furthermore, large sections of this legal system (such as the law of torts, contracts, property, future interests, corporations, commercial transactions) are similar to those of any other advanced industrial society. Finally, a most interesting book by a South African law professor and advocate, John Dugard, bears out this point.[10] Dugard is an avowed critic and opponent of the policy of apartheid, but he never questions the fact that the law of South Africa constitutes a proper legal system: he refers to it frequently and casually in these terms, and at one point he explicitly states that "the apartheid order is a legal order."[11] Thus, his work is not devoted to disproving the preceding statement but rather to a detailed exposure of those substantive and procedural features of this legal system that flesh out the policy of apartheid and to an explanation of the constitutional provisions that make the application of this policy possible: with regard to this latter point, he mentions especially the central role of the doctrine of absolute parliamentary supremacy and the consequent absence of anything equivalent to a bill of rights and a policy of judicial review.[12] It would therefore appear that even those who abhor the policy of apartheid acknowledge that it *is* a legal system (in the full sense of the term) that serves as the basis and framework of this policy.

As regards the moral aspects of the issue, it is equally obvious that this legal system contains important elements and supports basic policies

[10] See John Dugard, *Human Rights and the South African Legal Order* (Princeton: Princeton University Press, 1978).

[11] Ibid., p. 391. Cf. also pp. 36, 49, 53.

[12] On this latter point of great significance, cf. esp. pp. 3-53.

that are unjust and immoral. A large proportion of the population of the country (some four-fifths) is oppressed, exploited, disenfranchised, segregated, and excluded from most of the amenities and even necessities of civilized life. In sum, the legal system is stigmatized as sanctioning racism and discrimination in their most blatant forms, thus trampling on the most elemental rights of most of its subjects.[13] Seen in the light of the situation in the typical Western society and judged by Western standards, such a legal system is to be morally condemned; and this tempts its critics to suggest that it is not a legal system at all but rather an organized reign of terror.[14]

Up to this point, everything would appear to be clear-cut: the law of South Africa is a formally sound and actually efficacious legal system, but it is grossly inequitable and it supports a repressive social order. This conflict of the legal and moral aspects forces the practical issue: What should and can be done to correct the situation? And now the problem becomes acute and difficult.

Perhaps the most obvious—and appealing—way to deal with the mat-

[13] It is only proper to note that the South African regime vigorously denies the correctness of this characterization. The government describes its policy as one of "differentiation without inferiority" and "separate development." And it has announced and partly implemented a plan to create separate independent states for its various ethnic groups, allowing each group self-determination in its own territory (see ibid., pp. 53-55). Thus it is South Africa's announced intention to do away with the policy of apartheid and to solve its racial problem by excising from its body politic the elements that have made that policy necessary and have created the problem: it will cede territory to each ethnic group, and these can then constitute their own governments and cultures. In theory, this is a reasonable solution. Regarding its outcome in practice, one can only wait and see. Professor Dugard is openly skeptical of both the sincerity and the practicality of the policy. The plan is in some ways similar to, though in others quite different from, that followed by the United States in its treatment of the American Indians: if that analogy holds, the outlook for the African blacks is not promising. In the discussion that follows, I assume (what seems to be certain) that large numbers of blacks will continue to live and work in South Africa proper: therefore the problem will remain, even if reduced in scope.

[14] With regard to this point, it is worthy of remark that doubts never seem to be cast on the standing of the "legal" system of the United States during the almost one hundred years between the adoption of the Constitution and the ratification of the thirteenth, fourteenth, and fifteenth Amendments. Yet this Constitution—and hence the "legal" system based on it—explicitly sanctioned slavery, allowed for the unlimited importation of more slaves for some twenty years, and provided that slaves who escaped to a free state and were there captured must be returned to their owners (Article I, section 9, paragraph 1; Article IV, section 2). In short, slaves were chattel, on the same footing as cows and horses—although perhaps somewhat more valuable. But I have never heard anyone ask if this "legal" system really was a legal system. And it is worth remembering that the way in which we of the United States have treated our own native population, the American Indians, is hardly a model of morality and benevolence—or even, it now appears, of legality.

ter is simply to extend by analogy Hart's dictum regarding particular laws that are legally valid but morally reprehensible. We could then say of the South African legal system that it is both efficacious and legitimate (it exists and functions both de facto and de jure) but that regarding its policy of apartheid, it is "too iniquitous to be applied or obeyed." But this is to counsel revolution and a radical transfer of power; and it is doubtful that even if this could be effected, it would produce a balance of benefit over harm. When we espouse this course we commit three serious mistakes: we allow our pursuit of our ideals to blind us to the realities of the situation we seek to mend, we adopt a dangerously simplistic view of the problem posed by this situation, and we do this because we equate the South African situation and problem with those we are familiar with in this country. But the circumstances that hold in South Africa (as in Rhodesia) are vastly different from and more difficult than those that have finally been faced (but still only partly corrected) by the United States in the last few decades. There is little similarity between the two cases, save for the gross fact of racial discrimination; and even taking this factor into consideration, it will be seen that the proportions of the races concerned, as well as their past and present circumstances, are utterly incommensurable. In addition, there is the important fact that the legal doctrines and techniques that were available to deal with the problem in this country are largely lacking in South Africa.[15]

Furthermore, it is interesting to note that even Professor Dugard, who is himself a dedicated apostle of change, rejects this solution by revolution. In a significant passage, he has this to say on the issue:

> There are critics of the apartheid order who choose to see it through the eyes of Radbruch, who would wander through the South African statutes identifying those which qualify for the pejorative term

[15] I was made acutely aware of these differences some years ago when Professor Pierre J. Hugo of the University of South Africa in Pretoria, who was an outspoken critic of apartheid, came to the United States (and especially to the South) to study the procedures and precautions that had here been employed in the process of integration. Since the University of Alabama had recently integrated its student body quietly and successfully and since I had published an article on the question ("Segregation and the Professor," *Yale Review* 45, no. 2 [1956]: 311), Professor Hugo spent several weeks at the university discussing the problem with myself and others. This was an extremely interesting experience for me (and I believe for Professor Hugo also), but I had talked with him for only a few hours when I told him that I was afraid that there was very little that he could learn from me, or from the experience at the University of Alabama, or indeed from any other persons or experiences in the United States that would offer any light and guidance in dealing with the South African problem, for it took only a short while for both of us to realize that the situations in the two countries have only the most superficial resemblance to one another.

"statutory injustice" for use at the day of reckoning before South Africa's Nuremberg trials. This is not a helpful exercise, at least in the author's opinion, as it presupposes a violent revolution, an Armageddon, after which old scores will be reckoned with the full majesty of law and might in the hands of the other side. For anyone who believes that a peaceful resolution of the South African racial issue is still possible, this is a singularly unconstructive approach as it fails to recognize that a new approach to the legal process may yet forestall the grim prospect of such proceedings.[16]

In short, Dugard feels that such a course would merely reverse the roles of oppressed and oppressors, leading to at best a witch hunt and more probably to a holocaust.

If violent revolution with its total and immediate transfer of power is renounced, what is to be done to bring a hitherto repressive legal system and social order into line with Western moral and legal values? In order to answer this question and thus to ensure the adoption of a practical and reasonable policy, it is essential first to obtain a full and balanced view of the actual situation. It will not do simply to stigmatize the present policy as "immoral" and to demand that it be abolished forthwith, since this is as grossly simplistic as declaring that a person is ill and ought to get well. Instead, we need to specify more closely just what constitutes and follows from this "immorality." What iniquities—what deprivations and abuses—does apartheid impose on those who are made subject to it? And what are the consequences of such treatment and its effect upon those who suffer it? Only when we have adequate answers to these questions can we spell out in some detail the goals that must be sought and the steps that must be taken in order to cure the ravages of apartheid.

One way (there are undoubtedly others) to achieve such a comprehensive grasp of this problem is to examine it in the light of the matrix of positive law that was developed in the early chapters of this book. That is what I shall now do. And I would emphasize that I seek only to expose the full dimensions of the problem posed by the present evil of apartheid and to indicate in what the correction would consist. I do not pretend to

[16] Dugard, *Human Rights*, pp. 399-400 (fn. omitted). Dugard pins his hopes on reforms at two levels: the mode of legal thinking and the constitutional basis of the legal system. As regards the first, he urges the rejection of the rigid positivism that has been dominant and the adoption of a "realist-cum-value-oriented" philosophy—a modernized and moderate natural law position. As regards the second point, he argues for a new constitution with an explicit bill of rights, limitations on the power of parliament, and provision for judicial review. These legal reforms are undoubtedly important and indispensable, but as the ensuing discussion will make clear, they are not nearly enough by themselves.

know through exactly what policies, procedures, and practices these goals could be attained.

Stated first in general terms, the effect of apartheid is to confine all black people[17] to the regime of Necessity, denying them any but the most limited access to the regimes of Possibility and Purposiveness. This effect can be spelled out by briefly tracing its course through the several dimensions of order.

In the dimension of the Many, blacks are denied any meaningful individuality and are treated as though they were all identical in background, ability, and training. As far as law and society are concerned, any black's character is determined by the simple fact of his class membership, with little regard for what any particular black may be as a unique person. In the dimension of the One, blacks are completely dominated by the political and legal order and are placed in a subordinate social position. They have no effective representation in parliament and so no influence on government policies and decisions. They do not enjoy either equal protection of the laws or due process of law, but are subject to special and pejorative legislative enactments and judicial procedures. In the dimension of Process, the lives of blacks are very largely subject to the operation of action and reaction. They are acted upon and repressed by political power, police force, and economic pressure; and they have little choice but to react with either compliance, however sullen, or violence, however futile. The field of action left open to them and the resources they can deploy to exploit this are so restricted that they have little chance to develop their potentials and determine the course of their lives. Finally, in the dimension of Pattern, blacks are held fast in a web of relationships that is closed, rigid, and minutely defined. Both the status that blacks occupy and the functions that they perform are determined by this antecedent framework, which sets strict terms for such basic conditions of human existence as marriage, family life, education, employment, wages, the acquisition and use of skills, and even physical movement.

To the extent that these four conditions of Necessity are forcefully and arbitrarily imposed upon any members of a society, that society is clearly unjust. This analysis spells out with some specificity and precision what is entailed when a legal system and social order are declared to be "immoral" and "iniquitous." When these conditions are imposed upon a very large majority by a correspondingly small minority, the

---

[17] Following Dugard and common South African usage, the term "black" includes all nonwhites: i.e., native African blacks, Asians, and those of mixed blood (the "colored").

human harm that is done is magnified. Unfortunately, the difficulty of rectifying the situation is similarly magnified. Suppose now that such a society is to mend its ways and create a social order dedicated to justice and equality among the races. How is it to proceed?

Stated first in general terms, the answer is obvious: those who have been confined to the regime of Necessity must be afforded effective access to the regimes of Possibility and Purposiveness. But even this general statement contains one essential proviso: *the passage toward these latter two regimes must be effected in such a way that they are achieved concurrently*. The fatal mistake that threatens this effort is to conclude that since the wrong has consisted in confining people to the conditions of Necessity, the way to right this wrong is simply to loose their bonds and open to them the conditions of Possibility. But as we saw earlier, the regime of Possibility is incomplete: it demands that a proper use be made of it. This use is defined by the conditions of Purposiveness. Blacks and whites—a majority and a minority, the oppressed and the oppressors—have lived for generations under one set of conditions. It is now proposed that these conditions shall be radically altered and the two groups live together on quite different terms. This cannot be done by proclamation and fiat. Rather, both groups must be carefully prepared for the new relationship and way of life that they are to share. The briefest examination of the consequences and demands of this transition is enough to make its scope and challenge apparent.

Access to the conditions of Possibility for those who have hitherto been excluded from them would have the following outcomes. Blacks would be treated as individual persons rather than class members, and their differences of ability and energy, taste and talent, would be allowed to manifest and express themselves. They would have standing as political and legal equals, with a voice in the determination of government policies and the full support of the legal apparatus. Concurrently, blacks would exercise the same measure of self-determination that pertains to other citizens, choosing their goals in life and the courses toward these. Finally, the social order as a whole would become open and flexible, allowing blacks to acquire the education and training, and to find occupations and positions, commensurate with their abilities. Finally, and to point the obvious, as blacks gain access to the regime of Possibility, the whites' control and exploitation of its conditions will be curtailed. This curtailment will be particularly significant in the dimensions of the One and Pattern, for whites must now share the political power and economic benefits that they have previously monopolized.

The achievement of these conditions would be quite simple in principle, imposing only two requirements: the political and legal barriers that have hitherto blocked the way must be removed; and whites must accept the new regime and cooperate at least minimally in furthering its conditions. Achieving this in practice is clearly another matter. But that point can be waived for the moment, for even in principle, this is the barest beginning of the passage toward freedom and equality for the blacks. Loosing the bonds of Necessity, but being by itself incomplete, Possibility opens the door to disorder, holding the promise of reconciliation and progress but also posing the threat of dissension and retrogression. If this advantage is to be seized and this danger avoided, the amorphous conditions of Possibility must be given a form and content. This is the challenge of Purposiveness. As we briefly rehearse its conditions, we can realize the complexities and difficulties that are hidden by the verbally simple demand to "end apartheid."

In the dimension of the Many, this will require an intensive effort of cultivation directed—though in very different ways—toward all segments of the society. The oppressed, who have been deprived of all opportunity to develop their potentialities, must be educated and trained. This process must render the blacks literate and articulate, discern and discipline their various talents, and prepare them for the whole gamut of social roles. As regards those who have been the oppressors, this effort must be directed chiefly toward their emotions and motives: their stereotypes must be eradicated, their prejudices overcome, and their self-interest tempered with sympathy and a dedication to new ideals.

In the dimension of the One, an altogether new authority relationship must be forged. As matters now stand, blacks have seen the legal system in the narrowest Austinian terms, simply as an instrument of coercion: they have submitted and obeyed because of the sanctions that were threatened. Conversely, whites have employed the law as a tool of domination and exploitation. To transform such a regime of oppression and submission into a viable authority relationship requires that three steps be taken concurrently: a common set of values and purposes must be projected; authority must be vested in leaders who have the ability and the will to exercise it impartially in the general interest; and all groups must have confidence in these leaders and the courses they set.

In the dimension of Process, both whites and blacks—both oppressors and oppressed—must be made to realize and acknowledge that responsibility for achieving the new state of affairs rests primarily upon them, not upon the legal system and its apparatus. The most that the law can do is to define the new order and to punish violations of it after their occurrence. The effective achievement of this order depends upon the voluntary, informed, and conscientious efforts of all concerned. Blacks must learn to use their new freedom with both initiative and patience, being always aware that success cannot be granted to them (as failure was imposed), but that it rests in their own hands. Whites must cooperate in an enterprise that will certainly entail sacrifices on their part, and they must educate and train people who will then compete with them instead of serving them.

In the dimension of Pattern, the social order must be prepared to accept an enormous influx of trained persons who are eager for the positions and rewards for which they are now qualified and which they have been led to expect. A vast new amount of social room must be provided, as well as paths of access to—and, alas, egress from—its favored positions. The new order will have to accommodate an unprecedented flow of social movement, with all of the potential for conflict and frustration that this entails.

This bare and pedestrian recital (which merely propounds the problems that are raised by a legal system that is formally valid but materially unjust and proposes no solutions to them) should still suffice to make two points clear beyond cavil. First, these problems are extremely complex and difficult, and they are greatly magnified when it is a large majority of a population that has been unjustly deprived and exploited. Second, the power of law by itself to correct this situation is severely limited. Such legal reforms as those endorsed by Professor Dugard can furnish the impetus and framework for realizing the conditions of Possibility, although these must be enacted and implemented by an entrenched minority that can hardly be expected to accept them willingly. And law can do even less than this to promote the conditions of Purposiveness. Indeed, as I have argued at length, if law seeks to take an active and guiding role in this effort rather than a merely supportive one, it threatens to do more harm than good.

In such a situation as that just considered, the legal system is undoubtedly valid: in its structure and functions, law is serving as a principle of order. To quote Professor Dugard once more: "The apartheid order is a legal order." But the order that law here supports is grossly unjust. To remake the legal system into an effective instrument of a just society is quite simple in principle and on paper. One need only adopt a new constitution containing especially the provisions noted earlier: a bill of rights, limitations on the powers of parliament, and judicial review.

But to remake the social order is a task of altogether different magnitude, for the problems that arise here have moral, social, economic, and political dimensions that law can barely reach and cannot at all grasp. In a perceptive passage in *The Concept of Law*,[18] Hart has argued persuasively that it is advantageous, for both theoretical and moral reasons, to recognize that laws can be iniquitous but still valid, instead of holding that iniquitous "laws" simply are not laws at all. To Hart's arguments, I would add one of a practical nature. If we think of iniquitous law as not really law—and even more, if we think of an unjust "legal" system as not actually a legal system—this has the effect of focusing our attention solely on the legal aspect of the matter. And this in turn leads us to treat the problem in strictly legal terms: since the supposed "law" is not such, there is no real law present, and all we need to do is to enact laws that will right the actual wrongs. And that is quite certainly a self-defeating policy.

In this chapter, it has been my purpose to explore the possibility that law necessarily transforms the goals of social justice in seeking to secure them. I would hope that the immediately preceding pages have established the fact and depicted the manner of these transformations. The particulars of the four episodes that I have traced in detail also point to certain general conclusions, which can be drawn in a few words.

Throughout its history, law has acted in a more or less balanced conjunction with various other institutions and organizations, each having a power and exerting an influence of its own. Sometimes law acts with these forces, as when it reinforces and organizes their efforts: cases in point are the law of tort and contract, criminal and administrative law, the concept of liability, and the legal formalization of authority; sometimes it acts against them, as when it restrains and corrects their abuse of power: this is exemplified in such legal doctrines as those of equality, freedom, individual rights, due process, and *ultra vires*. But always there has been the recalcitrance of other forces (in Aristotelian terms, the material substratum that both supports and resists) upon which law exerts itself to impress its form. If this resistance is negated or removed—if these forces are undermined externally or decay internally—law inevitably overshoots its mark, with the consequences we have already seen. The outcome is exactly analogous to what we familiarly experience when we step on a stair that is not there or push violently against a door that proves not to be stuck: we achieve a great deal more than we planned for, and wind up badly off balance if not flat on our faces. In similar circumstances, law encounters a similar fate. In sum, and to use a different figure of speech, what we meet with here is the legal equivalent of Gresham's principle, with bad law driving out good.

[18] Hart, *The Concept of Law*, pp. 203-207.

CHAPTER XIX

LAW AND
THE SOCIAL ORDER

I DEVOTED the first part of this book to developing a theory of positive law and its place in the natural order—in the single vast "realm and rule of law" that earlier writers took as their universe of discourse. For the past several chapters I have been examining the place of law in the social order and the role of legal action as one form of social control. Here I have been particularly concerned with three issues: the reach and the limits of legal effectiveness; the transformations that law effects in the goals of social justice as it seeks to promote these goals; and the undesirable outcomes that could be anticipated if the legal apparatus were to dominate other institutions and impose its views upon this common quest.

These latter discussions might invite the view that the legal apparatus is hopelessly crude and quite inadequate to the tasks it undertakes, spoiling whatever it touches. To draw that conclusion would be simplistic and a serious mistake, for what these discussions do in fact point to is the more complex conclusion that law is an indispensable but supplemental instrument of order and justice. I have tried to keep these aspects in balance, and to expose them in concrete terms, while following the law in its pursuit of the four conditions of social justice. It is the more important that this same measure be preserved in summarizing the lessons of these analyses and arriving at a general view of the place of law in the social order.

Law is indispensable because it supplies the compelling social need for a force that is at once *sovereign* and *principled*. Despite current usage, the term "anarchy" does not mean chaos or disorder: it connotes a state of affairs in which there is no single ruler or governor, no central source of direction and control. But the fact of anarchy, the existence of such a state of affairs, would very surely produce disorder verging on chaos. A complex society, composed of heterogeneous elements and competing interests, must have an instrument through which it can speak with a voice that will be heeded by all: it needs a locus of sovereignty that receives habitual obedience and that is able to support its decisions with force when need be. At the same time, this sovereign power, which by definition escapes external control, must be governed by its own internal principles—by self-imposed provisions and mechanisms that govern the use of this power and prevent it from becoming autocratic and arbitrary. Law is by far the best instrument yet devised to meet this need.

Because no institution can dominate circumstances or rise above its personnel, performance always falls short of promise. But the idea and the apparatus of law have been highly successful in winning the respect and allegiance—or at worst the submission and compliance—of the general populace and of other institutions. And the law has been even more successful in imbuing those who serve it with a dedication to its purposes and values, to the spirit of legality itself. Furthermore, the procedures that law requires are spelled out so carefully that they furnish their own protection against those who would abuse the power that their position in the legal apparatus puts into their hands. It is this exercise of sovereignty in accord with principles that constitutes the great and indispensable contribution of the institutions of law.

But although law is sovereign and indispensable, it is neither omnicompetent nor self-sufficient: rather, it is heavily dependent upon other institutions both to accomplish what it cannot do and to support it in its own work. As we have seen in detail, the legal apparatus has but a severely limited capability to promote in any positive way the substantive goals of justice. The conditions of cultivation, authority, responsibility, and continuity largely escape direct legal action. The realization of these goals requires that human character be firmly molded in definite ways and that human conduct be channeled along specific courses and governed by established standards. And these are undertakings that must be carried on by other social agencies: they lie within the province of morality rather than law, and the tasks they impose have traditionally fallen primarily upon the triad of family, church, and school, with secondary support from custom, tradition, the neighborhood, and professional and vocational associations.

But the conditions that are envisaged by the concept of justice are counsels of perfection. They presuppose that social institutions function in a completely effective and disinterested manner and that individuals conform and cooperate willingly and without fail. In fact, it is these assumptions that fail: institutions and individuals alike deviate from the courses, and fall short of the standards, that the ideal of justice prescribes. It is primarily to contain these shortcomings that law intervenes in a supplemental role.

Again speaking generally, this intervention takes two broad forms: the correction of institutional abuses and the restraint of individual defiance. The legal apparatus cannot duplicate the positive accomplishments—the formation of character and conduct—of more intimate social agencies, but it can supervise their work and keep them up to the mark they themselves proclaim. And by the threat of detection and punishment, it can deter men from antisocial behavior. The legal doctrines of equality and freedom cannot issue in cultivation, but they can minimize discrimination and repression. Legal formalization cannot create a vital authority relationship or assure effective leadership, but it can provide controls on the ways in which authority is acquired and exercised. The sanctions of civil and criminal liability cannot make men responsible agents, but they can induce men to employ forethought and caution. Contract and administrative law cannot generate a sense of community and cooperation, but they can regulate the pursuit of self-interest and protect the public interest.

Given the imperfection of men and institutions, the intervention of the legal apparatus is inevitable, and the transformations it works on the goals of justice are necessary adjuncts to progress toward these goals. But given the limitations of legal effectiveness, the continual presence of these other social institutions is equally indispensable: their prior accomplishments are the necessary support, and the outcomes they seek are the final ends, of law. The relationship between the legal apparatus on the one hand and other social institutions on the other is thus thoroughly symbiotic: they have complementary roles, and neither can survive without the other.

This fact places law under a double obligation. As sovereign instrument of order and justice, protector of the public interest and the general welfare, law must be zealous in maintaining its supremacy. It cannot afford to bow before the threats of other institutions and organized groups when these use whatever pressures are available to them to assert their claims and further their interests. With the exception of the appeal to force, the legal apparatus is the final arbiter, and it must have the last word. But it is equally incumbent upon law to protect and foster the other institutions upon whose contributions it so heavily depends. Stated positively, this has several meanings: law must acknowledge the limitations that its apparatus imposes upon it; it must respect the probity and integrity of other institutions and professions, assuming their sincerity and competence unless there is strong evidence to the contrary; it must accept these other forces as allies in a common undertaking and support them in their distinctive roles; and it must exercise restraint in its position of overlord. These same points can be made (perhaps even more emphatically) in negative terms: law should not usurp the functions of these other institutions; it should not intrude too much upon their operations nor assert too close a control of their decisions; it should not regard them with suspicion and call upon them to justify their every action; and finally, the legal apparatus must not impose upon other institutions and professions its own procedural methods and standards.

In summarizing a long discussion of the proper role of law, Roberto Unger puts the matter succinctly: "The laws should complement and police rather than smash the internal rules of private institutions."[1] Unfortunately, as Professor Unger himself emphasizes, it is impossible to draw a sharp line between these two operations of the law, which is simply to say that no theoretical formula can define with precision the proper relation of law to other social institutions. Nowhere does this difficulty present itself with greater urgency than when moral issues are at stake, for these touch the lives of people very intimately and directly and so arouse intense feelings. The problems that occur in such cases are pointedly exemplified in the dispute between Lord Devlin and his critics.

This is ostensibly a dispute about a matter of principle, focused on the question of whether or not law should engage in the "enforcement of morals," with Devlin upholding the affirmative and his critics the negative. But what appears verbally to be a clear-cut issue soon exposes itself as a series of arguments about subsidiary considerations, so that the issue is never really joined: indeed, it cannot be, for this is not a simple question of either/or. Rather, everyone is agreed that a large part of the body of the law consists in the recognition and enforcement of what were originally only moral duties and norms, and no one denies that it is both proper and necessary for law to continue to reflect morality.[2] The

[1] Roberto Unger, *Law in Modern Society* (New York: Free Press, 1976), p. 109.

[2] For instance, in *The Concept of Law* (Oxford: The Clarendon Press 1961), H.L.A. Hart puts the matter in this way:

The law of every modern state shows at a thousand points the influence of both the accepted social morality and wider moral ideals. These influences enter the law either abruptly and avowedly through legislation, or silently and piecemeal through the judicial process. . . . The further ways in which law mirrors morality are myriad, and still insufficiently studied: statutes may be a mere legal shell and demand by their express terms to be filled out with the aid of moral principles; the range of enforceable contracts may be limited by reference to conceptions of morality and fairness; liability for both civil and criminal wrongs may be adjusted to prevailing views of moral responsibility. No "positivist" could deny that these are facts, or that the stability of legal systems depends in part upon such types of correspondence with morals. If this is what is meant by the necessary connexion of law and morals, its existence should be conceded. (Pp. 199-200)

critical question is when and why, under what conditions and toward what ends, law should intervene in this field and whether it should support or challenge some current moral injunction. Even at the level of theory, it is extremely difficult to frame any general propositions that will identify the circumstances that justify legal enforcement of morals. When it comes to particular cases, agreement is yet more difficult to reach: for here unverifiable opinions and unconscious biases play a large part in determining one's position. And since theoretical arguments invariably appeal to concrete cases for illustrative purposes, these latter often have a strong, if hidden, influence on the attitudes of the disputants.[3]

However, it is at least possible to disentangle the principal issues that control decisions in these cases. There are, I believe, three such issues that are always involved—although it is very infrequently that they are clearly distinguished and explicitly dealt with. The first and most basic of these hangs on the distinction between the areas of *public* and *private* morality. This distinction and the doctrine based on it, made familiar by the writings of John Stuart Mill, hold that there are some patterns and standards of behavior, some duties and prohibitions, some obligations that all persons have toward others that are essential to the sound and peaceful life of society: these constitute the field of public morality. This field includes those bodies of rules and approved practices known as custom, convention, tradition, the proprieties, professional and commercial usages, marital and sexual arrangements, parental and filial duties, the rights and obligations of citizens. In this sense, the term "morality" carries very much of the meaning of its progenitor, "the mores." Legal enforcement of public morality is regarded as justified because this is felt to be necessary to assure social peace and order, to prevent corruption and abuse, and to protect all from behavior that is potentially injurious or offensive. Broadly speaking, this field covers those practices involving interpersonal relations that have a direct impact upon others beside the

---

Here, as always, Hart is insisting not upon the *separateness* but upon the *distinctness* of legal validity and moral rightness. As I have already argued at length, I believe that his position is unimpeachable.

[3] This factor would clearly seem to have played a decisive role in the dispute between Devlin and his critics. The example on which the argument centered (homosexuality between consenting adults) had two unfortunate effects on the course of the dispute: it served as a tempting red herring, and it put Devlin at a severe disadvantage. If the chosen example had been affirmative action, the right to treatment, truth in advertising, or abortion, the course and outcome of the argument might have been very different.

agent. There remains a large area in which what people do, what practices they choose to follow, and what standards they adhere to have only a slight and indirect effect (if any at all) on anyone other than themselves—and certainly not on the public in general. This is the field of private morality, and into this the law should not intrude.[4]

This is all very good as an abstract statement of doctrine, and it enunciates a principle that should certainly be borne in mind whenever legal intervention in matters of morality is contemplated; but it is just as certainly not a touchstone that yields automatic decisions in concrete cases. Even the most private actions, and the tastes and preferences that underlie and dictate these actions, will almost surely have at least some impact on the lives and concerns of others. A tendency toward deception and exaggeration, a fondness for salacious literature, an inclination toward alcoholism—such seemingly minor matters as these can have a quite disproportionate effect on one's relations with wife or husband, children, and friends; and if they become habitual, as they easily do, they can spread into larger public consequences. Thus the seemingly personal and innocuous merges into the publicly harmful by indiscernible steps.

This complication leads to the second issue just mentioned. This has to do with the question of how imminent and dangerous the threat to public morality must be in order to justify legal intervention. How seriously must the health, safety, and well-being of how many persons be adversely affected before the law can properly step in to correct the situation by prescribing or prohibiting certain types of conduct? Again, this question obviously permits of no precise and general answer. Opinions will differ in their assessment of the harm that is threatened, the effectiveness of legal action, and the availability of other less drastic measures. And in addition to these imponderables, there is the possibility that the legal apparatus, remote from the situations it is seeking to regulate, dependent on its limited array of procedures and techniques, and having to frame its directives in general terms that will cover a variety of cases,

---

[4] Linguistic usage is not precise or constant, but it is nevertheless indicative of popular sentiments and attitudes. And I believe that one can detect a significant difference in the meanings that the term "morality" carries in its familiar employment in the United States and in Europe. In England and on the Continent, moral issues are still closely associated with the mores, and the use of the term in ordinary speech refers to the patterns and practices of public morality: this is clearly brought out in the common French phrase, *l'ordre public et les bonnes moeurs*. In the United States, on the other hand, the term "morals" invokes the field of private morality, especially sexual behavior. One is led to suspect that this difference in usage has contributed substantially to the misunderstanding between Lord Devlin and his critics.

will do more harm than good. The unanticipated and unwanted consequences of legal intervention seem sometimes to outweigh the intended good that it is able to achieve.

The factors that argue for and against legal intervention and the difficulties that can occur when enforcement is undertaken can best be exhibited by a brief reference to actual instances. In the United States, this intervention of law in support of public morals and social order is most familiar in the context of obscenity. In England, this matter traditionally fell under the jurisdiction of the ecclesiastical courts, so that when the common law courts of the new nation confronted the issue, they had to start more or less from scratch. After all these years, they are still in much the same position. Judges at all levels, from municipal courts to the Supreme Court of the United States, have sought for a formula that would settle the question. But all they can do is vacillate helplessly between protecting the "young and susceptible" against the lure of the "lewd and lascivious" and protecting the "mature and sophisticated" in their enjoyment of art and literature with a potentially dangerous content, usually sexual. Public morality wins in one case, the First Amendment in another, the doctrine of "redeeming social value" tries to mediate between them, and finally the courts decide to leave the decision to "local standards." And then the process recommences.

A similar issue, posing similar problems, has recently arisen in a different context. It would be generally acknowledged—indeed, it is commonly assumed—that manufacturers have a clear moral duty to be truthful in describing the merits of their products, to take all reasonable precautions to assure that these are safe, and to warn of any dangers involved in their use. But when they fail to do so, under what circumstances should the law intervene to enforce this moral duty with legal regulations and sanctions? How much harm might be caused by the deception? How many people will be deceived? To what extent should consumers themselves be expected to use their intelligence to evaluate the claims made by manufacturers and to use their products with care? What difficulties can be expected in framing regulations, and to what problems might these regulations lead?

These and other questions require careful consideration in each particular case, and even then opinions will differ. Until quite recently it was felt that practices in this field were best left to the business sense and morality of manufacturers and to the good sense and skepticism of consumers. But the pressure of competition led to extravagant claims by the former group, while the latter group showed symptoms of being distressingly credulous and easily gulled. Legal intervention was thus decided on, and there are now detailed regulations governing truth in advertising and fulness of information in labeling. As a consequence of this, several firms have been compelled to spend huge sums in publicly repudiating the claims they had for years been making; automobiles are recalled by the million; news releases give the impression that everything we eat or drink is an almost certain cause of cancer; and the labels on products have to include so much information, and hence are printed in such small type, that they can only be read with a powerful magnifying glass. It may be that abuses had become so great in this area, and the moral sanction so weak, that something needed to be done. But this case illustrates perfectly the difficulties that law both encounters and creates when it tries to determine such questions as whether silence constitutes deceit, when a boast becomes a lie, and how much protection people require—or deserve—against their own gullibility and carelessness.

Another case illustrates a different aspect of this problem. Certainly, no one would deny that children must be protected against abuse and exploitation: we all have a moral duty in this regard. When greed and poverty threaten to erode the moral sanction, child labor laws are enacted and the Department of Labor is authorized to issue regulations in this area. For a good many years, it has been customary for entire families, including children as young as ten or twelve, to work together harvesting potatoes in northern Maine. It is the general insistence that this is a boon to all concerned and a threat to none: the potato farmers get the needed supply of casual labor for the short harvesting season; poor families get badly needed money; and the children work hand in hand with their parents and older siblings, carefully watched over, getting healthy outdoor exercise, and learning the value of both work and money. But now, not trusting to the moral sense and decency of the farmers or even to the love and concern of the parents, the Department of Labor has issued detailed regulations governing the conditions under which children can work; and the requirements of these are so stringent that the employment of children in the potato harvest is made practically impossible. In its well-intentioned interest in the health and safety of children (and probably with industrial conditions and migrant labor chiefly in mind), the Labor Department has superseded parental discretion in the care of their children, told farmers how to harvest potatoes, and assured that tons of potatoes will rot in the ground, thus contributing to the world food shortage. As one irreverent Maine commentator remarked, the good intentions behind these regulations will pave a long stretch of the road to hell. As might be expected, the Maine congressional delegation has descended en masse on the Labor Department to get these regulations rescinded or amended—which shows that when law seeks to intervene in such matters, it is apt to encounter not only external difficulties but also internal opposition and conflict.

The third issue that must be resolved in deciding on legal intervention is at once the simplest and most elusive of all, and I shall deal with it briefly. This concerns the criteria and principles to be appealed to in determining whether legal action to enforce some moral duty or to support public morality, safety, and well-being is justified in a particular case. Is one to apply the Utilitarian standard, balancing the possible good to be achieved against the possible harm to be caused, bearing in mind the greatest happiness of the greatest number and with an equal consideration for each person affected? Are there some absolute principles or values, such as freedom of speech, respect for individual freedom and privacy, equal protection of the laws, and the national security, that control decisions, whether in the sense of forbidding or justifying legal action? Is one simply to rely on the democratic rule and count heads for and against? Should one accept the "good reasons" doctrine and demand a sound logical argument to justify intervention? Or, finally, is one to espouse the emotivist position and hold that if enough people feel strongly enough about a certain practice to insist that it must be enforced or prohibited, that settles the matter?[5] Since philosophers have been trying for several thousand years to settle this problem, with a notable lack of success and with disagreement still rampant, it is too much to expect legislators and judges now to proclaim the correct solution with a unanimous voice. Thus different officials apply different criteria and principles (and the same official will apply various ones as the occasion seems to demand), with different results being reached in different jurisdictions and split decisions abounding.

---

[5] It was Lord Devlin's seeming adoption of this emotivist position that called down on him the special wrath and ridicule of his critics. In the first statement of his argument in the Maccabean Lecture in 1958, he did employ some very indiscreet language, which he qualified and largely withdrew when the lecture, along with other essays on the same topic, was published in book form (*The Enforcement of Morals* [Oxford: The Clarendon Press, 1965]). In the original lecture, Devlin said that legal enforcement of morals is justified when public feeling regarding some particular behavior (homosexuality, in this case) rises to the level of "intolerance, indignation, and disgust" and when the well-known man "in the Clapham omnibus" feels that it is "a vice so abominable that its mere presence is an offense" (p. 17). Devlin later acknowledged that these criteria were too extreme and exclusive as justifications for legal intervention; he introduced several of the other criteria and principles just referred to, such as the appeal to reason and respect for individual freedom and privacy; and he has since urged publicly that the laws and sanctions regarding homosexuality be relaxed.

To raise these issues is not to challenge in principle the need and the value of legal intervention in areas and affairs that are the immediate concern of other institutions, including as a notable case the force of public morality. Rather, it is merely to reemphasize that such intervention, which is the responsibility that sovereignty bears, should be undertaken with due restraint and caution. Describing this relationship in a geometrical figure of speech, John Austin pointed out that the circle circumscribed by morality is larger than and contains that circumscribed by law. This is certainly true; but it is a good deal less true than it was in Austin's day. The membrane that separates these circles has always been highly permeable: moral concepts and standards seep through in a steady stream to pervade the law; and the law thrusts through to enforce what morality preaches or to declare that some moral prohibition or command is legally invalid and will not be enforced. With the passage of time and shifts in the winds of doctrine, the line between these two has become more and more tenuous, until now it is almost illegible.

Most people would agree that the systematic exclusion of blacks from opportunities in education and employment is morally wrong, and there would be at least equally wide agreement that employers have a moral duty to protect the health and safety of their workers. But it is only in recent years that such racial discrimination by private agencies has been declared illegal and its practice reversed by stringently enforced regulations and programs. And it is even more recently that an agency—the Occupational Safety and Health Administration—has been created to establish standards and to inspect industrial plants and sites in order to ensure that proper measures are taken, instead of merely awarding damages after the event. And this coin has its other side. It long was (and it may still be) the general feeling that abortion is morally wrong; and there is strong support for the value of school prayers and the pledge of allegiance to the flag as legitimate means to inculcate important elements of public morality. But the law has recently intervened to declare that abortion is a legal right and that enforced prayers and pledges are unconstitutional violations of the First Amendment.

The difficulties and problems that these legal interventions have created, the objections and the overt opposition that they have aroused, are a familiar story. I have previously developed this theme at length in theoretical terms, and I have illustrated it with detailed analyses of some concrete cases. Regarding the instances just referred to, it is not to my purpose here to debate their propriety. Suffice it to point out that even where there is wide agreement on the ends pursued by the law (as would be true of the first two cases), there is much criticism of the legal means

employed and of the effectiveness of the measures adopted. And the latter two cases have been greeted with bitter complaints that law is systematically undermining morality, religion, and the social order.

There is a general outcome that is incipient in the cases just discussed
that merits particular attention. This is the possibility that continued
legal intervention of this scope and on this scale will impede the efforts
of other institutions, erode the force of other social sanctions, and
weaken the sense of individual responsibility and self-reliance. As law
preempts more and more of the fields and functions that have hitherto
been the province of other institutions, it tends to establish a monopoly
as the society's sole principle of order. The patterns of behavior prescribed by its substantive content then replace those of more private and
informal bodies, and its procedural rules render obsolete all other standards of conduct. I have already discussed the specific outcomes to which
such a course would lead. The overriding danger is that law, deprived of
these necessary adjuncts, would then prove ineffective and unable to accomplish what it has undertaken, thus leaving a gaping social vacuum. It
is easy to foresee what would fill this vacuum: either anarchy or
tyranny—or, more realistically, an intensification of both factionalism
and paternalism.

This situation can be summarized by saying that law must be master
in its own house, but it must equally remember that this is a house that
is staffed by many servants. Like any master, the law must supervise its
servants, lay down the lines of their general responsibilities, see that
they do their work properly, and make sure that they do not abuse their
positions to line their own pockets. But it is only a foolish master who
keeps a constant watch over the doings of his servants, nags them at
every step, and ends by virtually doing their work himself.

As Hegel saw so clearly, this is the quixotic outcome to which any
overlord is tempted. Since law is sovereign, and sovereignty is the ultimate overlordship, this temptation to intrude itself and impose its views
throughout the social order confronts law in an acute form. Should the
legal apparatus succumb to this temptation, it would undertake to
scrutinize every detail of the operations of other institutions: it would
demand that they explain and justify all of their decisions; it would
question the legitimacy and adequacy of their actions; and it would insist
that everything be done over again in its own way and under its vigilant
direction. Like the foolish master who is convinced that only he can do
things properly, the legal apparatus would end by trying to do everything itself.

By overreaching itself in this way, law would undermine its own position and defeat its true purposes, for this would mean that strictly legal concepts and criteria would compete with and largely supplant rather than supplement those of other institutions. I have already traced in detail the course that this movement would take if it were carried to its logical conclusion, and there is no need to repeat that journey. Its outcome can be quickly recapitulated. The substantive conditions of cultivation, authority, responsibility, and continuity would be transformed in ways to bring them within reach of law's procedural apparatus. The efforts of other institutions to promote these goals of social justice would be hindered, and their contributions to the social order would decline drastically. Thereafter, having deprived itself of these necessary supports, law would have its own effectiveness seriously diminished and would find that the social conditions that it actually furthered were quite different from those that it originally intended.

This simply repeats the by now familiar moral that law must assert its sovereignty but must not pretend to omnicompetence. For law cannot by itself secure the goals of social justice. If it is tempted, or forced, to try this, it betrays the ideal it seeks to serve. What law can do is guarantee certain rights and enforce certain duties that are themselves the necessary preconditions of justice. That is, the legal apparatus can assure an environment in which it is possible for other institutions to act effectively to promote a truly just society. For justice lies beyond the law, though it is only through law that it can be reached.

Throughout this book two themes have recurred with a particular persistence. One of these holds that positive law is a natural and necessary evolutionary development, an agent of social adaptation that is called into being as a supplemental principle of order when other forces and agencies prove inadequate to this task: law is sovereign and indispensable, but it is neither omnicompetent nor self-sufficient. The other holds that if positive law is to function effectively as a principle of order, its mode of being must be fully three-dimensional: the mediating order that law posits must be appropriate to the actual and ideal orders with which it deals. These two themes stress the importance of defining and maintaining the proper relationship between law and the forces and agencies that it supplements but cannot supplant.

One way to epitomize this relationship is to regard law as a second-order institution: it supervenes upon a social scene that has already been closely ordered by other institutions. Law's role is to further institutionalize these institutions. It does this partly by supporting their accomplishments and partly by supervising their activities, in both cases by throwing in the additional weight of its principles, procedures, and sanctions. This is what it is to be sovereign.

But sovereignty has its weaknesses as well as its strengths. The very fact of being a second-order institution means that law operates at a distinct remove from the people whose lives it governs and from the affairs that it manages. The other institutions that we have surveyed are more intimate, touch and attach men's emotions more intensely, and more obviously serve purposes that their members understand and value. Custom, morality, the family, religion, the schools, and professional and vocational groups—all are tied quite directly to human needs and concerns. They are expressions of deeply rooted drives, arising immediately from the human condition and serving as vehicles of basic human strivings. Though the words are dangerous, one wants to say that they are natural phenomena, spontaneously begotten rather than intentionally created.

The same is not nearly as true of the legal apparatus. Law is certainly not an artificial contrivance, a cultivated exotic grafted onto a society with which it has nothing in common and which it uses merely for its own sustenance: the whole force of my argument has gone to show that positive law is a coherent element of both the natural and social orders. But it is nevertheless the case that law is more remote and detached from the body of society than are other institutions. The very substantive completeness and procedural stringency of the legal apparatus tend to make it highly self-enclosed. Much of the strength and integrity—even the majesty—of the law derive from its determined adherence to internal principles, established rules, and formal procedures. But this insistence upon its own ritual also has the consequence of partly, and sometimes largely, isolating law from the needs of men and the pressure of circumstances. Just because it is so formalized and impersonal, the legal apparatus deals with men at arm's length rather than intimately, and its edicts often have the air of being issued by an alien power unfamiliar with the affairs of men and indifferent to its impact upon them. For good and for ill, the law filters the concrete human and social worlds through its own abstractions: only then can it "recognize" them.

These requirements of legal recognition afford law the high measure of impartiality, generality, and certainty that are the jewels in its crown; but they also entail the obvious risk that those who administer the legal apparatus will lose touch with the actualities of society and the temper of the people. It is the institutional substructure of society that mitigates these dangers. If other institutions perform their functions effectively and if they are sufficiently strong to secure respect for their views and values, they can serve as mediators between law and the society it administers. In this role, these institutions make two contributions of particular importance. First, since they are more closely geared to the various segments of the social order, they can assure that the legal apparatus is conversant with prevailing social conditions: the problems the society faces, the resources it commands, the expectations and tolerances of the people. This knowledge can go far to ensure that the measures that law proposes will be appropriate and acceptable. Second, since these institutions play the largest part in forming human character and conduct, they can assure that the legal apparatus will deal with a populace that has acquired the habits and attitudes, the training and discipline, the values and standards that are necessary to a decent social life. The institutional substructure transforms men from merely rational animals into reasonable creatures. In sum, these more intimate social institutions domesticate man and prepare him to be law-abiding, and they sensitize law and make it responsive to man's needs.

The organic theory of the state is both faulty as a description and dangerous as a theory, but it has its usefulness as an analogy, and as such it has been used to support the most wildly divergent purposes. To add one more variant to this theme, I would suggest the following. Law is the skeleton and the carapace of society: it supplies the framework of the social order, and it places bounds on the activities of all the participants in this order. But the flesh and blood, the nerve and muscle, of a society lie in its other institutions, for these fashion the character of the participants and determine the use they will make of the order that law provides.

INDEX

action-reaction, as feature of regime of Necessity, 33-34
alienation (the antisocial), 208-209
alpha, as type of leader, 162, 165-166
analytical jurisprudence, 67
anointed king, as type of leader, 162, 168-170
Anson, Sir William, 9
Aquinas, St. Thomas, 9, 64, 65, 316
Austin, John:
  on efficacy, 173-176
  on law as command of sovereign, 73, 173-174, 192
  on obligation, 192
  on relation of jurisprudence and legislation, 74
  on relation of positive law to positive morality and law of God, 66, 379
  on Utilitarianism, 73-74
authority, 39-40, Chap. XI passim
  character of, 39-40
  and law, 159-161, 173-184, 354-356
  and leadership, 161-165, 182-190
  misconceptions regarding, 154-156, 159-161
  as a relationship, 154-158
  See also authority relationship, leadership, obligation
authority relationship:
  as basis of legal order, 182-190
  character of, 154-159, 200, 202-203
  disruptions of, 2-3, 210
  See also compact, lived relationships

Bakke v. Regents of the University of California, 269-286
Bentham, Jeremy, 73-74
  on social reform, 151-152
  on use of hedonic calculus, 59-61
Bickel, Alexander, xii, 232n, 279n, 353n
  on civil disobedience, 209-210
  on consent, 210-211
Blackmun, Harry A., 287, 289, 297, 299, 300

Blackstone, Sir William, 65
bond, 198-199
Brennan, William J., Jr., 287, 291-293, 296-300
Bryce Hospital, 135-150 passim
  conditions in, 137-138, 141-142
  court orders and standards regarding, 141-142; benefits of, 150; deficiencies and difficulties in implementation of, 142-150
  Human Rights Committee, 136n, 137n, 142
  Office of Planning, Research, and Evaluation, 136n, 137n
Burger, Warren E., 287, 289, 297, 299, 300

Cairns, Huntington, 6n, 8, 22
Cardozo, Benjamin, 7, 22, 58, 66-67
Cherry, Charles, 280
civil disobedience:
  character and causes of, 202-206
  law's response to, 206-207
  variants of, 207-210
Civil Rights Act (1964), 287, 289-293
community, 231-232
compact, the:
  Bickel on, 210-211
  element in authority relationship, 154-155, 200-204
"compelling state interest" thesis, 269, 271-272, 288-289, 294-296
continuity:
  character of, 41
  and positive law, 51-52, 357-360
contract, 51-52, 360
courts, *see* judiciary
Cox, Alexander, 353n
cultivation:
  character of, 39, 348-350
  different views of, 332
  as goal of law, 53-55
  as transformed by law, 350-353

LIBRARY OF CONGRESS CATALOGING IN PUBLICATION DATA

Jenkins, Iredell.
  Social order and the limits of law.

  Includes index.
  1. Jurisprudence.   2.   Effectiveness and
validity of law.   3.   Sociological jurisprudence.
I. Title.
K230.J45S6   340.1   79-3216
ISBN 0-691-07241-8
ISBN 0-691-02007-8 pbk.